D0642139

Producing for TV and Video

Producing for TV and Video

A Real-World Approach

CATHRINE KELLISON

AMSTERDAM • BOSTON • HEIDELBERG • LONDON
NEW YORK • OXFORD • PARIS • SAN DIEGO
SAN FRANCISCO • SINGAPORE • SYDNEY • TOKYO

Focal Press is an imprint of Elsevier

Acquisitions Editor: Elinor Actipis
Project Manager: Dawnmarie Simpson
Assistant Editor: Robin Weston
Marketing Manager: Christine Degon
Cover Design: Cate Barr
Interior Design: Julio Esperas

Focal Press is an imprint of Elsevier
30 Corporate Drive, Suite 400, Burlington, MA 01803, USA
Linacre House, Jordan Hill, Oxford OX2 8DP, UK

Copyright © 2006, Cathrine Kellison. All rights reserved.

No part of this publication may be reproduced, stored in a retrieval system, or transmitted in any form or
by any means, electronic, mechanical, photocopying, recording, or otherwise, without the prior written
permission of the publisher.

Permissions may be sought directly from Elsevier's Science & Technology Rights Department in Oxford, UK:
phone: (+44) 1865 843830, fax: (+44) 1865 853333, e-mail: permissions@elsevier.co.uk. You may also
complete your request online via the Elsevier homepage (http://elsevier.com), by selecting "Customer
Support" and then "Obtaining Permissions."

Recognizing the importance of preserving what has been written, Elsevier prints its books on acid-free paper
whenever possible.

Library of Congress Cataloging-in-Publication Data
Application submitted.

British Library Cataloguing-in-Publication Data
A catalogue record for this book is available from the British Library.

ISBN 13: 978-0-240-80623-5
ISBN 10: 0-240-80623-9

For information on all Focal Press publications
visit our website at www.books.elsevier.com

05   06   07   08   09   10   10 9 8 7 6 5 4 3 2 1

Printed in the United States of America

Working together to grow
libraries in developing countries

www.elsevier.com | www.bookaid.org | www.sabre.org

ELSEVIER   BOOK AID International   Sabre Foundation

Contents

Preface

Like many of the people you'll meet in the pages of this book, I didn't start off as a producer. Writing was my passion. I liked the process, and wrote professionally for years — screenplays, short stories, magazine articles, movie reviews, educational curricula. Then, somewhere down the line, I was offered a job at NBC as a writer/producer. I knew what a writer did, but a producer . . .? Of course, I said yes immediately.

That simple "yes" was the launch pad for this journey called producing for television that has lasted over two decades with no sign of slowing down. I've written and/or produced hundreds of television hours — for broadcast and nonbroadcast, from two-minute movie trailers to two-hour documentaries, in almost every genre. These projects have exposed me to an extraordinary range of experiences. They've allowed me to research new ideas then write about them; to shoot on exotic locations; to understand the parameters of finance; to interview on-camera celebrities, academics, and visionaries; and behind-the-scenes, to work with teams of creative and talented people.

Producing for television — it has always felt natural to me. As the oldest of four kids, I mastered the skills of delegating, nurturing, cajoling, and outright bribery at an early age. I could convince my brother and sisters that making me a sandwich was an honorable task rather than drudgery. Hiring them with my babysitting money to do my chores became a profitable habit, and gave me time to dream about moving from our Nashville home to New York City, where I'd drive a taxi and write amusing-yet-heartwarming novels about my mysterious passengers. Around age twelve, I started a newspaper, *The Shack*. I gave each sibling a job: reporting a new deer sighting, drawing maps, making up riddles, selling ad space. I wrote the lead stories, designed it, and gave myself top billing. So, in essence, I've been producing all my life.

The creative potential of producing parallels my control issues, thanks to my parents who were independent filmmakers. With a small dedicated crew, they directed, produced, and shot documentaries in earlier times when nonscripted reality programming was a labor of love, poorly funded, and rarely seen by large audiences. They traveled around the globe, shooting for weeks at a time. They showed us exotic places with unpronounceable names, and told stories of trekking into villages where the only language was eye contact. They were filmmakers who loved what they did: the planning, the shooting, the weeks of editing, and they found challenges and payoffs in each phase.

This family collaborative, its passion — and fun — has shaped my world view of producing for television. Family has also been essential to producing this book. My mother, Allie Clayton, provided the graphic format design and transcribed hours of interviews. My oldest daughter, Joni Johnsen, was also a valiant transcriber and source of inspiration, as were Jonna McLaughlin, my middle daughter and her best friend Becky Teitel, who contributed their sage advice and experiences as students of producing, along with my third daughter, Simone McLaughlin, who essentially constructed the glossary. My husband, Jeffrey McLaughlin, shared his considerable knowledge of post-production, and supported me throughout the long writing process with his belief in my vision. Overseeing this family endeavor is the guiding spirit of my father,

John Clayton, whose humor, vision, and belief in his team were the stuff of legend. His grin could light up any set.

Writing this book has been a process of exploring my own experiences, then combining or contrasting them with those of dozens of other professionals. The first draft of every chapter was reviewed by a small team of college students of producing who contributed their candid feedback, and unique perspectives. Jackie Moldower bolstered my spirits with her unswerving support, extensive research, and review; she compiled much of the references. Adam Wager contributed an invaluable clarity to the text and its overall tone. Ashley Cooper Kerns and Joanna Kerns helped reshape and clarify the legal chapter. Daisy Montfort and Noah Workman chipped in long hours on behalf of this book. I'm so grateful for their dedication to my dream.

Adding another dimension to this text are the experiences and insights from the "guest speakers" in Chapter 11: Sheril Antonio, Sharon Badal, Veronique Bernard, Michael Bonfiglio, Salli Frattini, Barbara Gaines, Ann Kolbell, Matthew Lombardi, Jeffrey McLaughlin, Brett Morgen, Stephen Reed, John Rosas, Tom Sellitti, J. Stephen Sheppard, Valerie Walsh, and Justin Wilkes. I'm grateful to my colleagues at New York University — James Gardner, Patricia Lennox, Al Lieberman, Rick Litvin, Lynn McVeigh, Peter Rea, Paul Thompson — who believe in the power of television, and to Amit Das who convinced me to expand my *Producing for TV* syllabus into a textbook. I'm eternally grateful to Kent Cathcart who not only showed me the power of words early on, but provoked my spirit of adventure.

An integral part of the early development of this book are the proposal reviewers, Ivan Cury, Doug Smart, Don Smith, and Fred Watkins, and the reviewers of the final manuscript, Alec Hirschfeld and Lorene M. Wales. Each made significant contributions with feedback that proved both candid and encouraging. My heartfelt thanks also go to the folks at Focal Press: Elinor Actipis, Dawnmarie Simpson, and Christine Tridente, who provided constant support, encouragement, and invaluable direction through each and every phase of the book's development.

This book is the final outcome of collaboration, experience, curiosity, a bit of good luck, and a lot of hard work — a formula that's remarkably similar to producing for television and video.

Introduction

Know what you don't know.

—Stephen Reed, producer

If ever there was a succinct description of the television producer's job, *"know what you don't know"* defines it best. The producer in television and video has little choice but to be a lifelong learner, constantly researching, asking questions, and listening — in essence, knowing what you don't know.

There isn't one producer in the television industry or in the nonbroadcast realm who knows all the answers, or the tricks of the trade, or grasps the nuances of each and every detail on the producer's to do list. Although producers share certain skill sets, each genre in which the producer works is different. Each requires a unique result from its producer. This book strives to lay out the overall parameters of the producer's many roles and options, and the steps that are generally taken in producing quality programming for television shows and nonbroadcast video.

Before the TV producer, however, comes the medium itself. Television in the 21st century is pervasive. It reaches literally billions of people around the globe; for many of them, TV is their sole source of information and entertainment. You may be among the majority of people who watch it on a daily basis; or, you rarely, if ever, watch TV. Regardless of your own viewing habits, TV has had a resounding impact on the data, the culture, the changing trends, and the economics that inform your world.

Television has always held a unique position in our culture. In its infancy, TV was disdained as simply a passing fancy, "an inventor's will o' the wisp." Over the subsequent decades, its detractors have been harsh and outspoken, insisting that TV caters to the lowest common denominator, that it barrages us with negative impressions, controls the content and delivery of news, manipulates cultural trends, and encourages viewers to be active contributors to the consumer society. But now current research points to television as a vehicle that can actually make its viewers smarter as they navigate complex narrative plots, explore ethical issues of relationships that are central to reality programming, or use video as educational tools for learning.

Within this range of viewpoints, it's indisputable that the medium of television offers potential opportunities that are virtually limitless. This is where the producer enters the picture.

TV Is the Producer's Tool

A television is simply a mechanical device that can receive electronic signals. It's like a blank canvas waiting for the artist's brush. The producer can use the tool of video to create an image on the screen just like painting that canvas. With video, the producer can stand up to television's critics, using his or her creative vision, technical know-how, and a rather extraordinary set of skills to produce unique, solid programming for broadcast and nonbroadcast television.

Television Lives within an Historical Context

May you be born in interesting times.

—Ancient Chinese curse

Today's world certainly lives in "interesting times." Few periods in human history have been as dramatic or as enlightening. For most Americans, TV is the primary medium that reflects — and influences — what is happening in the world around them, as well as how they perceive this world.

Television has a century of creative and technical history behind it, rich in insight, providing a foundation for the contemporary programs we watch today. We can see Steve Allen's late night humor and hosting style from the 1950s in the current shows hosted by David Letterman and Jon Stewart. Superior live presentations from dramatic series like *Playhouse 90* or *Hallmark Hall of Fame* upped the ante for superior acting, writing, and directing that is still seen every night in dozens of network and premium cable programs, such as *The West Wing, Deadwood*, and *The Sopranos*. In the early days of childrens' television, we met *Mr. Wizard* and Mr. Rogers who paved the way for today's popular *Sesame Street* and *Dora the Explorer*.

Yet television's detractors target the predominant themes of competition and humiliation in "reality shows," or the evening news broadcasts — once reported by courageous pioneers in journalism like Edward R. Murrow and Walter Cronkite — in which news is limited by media conglomerate dictates, and focused on the sensational and shallow. Explicit music videos and adult-only channels have lowered the bar of constraint, as mature content seeps into family programming; concurrently, the vital issues of censorship and freedom of speech are increasingly being challenged, even curtailed under political and economic pressures The pros and cons of television are in constant flux, and the debates will surely continue to flourish.

So where does it all go from here? What is television's future? That answer is up to the producer. In the midst of this ever-evolving vortex called television, the producer can choose to go with the flow or change the direction of the current.

TV Is a Unique Medium

An effective producer takes advantage of television to create compelling entertainment, in-depth information, or educational content. Television is a stabile medium, an industry unto itself that is no longer the stepchild of the feature film industry, or an offshoot of radio. It's here to stay. Much of television's quality programming and technological advances have crossed over from "craft" to "art," and the television industry is now a thriving, multibillion dollar business that circles the globe. More than any other medium, television creates the strongest impact and influence on our world.

As a true synthesis of creativity and technology, television and video-based content is a major conduit for transmitting an idea. Whether for network or cable, corporate or nonbroadcast, this content has the potential to offer stimulating entertainment, the news as it's happening, political opinions from all sides, and top-notch education. It's also the strongest selling tool, convincing us to buy products, data, and lifestyles. Television and video content can reflect trends or start them. It can mirror our identities, even form them.

The TV set is a staple in most households. It's a familiar voice in the background, an antidote to loneliness. As with a family member, we can enjoy it, tune it out, argue with it, or laugh out loud. We don't have to leave the house, hire a babysitter, or pay the high price of admission for feature films and documentaries — we'll eventually see them on our TV set.

The TV Producer Is at the Core

Some producers in television are responsible for bringing the entire project to life, from a simple concept through development to its final broadcast or distribution. Other producers work on specific areas of a project and are a valuable part of a larger team of producers. The parameters of the TV and video producer's functions cast a wide net; it's the least understood job in television. It's also the most demanding and time-consuming job, and yet a natural-born producer loves (almost) every minute.

The skills needed to be a producer are rather like the tiny pixels in a television image. Each skill deals with detail, and each detail is important — like a pixel — and it takes thousands of them to create an image on the TV screen. This book explores these details as they pertain to each stage of producing a project.

- Stage One: The Idea (Project Development)

- Stage Two: The Plan (Preproduction)

- Stage Three: The Shoot (Production)

- Stage Four: The Final Product (Post-Production)

- Stage Five: Next Steps (Wrap up and Distribution)

Producing isn't just about mastering the details. A producer also has a clear vision of the "big picture" of television: the current marketplace, the audience demographics, the trends of the day. She reads the industry publications, actively watches programming in specific genres, and seeks out learning opportunities.

The Professional Opportunities in Television

According to the Bureau of Labor Statistics, "employment in the motion picture and video industries is projected to grow 31 percent between 2002 and 2012, roughly double the 16 percent growth projected for all industries combined." Demand for content comes from networks, cable and premium channels, satellite, as well as from the many venues in non-broadcast. And the international market continues its consumption of the latest hit show or newest format idea from America that can increase their audience base and advertising revenue. As an industry, television offers a range of options to the beginning producer — from a staff position at a national network to working with a news producer in a local television station. Producers in video may opt for being freelancers or independent with their own small companies that produce content for broadcast, corporations, documentary channels, or educational distribution. Like the industry itself, the options for a producer are expanding on a daily basis.

The TV Producer in the Digital Domain

TV and video producers now work almost exclusively in the digital domain. Most of the producer's integral tools are digital — the cameras, the formats for shooting the image and recording the sound, the editing and mixing systems, and the broadcasting technology — and each aspect of the production and post-production process takes full advantage of the technological advances in the digital world. We now live and work in the digital domain, and this book focuses primarily on these digital tools and the producer's relationship to them.

Organization of the Text

The Roles of the Producer — In Two Parts

A producer's role is as much about people as it is about the details of production. Working alone, the producer may have a marketable skill such as writing or directing, but the very role of the producer depends on working with others. The strength of this collaboration between the producer and the creative teams, the crew, the talent, the client, the vendors, and the dozens of other people along the way is what propels and accomplishes the five stages of production listed above.

The primary purpose of this book, then, is to look closely at this teamwork, and to explore the ways in which each individual on the producer's team function. What does a director of photography bring to the project? Will you need a location scout, and if so, what should you expect? How does the script supervisor make your job easier? At what stage do you hire the editor? Should you consult with an entertainment lawyer for each contract? And, most important, do you have the necessary "people skills" for holding this team together?

This book, designed in two parts, aims to answer these questions, and many more along the way.

Part One (Chapters 1–10) — There are five overall stages of producing for television, but this book devotes ten chapters to this journey. They provide the reader with a step-by-step explanation of the producer's jobs — from the initial idea of a project to its final distribution process — along with the steps following the project's completion.

Each chapter delves into a specific area of producing for TV and video. The first chapter offers an overall perspective on the many jobs and titles of a producer, and the second chapter reviews television's history, its current state, and its possible future. There is a chapter for each of the five stages of producing a project; each explores the details of budgets and breakdowns, legalities and rights, pitching and selling, as well as the important people skills benefitial to every producer.

In Part One, each chapter opens with talking points that cover the highlights and main points of the material. Each chapter is then broken into sections with specific information, guidelines, and suggestions. Various quotes and excerpts from the interviews in Chapter 11 scatter through each chapter, as well as commentary on the personal side of producing, called "*On a human level. . . .*"

Part Two (Chapter 11) — In Chapter 11, fifteen interviews with sixteen high-profile, experienced television producers and industry professionals take center stage. They talk openly about their jobs: what they do, how they do it, what makes one producer's job different than another's, the people they work with and depend on, their day-to-day functions, their tricks for balancing their professional lives with their personal ones. These interviews cover a range of producing jobs from executive producers in network television to independent producers of documentaries or nonbroadcast material. Industry professionals share their insights about topics ranging from legal issues to festival submissions.

These contributors actively work in broadcast, nonbroadcast, advertising, documentary, and alternative media. Just like a compelling guest speaker in the classroom, or a mentor in the workplace, each shares his or her own stories from the trenches and offers a unique perspective on producing for television and video.

Added Features

Throughout all the chapters in the book, each contributing producer and industry professional also shares pertinent information and producing clues through:

- *Top Ten Lists*: The top ten aspects of professional success as noted by its contributor

- *Sound bites*: Salient quotes from producers and other professionals in television and the entertainment industry; some are excerpts from the interviews in Chapter 11.

The Glossary

The terms, expressions, phrases, and explanations of a wide variety of the language of television are explained in the glossary. Each word in the text is italicized, referring the reader to the glossary for further explanation.

The CD

Television producers regularly use specific forms and legal agreements in organizing and protecting the project. In the CD that accompanies this book, you can find a variety of templates for most of the forms and agreements that producers use on a daily basis. The CD also offers a variety of Resources, including an extensive Books and References section, Web sites, and more.

Note to the Instructor ...

In addition to this textbook, the *Instructor's Manual* offers an overview of the material, as well as a per-chapter syllabus, and a variety of opportunities for classroom interaction and individual student projects.

To access the Instructor's Manual, contact your Focal Press sales representative or visit www.textbooks.elsevier.com.

Note to the Reader ...

You may be a student of television who has enrolled in a plan of study that explores the role of the producer in this medium. Or, you have an idea you think could work for television or video distribution. You may even be an experienced producer who is actively involved in producing content and can benefit from an updated primer on the technical and creative aspects of producing your project.

Regardless of the category into which you may fall, this book has been researched, designed, and written for you. It is the first book of its kind to fully explore both the "big picture" and the small details of producing for television. It can be part of an overall curriculum, or a helpful manual with creative and technical guidelines. Most important, this book aims to present the realities and possibilities for one who is ready to devote time, energy, and passion to producing quality programming and content for this extraordinary medium called television.

Put simply, this book promises to help you know more about what you don't know ...

PART I

The definition of a producer: An idealist, a realist, a practical dreamer, a sophisticated gambler, and a stage-struck child.

—Oscar Hammerstein

What Does a TV Producer *Really* Do?

This Chapter's Talking Points

I. The TV Producer's Domain

II. Defining a TV Producer

III. The TV Producer's Roles

IV. Titles and Job Descriptions of TV Producers

V. The Need for People Skills

VI. Summary

VII. Chapter Review Questions

I. The TV Producer's Domain

Television in the 21st century both mirrors and shapes the global village. And like the "real world" that television reaches out to, TV brims with possibilities and real challenges. The role of the producer in television and video is essential, and brings with it a virtually unlimited potential to educate, inform, and entertain. The producer's role also comes with heavy demands and responsibilities.

Popular demand and the appetites of commerce require a continuing stream of unique programming, or *content*, for television and video — from sitcoms on NBC, to internal corporate training videos for IBM, to segments for CNN cable news. For every show, a producer is in charge of satisfying both the client and viewer as well as best utilizing the talents of the cast and crew.

A producer's job description combines art with craft and commerce with technology. There is also a certain mind-set and personality as well as dedication, time, and problem-solving that comes with the position. Not everyone who wants to be a producer may be right for the job; whether you ultimately become a producer, work with producers, or simply want to think like one, this textbook helps you explore the many levels of responsibility and creativity that are involved in television producing. This chapter, as well as subsequent chapters, examines the producer's vast domain: what a TV producer needs to know about the many phases of a project's development and the benefits and challenges of producing.

> I love bringing talented people together. There's no greater feeling than standing on a shoot, sitting in an edit or watching the final product on TV, knowing that you as the producer pulled together an incredible, hard working group of people to create something.
>
> —Justin Wilkes, *excerpt from interview in Chapter 11*

Increasingly, a television producer who works with cable channels, independent productions, or in nonbroadcast is asked to be proficient in multitasking. She may not only write and produce a program or segment, but she might also shoot the program, edit the footage on a desktop system, mix the audio, and add narration or voice-over. The availability and low cost of equipment — along with decreasing budgets offered by the end user — make these skills valuable and increasingly necessary to the producer.

> Producers are risk takers, who seize an idea, run with it, and convince others to follow them.
>
> —Gorham Kindem, *The Moving Image*

A producer's talents and skills cover a broad spectrum ranging from creative to technological, idea to broadcast, and finance to marketing. In this chapter and throughout the book, we'll explore the producer's role: finding, writing, developing, and pitching an idea; budgeting a script; negotiating a deal; securing financing; and more.

Clearly, no one book can cover all the details a producer needs to know. So for each of the facets of producing covered in the following chapters, there is a wealth of resources available for more in-depth coverage including books that target areas like scriptwriting, legal, budgets, festivals as well as comprehensive Web sites, classes, and internships. These resources are invaluable; a strong producer keeps in close touch with industry trends and changing technology.

II. Defining a TV Producer

> I'm a producer. I do whatever is necessary to turn an idea into a finished product. That means at different times I've been a salesman, director, film editor, casting director, creative consultant — I've even driven the bus.
>
> —David L. Wolper, *Producer: A Memoir*

Without a producer, there is no project. The producer propels the project from an unformed idea to living-color broadcast. He can nurture the project from conception to distribution and might also be the writer, director, or the financing source. At various stages of production, he may bring in other producers who can help in handling the hundreds of details that need supervision or polish.

The producer is the first one on a project and the last one off, essentially the overall project supervisor who gets it off the ground, and then supervises every step of its development and production. Not every producer originates the ideas they produce. Sometimes a producer is brought in to work on a network or production company program after an idea has been created and sold. Either way, it's exciting and exhausting work.

A TV producer is different from a film producer. Conventional wisdom says that feature films are the realm of the director, theater is the realm of the actor, and TV is the realm of the producer. In most films, the producer acts primarily as the liaison between the studio and the production providing a strong support system for the film's director; feature film producers, increasingly, are shepherding their own scripts or heartfelt projects. Yet, in television, the producer is the governing force who can also double as the director. The TV producer usually hires — and fires — the director, writers, key department heads, actors, and other talent, crew, or anyone else needed to bring the project to life. In television, the director generally makes more of a technical contribution, working with the cast and crew on blocking and lighting and rehearsing lines, but it is the producer who makes the final decisions and takes on all the responsibilities.

> I carried my tape recorder with me everywhere as a kid. I had this odd fascination with recording things and playing them back. I taped everything. As I got into school, I brought my video camera to school. It was this odd fascination with wanting to play things back for some reason. By the time I was old enough to try and figure out what I was supposed to do for a living, all I really knew was I wanted to continue this process of recording something and making it into something.
> —Matthew Lombardi, *excerpt from interview in Chapter 11*

A. Who Makes a Good Producer?

If you can wake up each day excited to go to work, if you're eager to meet challenges and can handle a steady stream of demands and questions, if you are slightly type A or obsessive compulsive and like to run a tight ship while still having fun, you have the makings of a good producer. Combine those qualities with creativity and flexibility, an openness to new ideas and information, and a genuine like of people — or at least a respect for their talents — with an ethical and profitable approach to business. The majority of working producers enjoy their job. They like its random nature, and welcome the challenges. As you read the interviews with contributing producers in Chapter 11, you'll see that producers choose this work because it excites them.

A good producer:

- **Is a problem solver.** A producer anticipates what's needed. He's smart and plays fair. He's a nurturer, an arbitrator, a leader, and a team player. He's a risk taker and has prepared contingencies for any predictable scenario.

- **Is the master of multitasking.** Whether the project is a low-budget documentary or an expensive weekly episodic drama, the producer must juggle dozens of tasks at once. She might be an entrepreneurial executive producer who secures the financing and makes deals, or a producer commissioned by the executive producer to work on aspects of the project from start to finish, such as segments, post-production, music, etc. She might also be working in several stages of production at once.

- **Is a middle man.** The producer who's wise enough to be on set regularly (even though he may not be needed) becomes the point person for the director, the DP (*Director of Photography*), the actors, and the crew members who rely on his leadership. The producer balances the needs of the production with the needs of the talent.

- **Wants to know everything.** A good story and useful information are both at the core of a producer's craft. The world of producing changes daily; read everything at your disposal such as books, magazines, the industry trade papers, newspapers, plays, biographies, art and history, and philosophy. Look for ideas that interest you and could also appeal to a wide audience; you can find additional sources in Resource by Chapter at the end of the book. Know where the industry is going, look for the "next big thing," and try to capitalize on what's popular now.

- **Enjoys the process.** She's comfortable doing business *and* being creative. A strong producer doesn't need to know how to do everything herself — write, direct, edit, create sound design, and light and design sets — but she knows and hires the best people to do those jobs and creates a team that can work together for a common goal.

To paraphrase Gertrude Stein, a producer is a producer is a producer. In other words, the definition and job function of a producer relates to each genre he or she may be producing, but the skill sets are similar. A good producer can produce almost anything — a two-hour documentary, a half-hour sitcom, a thirty-second commercial, a corporate image piece, or a music video. The projects may differ in content and length and require certain skills that relate to a specific kind of television content, but the creative, financial, technical, and communication skills required are similar for all producers.

> I don't really think there is a "producer's personality," but I think there are many qualities that a good producer should have, if he or she wants to do his job well and also be able to sleep at night. Despite the clichés of what a producer acts like (sharp-dressed, fast-talking, megalomaniacs), I think that honesty is very important. Anything else will eventually come out anyway, so aside from basic ethics, there's really no point in making things up to cover your bases, or to convince someone of something that isn't true, just so you can get out of them what you want.
> —Michael Bonfiglio, *excerpt from interview in Chapter 11*

III. The TV Producer's Roles

The TV producer has the power to educate, entertain, and emotionally move an audience, yet getting to this stage takes time and energy. No matter what its length or content, each project goes through the following five stages of production, and each stage needs a producer or producers. There are always exceptions to these categories, but this is typically what lies ahead for the producer.

A. The Five Stages of TV Production

- Stage one: The idea (project development)
- Stage two: The plan (preproduction)
- Stage three: The shoot (production)
- Stage four: The final product (post-production)
- Stage five: Next steps (wrap-up and distribution)

In this book, there are chapters that encompass each of these five stages of producing for television or video.

1. *Stage One: The Idea (Project Development)*

Your idea can be a full-length script or a one-paragraph treatment that exists in some format. Over the stages of production it is developed, fleshed out, and possibly, produced. In the project development stage, explored in Chapter 3, the producer:

- Either originates or finds material to option, or buys all rights to produce it. This material can be an original idea, a script, a book, or an article from a newspaper or a magazine — any source constitutes "material."

- Evaluates the project for initial costs, funding sources, and likely markets.

- Develops the proposal and story synopsis as a basis for getting financing.

- Oversees the development of the idea, which for television might include the overall *Bible* that includes the plotlines and character sketches for a season of shows in a continuing series.

- Develops a rough estimate of the budget.

- Pitches the project to secure interest and ultimately financing for the entire project or for its initial development. A development deal can range from simply developing the script to producing a pilot.

- Negotiates and obtains contracts for licensing fees and other legal aspects of the project's distribution or broadcast.

- Selects, interviews, and hires a director who shares the project's visions and can deliver — on schedule.

- Selects and hires a writer or team of writers (staff and/or freelance) to develop the idea further.

- May consult with and hire additional producers, associate producers, and/or a production manager.

- May be hired by a production company as a staff producer and assigned to projects in which he or she may not have a vested interest.

2. *Stage Two: The Plan (Preproduction)*

The original idea has taken a more tangible form, and it can now act as a blueprint for the research and hiring of the essential crew members who will take it to the next stage. In the preproduction stage, explored in Chapters 4–7, the producer:

- Is established as the principal point person for the financing and/or distribution group, and is involved in negotiations, contracts, rights, and union discussions, as well as securing rights and permits for locations, music, and other elements.

- Breaks down a script or treatment and uses it to make a rough budget estimate.

- Continues consulting with the director on aspects of the script and production.

- Depending on the scope of the project, hires and consults with the line producer, location manager, director, cast, DP, production designer, editor, musical composer, and graphics and special effects personnel, as well as essential crew like camera operators, audio recordists, lighting designers and areas of production like make-up, wardrobe, props, construction, transportation, catering, etc. The director may or may not be involved in the hiring process.

- Hires and supervises legal consultants, accountants and auditors, production coordinators, office managers, script supervisors, producer assistants (PAs), interns, etc.

- Supervises the completion of the shooting script.

- Scouts and approves all locations (often with the director and/or DP).

- Consults with the production designer on sets, construction, props, and the overall look of the production.

- Consults with the DP and director on shooting format (Beta, high-definition, DigiBeta, DV, 24P, film, etc).

- Breaks down the shooting script to prepare the overall shooting schedule, call sheets, and production report forms (usually with the line producer and/or production coordinator and/or executive in charge of production).

- Negotiates with appropriate unions on contract and fee agreements.

- Prepares all contracts and deal memos, or oversees them after the unit production manager (UPM) has compiled them.

- Signs off on the final budget.

3. *Stage Three: The Shoot (Production)*

The first two stages have led to the actual shoot where the producer's initial vision can now be captured on video and audio. During the shooting stage, detailed more thoroughly in Chapter 8, the producer:

- Is generally on set or available on call at all times.

- Consults with the writer(s) and supervises any changes.

- Works closely with the line producer.

- Works with the production designer and approves all aspects of the production's look and appearance.

- Consults regularly with the director, on-camera talent, production designer, and other key department heads.

- Screens the dailies with the director (and often the editor).

- Prepares, balances, and/or approves the daily or weekly cost estimates.

- Stays on top of any press or publicity material generated and carefully supervises what's appearing in the media about the project.

4. *Stage Four: The Final Product (Post-Production)*

The tape and sound are "in the can" and now all the disparate pieces are ready to be joined together in the editing room. At this stage, it's unlikely that you can go back and either reshoot or create additional content, so it is up to you to make it work through careful planning for both the shoot and post-production. During the post-production period, which you'll explore in Chapter 9, the producer:

- Often screens and logs all footage, and supplies the editor with a "paper cut" that acts as a script for the editor, with notes, time-code references for footage, and reel numbers and logs, as well as listing all graphic elements and audio components. You can find out more about paper cuts in Chapters 4 and 9.

- On most projects, is fully present during the editing or comes into the editing room on a regular basis to review the editor's work in progress.

- Continues as the point person for the network or producing group regarding issues of the final cut, timings and show lengths, standards and practices, and various other delivery requirements.

- Keeps a close eye on the budget. Post-production can be one of the least controllable financial aspects of the project.

- Selects, negotiates, and books post-production facilities, such as editorial houses and editors, stock footage facilities, audio studios, composers and/or stock music supervisors, graphics houses and designers, etc.

- Is familiar with all footage, selected takes, B-roll, cutaways, etc. and/or works closely with an assistant who's familiar with the footage.

- Regularly supervises the editor and is responsible for the final cut, depending on contractual agreements.

- Works closely with the musical composer and/or stock music supervisor.

- Supervises all audio sessions including narration, dubbing, ADR, foley, rough mix, and final mix.

- Works closely with the graphics designer(s) on show titles, in-show bumpers, opening and end credits, special effects, etc.

- Signs off on the video master of the final cut for client delivery.

- May organize and conduct focus groups or audience testing and supervise any editorial changes that could result from their responses.

5. *Stage Five: Next Steps (Wrap-Up and Distribution)*

The project is edited and ready to go, whether to broadcast or to a client, but the producer must attend to several vital details. In the wrap-up stage, explored in Chapter 10, the producer:

- Pays and reconciles all outstanding invoices.

- Finalizes all legal contracts and other issues still outstanding.

- Reconciles all budget issues and submits a final report to the client.

- May distribute copies of the final product to key personnel on the production.

- May be involved in advertising and promotional campaigns, such as on-air promos, print ads, etc.

- May consult with the network or production company on publicity, such as special events, public relations photos and artwork, etc.

- May work closely with the network or production company on securing international broadcast, ancillary rights, licensing, etc.

- May coordinate press activities by keeping careful control of what material is appropriate for release to the press.

B. Why Become a Television Producer?

A producer's job is one that requires hard work over a long period of time. But most producers genuinely love their job, partially because they find its demands to be stimulating. Each TV producer started off somewhere — some began with an internship, others as a PA, a secretary, a production coordinator, or an assistant. Some producers made the transition from other careers as lawyers, writers, directors, actors, agents, or managers. In the last few years, universities and private institutions have offered classes on television producing. As you'll learn in Part Two of this book, most of the important aspects of producing are learned on the job and in the trenches of the real world.

Many producers began as writers who had an idea, a vision that they wanted to brand with their own unique voice. Because they wanted that voice to be heard, they refused to relinquish control over the development of the idea, and chose to become producers so they could protect that vulnerability and actualize their original idea.

> I do think there are a lot of creative advantages to television — the immediacy, the amount of financing, funding — making it vastly superior to film, particularly now in cable television.
>
> —Brett Morgen, *excerpt from interview in Chapter 11*

C. Creativity, Clout, and Control

Every producer is enticed by a potential payoff; this payoff can come as the result of a producer's *creativity, clout, and control*. Writers in TV, for example, don't always have the clout to be guaranteed that their script will be produced and aired as it was originally written. For the most part writers — even the best of them — are regularly hired, fired, and replaced. But when writers can develop producing skills or actually take on the producer's role directly, they can dramatically increase their chances of control over their project, especially if they can develop a reputation as a producer who can also write and/or direct. This overall concept of originating and nurturing an idea can be looked at more closely through three very different lenses:

1. Creativity: Inspired and Creative Skills

Your idea forms the essence of your project. You'll either write it yourself or you'll find an idea that's been originated by someone else. Then, you'll develop it and flesh it out, protect it legally, and finally, you'll produce it. Your team is the next creative component. These are the writers, actors, directors, crew, and production designers whose visions are aligned with yours. You want to create and build a team of talented people who can share your vision and bring positive energy into the process.

2. Clout: Networking and Contacts Skills

The eternal rule hasn't changed: it's *who* you know before *what* you know. Networking has become a way of life, so look for opportunities to meet people such as parties, festivals, organizations, school clubs, openings, and charity events. If there's nothing in your area, hone your producing skills by putting something together yourself.

- Keep your ear to the ground and know who's who and who does what the best.

- Follow the trends in television and other media, as well as their financing for them.

- Read the entertainment news. Know the current trends.

D. Control: Business Skills

- Research the areas of legal protections (copyrights, contracts, deal memos, and other forms of negotiation are covered in Chapter 5) that can protect your idea and the project.

- Fine-tune your skills in budgeting, costing out, rough estimates, daily costs, etc.

- Secure financing. You'll find more information in later chapters.

- Know your audience — both domestic and foreign. What are their interests and their demographics like age, income, ethnicity, education, etc.?

- Research the changing technologies in production and post-production.

- Find a distributor or global network of distributors who can give your project exposure and press and can create a buzz for your project.

IV. Titles and Job Descriptions of TV Producers

Unlike other areas in television, such as writing, directing, or acting, the producer is seldom covered by a union because the producer is generally in charge of the project. Although the Producers Guild of America offers various benefits to an experienced producer, its parameters aren't currently comparable to those in the traditional unions. It is only in the recent past that universities and independent film and television schools have offered courses in the arts and skills of producing. Producing has historically attracted the entrepreneurs and the rebels, motivating people who tend to think outside the box to venture into the real world and do it.

There are genuine producers and there are the wannabees. The title of "producer" can be given out freely as a reward, and it isn't uncommon for a so-called producer to know very little about the intricacies of producing. Instead, he may be a legitimate major investor or a minor con artist who wants to flaunt his credits on the big screen without doing the hard work. Because there is no governing body that controls the assignment of the producer title, a network or production company can bestow it on actors, agents, managers, or anyone else who has had some part in putting the deal together.

A. Producers' Titles

In scripted TV, producers can also be writers. From show to show and genre to genre, producers' titles and their job descriptions can vary considerably. Below, you'll find a sampling of titles that genuine, hard-working producers work under.

Executive Producer — This is the murkiest of all producers' titles because it covers the gamut of descriptions. It's meant to designate the person who makes the deals, finds the finances, and/or puts the package of writer, director, actors, and/or crew together. Usually he sets up and controls the budget. The executive producer may hire various crew and cast, and can be in charge of other producers for one or more projects. There may be several executive producers, also listed as co-executive producers, on a single project.

On a financial level, the executive producer might have single-handedly financed the project, even mortgaged his house to develop it, or he may have had just one brief meeting with an investor who said yes. He may be actively on the set and in the office every day, or he may show up only at the wrap party. The lead actress could demand the executive producer credit, and so could her husband or manager.

TOP TEN

The Top 10 Things You Need to Be a Good Executive Producer:
1. Loyalty to the host and show that borders on insanity
2. A long fuse
3. A small ego
4. Attention to detail
5. Organizational ability
6. Ability to make a split-second decision
7. Learn to take a joke
8. Pick your battles
9. Good listening skills
10. Snappy dresser

—Barbara Gaines, The Late Show with David Letterman, *excerpt from interview in*
Chapter 11

Showrunner — This job can be as ill-defined as the executive producer's job — and often, they are one and the same job. The term showrunner is informal, and not credited as such, although the person in this position is responsible for the overall creative direction of a series. She is primarily the writer and/or manages and guides other writers in creating the scripts; she may often rewrite scripts and make sure they're delivered on schedule. The showrunner on a reality show, talk show, news, specials, etc. is not as involved in writing and deals more with generating ideas. She may also be very involved in pitching a show idea to a network, casting the actors, and staying on top of a very long list of elements needed to produce a weekly show. Most important, the showrunner maintains the essential vision of the show. A showrunner can be a writer, a producer, or both, and she has the power to hire or fire, shouldering the burden of the show's success or failure.

Producer (also called senior producer, supervising producer) — She can be an entrepreneurial producer or a producer commissioned to work on the project. Either way, she starts the ball rolling, usually from concept to broadcast, by initiating ideas and hiring and coordinating crews. She can also be the writer and/or the director, or hires them; casts the talent; and supervises and controls the budget and the technical and administrative aspects throughout the project. She oversees contracts and negotiations, and may receive part of the final profits as well as a regular salary.

Associate Producer — Also called the coproducer or assistant producer, he is the producer's right hand and does specific jobs that the producer assigns. This can be on the creative side, such as helping with interviews on a talk show, and can also lean toward the administration side, such as making production schedules, allotting budgets to departments, booking talent and/or crew, research, interviewing talent, finding locations, etc.

Line Producer (also called production manager, unit production manager, producer, or coproducer) — The nuts and bolts of producers, she's most involved in the day-to-day operation from the beginning to the end of the project. She keeps budgets on track and compares estimated costs to actual expenditures. The line producer represents the administrative side of television. Rather than generating ideas, the line producer turns ideas into reality by figuring out the logistics of a project. She keeps the production on schedule (set constructions, props, wardrobes, talent releases, etc.). She breaks down the script into a storyboard and its components for production, and decides the sequence of shooting that's most cost-effective. She works closely with the producer(s) in various aspects of location scouting, transportation and lodging, as well as other aspects of production. It's a vital job as the line producer helps the executive producer, producer, and director do their jobs smoothly.

Staff Producers — Staff producers are hired on a permanent basis by a network or production company, and generally are employees with benefits. Their jobs usually involve producing an ongoing aspect of the show assigned to them: they interview potential guests, research stories, find and secure locations, etc.

Segment Producers — In news, reality-based programming, or talk shows, they are assigned to one of several stories aired within the program and produce their own segment. Some shows may have several teams comprised of a producer, PAs, a camera operator, and an editor who work together on their segment.

Independent Producers (also called independent contractors or freelancers) — They often own their own small companies with a capable infrastructure, and work on a project for a network or production company. They may have a complete staff and might not be required to work on premise; they get no benefits and usually pay all their taxes and other expenses from their production fees or salaries.

Field Producers — This area of producing means a producer is "in the field" or at a location some distance away from the primary producer. Many companies in New York or Los Angeles have a roster of field producers who are located around the country or abroad. They can be on the scene faster and less expensively, and usually work in areas such as sports, entertainment, and news.

Session Producers — Many aspects of producing require a producer to supervise for quality, time, and length, and to keep consistent with footage already shot. These producers arrange for and supervise recording sessions, interviews, voice-over narration, etc.

Post-Production Supervisors — As producers for the post-production stage, they're familiar with the footage to be edited as well as with all the graphic and audio elements. They work closely with the editor and later, with the sound designer and audio editor in all the audio mixes throughout the final stages of post-production.

TOP TEN

The Top Ten Things a Producer of Nonfiction Should Know:

1. Who is your target audience?
2. What is new/unique about this program?
3. How much is it going to cost or what is the budget?
4. Who is paying for it and what are their expectations?
5. Hire the best people you can afford.
6. Try not to cut corners on anything that is going on the screen.
7. It's all about the story.
8. It's all about the casting.
9. Ideas are easy, getting them made is hard.
10. You're only as good as your last production.

—Veronique Bernard, *excerpt from interview in Chapter 11*

V. The Need for People Skills

Although a producer's creative and business skills are essential to the success of a project, it doesn't stop there. People skills are an equally important facet of a strong producer. It can't be stated often enough: A producer can do nothing without a team. The producer builds her team on the talents of writers, directors, crew, actors, editors, composers, etc. Without them to actualize the project, a producer is useless. The producer uses her people skills to not only attract qualified people to the project, but to keep them engaged and collaborative. A strong producer relies on and employs the following abilities when working with the many people involved in actualizing a project:

1. **Collaboration.** A strong producer embraces collaboration and fosters teamwork by supporting each member of the team, and encouraging open discussion.

2. **Communication skills.** These skills are vital for effective relationships. Without them, you risk misunderstandings, even chaos in your project. Communication is either *verbal* (words as well as the tone and volume of our voice) or *nonverbal* (facial expressions, body language, and gestures).

    *   Verbal: Is *what* you said the same thing as *how* you said it? You say you're not mad but your tone of voice says otherwise. Say what you mean.

    *   Nonverbal: Do you look at people as you talk or listen, or are you distracted? Does your body language say that you are nervous or inattentive, or calm and in control?

3. **Conflict management.** Conflicts happen all the time — especially in the high-stress world of television. No matter how hard we try, some conflicts are inevitable and can't be resolved. But most conflicts can be *managed* effectively if you can grasp the cause of the conflict at hand and deal with it. As the producer, you are also the peacemaker.

    *   Embrace your options: Look for all possible solutions to a problem, and don't stay stuck on the problem — move on to solutions.

    *   Stay cool: Getting emotionally upset only contributes to the problem, and in the scope of things, is seldom worth the energy.

    *   Empathize: Everyone has a bad day — even producers. Sometimes a conflict is a poorly disguised call for attention or recognition. Listen to your intuition.

    *   Own it: If you've got a viewpoint or an emotion, own it. Take responsibility for how you're reacting to someone else's emotions or outbursts.

    *   Humor: The old saying inside the TV networks is "Hey, this isn't brain surgery." People respond to humor in almost every situation, and as stressful as producing can be, it isn't life or death. You can be serious about your work without taking yourself too seriously.

4. **Emotional intelligence (EQ).** In this growing field, initially developed by Daniel Goleman, a person's emotional strengths are considered as important as his or her intellectual abilities. A high EQ is measured by a producer's ability to show genuine empathy, respect, and sincerity, as well as real affection, for the team.

5. **Learning styles.** We are seeing impressive research over the last few years on the ways that people learn, both cognitively and emotionally. Researchers in this field have identified over twenty different ways that people absorb information. They're all effective, and when you can understand the different ways in which we learn, you can build strong communication with your team. Some of these learning styles include:

    *   Multiple intelligences: This was originally developed by Harvard professor, Dr. Howard Gardner. His research reveals almost a dozen distinct predominant intelligences that each of us can claim, such as a strong musical, mathematical, or athletic intelligence.

    *   Analytical learner: Another way of understanding a person's various learning styles, the analytical learner understands information best when he's presented in ways that are sequential, linear, organized, and delivered one step at a time.

- Global learner: The opposite of the analytical learner, this person sees the big picture first, then breaks it down into smaller and more manageable details.

- Visual: This style refers to a person who learns visually, by reading or looking at information, and then creates a mental picture from the data.

- Auditory: In this case, he absorbs information better when it comes through hearing the spoken word or audio. The auditory learner generally has strong listening skills and acute verbal abilities.

- Kinesthetic: To the kinesthetic learner, information is best conveyed through ways that are physical, spatial, or sensory, such as charts and 3-D modeling.

- Goal-oriented: This type of person tends to stick with a task until it's done, with no breaks or lulls, and with a focus that's almost single-minded.

- Process-oriented: Here, the process and the journey of reaching the goal can be as interesting as is the goal itself.

6. **Listening skills**. The ability to simply listen to another person can work wonders. Being attentive, not interrupting, and acknowledging that you hear the other person can be a surprisingly difficult skill for many people to develop. By suspending your own need to talk and control, you can make people feel valued.

7. **Leadership skills.** As the team's leader, the producer recognizes that the team is made of individuals, each with his or her own emotional needs, learning styles, problem-solving strategies, communication approaches, and personal issues that can influence professional function.

> Leadership has a harder job to do than just choose sides. It must bring sides together.
> —Jesse Jackson

The producer benefits — and so do the team members — when the needs of the team are taken into consideration with an eye on creating balance. The producer models behaviors and viewpoints that set a tone for the project and all its stages of production. Some of the essential ideals that the producer can embody are

- Commitment: If you don't believe in your project, don't expect anyone else to. Stand firmly behind it.

- Credibility: Though you want people to respect you, don't let your need to be liked get in the way of getting things done.

- Delegation: Hire the best people you can find, and learn what they do. Then, leave them alone to do their job. Check in regularly to confirm that the vision is intact.

- Motivation: Producers don't expect praise, but they lavish it on their team when it's genuinely earned. Find ways to show your thanks.

8. **Ethics**. The word ethics is more about strength of character than a spiritual or religious mandate. A producer who assesses his or her own ethical framework is more likely to create a project that's under control, stimulating, and a positive experience for everyone.

- Accountability: Because you're in charge, you're accountable to your team — it's their project too. Keeping up with changes in technology, creative trends, and the business of the TV industry is also part of your job.

- Honesty: Your word is solid enough to build your reputation upon it.

- Objectivity: You can listen to criticism without taking it personally, and can acknowledge all sides of an issue.

- Patience: Respect the fact that people work at different rhythms with varying working styles.

- Personal balance: The demands of the job can take over your life. With the right perspective, you can have a professional *and* a personal life.

- Avoid excess: Stress in television can result in producer burnout caused by too many hours, too little sleep, a diet of junk food, and the temptations of smoking, alcohol, drugs, and negative relationships.

- Relationships: It is possible to cultivate new friends who share your passion for producing without ignoring your most important supporters — friends and family.

- Daydream: Occasionally, you'll make the time to take a walk, a mental break, and a few deep breaths.

On a Human Level . . .

As the producer, you form the core of a project by encouraging collaboration and providing strong and balanced leadership. You know when to step back and let people do their job. You model patience, humor, and a clear vision of the project, supplying creative direction while balancing the time pressures of the budget. You are generous with your flexibility and encouragement, while staying connected to the realities of the budget and time constraints.

> I've found in life that when you refuse to settle for anything but the best, you very often get it.
>
> —W. Somerset Maugham

VI. Summary

A good producer is knowledgeable about the many elements of producing. He or she is also a good writer, director, or editor, or can do all three. A storyteller, an entrepreneur, a risk-taker — a producer has strong leadership skills and works well with a team. Another sure sign of a strong producer is an understanding of the larger context of television, including its past history, current status, and future potential. The goal of the next chapter is to provide that context.

VII. Chapter Review Questions

1. How do TV producers differ from film producers?

2. List three important skills and traits that a good producer has mastered. Explain why each is helpful.

3. List one role the producer plays in each of the five stages of project development.

4. Define "clout" in producers' terms.

5. What does the Line Producer do? How is this job different from other producing titles?

6. List two reasons why "owning" your emotions can help in managing conflicts.

7. What areas of producing might be impacted by a failure of leadership? A failure of strong ethics?

8. Define three types of learning outlined in the Learning Styles section. Include a constructive approach to working with each type.

9. How can "delegation" contribute to the fluidity of a crew and the execution of a project?

10. What have you learned so far about being a producer? Has it affected your career choices?

Television: "the art of distant seeing ... the possibilities of the new art are as boundless as the imagination."

—David Sarnoff, 1927

There's nothing on it worthwhile, and we're not going to watch it in this household, and I don't want it in your intellectual diet.

—Philo T. Farnsworth, one of television's inventors, to his children

TV: Past, Present — and Future

This Chapter's Talking Points

I. Television Is a Unique Medium

Television as a communications medium has had a singular impact on millions of people around the globe, and it wields an impressive influence on how we view our culture. Almost every American home has at least one TV set, and more than 40% of Americans have at least three. Since the 1950s, television has emerged as a global catalyst for social and political change, and has greatly affected how we learn and communicate.

TV lives at home base. It is a facet of our day-to-day lives that we can enjoy alone, or in a group, and its presence in the background can be a source of human contact. With its immediacy, television is, for many people, a primary source of information. TV can feel like a member of the family: familiar, frustrating, and often comforting.

TV has created a unique environment of "home entertainment." What we choose to watch can range from drama of superior quality to programs that challenge good taste. The range of programming comes to us through literally hundreds of channels that are brought to the viewer by cable and satellite, and even traditional rooftop or rabbit ear antennas. Yet television is a consistent source of contention and controversy. Its critics argue that the full potential of television may never be reached, or that entertainment panders to the lowest common denominator. Ultimately, the validity of these arguments rests on the shoulders of the television producer who has the skills and the capability to put these criticisms to rest.

II. How TV Works

Television *content* (a catch-all phrase for programs, news, information, music) comes into a television set through broadcast signals. These signals hold data — an image, sounds, graphic art, electronic lettering — that is re-created in your TV set as clear images and audio. There are four broadcast signals. Each signal separately controls the:

- Brightness of the image

- Color of the image

- Audio from the image

- Synchronization of the transmitter and the receiver (your TV set)

Broadcast signals are transmitted through virtually the same radio waves that deliver a radio show. These radio waves travel through the atmosphere at the speed of light, and can accommodate vast amounts of information. Television's video signals are heavier, don't travel as far, and use about one thousand times more *bandwidth* (channel space) than the transmission of an audio signal. With the advances in today's technology, programming can be transmitted by discrete digital signals delivered via *fiber optics*, opening up potential levels of interactive use.

III. The Impact of Human Vision on TV

As we look at an image, this picture stays imprinted on our retina for a fraction of a second. This phenomenon is known as *persistence of vision*; as we watch a sequence of rapid images at the right speed (25 to 30 times a second), an illusion is created of a complete and uninterrupted picture.

In early television, scanning wheels created a broadcast picture by scanning an image slowly, line by line; the blurry images on the earliest sets were built with 48 scanned lines. Now, modern color sets reflect a picture that's comprised of several hundred scanned lines. These lines contain over 100,000 picture elements known as *pixels*. Our TV screen is coated with fluorescent compounds consisting of millions of miniscule dots that give off light as they're hit by electrons at high speed.

For an image to be transmitted by electronic impulses, it is first broken down into tiny pixels using a scanning process. Thousands of these pixels form lines that are rapidly transmitted, one line at a time. Even though the screen never has more than one pixel displayed at once, the electron gun scans the screen so quickly that we see a complete picture, not the separate elements it is composed of.

Each of these tiny pixels is shaped like a rectangle and is made from three colors: red, green, and blue (RGB). The pixels are combined on a phosphor screen, close enough together that they appear to be just one color. These lines, in order to be seen by the viewer, must be reproduced one by one and rapidly reassembled into the original image. This whole process results in a video signal.

Modern television sets in America receive programming that has been transmitted as 525 rapidly scanned lines; most other countries broadcast in 625 lines, which gives their picture a higher resolution or clearer picture. Early mechanical TVs could only broadcast a 48-line image; the electronic *kinescope* boosted the count to 60 lines. NBC broadcast 120-line images in 1931 and then improved their system to 240 lines two years later. By 1940, NBC had televised a 507-line picture, and one year later, the National Television Standards Committee (NTSC) adopted what has been the American broadcast standard ever since — a 525-line, 30-frames-per-second picture — called the *NTSC format.*

A television camera, like a film camera, is pointed at an image, and the opening of the camera's shutter allows that image to enter the camera. But the way TV captures that picture is different from film. In film, images are captured on film coated with an emulsion that has been chemically treated to be sensitive to light. It is must be developed in a film lab before it can be viewed. In television, the image is transposed *electronically* — either to videotape or directly to digital storage — and can be seen immediately.

Since 1941, standard American TV sets have an *aspect ratio* of 4:3 and a shape that is almost a square, a little wider than it is tall. More recently, *high-definition television* (HDTV) has vastly improved our television image. For example, an HDTV set has a larger aspect ratio of 16:9 and is one-third wider than the current NTSC picture. This aspect ratio accommodates the way our eyes naturally see an image. With HDTV, we see more of what is in our field of vision. It gives the image a finer resolution, with more clarity of detail and almost twice as many lines and pixels as NTSC television. HDTV has smaller pixels that are square rather than rectangular and are closer together.

Regardless of how it may be transmitted or the size of the TV set, television is increasingly a part of our daily culture. TV surrounds us, not only in our homes, but in the office, the supermarket, at dentists' and doctors' offices, in a bank line, on a long airplane flight, and even in some New York City taxis. To best study this phenomenon, you need to explore the rich history of television's early beginnings.

"An unexamined life is not worth living." If you are interested in developing an art form and you consider yourself to be in an art form, you must, must, must know what came before you. How things work, what the traditions were. The people who are the most informed are people who can take the most risks and be successful. The people who aren't aware of the history are the very safe ones who don't change things. They are only building on what's been done before.
—Sheril Antonio, *excerpt from interview in Chapter 11*

IV. The Creators of Television

If it weren't for Philo T. Farnsworth, inventor of television, we'd still be eating frozen radio dinners.

—Johnny Carson

While exploring the earliest beginnings of television, determining the "truth" of its ancestry can be as frustrating and fuzzy as its first broadcasts. One example is a perennial debate that continues among TV historians: Who can legitimately claim the title of the inventor of television?

- In 1883, German engineer Paul Nipkow designed the primary component of early mechanical television systems called the *scanning disk*. The disk was punched with holes that created a spiral from the outside into the center, and each hole vertically scanned one line of an image. Each line was transmitted to a selenium cell, transferred to an electronic signal, and re-created in the receiver by a similar disk. Nipkow called his early design an "electric telescope," although he never actually built the device itself.

- Often called the pioneer of mechanical television, John Logie Baird was a Scottish entrepreneur with an engineering background who was the first to transmit an image using a mechanical television system in 1924. His first public showing of "television" was held in a department store in London, though only silhouettes could be seen of the images. Three years later, Baird had so improved his system that the British Broadcasting System (BBC) adopted it for the broadcast of experimental programs. By 1930, the British public could buy Baird kits or ready-made TV sets to receive the broadcasts.

- Widely known as the father of electronic television, Philo T. Farnsworth was a Mormon teenager who dreamed of a concept for television while plowing his field. By the age of 21, Farnsworth had designed the first all-electronic television system that had its first public demonstration in 1928. His "Image Dissector" camera pick-up tube recorded moving images that were coded through radio waves, then reconfigured back into a picture on a screen. Farnsworth's invention in tandem with Zworykin's "Iconoscope" (see later in the list) combined to create electronic broadcasting in 1939, although bitter litigation between the Radio Corporation of America (RCA) and Farnsworth's company has historically eclipsed his essential contributions to television.

- Another contender for the title was Charles Francis Jenkins, whose wealth and intelligence enabled him to develop "radio movies to be broadcast for entertainment in the home." In 1925, he broadcast a ten-minute film of a small windmill over a five-mile distance. His "radiovision" depended on Nipkow's scanning disk as its basis.

- Vladimir Zworykin was a highly educated Russian immigrant whose research was substantially financed by powerful RCA. His research contributed to RCA's domination of the infant television market — first manufacturing TV sets, then setting up the National Broadcasting Company (NBC) to provide programming for the sets. Zworykin's efforts resulted in the Iconoscope, an early electronic camera tube that he patented in 1923, as well as an all-electronic TV receiver that utilized Zworykin's picture tube, which he called a kinescope.

Internationally, other scientists and inventors were experimenting with similar ideas.

- In 1897, German physicist Karl Braun invented the first cathode-ray tube, which forms the basis of all modern TV cameras and sets.

- Russian Boris Rosing was also exploring the cathode-ray tube by 1906. He has been credited with discovering the theory for electronic television via wireless transmission in 1911 by using the Braun tube and the research of others before him. One of Rosing's students was Vladimir Zworykin whose work would be integral to the advancement of television.

The work of these early inventors and scientists clearly shows television to be the result of experimentation, labor, and the passion for their vision of "distance seeing." Yet, the possibility of communicating through images has intrigued thinkers and dreamers throughout human history. In ancient Greece, Aristotle was convinced that we were surrounded by invisible particles that combined to form images of matter. He was unable to prove his own theory, yet

Aristotle's vision has propelled two millennia of experimentation, and television stands as an actualization of his curiosity.

Today, what we watch on television seems effortless. Yet the making of any program relies on producers, writers, directors, actors, and a complete crew. It requires money to finance it and time to complete it. A TV show depends on camera and audio equipment to videotape the image and record the audio, and then relies on technology to broadcast and transmit the picture and sound. It needs satellites, cable, electricity, and hundreds of other components to complete the broadcasting process.

This broadcasting process that we, as viewers, now take for granted has been crafted by the labors of some extraordinary thinkers, as you'll see in Section V below.

V. Television's Evolution

Guglielmo Marconi took an active part in the invention of television. A bright and wealthy Italian inventor, Marconi discovered a method of transmitting Morse code over limited distances by using electromagnetic waves. In 1896, Marconi's "wireless" telegraph reached all parts of the world after he telegraphed the letter S, in Morse code, across the Atlantic Ocean, over 2,000 miles away. He quickly formed a company called the Marconi Wireless Telegraph Company of America, which claimed responsibility for *the broadcast* — a transmission of sound waves that could move in all directions, follow the earth's curvature, and that was able to be picked up by a receiver on the other end.

An ambitious young Russian immigrant named David Sarnoff, who worked as an office boy at Marconi's company, was astute enough to realize the potential of the company that was growing rapidly around him. Taking engineering classes at night, Sarnoff used his considerable energy to grasp and master this enterprising technology. In just a few years, Sarnoff became a governing force at RCA and eventually was one of the founders of NBC.

The dawn of the 20th century ushered in the concept of "distance vision" at the 1900 World's Fair in Paris. During the First International Congress of Electricity, a Russian named Constantin Perskyi was the first person known to bring the word "television" into the public's consciousness. This dim concept was already taking root in the minds of other inventors and scientists around the globe.

> Television was the most revolutionary event of the century. Its importance was in a class with the discovery of gunpowder and the invention of the printing press, which changed the human condition for centuries afterward.
>
> —Russell Baker

A. Early Television and Commerce

Television as an industry began with the radio. At the end of World War I, General Electric joined forces with three powerful companies — AT&T, Westinghouse, and United Fruit — to form a company known as RCA. The purpose of the alliance was to manufacture and sell radio receiver sets. Although the original company eventually unraveled, RCA survived as an independent company, buying out all the assets of Marconi's company.

In 1926, NBC became a wholly owned subsidiary of RCA. The overwhelming popularity of their radio audience required them to add a second radio network, and the two networks were soon dubbed "NBC-Red" and "NBC-Blue." By the early 1930s, RCA was gathering resources and power — it manufactured radios and it owned two networks of radio programming and a growing number of stations. More significantly, RCA controlled the contracts of the most popular radio stars, writers, and producers. NBC now ruled the airwaves.

As NBC was gaining supremacy, Columbia Phonograph Broadcasting System (CBS) was formed. In retaliation, NBC announced its intention to merge with the Victor Talking Machine Company, and when Columbia realized that this merger with its main competitor could expand their enterprise, they entered the radio business by merging with United Independent Broadcasters. Although they eventually dropped out of the merger, the name of CBS stayed on with the new company. Now NBC and CBS were rivals, and the concept of network competition was introduced to advertisers and audiences.

VI. Television's Transitions — From the 1920s to the Present

Television began as the product of technology, and the creative and informational components of television would soon follow in its wake. In labs around the globe in the 1920s and 1930s, talented scientists, engineers, and inventors were driven by their vision and passion — designing components that would ultimately be brought together as television.

A. Mechanical Television

Early television was primitive, with limited audio and an image that was small and blurred. It was based on a mechanical system with a rotating scanning disk as its basis. An image was first mechanically scanned, then transmitted mechanically. The transmitted image was received on a set — again, mechanically. The design for the scanning disk was invented by Paul Nipkow in 1884, and it was used as the foundation for other mechanical television systems that were being explored by inventors like Baird, Jenkins, Ives, and others.

Charles Francis Jenkins successfully transmitted an image that was mechanically scanned in 1925. Two years later, Dr. Ives of Bell Telephone Labs introduced his television research program by transmitting an image of a tap dancer on top of a New York skyscraper, which was carried through phone wires. Another engineer, Dr. E. F. W. Alexanderson, demonstrated a television system that operated on revolving mirrors. This led to more sophisticated scanning disks and expansion of the components. And in 1928, his first regular broadcasts began in Schenectady, New York. Unfortunately, very few people owned the Alexanderson TV sets that were necessary to watch the telecasts.

In 1928, Baird Television was the first all-mechanical television system. This system appeared to be satisfactory, and it would be several years before investors would fund the research into a better way to capture, transmit, and receive an image using electronics — moving away from the more cumbersome mechanical system.

B. Electronic Television

Meanwhile, research into *electronic TV* was energizing television technology. The basis for this new all-electronic system was the cathode-ray tube, which was originally explored by early inventors such as Rosing in Russia and A. A. Campbell-Swinton in England. Philo Farnsworth's extensive work with his Image Dissector, along with Zworykin's Iconoscope, was promoted by the ultimate catalyst — millions of research dollars invested by RCA who, with the entrepreneurial genius of David Sarnoff behind it, proved instrumental in developing a television system that was powered by electricity. By the late 1930s, both the camera and the receiving TV set were electronic, and mechanical television was a thing of the past. The first all-electronic TV set had a 14-inch tube and was manufactured by DuMont in 1938. It was called "The Clifton."

By the end of the 1920s, there were fifteen experimental television stations in America, which transmitted limited programming via the mechanical television system. However, the devastating crash of Wall Street brought most research into television to a halt.

C. Television's Experimental Steps (the 1930s)

Although television could now be viewed in some areas in America, radio continued to capture everyone's attention. Live radio shows and personalities were wildly popular and radio was inexpensive to produce, transmit, and receive. Television was still considered a speculative venture. Costs were high: facilities had to be built and programs written, produced, and paid for. TV sets were not only expensive, they were hard to find and only limited programming was available for viewers.

Yet the *idea* of television was thrilling: an image could actually come into our homes — television was like radio, but with a picture. In reality, TV was still in its primitive form. The images were blurry, the audio was scratchy, and the picture barely visible on available 2- or 3-inch screens. Many sets even came equipped with an attached magnifying screen. In 1930, NBC inaugurated its first experimental TV station in New York, W2XBS. Its debut broadcast was a very fuzzy image of a Felix the Cat statue. One year later, CBS followed with what could generously be called the first television "spectacular," which featured George Gershwin playing the piano and Kate Smith singing. But television continued to be cynically regarded by most Americans as just a passing fancy.

Behind the scenes, the government was reviewing both the technical and ethical advances being made in radio and television — measuring their effects not only on the viewing public but also on business. In 1934, Congress established the Federal Communications Commission (FCC), whose purpose was to patrol the airwaves with the understanding that because the airwaves were essentially owned by the public, all private businesses that controlled and owned radio and television stations must be regulated and issued licenses in order to use these airwaves.

A landmark breakthrough came in 1936 with the introduction of coaxial cable. This transmission device was constructed of a hollow tube that housed wires that transmitted electrical impulses of different frequencies without combining them. This prompted the FCC to create the NTSC. Comprised primarily of engineers, the NTSC researched and recommended a comprehensive set of standards for electronic television that was adopted in 1941. The majority of their guidelines are still in effect today.

As it had with radio, RCA expanded its energies into building and selling television receivers, or TV sets, and then creating programming that consumers could watch on the sets they purchased. The theme of the 1939 World's Fair in New York City was "The World of Tomorrow," and it was an ideal forum for NBC to be the first network to broadcast a head of state — President Franklin D. Roosevelt. Although television had been pushed into the background by radio for over a decade, the World's Fair provided RCA with a promotional spotlight that planted television firmly in the country's consciousness. In other parts of the world, Germany and France began limited broadcasting in the 1930s, and in Canada, the Canadian Broadcast Company (CBC) was formalized in 1936.

D. Television in the Trenches (the 1940s)

In the early 1940s, the war was escalating in Europe and dominated everyone's thoughts. People stayed glued to their radio; it ruled every waking hour and connected Americans to the battle-fields with an urgency that diminished continuing research into television. Increased war efforts forced stations to make cutbacks. There were fewer broadcasts as employees went to fight in the war, and available programming was drastically reduced.

But radio flourished, and NBC had become so popular that the company divided their extensive radio shows (and limited experimental TV programming) into two networks, the Blue and the Red. The Blue network broadcast programs that were more cultural in content — like drama, music, and thoughtful commentary — while the Red network favored entertainment and comedy. Eventually, almost 250 stations across the country received programs from NBC's two networks. Fearing the possibility of a monopoly, the FCC ruled that one company couldn't own more than one network. RCA was forced to sell its Blue network in 1943, which eventually became the American Broadcast Company (ABC). Within the decade, the three networks — NBC, CBS, and ABC — would be in fierce competition, with the DuMont network close behind.

In 1941 both CBS and NBC officially became what we now call "commercial television." The fledgling DuMont Television Network had also begun limited broadcasting, and by 1942, it was one of the few sources for TV programming. This innovative network from New York City, formalized as a network in 1946, was the creation of Dr. Allen B. DuMont, one of the original pioneers in electronic television who had premiered his innovative and high-quality TV set at the 1939 World's Fair alongside RCA.

DuMont was equally as creative in his programming choices as he was in his technological advancement of television. The DuMont network was determined to provide comedy and entertainment for Americans to combat the stresses of the war, and introduced many of television's early legends: Ernie Kovacs, ventriloquist Paul Winchell and Jerry Mahoney, and Fred Waring's famous glee club. However, the network had been forced to broadcast on a UHF frequency rather than the standard VHF, and the growing popularity of the other three networks finally forced the DuMont network off the air in 1956.

As World War II drew to a close, ongoing research into television's potential benefit to the war efforts ultimately thrust America into the forefront of technology and creative programming. Our major competitors at the time were England and Germany, both of which had essentially stopped all research during the war years. American companies were exploring and refining color TV with CBS developing a color disk that could be placed over the black-and-white image. But ultimately it was NBC who perfected the technical ability to make a TV set "compatible" — a color broadcast could also be watched on a set that was a black-and-white receiver. By the mid-1940s, the country's nine original commercial (nonexperimental) TV stations had expanded to 48 stations. Less than 7,000 functioning TV sets were capable of receiving programs in homes around New York, but by 1948, sales of TV sets had grown by over 500%. Most viewers, over one million of them, watched TV in public places like bars, restaurants, and hotels, or in stores that sold TV sets.

In spite of radio's ongoing popularity, TV was rapidly catching up. It offered the additional advantage of seeing images as well as hearing them, which gave viewers the ability to watch sports and dance in action, to see news as it happened, the beauty of scenic locations, works of art, the facial expressions of an actor, the pratfalls of a comedian, and the eyes of a politician.

TV capitalized on radio's lack of visuals with the introduction of shows like *The Texaco Star Theater* with Milton Berle in the fall of 1948. "Uncle Miltie's" energy, unique humor, and famous guests revolutionized television programming and vastly expanded the number of people buying TV sets. At the time, the average cost of a television set was $500, even though an average annual salary was less than $3,000. In 1946, about ten thousand TV sets were in use; by 1948, 400,000 homes in America had sets; and four years later, nineteen million TV sets were in active use. By 1956, 85% of American homes had sets.

On the heels of Milton Berle's show — which ran until 1956 — came Sid Caesar and *Your Show of Shows*, a 90-minute weekly comedy show that featured groundbreaking humor, clever writing, satire, sketches, and acting. Although its final episode was broadcast in 1954, its influence rippled indelibly through television humor in shows like *Laugh-in* and *Saturday Night Live* decades later.

Ed Sullivan was a rather stiff master of ceremonies with a dry delivery, yet his early show, *Toast of the Town*, and, later, *The Ed Sullivan Show*, attracted top talent, such as Dean Martin and Jerry Lewis, Elvis Presley, Ingrid Bergman, and the Beatles who all became entertainment legends.

Advertisers recognized the inherent value in television as a marketplace in which to sell products. As they began to invest their revenues in the creative aspects of this new medium, the technical designers and engineers were keeping pace by building sound stages, facilities, and transmitters. Radio stations, fledgling television stations, and newspapers were lining up for TV licenses while producers, directors, and writers were busy creating the next big show. Television's time had come as evidenced by personalities like Faye Emerson, Perry Como, Gene Autry, and William Boyd and shows like *The Lone Ranger, Hopalong Cassidy, Howdy Doody, Meet the Press*, John Cameron Swayze's *Camel Newsreel Theater*, and *Kraft Television Theater*, which aired on both NBC and ABC.

E. Television's Golden Age (the 1950s)

The 1950s has justifiably been called The Golden Age of Television. With the end of World War II, the economy had recovered and stabilized, and television had become so popular that magazines regularly featured articles on home decorating with the TV set as the centerpiece. The dining room table had been replaced by frozen dinners on a TV tray, and *TV Guide*, launched in 1953, was on the coffee table.

TV producers and writers freely took their programming ideas from radio and traditional theater. TV news, for example, consisted of the anchor simply reading the newspaper and wire reports into camera, with none of the visuals we expect in today's news broadcasts. CBS and NBC created legendary television with innovative anthology programming such as *Kraft Television Theater, Studio One, Playhouse 90, Philco TV Playhouse, General Electric Theater* (hosted by Ronald Reagan for eight years), and *The U.S. Steel Hour*. By the mid-1950s, there were 14 live-drama series from which to choose. Early television was transmitted live — broadcast from the studio to the viewer with all its visible glitches and mistakes.

As programming boundaries expanded, television shows and the creative minds behind them grew bolder. Brilliant young comedic minds like Ernie Kovacs and Sid Caesar wrote witty and irreverent material, and used TV's technology to produce special effects that played with the material at hand. Television was moving away from simply adapting traditional radio formats to new and innovative programming concepts.

Yet with all its creative departures, the technical limitations of live broadcast had traditionally restricted television's ability to produce and transmit a show from any location other than from television studios, most of which were then in New York City. However, when videotape was introduced in 1956, this invention allowed programs and shows to be first taped, edited, then broadcast from a wider range of locations. This offered viewers much clearer images and audio. Videotape made it possible to record and archive programs; it was electronic, more flexible, and less expensive than film. Prior to wide use of videotape, the only way to record a broadcast had been to aim a film camera at the television set as it received the live broadcast and to film it; the result was called a *kinescope*. The first broadcast use of videotape was a segment in color on the innovative *Jonathan Winters Show*.

Coaxial cable, which had originally connected only New York and Philadelphia, eventually worked its way to the West Coast; its cross-country completion was celebrated in the fall of 1951. NBC could now broadcast coast-to-coast over its 61 stations. The same year, the first experimental color TV transmissions were attempted, but were a failure because black-and-whites sets still couldn't pick up color transmissions. Although CBS had developed a color disk that could be placed over the black-and-white image, it was NBC who ultimately perfected the technical ability to make a TV set compatible. Two years later, the problem was solved and "compatible color" was successfully broadcast.

The creative borders of television were changing, as the dramatic long-form productions gradually took a back seat to shows like Jackie Gleason's *The Honeymooners* and *I Love Lucy* with Lucille Ball and Desi Arnaz. These shows captivated viewers with their familiar and lovable ongoing characters. *I Love Lucy* was also the first show to have "repeats," introducing the lucrative concept of syndication where repeats could be sold to various stations. By 1960, only one of the original drama series was still broadcasting and the sitcom was born.

Quiz shows were another popular genre in the 1950s. *Twenty-One, Tic Tac Dough, The Big Surprise, You Bet Your Life* with Groucho Marx, *What's My Line?*, and *The $64,000 Question* swept the ratings, as Americans enthusiastically played along with the contestants. But when a contestant on *Twenty-One* admitted to being provided with the answers to the questions, the genre was permanently tainted and mutated to milder shows, such as *Queen for a Day* and *Let's Make a Deal*. These shows were now governed by strict regulations that are still enforced on similar shows today.

The technology of television was getting better, faster, and most important, cheaper. As the sales of TV sets flourished, movie theaters and the established motion picture studio system were threatened by this burgeoning medium. Television's explosive growth alarmed the FCC. The mounting technological and ethical questions hadn't been anticipated, and the establishment of monopolies was only a matter of time. It was becoming an overwhelming issue, and in 1948, the government stopped issuing any additional broadcasting licenses and focused their resources on the rapid expansion of television as a powerful business and cultural force to be reckoned with.

It took the FCC four years to draft and finally agree upon a statement of principles that would govern television and the standards with which it operated. The political and electronic complexities were regulated by a set of guidelines established in 1952 that set new standards for flourishing areas of television, as well as for future media advances that were then still theoretical.

The FCC guidelines included the assignment of very high frequency (VHF) and ultrahigh frequency (UHF) channels. These new standards for engineering and technology applications defined public service and educational programming, and set channels aside that were only for educational and public access use. It took the FCC over a year to review the various color systems that were still experimental, finally agreeing on one color system that could be transmitted by all the networks and received by all color TV sets.

Cable TV was launched in 1950 as an effort to provide television to homes in rural areas that were unable to receive broadcast signals due to their distance from major transmission towers. As television viewing exploded in the urban American cities, the demand increased among people who lived in more remote areas for both outlets through which they could buy TV sets as well as ways to receive programming on them. Cable TV was able to provide the programming, and television dealerships in rural areas grew exponentially.

In 1951, the merger of ABC with United Paramount Theaters created a huge leap in creative programming that catapulted the young station into direct competition with NBC, CBS, and DuMont. When DuMont finally went out of business in 1956, the remaining three networks began a battle for domination that continues to this day: vying for advertising dollars, viewer ratings, and programming originality. This competition led to the development of the "network system" that included production services for writing and producing programs, sales and distribution of these programs to the network affiliates as well as their Owned and Operated (O&O) stations, and the generation of advertising dollars with which to subsidize the network.

The first political TV ads had an explosive effect on television viewers, and possibly, on the outcome of an election. In 1952, presidential candidate Adlai Stevenson bought eighteen half-hour time slots in which to get his political message across to the American people. But they proved to be too long and tedious for most people to watch, and viewers got angry when his speeches interrupted their favorite shows. His rival, General Dwight D. Eisenhower, was wisely advised to make his own TV ads short and sweet, and his first political ads were brief 20-second spots that aired before or after popular shows like *I Love Lucy*. Though the ads may or may not have been direct contributors, Eisenhower won the 1952 presidency.

It was during the 1952 political convention that the term "anchorman" was first used to describe Walter Cronkite's convention coverage for CBS. His intelligent and thoughtful observations on the political arena and its politicians won him the title of "the most trusted man in America." Cronkite's nightly broadcasts emphasized television as an increasingly important source of news and information for most Americans.

TV bore witness to another kind of politics called McCarthyism. The House Committee on Un-American Activities (HUAC) had begun their investigation of the film industry in 1947 in their sweep for "Communist infiltrators" and their witch hunt soon spilled over into broadcasting. Dozens of writers, producers, actors, and directors who were suspected of having left-wing tendencies were fired and blacklisted, which prevented them from being employed anywhere. CBS required its employees to sign an oath of loyalty, yet it was the network's esteemed journalist, Edward R. Murrow, who ultimately broke the back of McCarthyism. In Murrow's courageous documentary in 1954, he exposed Senator Joseph McCarthy with his legendary quote: "His mistake has been to confuse dissent with disloyalty." Within months, McCarthy was censured by the U.S. Senate; television had effectively ended his reign.

The Golden Age of 1950s television saw the creation of *I Love Lucy* in 1951. This was the first sitcom shot with the now-standard three-camera setup, along with family shows like *The Adventures of Ozzie and Harriet* and *Father Knows Best*. In 1952, Dave Garroway was the original host of the *Today Show,* the first magazine-format program. One year later, *TV Guide* began publication. The country's first "adult western," *Gunsmoke,* began in 1955 and ran for twenty years. *The Mickey Mouse Club* put ABC on the map as a youth-oriented network in 1955. The teen hit of the decade was *The Many Loves of Dobie Gillis* with Warren Beatty and Tuesday Weld, and Rod Serling's sci-fi series, *Twilight Zone,* aired from 1959 to 1964 on CBS. It also the first network to introduce 30-minutes soap operas rather than the traditional 15-minute dramas, and both *As the World Turns* and *The Edge of Night* began airing in 1956. *Broadway Open House* with Morey Amsterdam was the first late-night variety show, setting the stage for *The Tonight Show* and *Late Night with David Letterman*.

F. The First Television Society (the 1960s)

By the 1960s, Americans had become known as the first television society. Both the subtle and overt influences of television permeated the culture, and over 90% of American homes had at least one television set. The three networks — NBC, CBS, and ABC — dominated the country with roughly 200 affiliate stations each in the major metropolitan areas.

The networks produced the vast majority of their programming in their Los Angeles and New York studios, seldom subcontracting any productions out to independent producers or filmmakers. The network system included the now-essential program sponsor (soap products, automobiles, cigarettes) along with an advertising agency that created the commercials for these sponsors' products.

By 1960, there were 640 community antenna television (CATV) systems that delivered all available channels from nearby metropolitan centers to more isolated areas. These fledgling independent and public television stations were new and inexperienced, and offered little competition to the networks that targeted their programming to a mass audience. The immediacy of satellite programming brought the news of the world to Americans in real time. Now, we could see events as they happened.

As television became more popular, it attracted producers, writers, directors, and actors who had previously worked only in film. There were many advantages to this medium: the exposure of TV was much wider than that of the motion picture, millions of people watched TV regularly and seldom went to movies, and it was more cost-effective to produce programming for television than for film. Movie studios saw the potential of television as a next step for their films after a traditional theatrical release, and they began channeling more financing into television development departments.

It wasn't until 1964 that the FCC finally approved RCA's color system, opening the airwaves for broadcasting programs in bright, highly refined color. Although CBS had first originated the color system, RCA quickly flooded the market with black-and-white sets that could also receive programs (in black-and-white) that were broadcast in color. By the mid-1960s, NBC was producing the majority of its prime-time programs on color film.

The 1960s produced some technical elements that we now take for granted:

- Electronic character-generator. Also known by its brand name of *chyron*, it could superimpose words over a picture and create opening and closing credits as well as lower-thirds that spelled out the speaker's name and occupation or location.

- Slo-mo. The ability to record a picture (say, of a baseball play), and replay it in slow motion, repeatedly.

- Other equipment and technology were unveiled, such as color videotape machines, videotape cartridge systems, portable small cameras known as "mini-cams," and remote-controlled operation of radio and TV stations' transmitters.

The growing influence of television was incontrovertible. When a charismatic and articulate John F. Kennedy debated a badly shaven, shifty-eyed Richard Nixon on television in 1960 in the "Great Debates," the disparity between the two men was obvious to voters. This was made even sharper through a new device called a *split screen*, which was used for the first time during the debates. Interestingly, audiences who had listened to the debates on radio picked Nixon as the winner.

Television featured prominently in national tragedy as well. Almost every American, 96% of the population, followed John F. Kennedy's funeral on television after his assassination in 1963. Days later, when Kennedy's suspected assassin — Lee Harvey Oswald — was murdered on live television by Jack Ruby, the stark immediacy of television stunned Americans.

The Vietnam War was the first war that the world watched as it was being waged. The first satellite link to Asia brought the harsh reality of the front lines to a public whose dissatisfaction with the war was growing. When CBS aired a report that exposed the cruelty of a group of U.S. Marines in a Vietnam village, President Lyndon Johnson angrily attacked the network as being unpatriotic. As a counterpoint, Walter Cronkite said at the end of a documentary he had produced in 1968 on the state of the war: "It is increasingly clear to this reporter that the only rational way out will be to negotiate." A defeated President Johnson reportedly said, "If I've lost Cronkite, I've lost middle America."

TV documentaries reached new heights in intelligent and courageous exploration of issues from civil rights to communism. A historical example was NBC's *The Tunnel*, which filmed the escape of East German refugees who had burrowed escape tunnels under the Berlin Wall. Other highlights of the 1960s included the 1962 launch of Telstar and Relay, the first television satellites to transmit transatlantic images. ABC debuted *General Hospital* in 1963, and *Days of Our Lives* on NBC followed in 1965. The Beatles made their hugely popular first appearance on *The Ed Sullivan Show* in 1964, and a year later, Bill Cosby became the first African-American actor to costar in a continuing drama, *I Spy*. Congress created the Public Broadcasting System (PBS) in 1967 that, two years later, debuted *Sesame Street* for children. NBC became the first all-color network in 1966, the same year that the network premiered the made-for-TV movie genre with shows like *Columbo, McMillan and Wife,* and *McCloud* that featured continuing lead characters. Three years later, over 600 million people around the world watched the first TV transmission from the moon on July 20, 1969. Humor got a needed boost with shows like *Rowan and Martin's Laugh-in, That Was the Week That Was,* and *The Smothers Brothers Comedy Hour;* all succeeded in reflecting the chaotic era of the 1960s with satire and irreverent wit.

G. Television in Transition (the 1970s)

Television grew progressively bolder in the 1970s in the wake of Woodstock and with the end of the Vietnam War. TV shows reflected the social and emotional changes of the growing youth culture, and the content of the traditional program shifted to more outspoken and outrageous material. In 1970, the networks cancelled at least 30 series that had been hits in the 1960s and replaced them with a new approach to programming that was directly targeted to the younger audience.

All in the Family broke new ground as the first prime-time sitcom to bring hotbed issues like racism, bigotry, and sexism into America's living rooms. *The Mary Tyler Moore Show* proved that a single professional woman could succeed on her own, addressing pertinent issues facing the working woman in the workforce. *Bridget Loves Bernie* was a forum for ethnic comedy, and also showed its main characters in the bedroom. And *The Partridge Family* brought popular music to the sitcom.

The prime-time drama became another staple of TV viewing. America was fascinated by the professional and personal lives of doctors, lawyers, and police officers featured in shows such as *Kojak, Starsky and Hutch, Baretta,* and *M★A★S★H.* The genre of the "super woman" forged new icons in the 1970s with shows like *Charlie's Angels, Police Woman, Wonder Woman,* and *The Bionic Woman.* The characters reflected the burgeoning woman's movement, while sitcoms like *Laverne and Shirley* and *Phyllis* gave working women a playful dimension of fun.

The 1970s ushered in an innovative dimension of immediacy in reporting the news of the day. Sony's "portapak" video camera had revolutionized *electronic news gathering* (ENG) with its portability and low cost. Along with satellite relay and distribution systems, local, national, and international news broadcasts — live and prerecorded — closed cultural and national boundaries.

This decade also saw the emergence of cable channel services that offered more specialized programming such as movies on HBO, children's shows on Nickelodeon, live broadcasts from the House of Representatives on C-SPAN, sports on ESPN, and Ted Turner's "superstation," WTBS. Cable television became increasingly popular for specific events like baseball and basketball games and hockey in areas with a loyal fan base. By 1971, New York cable, for example, had over 80,000 subscribers.

Television in the 1970s heralded such classics as *M*A*S*H*, which began in 1972 and ran for 11 years. The mini-series *Roots* focused on African Americans and their ancestors and attracted a record-breaking audience of 130 million viewers. PBS, which had been created in 1967, unveiled several unexpectedly popular hits such as *Upstairs Downstairs, Masterpiece Theatre, Nova, Crockett's Victory Garden,* and *The French Chef* with Julia Child. *Mork and Mindy* introduced Robin Williams to viewers, and the debut of *Dallas* in 1978 delivered the sex of daytime soap drama to prime time. Both *Saturday Night Live* and *The Phil Donohue Show* created new programming models that are relevant today. During this time the FCC ruled that shows broadcast during the Family Hour (7 to 9 p.m.) must be "wholesome" for family viewing.

Advancing technology offered the videocassette recorder (*VCR*) in 1972, followed four years later by Sony's Betamax VCR (selling for about $1,300). By the next year, RCA had introduced a competitive standard, VHS, which would dominate the market and push Betamax into obscurity. The improvements in fiber-optic cable in 1970, delivering 65,000 times more data than copper wire, improved television delivery to American homes.

H. Television Merges with Electronics (the 1980s)

With the widespread popularity of VCRs, viewers could now record their favorite program on VHS tape and watch it at their leisure. Video stores popped up in every neighborhood with recent movies and video games to rent. The television set was evolving from a passive medium to an interactive device. The impact of the VCR was especially harsh on advertisers who grew apprehensive, because viewers could completely tune out Madison Avenue's expensive commercials. The film business was equally concerned as bootleg copies of movies became widely available.

Creatively, producers became more aware of television's potential to reach an audience through innovative programming enhanced by special effects. These effects could be created through more sophisticated video editing systems and included innovative uses of texts and fonts, moving logos, digitized backgrounds, page turns, multiple pictures on a screen, and layering pictures on top of one another. At first, the costs were high and time-consuming, but by the mid-1980s, these effects became easier to produce and less costly.

Television in the 1980s was highlighted by the emergence of new cable outlets such as Ted Turner's TNT and the Cable News Network (CNN), an all-news channel along with Bravo, the first network dedicated to film and performing arts. MTV premiered as a revolutionary station that was specifically targeted to the growing youth culture, showcasing a new format known as "music videos." These music videos promoted recording artists and their labels, and influenced the creation of programs like NBC's *Miami Vice,* which went on air in 1984. Independent production companies broke new ground with shows like *Hill Street Blues, Cheers, St. Elsewhere, Cagney and Lacey,* and *L.A. Law.* In 1983, Vanessa Williams was the first African-American woman to be crowned Miss America, and the middle-class African-American family was the focus of the ratings hit, *The Cosby Show,* soon to be followed by shows like *A Different World.* In 1986, *Oprah* became the first major talk show to be hosted by an African-American woman. Sitcoms with underlying cultural issues were ratings bonanzas, for example, *Roseanne, Saved By the Bell, Growing Pains, Three's Company, Who's the Boss, Facts of Life,* and *Different Strokes.* And in 1985, *Live Aid* raised millions of dollars for famine relief with its 16-hour global broadcast of musical artists and cultural icons.

I. Television Moves Toward the Future (the 1990s)

Cable gave viewers an increased accessibility to world events, and in 1991, the world watched the Persian Gulf War as the United States dropped "smart" bombs on Baghdad. Three years later, millions of Americans were riveted to cable news stations to watch the saga of O. J. Simpson unfold, from the white Bronco chase to the infamous final verdict.

The popularity of cable had a direct impact on the major networks as three new stations, Fox, UPN, and the WB, reached audiences with improved cable technology and direct-broadcast satellite (DBS). As competition grew between cable and networks, the focus of television programming became increasingly unconventional. When talk show hosts, for example, explored raw topics with confrontational guests, their ratings soared. Cable sex shows and adult cartoons were in sharp contrast to a more sophisticated crop of made-for-TV movies dealing with mature issues like changing family values, gender bias, AIDS, homosexuality, and domestic abuse. In response to violence and sex on TV, the public — and subsequently the government — forced the broadcasting industry in 1996 to adopt a rating system for every show: TV-Y, TV-Y7, TV-G, TV-PG, TV-14, and TV-MA. Newer television sets were equipped with a "V-chip" that could be programmed to block unsuitable programs.

The focus on HDTV was substantial in the 1990s. The broadcasters saw that HDTV broadcasts were sharper and clearer than traditional television, and the sets themselves were bigger. The inevitability of HDTV was declared in 1997 when the government allotted $70 billion worth of broadcast spectrum to TV broadcasters. This gave each broadcaster an extra channel for broadcasting programs in high definition along with their analog signals. The goal of totally phasing out low-definition broadcasting was originally set for 2006, by which time all broadcasts would be totally digital. The mandate then required all broadcasters to give back their original channels (extra broadcast spectrum) to the government.

As personal computers became more user friendly and less expensive in the 1990s, the popularity of the Internet focused on the potential of interconnectivity between computers and TV, both creatively and economically. Experiments in digital audio and video, fiber optics, and HDTV moved from theory to actuality, and digital technology promised to energize the TV industry.

Television in the 1990s included the ratings domination by NBC with shows such as *The Cosby Show, Mad About You, Seinfeld, ER, Cheers, Friends, Veronica's Closet, Golden Girls,* and *Frasier.* CBS offered programming like *60 Minutes, Murphy Brown, Murder, She Wrote,* and *Everybody Loves Raymond.* And ABC aired popular shows like *Home Improvement, NFL Monday Night Football, The Practice, NYPD Blue, Who Wants to Be a Millionaire?,* and *Roseanne,* which featured the first "gay kiss" on television. Other shows like *Ellen* and *Will and Grace* challenged sexual stereotypes, and each major network had its own news magazine — *Dateline* (NBC), *20/20* (ABC), and *60 Minutes* (CBS). PBS debuted *Charlie Rose* and Bravo premiered *Inside the Actor's Studio* — both becoming enduring classics as well as targets of late night comedians. *The X-Files* and *Star Trek: Deep Space 9* brought sci-fi fans back to television.

J. Television in the 21st Century (2000s)

> Television! Teacher, mother, secret lover.
>
> —Homer Simpson, *The Simpsons*

The ongoing evolution of television continues to have a singular impact on global society. Virtually every household in America has at least one television set, most homes have two or more, and approximately one billion sets are watched around the globe. It's estimated that the average American watches seven hours of television a day. Viewers can watch TV on tiny pocket televisions and large plasma screens; TV sets are in the home, in cars, and in the workplace.

There are hundreds of programming sources, which include cable and network broadcasters, video-on-demand, pay-per-view, television via the Internet, and straight to DVD. The strength of our attachment to television is reflected in a *TV Guide* poll in the mid-1990s in which one out of four Americans declared that even if they were given one million dollars, they wouldn't give up their TV.

Technology is increasing ways in which a television image can be transmitted, although in mid-2005, some 19% of American homes were still using rabbit ear antennas. Some of those transmission services include:

- **Satellite dishes**: Large dishes that pick up video signals. The systems depend on frequency modulation (FM) to send the video.

- **Direct satellite system (DSS)**: Smaller dishes receiving transmissions operated at a higher frequency and whose signals are converted to digital data.

- **HDTV**: Higher resolution allows pictures to be transmitted in finer detail. There are 1080 lines, compared to the current 525, and its digitally transmitted picture is one-third wider.

Now, the traditional movie studio system and the top three networks have been replaced by unprecedented consolidations of big business with film and television powerhouses known as *conglomerates*. Entertainment, news, and information are increasingly demanded by — and fed to — the American public, whose appetite is voracious. The result is an entertainment industry worth billions of dollars annually that circles the entire globe. The control of these few powerful conglomerates spreads over vast domains of entertainment and information: from theme parks and newspapers to home video and publishing, from motion simulator rides to blockbuster movies to advanced video games and Internet networks. They're all connected through commerce and have real consequences on our expanding culture. The implications of the conglomerates' influence on the viewing public has sparked vigorous debate, and is a vital subject for more exploration and study by a committed student of television. Additional resources can be found in the Appendix contained on the CD included in this book.

> I believe television is going to be the test of the modern world, and that in this new opportunity to see beyond the range of our vision, we shall discover a new and unbearable disturbance of the modern peace, or a saving radiance in the sky. We shall stand or fall by television — of that I am quite sure.
>
> —E. B. White

Television in the early 21st century reflected the unimaginable images of terrorism in the weeks and months following the attacks of September 11, 2001. Cable and network news covered the ensuing wars in Afghanistan and Iraq, as well as the increase of international debate on America's involvement in world politics. News broadcasts relied more heavily on graphic elements, musical effects, and added a running "ticker tape" below the anchors to cover additional news not included in the broadcast itself.

Comedy is a welcome relief in times of political crisis, and shows like *Everybody Loves Raymond, Friends, Cheers, Frasier, Sex in the City, The Simpsons, Will and Grace*, and *Whose Line Is It Anyway?* appealed to all age groups. Episodic series such as *The West Wing, ER, Lost, Boston Public, NYPD Blue, Desperate Housewives*, and *24* continued to broaden themes and storylines. HBO saw a dramatic increase in subscribers — and Emmy awards — with shows like *The Sopranos, Six Feet Under, Deadwood*, and an impressive roster of quality documentaries. Talk shows reached new highs — and lows — with *The View, The Rosie O'Donnell Show, Ellen DeGeneres, Sharon Osbourne, Oprah, Dr. Phil*, and *The Martha Stewart Show*. Children's television targeted diverse audiences with dimensional writing and production value on *Nickelodeon, Noggin*, and PBS with shows like *Zoboomafoo, Dora the Explorer, Zoom*, and *Sesame Street*. News blended with satire in programs such as *Politically Incorrect, South Park, Saturday Night Live*, and *The Daily Show with Jon Stewart*. Advertisers were attracted to sponsor shows aimed at the growing market of "tweens," teens, and young adults with shows like *Buffy the Vampire Slayer, Ally McBeal, Dawson's Creek, The O.C., Felicity*, and *The Real World*. "Format" shows that started in other countries came to America, reconfigured in programs like *American Idol, Survivor*, and *Who Wants to Be a Millionaire?*

The genre that has changed the content of American television in the early part of 21st century is that of the reality, nonscripted program. *Trading Spaces, The Apprentice, The Bachelor, Road Rules, Fear Factor, Temptation Island, Survivor, Extreme Makeover*, and others have been ratings bonanzas. The seemingly global appeal of reality programming intrigues television scholars, and the considerably lower costs of producing these shows delights broadcasters. It has spawned two all-reality channels, and at least 150 reality shows have aired, are scheduled for air, or have come and gone.

The TV viewing public can be fickle and highly discerning with tastes and loyalties that shift with each television season. A program that feeds water-cooler conversation one week can be old news the next week, easily replaced with a better idea. Networks give their shows only a limited time to succeed, and cancel them if they don't perform well in their first few airings. Unlike the networks, cable and premium cable stations have more latitude in creating targeted programming that appeals to specific demographics and interests, though their budgets are lower. The changing horizons of television content in both broadcasting and "narrow casting" give producers new areas to explore in the future.

> Two words: branded entertainment. When TV first started, each program was sponsored, like *General Electric Theater*. I think we're going back to that now as a result of TiVo, which is going to open a lot of doors for producers.
> —Brett Morgen, *excerpt from interview in Chapter 11*

K. Television's Future

The future of television certainly relies on emerging trends in technology, but the primary function of television is storytelling. The stories it tells may range from harsh reality to total fiction, but a compelling and engaging story will always trump technology. The stories have yet to be told; however, we have glimpsed a few of the technological advances that are serious contenders for further transforming television.

1. *Digital Video and Television*

One of the distinct advantages of digital television is that, with the same amount of bandwidth, five times more information can move through a digital signal than an analog one (the current tranmission standard). A digital signal can transmit more data than an analog signal and stays consistent over wide distances. Digital transmission can also deliver data that gives our TV sets the potential to be interactive, in addition to HDTV programs, high-quality sets, and vastly improved digital sound with 5.1 channels of audio.

However, an analog broadcast doesn't automatically mean you'll see a picture worse than one that's digital. Digital images can be as bad as analog. HDTV can be broadcast over digital or analog signals. According to FCC regulations, all broadcasters must make the transition from the traditional one-channel analog signal to digital signals by 2006. Although it is expensive and time-consuming to modify the technology and replace the equipment, broadcasters, advertisers, and producers are convinced it will pay off over time.

2. *Interactive TV*

Interactive television (ITV) involves a digital signal that can transmit a multitude of images and sound as well as graphics, games, forms of information, and whatever available data a broadcaster wants to add to its signal. It achieves a real convergence with computers and the Internet because digital TV can implant interactivity within the signal. A growing number of TV viewers are simultaneously surfing the Internet, and broadcasters are researching ways to unite the two. The future of television includes TV on the computer, the Internet on television, and more. ABC, for example, airs several shows with an Internet component of "Enhanced TV" that encourages viewers to play along with game shows. And the introduction of "Mobisodes" promises to bring mini-episodes of television programming into the cell phone marketplace.

3. *Multi-casting*

Broadcasters who transmit their programming through digital signals have a choice of sending out one high-quality, high-definition picture. Or, by using the same amount of signal, a broadcaster can "multi-cast" four regular, standard-definition pictures. For example, during the day, a broadcaster might offer four standard-definition programs such as a documentary on one channel, a kids' program on the second, global news coverage on the third, and a gardening show on the fourth channel. But in prime time, the same broadcaster airs just one program in high definition, such as an original drama with high production value and a stellar cast of actors.

> Having moved away from broadcasting to narrow casting with the advent of cable and the multichannel environment, the next stage is even more niche programming where everyone can program their own channel and personal viewing schedules. The growth of video-on-demand (VOD) is apparently the next big thing in television. This will individualize TV viewing even more and move it further away from the communal experience of its origins. Advertisers will have to rethink their strategies to reach their target audiences, and the very nature of TV advertising will change drastically.
> —Veronique Bernard, *excerpt from interview in Chapter 11*

On a Human Level . . .

You have explored the intricate facets of television's evolution as a medium as well as its technological advances, and both have developed over a relatively short span of human history. Television is always moving forward, regardless of its high and low points. You can parallel the growth of television with your own development as a producer. Each step you take depends on the step you took before, how well you understood it, what lessons you learned, and how you applied the knowledge.

> Television is the newest and most controversial wonder child of modern science and industrial ingenuity, and because it appeals to both the eye and ear simultaneously, television may make the greatest possible impression on the human mind.
> —Eleanor Roosevelt

VII. Summary

This chapter has only touched on the rich legacy of television's past, its rapid transitions, and the unlimited possibilities of this medium's future. The resources for further study are plentiful, and you're encouraged to explore them. They will add to your resources as a producer and help you enter into a project armed with the experience and wisdom of the TV pioneers who started it all. In the following chapter, you will begin to focus on the core of a project — its story.

VIII. Chapter Review Questions

1. Discuss the integral advances dating back to the time of radio offered by television in its early phases.

2. Define: *persistence of vision* and *pixels*. What is their connection?

3. Choose three of television's creators and discuss their contributions to television.

4. Who is Samuel Morse? What was his contribution to television's early beginnings?

5. Choose a decade in television history. In your own words, discuss its progress, the risks taken, and advances that specifically characterize that era.

6. Choose one highlight in TV history that you feel is significant.

7. What is the FCC? The NTSC? What roles do they play?

8. What was the first war that was covered by live broadcast. How did that affect viewers?

9. What are your own speculations about the future of television — technologically? Creatively? Economically?

We must not be distracted from one fundamental concept: the idea is king. Stars, directors, writers, hardware, special effects, new sound systems ... all of these can have a role to play in the success of a film, but they all must serve as humble subjects to the supremacy of the idea.

—Jeffrey Katzenberg, cofounder of DreamWorks SKG

Script and Project Development: The Big Idea

This Chapter's Talking Points

   I.   Think It

   II.   Write It

   III.   Develop It

   IV.   Summary

   V.   Chapter Review Questions

I. Think It

The story is king. Regardless of what genre of television project you may want to develop, a good story is its foundation. Whether it is a dramatic series or news show, a sitcom or a sports special, each genre revolves around telling a story that is compelling and engages the viewer.

The markets for strong story ideas are proliferating as the number of broadcast venues expands. Writing for television and video distribution platforms — such as network, cable, syndication, pay-per-view, DVD, and nonbroadcast — is a trend reflected by the Writers Guild of America (*WGA*), who report that 30% more writers earn their income from TV than from films.

Producers in television stay in touch with what is currently airing on TV, and what might be aired in the future. They watch television, and they read the regular publications and industry trade magazines that deal with the TV business, like *Variety* (daily and weekly), *Hollywood Reporter, Applause, The Ross Report, The Creative Director, Entertainment Weekly*, and *TV Guide*. As you begin to put the pieces together, the intricacies of the television and entertainment industry will become clearer and more accessible.

It can be tempting to discount the enormous market outside of America, yet this market has a healthy appetite for programs that we produce. Shows that might do moderate business in this country can make vast fortunes globally. As you research or watch TV programs in other languages, you become more aware of what sells globally.

> The beginning is the most important part of the work.
>
> —Plato

Turning your idea into a project is more of a challenge than you may think — the work is hard, there isn't always a payoff, and the competition is intense. The majority of new shows are written by seasoned television veteran writers because most television executives love familiarity, both in concept and talent. Few shows are the products of new writers. This can translate to repetition for the viewer, but it is comfortable for the executives. The following statistics can be a real test of your commitment to your idea:

- At least 100,000 scripts are written each year, and most are written badly.

- Of these 100,000 ideas, only about 10,000 get pitched to people in a position to develop an idea for broadcast.

- Maybe 250 to 300 of these 10,000 get to the finished script stage.

- Fewer than 10% of those are ever shot as pilots.

- Depending on whose statistics you believe, maybe half of these pilots get aired and even less continue on as series.

A. Ideas for TV Programming Are Everywhere

Maybe you have what you think is a saleable, viable idea for a TV show, or you may have strong writing skills but haven't yet found an idea that engages you. Here are just a few sources for your programming ideas.

- *Friends, family, or fellow students.* They have good ideas but aren't writers.

- *Total strangers.* People you meet on a plane or at a party; everybody has an interesting story to tell.

- *Newspapers.* Big city or small town papers report stories from real life.

- *The Internet.* A lot of sites now pitch scripts, talk about plots, etc.

- *Libraries.* Find out what books or plays are in the public domain, like Jane Austin, Charles Dickens, and Shakespeare. Adapt them, or "borrow" freely.

- *Book expos.* Publishers large and small promote their books and authors; find ideas among them. Option the ones you think you can develop. You'll find more information about options in Chapter 5.

- *History.* Truth is as interesting as fiction, and cheaper. Put your character in a real situation, or imagine what could have happened, if . . .?

- *Biographies.* Why are famous people interesting? Read them for ideas for stories as well as some of the techniques and skills that made them famous.

- *Steal from the best.* Read great books, narrative and nonfiction, and see if they inspire any ideas in you. Something a character does or says might compel you to take a different direction that becomes your own.

- *Your own creative well.* Inside that brain of yours is an endless pool of ideas. You just have to tap into them. That's the same brain that dreams with astonishing results. Try some techniques, like giving yourself a problem to solve right before you go to sleep. Get into your subconscious and see what's in there. Keep a notebook or tape recorder with you and jot down ideas, snatches of conversations you hear, a sight gag, or an incident you see on the street.

Successful businesses have mission statements — a good TV producer has *a vision statement*. Author Laurie Beth Jones calls this ". . . a picture of how the landscape will look after you've been through it. It is your 'ideal'." Whether the idea you have is your own original concept, or one you acquired from someone else, your vision statement helps you define the effect you want your idea to have on a viewer.

> At the end of the day, you're telling stories. You have to be able to structure a story so that someone knows what you're talking about. One of the functions of a news producer is to write a story in collaboration with the on-air talent. If you don't have the writing skills to write a story and collaborate with someone who may have a different vision for that story, you're not going to be very happy.
> —Matthew Lombardi, *excerpt from interview in Chapter 11*

II. Write It

The television industry has a strong foundation of producers who started as writers. They had an idea they were passionate about, that they wanted to nurture and protect, but were reluctant to relinquish control to a production company or network that might not give it proper close attention. These writers learned how to produce to protect their vision. In television, the writer/producer can be a major player, and is known as a *hyphenate* — a creative person with two (or more) specific skills and one who can do twice as much work (and often earn twice the money). The title and the job can change with each show and its circumstances. As you learned in Chapter 1, the producer's titles can range from executive producer or showrunner, to coproducer or associate producer, to line producer or consulting producer — all depending on the individual project.

As the public's appetite for new television programming and content keeps changing and evolving, producers are challenged to find bright new ideas or capitalize on popular formats and topics that can satisfy the viewers. Whether you're writing the script yourself or working with a scriptwriter, it is in your best interest, financially and creatively, to know what makes a good script. Producers, directors, actors, and crew all depend on the script as a blueprint to construct their part of the project. The producer also needs a script to create a budget by breaking it down into specific departments, or accounts, as you'll see in Chapter 4.

Writing for television is not the same as writing for film. One essential difference is the people at the core of the story. In a feature film, the characters and their storylines are introduced, the story begins, peaks, ends, and everything is resolved. When the movie is over, so is the story. Yet in most genres of TV programming, the characters and their storylines continue with characters who are ongoing and familiar. TV writers can capitalize on that endurance by first creating strong characters and then writing storylines around them, building on their reactions, and constantly testing them. Viewers rely on this familiarity with the characters and their storylines. The audience gets to know them well, and brings their own cumulative memories and experiences of the show to each episode.

Art theorist, Steven Pepper, has called this phenomenon "aesthetic funding," adding that "a late perception in a series . . . carries to considerable degree the results of previous perceptions as its constituents." Simply put, an episode of *Friends* that we're watching now is enriched and added to by previous episodes of *Friends* we have seen in the past. Each viewing adds to the experience, and results in the viewer's aesthetic fund. It provides a meaningful context for the intimate details and character traits, and gives every aspect of the show an extra significance.

A. Television Programming Genres

As a producer, you may be interested in developing a project in any of the following genres of television and nonbroadcast programming:

- *Reality/nonfiction*: Make-over, competition, documentary, biography, nature, travel, "making of," interviews

- *Sitcom*: Family, teen, smart, silly, spin-off characters

- *Episodic drama*: Police, law, forensics, medical, firefighters, family, political, edgy, young adult

- *News*: Local and national news, entertainment, politics, weather, magazine format, special news reports

- *Children's*: Cartoon, educational, puppets, classroom

- *Talk*: Daytime, late night, women's issues

- *Soaps*: Daytime, primetime, novellas

- *Sports*: Event coverage, games, playoffs

- *Game and quiz shows*: Words, numbers, trivia

- *Movies of the week*: Network and cable

- *Infomercials*: Cable and nonbroadcast

- *Corporate*: Corporate image, training, industrials, promotional

- *Advertising*: Commercials, trailers, promos, DVD special features

- *Music videos*: Broadcast, point of purchase, special features

B. From Idea to Script

A television script translates an idea into a specific format that can act as a blueprint for production. At its core is a good story, one that grabs the viewer's attention and holds it. It includes the following components:

- *An amazing hook*: Something unique about the story — a character, a location, a texture — is edgy and different, and stands out from the others.

- *A protagonist*: The traditional hero who is somehow unique yet familiar, vulnerable yet courageous, someone the viewer can care about.

- *An antagonist*: A bad-guy role, someone who creates conflict, tension, and challenges the good guy or the overall plot in some major way.

- *A buddy*: The main character has a friend or sibling who's a sidekick or performs essential functions, like the conscience, the helper, the smart one, the comic relief — even the character who's sacrificed in the end.

- *A challenge*: The character must confront a challenge and either wins or loses in the process.

- *A conflict*: The character must make choices and each option has consequences. Plus, the conflict must be resolved in a way that convinces and satisfies.

- *A contradiction*: A situation that seems good but turns out to be bad, or vice versa.

- *A demon*: Something that happened to the character before the story starts that haunts and influences his or her actions now.

- *A heartstring*: Romance, vulnerability, sex — all help the viewer understand and bond with the characters and their lives.

- *An "up"ending*: Happy endings sell, often with some form of redemption or measurable growth of the character that makes the viewer feel good.

> The purpose of art is to lay bare the questions that are hidden by the answers.
> —James Baldwin

1. *Length*

In commercial television, the script must also factor in commercial breaks. These breaks include regular commercials, promos, and other material supplied by the local station affiliate. A one-hour show actually only broadcasts about 44 to 48 minutes of programming, along with 12 to 16 minutes of breaks. The script is generally about 50 to 55 pages long. A half-hour show runs 22 to 24 minutes with 6 to 8 minutes of commercial breaks. The traditional guideline is that one page equals one minute of action; this can vary with the genre.

2. *Commercial Breaks*

When a show goes to commercial, that interruption needs to be seamlessly integrated into the storyline without losing action or suspense or pacing, while still maintaining the plot's thread. The same applies to coming back into the story from the commercial. Unless you're writing for noncommercial television, these breaks come with the territory. Count the number of breaks in a TV show that's similar to yours. How often do they come? How long are they? How many breaks in a half-hour or one-hour show?

3. *Acts*

Most half-hour TV shows are divided into three segments, and the majority of one-hour shows into six. Regardless of length, both ideally reflect Aristotle's classic three-act format that has a beginning, a middle, and an end.

   Act 1 — Roughly 25% of the story. There is a set-up (location, relationships between characters, what's going on), an event propels action, the feeling of the show is conveyed, a running theme is presented, and a turning point leads into Act 2.

   Act 2 — Roughly 50% of the story. Subplots and other characters are introduced; relationships and characters further develop; increased conflict, complications, action; and a turning point that leads to Act 3.

   Act 3 — About 25% of the story. The pace picks up, questions are answered, conflicts get resolved, and the story comes to a climactic and satisfying end.

   Other forms of programming might be spaced into four or five parts — a teaser and four acts, or it could run to five acts. Some shows may add a short end tag, too.

- *The teaser*: 3 to 5 pages, with a plot set-up that hooks the viewer

- *Act 1*: 13 to 15 pages (the beginning)
- *Act 2*: 12 to 13 pages (the middle)
- *Act 3*: 11 to 12 pages (more of the middle)
- *Act 4*: 11 to 13 pages (the end)
- *Tag*: 1 to 2 pages (wraps up a plotline or teases the next episode)

4. Dramatic Plotlines

Most one-hour drama series rely on, and interweave, three story lines:

- *The A story*: Propels most of the episode's storyline
- *The B story*: Storylines that focus on primary or supporting characters; sometimes, they may carry over into subsequent episodes
- *The C story*: The comic relief that deflates tension

C. Sitcoms

Generally, sitcoms tend to open with a funny teaser and have two or three acts. A few sitcoms break this mold and use the ABC format, like *Friends*. Other sitcoms devote their half hour to one main story. *Seinfeld* was a unique concept in that each episode featured four plotlines that resulted in one conclusion and satisfied all four conflicts.

1. Camera Angles

It isn't difficult to grasp the language of camera angles, and by using these terms correctly in your script, you can convey the texture and feeling you want your script to invoke. You can explore this more fully in Chapters 4 and 8.

2. Script Formats and Styles

Most writers prefer to begin writing their scripts by first outlining their idea into acts or segments. Then, they expand that into a treatment form before they finally flesh out the story in a full script format. Though outlines and treatments are shorter than full scripts, they act as a clear map for the writer and can highlight problems early on. An *outline* is usually 1 to 3 pages, almost a sequential laundry list of the show's beats that is used by the writer as a basic guideline. A *treatment* is traditionally written in paragraph form rather than script format, and can run from 3 to 10 pages, sometimes longer. In most cases, development executives only read the treatment for the program idea. If they are interested in what they read, they'll ask for a full script. You can find more information about treatments in Chapter 6.

A professional TV script is easy to read and follows a specific script format. Using a different format only marks you as an amateur. Here are the basics:

- It is neatly typed with no erasures, scribbled notes, or correction fluid.
- Each page has $1\frac{1}{2}$-inch margins and paragraph separation.
- The paper is simple 20-pound, white, and $8\frac{1}{2} \times 11$ inches.
- It's only printed on one side.
- Each page is divided into frequent paragraphs so the words don't run together.
- Scripts are typed in Courier or Times New Roman, with a 12-point font. Avoid fonts that are overly florid, they're a sure mark of an amateur.

- Each page is numbered and followed by a period on the upper right corner.

- Each page is double- and triple-checked for spelling and punctuation.

- The finished script is bound in plain card-stock covers with brass brad closings.

D. The Title Page

A descriptive, short title is vital to a busy development executive or potential buyer. It can also signal the tone or direction of your show. On the first page, the title is written in all caps and centered about halfway down the page. Under the title, type "written by" or "by" the author, which is also centered. In the lower right corner is the author's name, and/or his or her representative, with a contact phone number and/or e-mail address. In the lower left corner, type the copyright symbol, the year, and the author's name.

Scripts for television can be formatted in several ways, depending on the show and its genre. It can follow the traditional screenplay format used in writing films as seen below, or it can be formatted with vertical columns for audio, video, and graphics directions. Here's a short scene in a TV drama that uses the traditional script format.

```
FADE IN:

INT — LUXURY CAR — NIGHT
```
(A descriptive header, always capitalized, explains if the scene is INTerior or EXTerior, its location, and is DAY or NIGHT)

```
Two men sit in grim silence in the back of a cruising limo. The lights
of passing cars flit over their faces, and we see that MAN #1 is the
much older alpha dog, while MAN #2 is clearly afraid of him.
```
(This is the action)

(The first time a character is introduced, his or her name is in all caps.)

```
                        MAN #2
```
(character name)

```
                (quiet desperation)
```
(parenthetical description)

```
        Dad...you gotta pay her back!
```
(dialogue)

```
                    MAN #1
        ...you eat yet? You look real bad. Green.
                (taps on the limo
                    window)
            Hey, you. Boy! Pull over to the next burger joint.
INT — FRONT SEAT OF LIMO — NIGHT

The LIMO DRIVER'S eyes reflect in the rear view mirror. They shine with
hate. PULL BACK [camera direction] to see the 60-ish driver barely able
to hide his anger. His right hand moves down to a pistol on the seat. He
caresses it as his left hand guides the wheel and he's humming "Amazing
Grace" under his breath.
```

The same script, written in a more TV-friendly format, might look like this:

```
AUDIO                              VIDEO
                                   Two men sit in the back of a
                                   cruising limo. Passing cars light
                                   their faces. MAN #1 is older,
                                   MAN #2 is clearly afraid of him.

Man #2:   Dad, you gotta pay her
back!
Man #1: ... you eat yet? You look  Man #1 taps on the limo window
kinda pale ...
Hey you. Boy. Pull over at the
next burger joint.
```

You can also add other information to this format, such as graphics (lower thirds like name, location, title), transitions (a dissolve or wipe), and duration (the length of a sound bite or visual action). Any voice-over or narration is written in the Audio Section.

E. Script Components

A strong script provides the reader with a clear format and brief descriptions of the action. Your script also includes dialogue that reflects the characters. Good dialogue gives important plot information, reveals characters' motivations, and propels the flow of the story line. Below are a few components of compelling dialogue.

- Dialogue should create the *illusion* of reality, not reality itself. Conversation in real life can be tedious and boring.

- Each word and every line advances the plot, explains the character, or provides further story exposition.

- When dialogue is used sparingly, less can be more. Pure silence can be eloquent at the right time.

- One perfect adjective is better than two or three that are not.

- Adding action to a character's dialogue creates momentum. An actor can be talking or yelling as they walk or run — it is preferable to talking heads. Sitcoms, for example, tend to place their primary sets in a living room in front of a staircase. A room with multiple entry and exit points allows for characters to enter and exit freely.

- By knowing your characters and how they speak, you can give them nuances and speech patterns, or unique phrases that only he or she would use.

- Read your dialogue out loud to yourself. Record it into a tape recorder. How honest does it sound to your ear when you listen back?

- An honest writer is a rewriter. Even the most seasoned writers rewrite until they're satisfied. They can sense when it works — it's a gut feeling. By listening to your own intuition and pushing your ego aside, you can more easily review your work. If you're still not sure, show it to another writer, a professor, or someone who can be totally honest.

  Don't say it if you can show it instead.

F. The Spec Script

Some writers have gotten into the television industry by writing a *spec script* — one written on speculation for no pay. Its sole purpose is to showcase your writing talents. Most spec scripts are written for a current TV show that is popular; one that you like and watch regularly. Your lawyer, agent, or an inside connection sends it to development execs who may be looking for new writers. A good spec script can be a major factor in their hiring decision. In writing a spec script, know the show inside and out. Study the characters, their histories, and how they speak. Watching at least a season of the show gives you the overall perspective as well as small pertinent details. You want to study the format of the show, including the number of acts and the script format (how do they show dialogue, action, headings, etc.). Create a plotline that has not been used before on the show. If you decide to send a spec script for a specific show to an exec who works on that show, they know their own show well, and will easily spot any flaws.

G. Working with Others

1. *Working with Other Writers*

Writers in television take different approaches to their work. Some work best alone, while others like to write with one or more partners. Many writers are part of larger writing teams, and thrive on the ongoing stimulation and pressure. Finding the writing style that fits your personality is integral to your creativity — and to your own brand of discipline. As you'll see throughout this book, virtually every aspect of television involves other people. Television is a highly collaborative medium, so by talking to other writers and producers, joining a writers' group or starting one, taking a class, and reading books about writing for television, you can expand your creative horizons.

2. *Writing with a Partner*

Having another source of ideas in the writing process can be stimulating as you bounce ideas off one another, experiment with dialogue, and discover plot counterpoints and narrative beats. Often one person can originate the dialogue while another acts as the wordsmith. Writers have different skills and when they're combined collaboratively, the results are tangible.

A script is a valuable commodity. If it sells, you can both be paid well. But before you pitch your idea, you and your partner want to discuss the pertinent details of your partnership. For example, talk over how you'll share writing credits, percentages and profits, and who's doing what aspect of the writing process. Write these details down in a *deal memo*, a process you'll explore in Chapter 5, and sign it. This helps to avoid hard feelings or any disagreements between you and your partner in the later phases.

3. *Working with a Writing Team*

A writer can be hired as a staff writer on a specific TV show, or can be a member of a group of independent writers. In both cases, a successful writing team creates the script from the many details contributed by each writer. On most established shows, the writing team is closely supervised by the showrunner who acts as the head writer and team leader throughout the life of the series.

As a staff writer on a show or series, you are likely to enter into a contract situation that spells out the parameters of your pay, credits, time frame, responsibilities, length and genre of the show, and so on. The WGA Web site (www.wga.org) can give you specific pay scales for various writing situations. If you're working with an independent team on speculation, clarify everyone's specific responsibilities within the group and put together a deal memo between all the contributing writers. You can find further information about deal memos and other contracts in Chapter 5.

4. *Working with an Agent*

An agent from an established talent agency, such as CAA and ICM, acts as the middleman between buyers and sellers. An enthusiastic agent who believes in you and your material can provide essential access to the right people. Agents usually take a commission of 10% for their services, which can include finding a buyer for your script, getting you a writing job, and/or negotiating final deals.

Yet finding an agent can be a frustrating catch-22 for new writers. Typically, an agent only wants to represent established writers, but how can you establish yourself without an agent? If you've already sold your script or have the promise of a sale, agents will pay more attention. You can research agents for writers through the WGA. You can find actors' agents through the Screen Actors Guild (*SAG*), and directors through the Directors Guild of America (*DGA*). If you strongly believe in your project, try using polite persistence to make contact with an agent you think is right for your project. It can be challenging to get an agent to read your script — but it isn't impossible.

5. *Working with an Entertainment Lawyer*

Lawyers who specialize in entertainment are aware of the current trends in the television industry. Because they have strong connections with producers, directors, actors, and other writers whom they also represent, they're in the position to connect them with one another. As you will see in Chapter 5, lawyers can charge by the hour or by the project, and these fees can vary significantly, depending on the lawyer and the project's demands. Some lawyers may stay with a project from start to finish, and are a permanent line in the project's budget. For a low-budget project, producers can obtain reasonable or free legal advice from organizations of volunteer lawyers, university law departments that offer programs in entertainment law, on the Internet, and from several texts listed in the attached CD.

> Do you really need a lawyer? If you are making a $15,000 movie as a thesis project, then maybe not. But if you have any notion of ever doing anything with it beyond showing it to the department, then you probably will need to get a lawyer involved at some point because nobody will distribute it unless they know that you have all the rights that you need, or all the clearances that you need and there won't be a bunch of claims flying in as soon as this thing ends up on television somewhere.
> —J. Stephen Sheppard, *excerpt from interview in Chapter 11*

6. *Working with a Manager*

The same way that agents and lawyers are well connected, managers are skilled in networking. Unlike agents, however, managers are not required to adhere to the same restrictions that restrain agents. If you have a manager who makes a deal for you, you'll still need a lawyer or agent for final legal negotiations. Managers generally charge 15% commission.

III. Develop It

The script development stage refers to the early phases of a project in which you polish your rough idea into a treatment, proposal, and/or script format. During the development stages, a producer considers potential directors, crew, talent, and the overall budgetary issues within the project. This phase can have several scenarios. Below are three:

1. You are developing an idea that is either your own original premise, or it belongs to someone else and you have legally optioned it for a period of time.

2. A production company or a network has put up some development money so that a writer can develop and flesh out a producer's idea.

3. Sometimes a private investor might see the potential of your idea, gives you a fee to take it to the next step, and expects a cut of any profits.

Each development option has its pros and cons.

— In the first scenario, you own the idea or have optioned it — no one else controls it. You will be financially subsidizing yourself.

— In the second example, someone else's money is involved, which gives them more control, although your own money is not on the line.

— In example three, investors have little assurance that the script or project will sell. They may demand a high return on their investment — often two to three times the initial investment. But it may be worth it for the security their investment provides.

The phrase *development hell* refers to getting stalled at various stages during the development process. Sometimes these delays are caused by writer's block, a conflict of ideas, the sudden firing of an executive, a cut in the budget, or an actor demands a bigger part.

A. Protect and Control Your Idea

Before you fully commit yourself to developing a project, you must first legally protect it or own it. If you are not legally protected, you could be wasting your time developing an idea for which you have no rights. Submitting an idea that you don't own can invite a lawsuit. In Chapter 5, you can find more information on the legal issues listed below:

• If the idea belongs to you, you must first protect it.

• If the idea belongs to someone else, you must option it.

• If a book, short story, article, or other material forms the basis for your story, you must get the rights from the author or from the author's legal estate. This doesn't apply if the work is in the *public domain.* The work of authors such as Jane Austin, Shakespeare, and Charles Dickens are in the public domain and can be freely adapted.

• If you are concerned that your idea could be plagiarized, most companies or people to whom you would submit your project will insist that you sign a *submission release* (an example can be found on the CD contained in this book) before they will read or consider it. You can find more information in Chapter 5.

Ownership and control are both important concepts for a producer. Let's assume you have an original idea that you think can be developed into a program concept. After you have fleshed it out into a treatment or script format, your next step is to legally protect it.

• *Copyright it.* Go online for forms at www.copyright.gov or call the hotline (202) 707-9100. The U.S. Post Office provides copyright package # 110 that you can fill out, and in either the end titles or on your cover page, list the copyright notice; for example, ©2005 CKNY Productions. (The date indicates the year of first public distribution.) Send the paper work, which is a nonreturnable copy, with a check or money order via certified mail. You will receive a certificate of registration and a registration number.

- *Register it with Writers Guild of America.* You can register either your treatment or script by mail, or online at www.wga.org. It costs roughly $25 to register it, and WGA holds it for five years. You can reregister it then.

B. If It Is Someone Else's Idea, Buy or Option It

Let's say a colleague of yours has written a script that has real potential. You may be considering producing it, or at least developing it further. But first you must either buy the full rights from your friend, or agree on an *option agreement* that gives you the exclusive rights to develop and pitch the idea, and eventually, to purchase these rights. An option is taken on a script for a period of time, usually six months to a year, during which time you are the only person who can legally develop and pitch the idea.

If you have found a short story, a novel, a magazine article, or another source for your story idea, you may need to negotiate any rights involved, or either option the rights to adapt it, or purchase them outright. An entertainment lawyer can locate the rights holder, or you can contact the publisher's subsidiary rights department yourself. You'll want to verify that no one else has optioned it, determine who holds the copyright, and be sure that there are no outstanding liens on the work.

C. Find the Best Market for Your Idea

The markets for good ideas are opening up to newer and edgier program material. In major markets cable and subscription channels are available, and in smaller markets nonbroadcast, educational, advertising, and industrials are seen. But you've got to sell the idea first. Breaking into the business can be a real challenge. Every successful writer and producer did it somehow and so can you.

The television industry continues to evolve, and though there are no set formulas, the following descriptions give you several directions in which you can go.

- Every network, studio, cable broadcaster, syndicator, and production company has a *development department*. This department looks for ideas — treatments, scripts, books, articles, news stories — that can be adapted for broadcast. Then, they work with either their own production department, or with an independent production company, to further develop the show.

- Networks and cable broadcasters may develop and/or produce their own programs in house. For example, NBC Universal may produce a show through their production arm, NBC Studios.

- The network or other client may rely on independent production companies with whom they have a strong relationship and lucrative history. These companies work closely with the development executives in the scripting, casting, shooting, and post-production of sitcoms, episodic dramas, format shows, and more.

When pitching your project to a specific venue, be certain that it is the right fit. You wouldn't bring a soap opera to a sports channel, or a music video to an all-news channel.

- If you want to interest a production company in your idea, make sure they have experience in — and enthusiasm for — projects similar to yours. You can locate production companies by watching shows you like, looking at the show's end credits, and then tracking the company down and researching their history and procedures. You can read *Variety* or *Hollywood*

Reporter for the shows in production that list the names and addresses of the production companies involved. You can also go to www.wga.org and click on the TV market list.

- If you want to pitch your idea to a particular network or cable broadcaster, carefully watch the programming shown on that channel. Be aware of what they may be developing for the future as well as their current programming.

- If you want to create a project that engages your audience, understand who your viewers are. Research projects that are similar to yours, and study their ratings, advertisers, demographics, and other statistics. Provide substantial proof that your project can create a revenue stream for the buyer.

- Most production companies or networks who do agree to read your idea or take a pitch meeting will ask you to first sign what's known as a submission agreement or a *release*. This protects them from any claims you may have later if you think they've stolen your idea. Each organization has its own regulations. Very few will accept unsolicited material, and most only accept proposals or take a pitch meeting after they have been contacted by an agent or lawyer. You can find a sample of the submission release on the CD.

D. Getting a Pitch Meeting

One consistent thread runs through development departments — they almost always work with known commodities. This includes writers and producers who have experience and credits, are usually members of the Writers Guild of America, and are reliable. When one of these established *creatives* (writer, producer, director) has an idea, he or she:

- Calls an agent, an entertainment lawyer, or an executive in the development department of a network, a studio, or a production company for which the idea is best suited.

- Sets up a *pitch meeting* (see Chapter 6) in hopes of convincing everyone to commit to further development.

- Pitches the idea verbally in the meeting.

- Gives the executive a leave behind — a page or two on the project's story synopsis, the creative team, potential talent, and crew.

- Hopes that the development executive likes the idea enough to take it to an executive further up the corporate ladder who either approves it for further development or rejects it.

- Understands that if it is approved for development, the executive in charge works with the producer on refining the idea. It helps if the producer is also the writer but if not, the executive and the producer find a writer they both like. Sometimes, a showrunner is brought in at this stage to help guide the vision and hire writers.

- Is emotionally prepared if the project hits a brick wall. As it makes its way up the corporate ladder, the project and script are reviewed by the top executives in charge of shows that are currently airing. The execs might also have deals around these shows that include guarantees of future buys. This means that the executives have promised to buy more programming from the same suppliers who are producing their current shows. To make sure they have enough content for each TV season, they tend to overcommit to these suppliers. This translates to fewer available time slots or less money for developing new projects.

Getting in the door to pitch your project often depends on your connections. An agent, manager, lawyer, or referral from a colleague or friend can provide an opportunity for a pitch meeting or phone call. Or, you can take a chance. By researching the network or studio, or the production companies and the networks they produce for, you're more likely to find the right person to approach with your idea. (In Chapter 6, you'll learn more about the format of your pitch.) If you send it, if they read it, and if your idea is right for them, it could signal success. If not, focus on other opportunities for your project.

Potential buyers and development executives seldom have the autonomy, time, and/or funding to buy ideas from producers or writers with no proven track record. However, there are venues that are more receptive to innovative projects. As you will read in Chapter 6, the proliferation of new cable channels and premium cable networks has created a demand for programming that can potentially be supplied by independent producers and production companies with compelling ideas.

E. Selling a Pilot

The continuing evolution of the creative and economic aspects of television has altered the traditional industry calendar for pitching, selling, developing, and producing pilots for new programming content. The current timetable follows these guidelines:

- *November–December*: New and returning shows debut in the fall. Networks, studios, and most production companies read scripts and take pitches for shows for the following fall, or for mid-season replacements.

- *January–March*: The few scripts that have survived scrutiny and executives' changes are shot and edited as pilots.

- *March–April*: The executives review the finished pilots and suggest changes.

- *March–June*: Most TV writers get hired during this "staffing season."

- *May*: The pilots that have been selected for the networks' fall line ups are traditionally announced and shown to network affiliates and advertisers in large industry gatherings known as the "up fronts."

- *May–August*: The successful pilots go into full-time production so they can fill their order of shows for the fall season, as possible mid-season replacements, or for the following spring.

- *May–June*: Many studios, networks, and production companies look for new ideas in late spring and commission them to be further developed over the summer.

- Mid-season shows don't have specific times and hire writers throughout the year.

- The current trend is moving toward a year-round approach, where a pilot might debut in the middle of the summer, in other time slots, or in later seasons.

F. The Impact of Budget on a Script

TV is all about business. It is an industry driven by revenue and profit margins, and your idea could translate into a business opportunity from which broadcasters and clients profit. Development executives must focus on this bottom line, no matter how creative or compelling the project.

If your project is expensive to produce, it already has one strike against it. A vital part of the producing process is maintaining your creative vision and still operating on a tight budget, as you will see in Chapter 4. If you are using union actors, for example, don't write lines for them if they are not essential — a spoken line costs more than hiring an extra with no lines.

Minors under 18 must have a tutor on set, which involves extra paperwork. Each aspect of your project costs money, so look for ways to cut costs. As you write and develop your idea, keep the following categories in mind.

- Screenplay and/or story rights

- Cast

- Crew

- Director

- Producers

- Locations

- Period pieces

- Special effects

- Post-production

- Music

- Miscellaneous items like overhead, contingencies, legal and finance charges, etc.

- Advertising and marketing costs

Experienced writers keep their plotlines simple, and try to avoid complicated locations, building sets and studio space, a large cast, destruction of expensive locations or items, stunts, expensive post-production dependencies, and other extras that expand the budget. Often, the story can survive without them.

1. *Options for Self-Funding*

Depending on the kind of program you're developing, you may choose to completely bypass the traditional broadcasters so that you can own it — and control it. This approach is risky — it could deplete your savings or ruin your credit. Or your risk could pay off.

Producers might subsidize their projects with their own money, or they can be financed by investors, corporate sponsorship, foundation grants, bank loans, fundraising events, donations, or even bartering goods or exchanging services.

Make a list of the people who could help you, and be clear about what you are asking for. You may want them to finance your entire project, or to simply invest enough money to cover certain stages such as development or post-production costs. Your list could include many of the people listed below.

1. Family and relatives

2. Other writers and producers

3. Fellow students

4. Coworkers

5. Writers

6. Directors

7. Producers

8. Lawyers

9. Agents

10. Managers

11. Investment Brokers

12. Actors

> You've got to write what you want to produce, or at least the first few shows, because otherwise, it will pretty much be taken out of your hands. Even if you don't have the desire to be a writer, take writing classes because you should know how a script is put together, even if you are the post-production supervisor.
>
> —Valerie Walsh, *excerpt from interview in Chapter 11*

On a Human Level . . .

The writing process can be painful. Translating a vague idea to a tangible script is fraught with pressures and uncertainties, and you worry that when it's read, people may respond with rejection or apathy. It seems endless. Your calls and query letters go unanswered. But keep in mind that every successful project on TV went through the development process — and survived it.

> I don't think art alone changes people, but consciousness, the life of the mind, is a critical force for change, and art helps the shaping of consciousness.
>
> —Tony Kushner, playwright.

IV. Summary

Throughout this chapter, you have weighed the harsh realities of developing an idea against the promises of success that lure writers and producers into the world of producing for television. In the next chapter, you will explore how these ideas translate into the reality of budgeting.

V. Chapter Review Questions

1. Devise a comprehensive strategy for informing yourself of current trends and producing deals in the television industry.

2. What are four good sources for story ideas?

3. Write a mission statement for your life and one for your project. In what ways do they connect?

4. What is the primary difference between writing for television and writing for film?

5. What is your favorite television genre? Why?

6. Write a sample scene. Use a professional script format.

7. Name five components of dialogue that you find compelling. Why?

8. Would you rather write alone, with a partner, or as part of a writing team? Why?

9. What is the importance of legally protecting your idea? How can you protect it?

10. Name six major story ideas that can impact your budget. What are some low-budget alternatives?

The TV business is a cruel and shallow money trench, a long plastic hallway where thieves and pimps run free, and good men die like dogs.

—Dr. Hunter S. Thompson

Breakdowns, Budgets, and Finance: Connecting the Dots

This Chapter's Talking Points

I. Break the Idea Down

II. Budget the Idea

III. Find the Financing

IV. Summary

V. Chapter Review Questions

I. Break the Idea Down

Making a budget for your project obligates you to predict the future. It requires you to examine each aspect of your project, give it a face, and assign it job descriptions and a set of parameters. Without a realistic budget, your project faces confusion and failure. Budgeting can be daunting, even for seasoned producers, yet with time and some practice you can understand and eventually master the budgeting process. As a guideline for this process, you can refer to the comprehensive budget template in the CD offered with this book.

Designing a budget is a process during which the producer evaluates the project's vision, then translates that vision into time and money. Costs have an enormous range, and if a dozen producers were to budget the same script, each would come up with different totals and calculations. One story can be told in many ways, and the best budgets emerge from solid research and cost comparisons, studying other producers' budgets, talking to people with budgeting experience, and practice.

The now-classic television series, *Friends,* first started with six unknown actors who were paid modest salaries. But by the time the show left the air, each actor had become a TV star, earning a million dollars per episode. Although these stars boosted the audience and advertiser appeal, the talent budget alone was six million dollars — per episode. Other costs rose, as well, as producers created new swing sets and added guest stars. Yet its high ratings, and subsequent sales to syndicators and international markets, allowed NBC to pay the increased costs. Money is *always* at the core of every television show, so the producer's job is to achieve the best quality for the lowest cost.

A. Understand the Big Picture of Production

The producers work closely with people who can transform an idea into a finished product, such as the director, talent, crew, heads of key departments, and others. Whether the production is large or small, the producer (or a team of producers) is at its core delegating, supervising, and making decisions throughout the project.

B. Create a Production Book

A good producer is organized, and an essential tool in that organization process is called a *production book*. Producers generally keep a separate production book for each project — a three-ring loose-leaf binder with tab dividers for each section. It includes most, if not all, of the following categories:

- A Contact list including names and phone numbers for talent, crew members, and other essential contact information
- A procedural breakdown of the responsibilities of the various staff members
- The script and any revisions
- Shooting schedules and call sheets
- Scene breakdowns
- Storyboards
- Props
- Wardrobe
- Transportation details
- Meals and craft service plans
- Location agreements and shooting permits
- Releases for talent
- Deal memos with crew
- Insurance information
- Budget

C. Break Down Your Idea or Script

There are several budgetary aspects to consider when you write or option material that is the foundation for a script or project.

- Allow yourself or your writer(s) adequate time to develop your script. You don't want it rewritten on set when time and money is at a premium.

- Most scripts require tweaking and revisions. Include money in your budget to cover an outline, a treatment, and at least two rewrites before you start shooting.

- Most scripts must get final approval from development executives or clients, which can result in additional changes to the script or overall project structure. The time required for the writer(s) to complete any rewrites is an added budget item.

D. Script Breakdown

Every script is a compilation of scenes, and each scene has certain requirements that cost money. Does the scene call for three actors or only one? Is the scene being shot with multiple cameras and lighting, or just one handheld camera using available light? What props or greenery or furniture are in that scene? Every component has a direct relationship to the budget and the shooting schedule. A *breakdown sheet* helps the production staff understand what is needed in each scene. It can be compiled by hand or by using special software. An example is provided in the included CD. It makes the process easier, and provides a concise blueprint that helps to make the scenes work. The breakdown is fully explored in Chapter 7, and includes any or all of the following categories:

- The scene number and name

- The date of the breakdown sheet

- The project title

- The page number of the script

- Location (on set or on a real location)

- Interior or exterior (shooting inside or outside)

- Day or night

- Brief scene description (one or two lines)

- Cast (with speaking parts)

- Extras (no speaking parts, either in the scene or in the background)

- Special effects (this ranges from explosions to blood packs to extra lighting)

- Props (anything handled by a character in the scene, like a telephone or pencil)

- Set dressing (items on the set not handled by the character)

- Wardrobe (any details that are pertinent to that scene, like a torn shirt)

- Make-up and hair (special effects, like wounds or aging, wigs or facial hair)

- Extra equipment (jibs, cranes, a dolly, steadicams)

- Stunts (falls, fights, explosions requiring a stunt person and stunt coordinator)

- Vehicles (cars or other vehicles used by characters in the scene)

- Animals (any animal that appears in the scene comes with a trainer, or *wrangler,* who takes charge of the animal during production)

- Sound effects and/or music (anything played back on set, like a phone ringing, music for lip-syncing, or music the actor is reacting to)

- Additional production notes

E. Storyboarding

Storyboards are not necessary in each project, but for those who use them , they're useful tools for saving time and money. *Storyboards* are simple, cartoon-like sketches of each scene in a script. They're numbered boxes with a drawing inside; each box refers to a scene or shot number from the script. When the image or camera angle changes, so does the content of the box. Each sketch is a rough portrait of the scene being shot: the location of one character in relation to another, the surroundings, the colors or lighting in a scene. Storyboards can be a real advantage to a production as a kind of shorthand for the director, producer(s), Director of Photography (DP), art director, and production designer, as well as information needed in the budgeting.

Prior to shooting, the producer and/or director go through the script. They make a rough sketch of each scene (often with the help of a *storyboard artist* or special storyboarding software) that details every camera setup in that scene. Usually storyboards contain minimal black-and-white line drawings, although they can be in full color photography, even animated. In the case of unscripted programs, storyboards can help the production team to visualize and structure a location so that it looks natural but includes spots to place cameras or microphones. Storyboards are often used as a visual tool in presenting an idea for a project — often producers pitch and sell their project ideas by using imaginative storyboards as persuasive selling tools. You can find a storyboard format in the CD included in this book.

F. Shooting Schedule

The *shooting schedule* is a key component in creating a budget. If, for example, your show costs $5,000 a day to shoot and you have a 10-day shooting schedule, you'll need to budget $50,000. But if your shooting schedule goes off course and extends to 15 days, you've got a $25,000 difference to consider. It isn't unusual for the cast and crew of a one-hour TV show to work 16 hours a day; some shows shoot as many as 12 to 18 script pages each day. This translates to shooting a feature-length script in two weeks — an incredibly tough schedule. Chapter 7 looks into the fine points of a shooting schedule.

Several prime time television shows, both narrative and unscripted reality, now shoot with a method known as *cross-boarding*. Using this approach, the producer shoots scenes, consecutively, from two or three different episodes that all take place on the same set or location. In other words, in Episodes 110, 113, and 117 of *The XYZ Show*, Tommy and his kids are in the kitchen. Their lines are different and so are the props, the wardrobe and the story lines, but they all take place in the kitchen set. It is much more cost-effective to keep the crew in place and the set dressed and lit so that all three scenes can be shot in the one location.

II. Budget the Idea

Each producer has his or her own approach to budgeting. Some television producers divide their budgets into three main categories: *preproduction*, *production*, and *post-production*, while others isolate their costs into *above-the-line* and *below-the-line* sections. These distinctions will be covered later in this section.

Producers factor in *indirect costs*, like legal fees, accounting services, insurance premiums, and a contingency that covers unforeseen costs. Some charge a direct *markup fee*, which is a percentage added to the costs that cover office and personnel overhead. Other producers might hide their profit margin in other ways, such as inflated crew costs and facility rentals. The overall goal is to make a profit in the long run, or at the very least, not to lose money.

Larger productions depend on budgets that cover pages of spreadsheets calculated on software. Smaller productions might only need a page or two to keep track of their costs. As the producer, look for the right budget template that works best for each project, or work closely with the production manager or the line producer in keeping track of daily costs and the overall budget.

> You have to be flexible. You have to be willing to roll with the punches, you have to believe in what you are doing and believe you can do it. If someone is telling you something is impossible, it is usually not. Anything is possible. There are some things that are impossible for budgetary reasons, but there are always compromises and ways to make your vision come to life.
>
> —Tom Sellitti, *excerpt from interview in Chapter 11*

A. Budgeting Costs

Most television and video producers find it easier to look at their costs by dividing their budget items into three major categories:

1. Preproduction

2. Production

3. Post-production

1. *Preproduction Costs*

Costs tend to be lower and more controllable in this first stage of a project. Budget items usually include the producer's fee for taking meetings, hiring crews, casting actors or talent, coordinating stunts, planning the shooting schedule, booking hotel, meals, and travel, and generally planning the project's overall development.

The script is a vital component of the project, and the producer works closely with the writer(s) in the preproduction stage. Budgeting for a writer can be done in several ways. For example, the producer and writer might agree on a flat fee that covers all aspects of developing the idea, writing the script, and any revisions. A writer might also be paid in stages, such as 30% of the agreed-upon fee after signing a contract, 30% with the first draft, and the remaining 40% is paid after final acceptance. In this case, the fee may include a specified number of revisions. If that number is exceeded, additional fees for extra revisions may be negotiated as part of the contract. Writers may also require the assistance of a researcher or other resources as part of the story development.

Other preproduction costs could include designing storyboards, consultant fees, casting fees (casting director and facilities), space for talent rehearsals, production assistants, office rental, location scouting, messengers, meetings, and meals. If the shooting is in a foreign location, research must be done to learn each country's requirements for shooting. Any sets must be planned, constructed, painted, and moved to a sound stage that needs to be scheduled, and paid for. Careful preproduction planning is vital and saves money for the overall budget of the project. This is covered further in Chapter 7.

2. *Production Costs*

When the producer has thoroughly explored and mapped out everything needed to shoot the project, the production phase can be the quickest and least problematic parts of the project. The script has been researched and finalized, the crew has been hired, the talent cast, the heads of key departments have submitted their department's requirements with estimated costs for production, contingency money has been put aside, and the many other details have been finalized so that the actual shoot can begin. Chapter 8 explores the specifics of production.

3. Post-Production Costs

This is traditionally a challenging area for producers to accurately budget. As you'll learn in Chapter 9, there are many factors in the post-production process to consider. These include the hours of footage that need to be screened, logged, and loaded into the editing system; the skills and style of the editor, and the costs for the editor, editing facility, the audio mixer and the audio facility; any graphics, artwork, animations, text, captioning, credits, and other design effects; music, narration, voice-over, sound effects, sound design, and even foreign language translation.

B. Above- and Below-the-Line Costs

In the case of some television projects — commercials and more elaborate, big-budget television series or specials — the producer might use a budget format similar to a feature film budget. This format divides the productions costs into two areas: *above-* and *below-the-line* expenses.

1. Above-the-Line

These costs are project-specific fees or salaries paid to the creative personnel (producers, directors, writers, and actors, depending on multiple factors including union affiliation, time required, special perks, and star power). Above-the-line fees are paid in several ways:

- *Union fees*: If the writer is a member of the Writers Guild of America (WGA), that fee is stated in the WGA contract with the producer. The same applies to a director who's a member of the Directors Guild of America (DGA) and to a Screen Actors Guild (SAG) actor.

- *Daily or weekly fees*: The personnel agree to a fee to be paid daily or weekly.

- *Flat fees*: Often a producer agrees to pay a fee to an above-the-line creative in install-ments: one-third on signing a contract or deal memo, one-third on completion of principal photography, and the final one-third when the project is completed.

- *Producer fee*: Because the producer is usually the person deciding how fees are paid, this can be a very arbitrary fee. The producer(s) generally takes the project from start to finish, and works longer than most everyone involved. Some producers take weekly fees, others work on a flat per-project fee. A producer might also defer payment until the project is sold in exchange for a bigger fee at the back-end of the deal, although there are seldom little, if any, profits to be made in the majority of projects.

2. Below-the-Line

These costs tend to be more predictable, covering the technical crew and their equipment, resources, and standard expenses like overhead, insurance, and more. Below-the-line personnel can be union or nonunion; this depends on whether the company behind the project is a *union signatory* who has agreed to adhere to union regulations. There are several unions that cover professionals such as writers, directors, actors, camera operators and audio engineers, grips and gaffers, make-up and hair, wardrobe, and others.

Union members are protected by strict rules that include hours worked, overtime, meals and breaks, benefits, and pension and welfare (P&W). Nonunion members can be more flexible with the hours they will work, they aren't paid benefits, and their rates tend to be more negotiable than union members who are often bound by rate scales. Nonunion members can be as qualified as union workers, and often, union members will work on nonunion jobs. Membership in a union doesn't necessarily imply quality or experience.

C. Estimated versus Actual Costs

A production budget is often divided into two primary columns: the *estimated costs* (what the producers thinks a budget item will cost) and the *actual costs* (what the item really ends up costing). On some budget templates, the estimated column might be called budgeted costs. Many budgets add a third column to the right of the first two that lists the *plus or minus* amounts (also called over and under). This figure represents the difference between the estimated costs and the actuals. This plus or minus column provides an instant readout on the running costs, and lets the producer know if the budget is on track or if adjustments need to be made to keep costs in line with the budget.

1. *Estimated Budget*

In the early stages of developing your project, you may be asked by a potential buyer or investor for an estimated budget that details the possible production costs. Drawing up this estimate and putting specific figures on a sketchy idea can be a real challenge, especially for a beginning producer. Often the script hasn't been written yet, and there is little information that can act as a basis for a budget. Ironically, the producer is looking for development money to expand the idea into a format that can be broken down and budgeted. When a potential buyer asks for a rough budget estimate, your response might include one of the following options:

- Ask about the client's financing parameters. Most are experienced enough in the business, and have an amount in mind that they're willing to spend. For example, they may have only $300,000 to spend, but your budget estimate is $350,000. You might be able to trim your budget down by $50,000, or you can justify the reasons behind your estimate and convince them to raise their offer by $50,000.

- Give the buyer choices: a Plan A budget that reflects everything on your production wish list, and a Plan B budget that covers fewer extra effects, locations, and other items that add to a budget.

- The buyer may be willing to give you a small development fee for expanding your script, research, location scouting, or doing a script breakdown.

- A buyer may be so dedicated to your project that they can find additional money from other budgets, or they may genuinely not have the amount you've budgeted. Often their commitment to your project can motivate you to pare down your budget as much as possible and to somehow make it work.

- Don't be afraid of walking away. If, for example, a buyer won't budge from a $200,000 offer and you're quite sure that your budget of $300,000 is realistic and professional, you can politely refuse their offer and look elsewhere. The skills of negotiation can be developed over time; meanwhile, an agent or entertainment lawyer can be a tremendous asset in making a deal.

2. *Actual Budget*

In the attached CD, you can find a sample project budget that has several columns. One is labeled actuals and the other is labeled estimated. The figures in the actuals column represent what was *actually* spent, rather than what was originally *estimated* (seen in the other column). Consider the example of a producer who budgets enough money to cover a three-day shoot on a beach. Suddenly, an unexpected storm shuts down the entire production for all three days. The production has stopped, but the talent and crew are still receiving full pay. After the storm passes, the producer shoots the necessary scenes for three additional days. In this example, the original estimated costs called for three days of shooting while the actual costs were for six days. This extra time and salary have to be covered in the budget, somehow.

> You have to know what things cost, because you have to know when you can say yes and when you can say no. We've got $30K to do this, and $30K seems like a lot but then you realize that $30K covers your travel, your crew, three days of shooting, your transfers, expenses, editing, the mix . . . you have to know what is in the budget. What is allocated for what portion, and realistically, can it be done?
> —John Rosas, *excerpt from interview in Chapter 11*

D. Researching Budget Costs

Putting a budget together relies heavily on research. The producer must make phone calls, surf the net, compare prices, talk to other producers, and read books and industry trade publications. It also helps to look at other producers' budgets to see how they have calculated their costs.

Almost every item included in a budget can have a low-to-high price range. Say you plan to shoot a TV documentary with a small two-person crew that includes a video camera, microphones, and their operators. The costs for a professional crew could range from $1,000 to $50,000 — per day! In this case, the lower costs would cover a crew that specializes in shooting news, interviews, and documentary material. In the world of high-end commercials and episodics, these costs can be considerably higher.

While budgeting any project the producer takes all of these variables into consideration, with the goal in mind of creating the highest quality product for the least amount of money. The producer finds the best people, equipment, services, and locations, and makes it all work within the budget. Creating a budget generally follows the following procedural process.

E. Creating a Working Budget

Break down your script or your treatment to determine specific factors that contribute to a realistic budget. These factors include:

- The number of preproduction days: Developing your script, location scouting, interviewing and hiring crew and talent

- The number of shooting days, on set and on location: What sets are needed, what locations and where, your *shooting ratio* (how much material shot compared to what's actually used in the final version), which talent and crew are working on what days and their costs, and equipment rental charges

- The number of days in post-production: logging and screening your footage, making notes for your editing script, planning and completing graphics, theme music, sound design, editing, and the final mix

1. *Budget Formats*

An effective budget outlines each and every category involved in every phase of the project. Each category in the budget is known as a *budget line*. There is no one standard budget form that's used by all producers. Depending on the project, a budget could be one short page or a dozen. Some budgets are separated into above-the-line and below-the-line costs; other budgets are divided into preproduction, production, and post-production categories. But all budgets must clearly specify what money gets spent and where.

2. *The Top Sheet*

Most longer form budgets begin with a *top sheet*, a brief summary of the project's costs in each department. It gives the producer a valuable overview of the budget at a glance. A blank top sheet, known as the Project Costs Summary form, can be accessed in the accompanying CD.

3. *The Detailed Budget*

A *detailed budget* addresses every aspect of the project's production. Each detail in a script or project translates into a cost that's part of a key budget category, or *account*. These accounts include all the departments and all expenses. Budgets are seldom distributed to anyone but the producer, director, line producer, and/or the production manager. A detailed budget varies in length, depending on the project.

4. *Budget Lines and Categories*

While creating a budget for a project, you might include any or all of the following categories:

- *Producers*: Each project has at least one producer with specific responsibilities. The primary producer is usually at the helm of the project from day one, and gets paid until the project is completed. His or her time must be budgeted for meetings, pitches, and day-to-day development in the beginning, all the way through production and post-production, and continue through consulting on marketing and distribution at the project's end.

- *Screenplay and/or story rights*: If the script isn't the producer's original script, then the producer must pay for the rights to use someone's else's story, script, article, book, or idea. Reality shows often require rights and releases.

- *Writer(s)*: Regardless of the source of the idea, a writer or team of writers is hired to flesh out the idea or refine an existing script.

- *Director*: A director with experience, vision, patience, and the ability to work fast is a major benefit to any show. He or she may be expensive but can save you money over the long run.

- *Actors*: Well-known stars can escalate a budget, but their names attract viewers and necessary sponsors. Unknown actors charge less, and with the right script, director, rehearsal time, and network promotion, they can create a hit show.

- *Talent perks*: Stars often demand extra benefits such as a personal makeup artist, a wardrobe stylist, a physical trainer, special trailers, travel accommodations, secretaries, and nannies.

- *Crew*: A crew can consist of 1 to 2 people or hundreds — it depends on the project as well as any necessary union regulations. Basic personnel might include camera and audio operators and their assistants, a director of photography, assistant director, a prop master, electricians (gaffers), grips, a stylist, a script supervisor, scene artists, set designers, carpenters, still photographers, a location scout, craft service, ambulance or paramedic/nurse on call, a tutor for minor children, choreographers, stunt coordinators, and others.

- *Staff*: The project usually employs production secretaries, administrative staff, production assistants (PAs) and interns, who are assigned to areas in which they're needed.

- *Locations:* Costs for locations could include scouting fees, transportation, hotels for cast and crew, meals, location and permit fees, and equipment rentals. A location can be less expensive than building a set, although locations can have their own challenges: audio problems that can't be controlled — like airplanes and air conditioners — or inadequate electrical power for cables and lights. Foreign locations create additional costs like varying personnel rates and wages, travel expenses, taxes, and currency exchange rates. However, these costs, when compared to domestic costs, might still be less expensive.

- *Set construction*: Sets can be elaborate and handcrafted, they can be computer-generated, or they can be minimal and simple. This area might require a production designer, set designer, construction costs, and personnel such as artists, painters, and carpenters.

- *Hair and make-up:* The needs of this department depend on the project's talent requirements and size of the cast, which includes supporting characters, minor children, and extras. Special effects, such as fake blood or wounds, toupees, hairpieces, or wigs are also taken into account.

- *Period pieces*: Recreating another time period automatically increases the budget in virtually every below-the-line area including locations and sets, wardrobes and props, researchers, and production designers.

- *Special effects*: This category includes extra costs like explosions, stunts, smoke, special lighting, car chases, gun shots, and rain.

- *Music and sound effects*: Most programs include show themes and filler music that has been especially composed for the program, as well as additional sound effects and voice-over narration. Occasionally, a sound track or theme song can become a popular hit. For lower budgets, stock music is an excellent alternative.

- *Transportation*: Hauling equipment, cast, and crew from one location to another requires trucks, vans, and other vehicles, along with tolls, parking, gas, and vehicle maintenance, all of which can add to a budget's costs.

- *Meals*: Keeping fed and energized is essential in any production, large or small. Make sure there's at least one full-sized healthy meal per day, and keep a table of healthy snacks, a bit of junk food, and refills of coffee, tea, and water.

- *Security*: In many cases, a production needs the help of a security guard or team of guards to protect equipment, keep talent isolated from fans, crowd control, and to generally keep one eye on the big picture.

- *Post-production*: This area can be cheaper when producers and directors know how to shoot less, edit "in their heads," log and screen, and come prepared to the edit room. Costs include tape transfers, loading into an editing system, the edit time, music and sound design and mixes, and graphic elements

- *Animation*: If a show contains animated portions, or is entirely animated, this budget line can be complex, and might include artists, designers, colorists, software operators, and a variety of other personnel and equipment. However, animation can cancel out your costs for props, wardrobe, make-up, and so on.

5. *Additional Budget Lines*

The producer also factors in expenses such as office overhead, petty cash, finance charges, insurance and special riders, and payroll, accounting, and legal costs. Additional expenses could also include music licensing, stock footage, stock music, and research fees, transcriptions, and foreign translation.

- *Office overhead*: Whether you're renting an office space or using your apartment as a production office, you've got daily operating expenses such as rent, electricity, telephone (cells and land lines), faxes, cable, the Internet, copy machines, a VCR and monitor for screening demo reels and your own footage, and basic supplies like paper, pens, and staples. The standard overhead fee is 6 to 8%.

- *Petty cash*: Get into the habit of keeping track of petty cash. By using a Petty Cash Report form (like the example found on the CD), you can keep track of your costs (and receipts) for meals, taxis, tolls, copying scripts, and various odds and ends that can inflate the budget.

- *Finance charges*: If you're paying anything with a credit card, remember to factor in the monthly interest. That 4 to 21% can be significant on a large monthly bill. The same goes for production loans, car leasing, and other costs.

> There is a bundle of insurance coverage that a picture needs. It needs liability insurance, it needs property insurance, general liability if you smash your camera through someone's plate glass window, or if someone trips over a cable, or if you've rented a car and have an accident during production. Then, there is producers' liability, or errors and omissions, that protects against claims arising out of the content and copyright trademark, and libel and privacy claims. Insurance is a big item.
> —J. Stephen Sheppard, *excerpt from interview in Chapter 11*

Insurance

As the producer, you must protect yourself and your production with insurance. It's a necessity — you could lose everything from one lawsuit for a broken ankle or a damaged location. Regardless of size, all independent producers and production companies protect themselves with a Comprehensive General Liability insurance policy that includes liability and workers' compensation. In most cities and states, a certificate of insurance is necessary to get a shooting permit. Usually, a one million dollar minimum is required. Insurance coverage can cost from $3,000 and up per year, depending on what and where you're shooting; some entertainment insurance companies are willing to insure a production by the day or for the duration of the project.

Below is a list of coverage your insurance policy could include:

- *General liability*: Protects you against claim of bodily injury, property damage, and vehicular damage that's additional to auto insurance. You might also add riders or special coverage for stunts, explosions, cast insurance, props and sets, extra expenses, third-party property damage, equipment loss or damage, faulty stock, faulty cameras or audio equipment, excess liability, union insurance, animal injury or death, and more.

- *Workers' compensation*: Covers temporary or permanent loss of cast or crew (whether they're temporary or permanent actors), and pays for hospital and medical, disability, and death benefits. The rates depend on the nature of the work.

- *Entertainment package*: In addition to the two primary insurance policies, above, producers can also cover their project with an insurance package that protects against bad video stock, lost or damaged camera masters, video or film processing, lost or damaged props, sets, equipment, wardrobe, extra expenses, and third-party damage. Other additional coverage includes problems with the weather, the cast, excess liability, aircraft and watercraft, animals, vehicles, political risks, and unique sets or props.

- *Errors and omission insurance (E&O)*: Essentially insurance that protects the production against lawsuits involving authorship and copyright issues such as plagiarism, unauthorized use of ideas, characters, titles, formats, or plots. It also covers invasion of privacy, slander, libel or character defamation, and copyright infringement. It defines a clear chain of title: who wrote what, and when, and who ultimately owns any rights to any aspects of your project.

- *Institutional and educational insurance*: In some cases a college, university, or public or private school might provide insurance coverage for enrolled students. This includes general liability insurance, as well as insurance for video and audio equipment and third-party property. This insurance seldom covers a project that is shot in a foreign location, uses explosives or moving vehicles, or depends on stunts.

Payroll Services

Larger or more complex productions rely on a payroll accountant or service that regularly pays all personnel, takes out taxes when necessary, accounts for union costs, agents or managers' percentages, pension and welfare, and pays other costs.

- *Accounting fees*: Often a production hires an accountant or accounting service to keep track of all daily and weekly costs for the production, and issues regular reports on the budget's progress.

- *Legal fees*: Attorney fees can be nominal, or they can be significant. Almost all productions require releases and contracts with the creative teams, the talent, the crew, and other personnel, as well as negotiations with sound stages, facilities, and other businesses needed in a production. Although producers can often handle these areas, a lawyer may be brought on board to take care of more complicated issues. Many contracts are simple enough to be drafted by the producer using a deal memo, such as the Crew Deal Memo found on the included CD, as well as additional information in Chapter 5. More complex contracts and negotiations require consultation with an entertainment lawyer. A lawyer can bill by the hour or ask for a flat fee that extends over the project; legal fees generally account for 2 to 3% of the budget.

Music Licensing

Costs for music can be prohibitive and might include a composer, lyricist, musicians, and ultimately, the music publisher and the recording company. See Chapter 5 for more in-depth information on music rights clearances.

Stock Footage and Stock Music

To save the costs of either an original musical composition or preexisting music, producers often rely on *stock music* that is royalty-free and cost-effective. The same applies for *stock footage* that has already been shot and can be licensed. You'll find more information about this in Chapter 9.

The producer is also responsible for the budgeting of costs listed below.

- *Research fees*: Depending on the project, a researcher or team of researchers might be an integral part of the process, especially in the case of fact-based programming, documentaries, news, and some reality shows. A researcher can be a staff member or a professional, depending on the complexity of the research needed.

- *Transcription*: Many producers prefer to work with written transcripts of interviews and documentary footage that are word-for-word transcriptions, often with time code references.

- *Translation*: Certain projects might require a separate audio track for translating the dialogue into another language. This requires a translator to do the actual translation, a narrator to read it, a director or producer to oversee the audio session, and often subtitles.

- *Advertising and marketing*: Both paid and free publicity is vital to the success of a show. A producer may hire a still photographer to take publicity shots, as well as a publicist to make sure the stills are featured in articles or ads for the project. Other costs could include promos, printing and distributing posters, flyers, direct mail, newspaper and magazine advertising, as well as hosting screenings, and entering festivals.

- *Contingencies*: Most productions run into a problem somewhere: the location could fall through at the last minute, an actor gets sick, or the videotape gets shredded in the camera. A professional budget builds in a contingency that covers these realities for about 10% of the final total.

III. Find the Financing

In some projects, the responsibility falls on the producer to raise the financing. It can be challenging for both a novice and a veteran producer to secure enough money to create and complete a project. Yet everything you see on television was funded, somehow.

A. Possible Sources for Funding Your Project

Once you have created a rough budget for your project, you can focus on raising the funds. As you will learn in Chapter 6, one of the more effective tools is a solid *business proposal* that you can offer to potential financing sources. These may include:

- *Private investors*: This category covers a wide range of possibility, as well as rejection. You can approach people you know — like friends, family, coworkers, fellow students — or you can meet with business people you've never met who see the economic promise in your idea, are looking for tax advantages, or simply an ego boost. Ideally, your project will be successful, and your investors can see a return on their initial investment. But you don't want to promise anything that can't be delivered. However, assure investors that you will do your best to pay back their good faith in you, if not their monetary investment. Some investors are happy to simply be on set and watch the shoot, or have a small walk-on part in return for their investment.

- *Grants*: Grants are a source of money that could prove beneficial in funding phases of your project, such as the initial research, writing, or post-production; some may cover the entire budget. Grants are awarded by public and private foundations. You'll find more information on grants in Chapter 10 and in the attached CD under Grants and Funding.

- *Public foundations*: Various categories of financial aid and grants are given out to filmmakers, depending on the nature of their project. Organizations like the National Endowment for the Humanities (NEH), National Endowment of the Arts (NEA), and the American Film Institute (AFI) are better-known sources, though each state and local government also offers funds for projects that fit their grant's requirements. These sources are listed on the CD in the sections Grants and Funding and Web Sites, and are discussed further in Chapter 10.

- *Private foundations*: Most large corporations earmark specific funds to support projects in the public interest, and often to elevate their own public image. They may award full grants, fund part or all of a project, or underwrite projects that they want to be associated with. Public television, for example, might air a special or a series that is partially or fully sponsored by a public or private foundation.

- *Bank loans*: Avoid investing your own money if you can. However, if you're determined to make your project, and you know that you can pay the loan back later with interest, it might be possible to get a bank loan if your credit allows. If not, the bank will require a cosigner or collateral such as a car, house, or something else of value that you own.

- *Credit cards*: You may have a healthy credit rating and can afford to take out a cash advance to pay for production costs. But before you do this, add up the extra interest costs on the advance, and be sure that you can make your monthly payments. You don't want to lose your valuable credit rating over a project if you can find another financing source.

> There are no wrong answers in producing, only answers that will cost you a lot of money.
>
> —Valerie Walsh, *excerpt from interview in Chapter 11*

B. Bartering, Negotiation, and Tips to Save Money

An effective producer looks for areas of flexibility in the budget, pulls in favors when necessary, knows how to negotiate, and cuts costs wherever possible while still maintaining quality. The following are just a few creative directions you can consider as alternatives to actual financing.

1. Negotiation

A producer can often negotiate better rates. Few unions will agree to lower rates for their members, but nonunion actors, crews, writers, and directors, as well as equipment rental houses and post-production facilities may be willing to negotiate. Offering the employment security of several days or weeks of work can provide an incentive for reduced daily or weekly rates or a flat fee for the project. Some people are willing to work for half-day rates. Another potential area of negotiation involves *product placement,* in which a product is prominently placed in the shot, visible to the viewer, and integrated into the scene. A fee is paid for this service.

2. Deferred Payment

A project may have a modest budget but everyone involved wants it to succeed. To save money, a producer might offer a *deferred payment* to some or all of the people involved. This means that when (or if) the project makes money down the line, all who agreed to defer their salaries are paid later — often with interest or bonuses on top of their original salary agreement.

3. Courtesy Credits

A producer can often negotiate for expenses like air or hotel accommodations simply by giving these companies an acknowledgement in the end credits of the program. For example, you might see "round trip travel provided by British Airways," or "hotel accommodations provided by Marriott Hotels."

4. Hiring Union versus Nonunion Talent

There are pros and cons to each option. Hiring union members generally assumes that they are professionals with experience. However, unions dictate specific rates and rules for working conditions that producers and the union member must adhere to. There is also extra paperwork and payments such as P&W, benefits, and other costs. Nonunion talent and crew can be as experienced and professional as union members without the restrictions of a union governing their work. Producers often pay their crew the same rates as they would pay a union member, without having to deal with paying benefits and extra paperwork. Often, a union member will work on a nonunion production, although they can be in violation of their union depending on the situation. There are several unions that a television producer may be working with, depending on the circumstances of the production. They can be found on the Internet and in the CD, and include:

- Writers Guild of America (WGA)

- Directors Guild of America (DGA)

- Screen Actors Guild (SAG)

- Screen Extras Guild (SEG)

- American Federation of Television and Radio Actors (AFTRA)

- National Association of Broadcast Employees and Technicians-Communications Workers of America (NABET-CWA)

- International Alliance of Theatrical Stage Employees (IATSE)

5. *Money Back*

Occasionally, after the shooting has been completed, a project may end up with items that can be sold, returned for refunds, or exchanged for services, such as unused video stock, wardrobe, props, furniture, plants, or greenery.

6. *In-Kind Donations*

An inventive producer can save substantial costs in the budget by asking for donations of goods or services. Some classic examples of in-kind donations that are offered either at a lower rate or for free include no-fee locations, food and beverages from a restaurant or grocery store, vehicles, software, supplies, and videotape stock. Legal and accounting services, databases and computers, telephone and Internet, and video and audio post-production facilities are other types of in-kind services. This generosity is traditionally rewarded with a *courtesy credit*, which acknowledges and thanks the contributors by listing their names or businesses in the project's closing credits.

C. Student Budgets and Resources

Many students can take advantage of resources their school offers, either as part of tuition or for a small fee. These might include video and audio equipment, allotments of video stock, editing equipment, graphics tools, and music libraries, as well as student labor. A student can often benefit from the school's tax-exempt status and liability insurance. Students also qualify for lower student rates that could apply to van or car rentals, travel, and meals by joining various video and film organizations that offer student membership rates. Several professional unions, like SAG, Actors Equity Association (AEA), and AFTRA may give students concessions on rates for student projects made under the auspices of an accredited school. Many editing and audio facilities and businesses that provide software programs, as well as original music, or stock music and stock footage, offer lower rates to students.

The student projects come with guidelines, and must be made only for use in the classroom or shown in student festivals. A SAG actor, for example, may work on a student film under special union exemptions, but if the film is purchased for broadcast or offered for sale, the rates must be renegotiated at a professional level.

- School-sponsored grants, awards, and sponsorships

- Private investors like friends and family

- Professional business investors

- Festivals and public and private foundation grants

On a Human Level . . .

Budgeting can be daunting, especially in the beginning. Your original idea seems to pale in the shadow of a harsh dollars-and-sense scenario, which can dampen your initial enthusiasm and even create an urge to back off the project altogether. It's common to have "math anxiety" over budgets, or to become impatient. Stick with it, and know that even the most experienced producers share your feelings.

> Mistakes are the portals of discovery.
>
> —James Joyce

IV. Summary

The only thing more challenging than finding the money is managing it when it comes in. Creating a budget and sticking to it takes discipline, ingenuity, experience, and patience. Each project brings its own requirements and frustrations, yet each brings you closer to mastering the skills of budgeting. As you become more familiar with the budgeting process, your next challenge is to explore the legalities of the project. The next chapter guides you through the legal maze.

V. Chapter Review Questions

1. What is the first element of "reality" that you must consider when developing a project?

2. What is the purpose of a production book? A breakdown sheet? A storyboard?

3. Define cross-boarding. Give an example of its use.

4. Identify the key differences between hiring union and nonunion crew employees.

5. What are estimates versus actuals? Why is it helpful to track both throughout a project?

6. What is a budget top sheet?

7. What are three areas in which a lawyer can be of assistance to your project?

Let us never negotiate out of fear. But let us never fear to negotiate.

—John F. Kennedy

Legalities and Rights: Welcome to Reality

CHAPTER 5

This Chapter's Talking Points

I.   Own It

II.   If You Don't Own It, Get Permission to Use It

III.   Protect It

IV.   Double-Check It

V.   Summary

VI.   Chapter Review Questions

I. Own It

It's the producer's responsibility to legally protect the production. This involves a common-sense understanding of entertainment law, and an awareness of the contracts, agreements, and rules that are integral in each stage of producing your project. A deal may start with a hearty handshake and a verbal promise, but ultimately you want to make sure it's backed up with solid legal documentation.

This chapter explores the legal side of producing. Its purpose is to offer many of the legal basics that every producer should know. However, it is simply a guide, and a beginning producer should also consult other sources — books, publications, the Internet, an attorney or legal aid service — for further in-depth legal and business information. The attached CD provides a number of resources, including various legal agreements and releases. In this chapter, we explore the primary legal aspects involved in producing, such as owning or "leasing" the material in your project, protecting the components of your project, and then double-checking all the components to make sure that you can legally proceed in producing your idea.

A. The Entertainment Lawyer

Whether you are a new to producing or have years of experience, you want to build a strong alliance with an entertainment lawyer who can properly advise you before you enter into to any kind of binding agreement. Entertainment law is highly specialized, and a certified entertainment lawyer is not only competent in state and federal law, but is also familiar with the complex wording of contracts, releases, copyrights, and the dozens of other legal documents necessary to protect your project.

In addition to reviewing the legal documents involved in your production, some entertainment lawyers help in pitching projects or making valuable connections with financing, production companies, directors, or talent. If you don't have an agent, your lawyer might send an introductory cover letter to the networks, studios, and production companies first. Most executives won't take a pitch unless they know that you have legal representation. If an initial contact is made by an agent, the lawyer subsequently coordinates and drafts contracts or agreements.

Lawyers get paid several ways: by the hour, by the project, for a flat fee, or as an ongoing line on your budget. Some lawyers take a lump sum up front, either as a *retainer* (not used toward any fees; this money is paid to retain the lawyer), or as an *advance* that the lawyer works off on an hourly fee basis. Discuss the fee structure with your lawyer at the beginning of the first meeting, and come prepared with a list of questions. Each minute you waste costs money. Whatever the amount, sound legal advice is worth the investment and could save your project significant costs down the line.

If you can't fit the cost of an entertainment attorney into your budget, look for a legal aid organization in your area, consult with universities that have legal departments, or contact groups such as the Volunteer Lawyers for the Arts. There are also boilerplate contracts available through various sources — books, articles, the Internet — that can be customized for your project. There are also contract examples, and Web site resources listed in the CD included in this book.

B. Intellectual Property Law

Almost every project involves some aspect of intellectual property law. Any product of human intellect that is unique and has some value in the marketplace falls under the term, *intellectual property*. This includes ideas such as literary creations, inventions, and unique names, as well as publicity rights, unfair competition, and misappropriation. In essence, intellectual property rights allow an artist the freedom of creativity and the promise of reaping any benefits from his or her hard work. Intellectual property law covers three main areas of law:

1.   Copyright

2.   Trademark

3.   Patent

1. *Copyright*

Let's say you've got a great idea for a TV show about some college kids who live together and share their stories of romance and conflict with the audience. So far, it's just an idea and anyone can use it. This idea is the *core creative concept* at its most basic. But when you define the number of kids, give them specific names and individual characteristics, put them in a four-bedroom converted loft in Brooklyn, design specific storyboards for the sets, create lighting and colors specific to the program, and write a defined script that fleshes out the original idea, you've created the *expression* of this idea. It's this expression that is protected by copyright.

A copyright protects works that have been created and preserved in tangible forms of expression like written works, video and film, photography, music, multimedia, software, drama, pantomime, choreography, motion pictures, and sound recordings. It's a right that is granted to the author or creator of "original works of authorship," and includes having sole privilege of multiplying copies, publishing, and selling them. The symbol of a copyrighted work is ©.

A copyright only forbids actual copying. If a writer or musician creates work that is similar to someone else's and this similarity is genuinely a coincidence, it will generally not be considered an infringement.

The terms of most copyrights now run from the creation of the work until seventy years after the death of the author unless the work was copyrighted before 1978. In this case the copyright protects the work for ninety-five years. Foreign copyrights have various terms, depending on the country in which the work was originally copyrighted.

However, not everything can be copyrighted. Ideas, titles, themes, or general concepts aren't protected by copyright law until they can be written down, videotaped, or somehow made tangible. Facts are also unable to be copyrighted. You can't copyright the facts of a person's life or an historical event, but you can copyright the script you have written about the person or the event after you've gotten any permissions necessary from the subject of the script. Rights are usually not necessary when your project involves a public or historical figure, although there are always exceptions. So you want to be completely sure of your legal rights before you proceed in developing the project further.

A producer who is employed by a network, a production company, or other employer is often working under a *work-for-hire* agreement. This states that the employer owns the copyright to any ideas the producer may have developed while in their employment, along with all other rights. This is the usual trade-off when the broadcaster pays the bills or the financing. The producer can negotiate for revenues from foreign broadcast rights, syndication, home video rights, merchandising, books and publishing, and other possible bonuses, depending on the terms of the employment contract.

Once a work has actually been created, it is considered legally protected. When a copyright notice is attached, this puts others on notice to contact you for licensing fees and permissions. To register your work, affix a copyright notice to your work, along with your full name, and the date of the first publication. Then, fill out the registration form and mail or e-mail it with a fee, around $30, and copies of your work to the U.S. Copyright Office in Washington, D.C. at (800) 688.9889, or register your work online at http://lcweb.loc.gov/copyright.

2. *Registered Trademark*

The indication of a trademark is the symbol connected to it. A trademark includes any word, symbol, name, or device that distinguishes certain goods or items from another like it. Brands, consumer goods, even buildings and well-known landmarks can be trademarked. You'll need permission from the trademark holder before you can feature a trademarked item in any way. To check if something is trademarked (or patented, as discussed below), check with the United States Patent and Trademark Office at http://www.uspto.gov.

3. *Patent*

When the Patent and Trademark Office grants a property right to an inventor, this patent gives the right to the inventor to prevent other people from making, using, or selling the invention in the United States. The term of a patent is usually 20 years from the date on which the application for the patent was filed. Patent laws and clearances are seldom an issue in television production.

C. Fair Use

Under its terms, the Copyright Act allows some exceptions to using copyrighted material — footage, photographs, music — under a clause known as *fair use*. In the case of fair use, the producer isn't required to have a copyright owner's permission to use his or her material, and can use that work without consent or permission in a reasonable manner that poses no competition.

Fair use is generally applied when the public interest is served, say, for news reporting, criticism, teaching or scholarship, or commentary; an example might be the use of a short music segment or a film clip in a documentary or a news piece. Fair use also can apply in parodies of material, either to make a social comment or for humorous effect. But fair use may not always apply, and it can be easily misused or misinterpreted. There are four determining factors for fair use:

1. The purpose and character of the use, including whether such use is of a commercial nature or is for nonprofit educational purposes

2. The nature of the original copyrighted work

3. The amount and substantiality of the portion used in relation to the copyrighted work as a whole

4. The effect of the use upon the potential market or value of the copyrighted work

The concept of fair use can be speculative. Most networks, distributors, and E&O insurers require that the producer get releases to protect them from possible lawsuits or copyright infringement arguments. Some might insist on blurring out things like artwork or posters on the wall behind an actor, brand names on a T-shirt, or products with obvious logos. It's an ambiguous area of the law and currently under close scrutiny by independent producers and broadcasters because it raises important issues of free speech and creative freedom. Fair use is actually a defense to a finding of copyright infringement, an assurance that the defense is valid and legal rather than the claim. Consult an entertainment lawyer who has experience with issues of fair use; he or she can often negotiate for a lower fee or can assure the network or insurer that your claim is valid and legal.

D. Writers Guild of America Registration

Although it doesn't take the place of a copyright, writers can protect their work by registering it with the Writers Guild of America (WGA), the primary union for television and film writers that legally registers thousands of literary works each year. This registration establishes the completion date of a literary property, which includes written treatments, outlines, synopses, and scripts that have been written for radio, theatrical and television motion picture, video cassettes/disks, and interactive media. The registration provides a dated record "of the writer's claim to authorship" of the registered literary material. WGA, similar to copyrights, cannot protect a title. This registration is valid for up to five years, and it can be renewed for another five years. A non-WGA member can register a script for a small fee. Check their Web site, www.wga.org, for more details.

E. Public Domain

After the copyright of material expires, it usually falls into a free use area known as the *public domain*. There is an appreciable amount of available literary material, music, photography, and other artistic expression that is no longer protected by copyright and can be freely used by producers. This material includes works by Shakespeare, Jane Austin, and Charles Dickens, along with literally hundreds of other authors, artists, composers, and other creative artists.

Public domain material is appealing to producers and broadcasters because it doesn't require money to buy the rights. However, although the material itself may be in public domain, it may have been adapted or used by someone else, and that expression of the original work has been copyrighted. For example, the music of Chopin is in the public domain, but if the Boston Pops records it with their arrangement, their musicians, and their unique interpretation they own the copyright and their recording cannot be used without permission. Your option is to record the music of Chopin with your own musicians, only paying them and not the composer. Make sure any work you might be considering falls completely and legally within the public domain status. This clearance is usually a requirement for getting production insurance.

A producer might find that the copyright holder of a film clip or piece of music can't be located, nor is it clear if the material falls into the public domain category. This material is known as *orphan work*, and creates a legal nightmare for the producer. There is potential risk in using this material without permission, but if the producer can genuinely pursue all avenues available to find the copyright holder — and provide clear documentation and backup of all efforts and intent — they have a stronger case in proving deligence if there are legal ramifications later.

II. If You Don't Own It, Get Permission to Use It

If you didn't create your project idea yourself, it is owned by someone else. If you want to use it, you have to first get permission. This applies to almost every aspect of your project: the talent, the script, the music, clips, images, photographs, products with brand names, props, and more. It is the job of the producer to legally protect every single component with some form of permission attached.

> In the course of the life of a project, you have to start dealing with third parties, with other people. If a book, for example, is going to be the basis of a movie, or if there is somebody's story, somebody's life rights, or if you need to get particular access to a building or certain circumstances — these are all obvious triggers for a conversation with a lawyer. When you start dealing with third parties, you have to make arrangements with them, and you have to get certain rights or permissions or clearances from them. That's when it probably makes sense to start talking to a lawyer and make sure that you are getting what you need — and that you are not getting more than you need, not getting taken to the cleaners.
> —J. Stephen Sheppard, *excerpt from interview in Chapter 11*

A. Licensing

When work has been copyrighted — a screenplay, a drawing, an original idea — it must be either bought outright or *licensed* for its use in a project. The producer (or the producer's employer) becomes the *licensee* and pays a fee for the right to use this copyrighted material. The area of licensing is complex and covers artist representations and credits, copyright, promotional approvals, and more. Licensing can also be a highly lucrative opportunity for a producer, although it is a specialized area that requires specific contracts including exclusivity, duration of use, definition of media, insurance, and other issues. In addition to talking with an entertainment lawyer, producers might consult with a company that specializes in rights and clearances. Both are experts whose advice is almost mandatory when considering the area of licensing.

B. Literary Rights and Clearances

Without ownership of all rights inherent in your idea or script, you have no legal foundation on which to construct your project. You will need to either *option* (negotiate for exclusive, limited rights to the project in return for a fee or agreement) or buy the rights (negotiate to buy and permanently own all ownership rights) to any original copyrighted material that might be part of your project. The list includes books, manuscripts, articles, treatments, outlines, newspaper columns or stories, and biographies and autobiographies, as well as adaptation, dramatic, or public performance rights.

Say you have a novel you want to adapt into a two-hour network broadcast special. Your first step is to contact the author's publisher, agent, or attorney, or, if he or she has died, the author's estate. Then, you'll write a compelling letter that outlines your project and the significance of the requested material. You may want to option the material for a limited period of time (six months to two years, for example) so you can generate interest, raise funds, and develop the project. You may want to buy it outright, in perpetuity. Either option is open to negotiation and requires discussion between you, your attorney, and the holder of the copyright.

C. Location Agreements

Producers often rely on locations rather than a studio in which to shoot their project. A location can be a private home, a public museum, a restaurant, school building, a city street, a country meadow, or a playground. Using this site requires a location agreement between the owner of the location and the producer. The *location scout* or the producer also pays attention to properties around any shooting locations, and talks directly to neighbors or business owners who might have objections to shooting at that location. In some cities and public locations, the producer is required to obtain a shooting permit. Check with the local mayor's office or Chamber of Commerce for further guidelines.

A location agreement gives the rights for the production company to photograph and record at the location, and releases the owner from any rights to the photography and recording. Often, a location fee is paid to the owner, and property insurance is obtained to cover any damage to the property. You'll find a standard location agreement form in the attached CD.

> Despite the clichés of what a producer acts like (sharp-dressed, fast-talking, megalomaniacs), I think that honesty is very important. Anything else will eventually come out anyway, so aside from basic ethics, there's really no point in making things up to cover your bases, or to convince someone of something that isn't true, just so you can get out of them what you want.
> —Michael Bonfiglio, *excerpt from interview in Chapter 11*

D. Music Rights and Clearances

Most projects depend on music for an opening theme, closing credits, to add suspense or humor or emotion, and as another expression of your creative vision. But music is potential quicksand for a producer. Unless you are using original music that has been especially scored for your project, you must get *clearance*, or permission, for *a license* that grants you the right to use any preexisting musical compositions and recordings that are owned by someone else. If your music hasn't been licensed, it could mean delays, lawsuits, and even the possible termination of your project.

It falls on the producer or a music clearance service or lawyer to determine who owns the copyright, to negotiate for permission with the copyright owner to use it, and to pay the fees that are necessary to get the clearances. Some of the larger networks and cable channels have blanket license agreements, though not all music is covered under them. There are two kinds of music licenses. Most preexisting and/or recorded music requires that you get both:

- *A sync (synchronization) license*: The publisher owns and grants the right to include the actual composition or piece of music that is synchronized to the picture. The songwriter(s) of that composition assign their copyright to the publisher who shares any royalties; the song-writer(s) might also retain rights to grant the license. Some compositions can also have multiple publishers who own portions of it. These all need clearance.

- *A master use license*: The record label owns and grants the right to include a specific recording of the composition in timed relation to the picture or image. The artist(s) might also need to grant a separate license. Some recordings may include "samples" of other recordings that also require clearances.

Publishers and record labels have specific departments that deal exclusively with reviewing requests for licensing. They require detailed information about the project as well as a synopsis of the project, its genre and length, its overall budget including the music budget, the creative team (the producer, director, actors, and narrator), any funding or donors, their profit or nonprofit status, any distribution plans, and information and address for the licensee.

Say you want to use a 12-second excerpt from a popular song under the opening credits of your program. These details tell the publishers and record labels how and where the music will be used and for how long. Broadcasters and all involved in the process of music licensing use a *cue sheet*, a document that lists each time and place that music appears in the program. It lists the title of each composition, the use and timing of each music cue, the composer(s), publisher(s), and their performing rights affiliation. Broadcasters rely on cue sheets to calculate fees for music in their television programs that have to be paid to ASCAP and BMI. They then use the cue sheets to identify the publishers and composers who are to be paid and what percentage of the royalties they're entitled to receive. An example of a music cue sheet can be found on the attached CD.

Additionally, publishers and record labels both require details about how you plan to use their music in order to assess the rights and fees involved. The venue, too, makes a difference; fees are higher, as an example, for music used in a network broadcast than they are for an educational nonbroadcast venue. One fee might be charged for use, say, on a PBS show, but if that show goes to DVD, additional fees and rights issues apply. Additionally, publishers and record labels will want to know what territories the rights will cover, such as only North American rights and/or world rights, and for how long you want to retain the license (a specific time limit or for perpetuity). Publishers require the title of the composition, its writer(s), and its publisher(s) and record labels require the title of the recorded track, the performing artist, and the source of the recorded track.

If you have plans to shoot a performance where live music might be played, or if there is any inclusion of a song's lyrics in the script, make sure you have all of the necessary clearances before you shoot the performance. Before you go into the post-production phase, clear all music you intend to use in your opening main credits, montages, background songs, musical underscore, end credits, or anywhere else in the program. The Internet is an excellent source for access to performers, recording artists, songs and compositions, publishers, and recording labels. In some cases, you can actually submit your request for clearances over the Internet.

You may find, after all your research and negotiation, that you are denied clearance to use the musical composition or a recording. The Copyright Law gives the final say to the owner(s).

If you choose to move ahead without clearance, you're liable for copyright infringement and possibly other claims as well. Both ASCAP and BMI regularly monitor television and film as well as other media looking for potential copyright infringement. Their job is to protect the composers, artists, publishers, and record companies.

Third-party rights covers material owned by someone else, like TV or film clips, music, published literary material, and so forth, that you want to use in your program. These materials require rights clearance in perpetuity throughout the world so that the show can air over time and globally. Often budgets don't allow for this overall clearance, and may only cover a short time period or limited territory; for example, just three years in the United States and Canada.

1. *Original Music*

It often makes sense for a producer to totally bypass existing music and hire a composer to write and record original music instead. A talented composer might also own his or her own studio and equipment and can work closely with you to create a music track that compliments your production. Many universities have departments for musicians and film and television composers. Young composers are often eager to work and can bring an energy and originality to your project for lower fees.

You can consider hiring a composer on a *work-for-hire* basis. Here, all publishing and recording rights for any music composed specifically for your project by the composer belong to you. In exchange, you'll pay a fee and agree on screen credit. If you do have music composed specifically for your project, you want to avoid music that bears a strong resemblance to a well-known piece. Even this can bring on a lawsuit.

For any of these options, you're wise to work closely with an entertainment lawyer or a music clearance company. Both have established links with licensing departments and can navigate the system quickly and legally. For more complex projects involving music rights, you can hire a *music supervisor* whose job it is to research clearances.

2. *Stock Music*

A viable option to prerecorded or original music is *stock music* that has been composed and recorded especially for a stock music house. It's considerably cheaper and is generally royalty-free. The producer pays a one-time fee for an unlimited use of stock music, and the rights have been cleared for sale. The variations of available music are impressive, covering all genres, emotions, rhythms, and timing. Most music libraries also provide sound effects, which are referred to as *needle drops*.

E. Stock Footage

Similar to stock music, *stock footage* includes photographs, film, video, images, and even clip art that has been catalogued and archived for sale. It can be licensed and purchased, royalty-free, from organizations that specialize in stock footage. This footage is often shot in high-quality video or film, and can be an inexpensive alternative to aerial shots, time-lapse footage, or historically archived shots. Stock footage can also provide a background for blue-screen backgrounds, used in creating virtual sets. You will find resources about stock music and stock footage in the Web site section of the CD included in this book.

F. Network Clearances

You may want to obtain footage from a network, cable channel, studio, or a production company. They are likely to have a Rights and Clearances (R&C) Department that focuses on rights and clearances and handles requests by producers to use footage from the network in

TV shows, films, or news shows. First, they determine that the clips are not denigrating their company in any way, and that they own the legal rights to the material. The R&C Department considers the source of the request, how the clips will be used, what fees to charge, and the details of the licensing agreement. Some networks can charge as much as $200 per second or as little as $25, depending on the exclusivity and content of the material. Other fees can be considerably less, and occasionally might even be free. This depends on several factors: Is this for broadcast or nonbroadcast? Is the request coming from an educational, nonprofit source, or from a rival broadcast network that might profit by featuring the footage in a program?

1. *Most Favored Nation*

With some projects, such as documentaries and low-budget independent productions, the creative direction and story content is more important than the salaries to the producers, actors, writers, directors, and other participants. When, for example, the casting of a project is based on a *most favored nation* (MFN) clause, this ensures that equal opportunities are extended to all parties involved, and that all have agreed to receive the same salary and get equal treatment in terms of work conditions. They might also agree to alphabetized on-screen credits rather than ranking their names by star power and/or salary levels. Everyone gets the same amount and shares equal parity. Salaries under most favored nation generally tend to be union scale plus 10%. As another example, MFN can also apply to a sound track; when one artist agrees to take a specific fee for use of a song, all other artists agree to the same fee for their songs.

2. *The Right of Publicity*

This area of the law addresses our basic right to prevent someone from using our name, our image, or our voice for commercial purposes without first getting our permission. Even a celebrity look-alike or sound-alike can be fertile grounds for a lawsuit. Although the right of publicity usually affects celebrities who have been exploited without their permission in advertising or in some other form of media, it can apply to any of us — even to using a full name in some context that might actually belong to someone who'll object, especially if this name can be legitimately associated with a specific person. Producers are especially diligent in this area, knowing that each state has its own laws.

The easy solution is to get written permission from every person you may be shooting or recording, from regular citizens to politicians and well-known public figures. Make sure that this release is easy to understand. You can find examples of release forms in the book's CD; look for the one that's appropriate for your needs.

III. Protect It

In the world of ideas, concepts for TV shows often simultaneously emerge from different pockets of the collective consciousness. Your sitcom pitch about modern-day pirates, for example, may be unique to you, but the network may have genuinely been developing a similar idea for months. Because of their understandable aversion to plagiarism lawsuits, the group to whom you're pitching will usually require you to sign what is known as a *submission release*, especially if you don't have representation by an agent or lawyer. Essentially, this release says that you are the owner of the material, that you have given them your permission to read and consider your pitch and share it with others in their company, that they are under no obligation to use the material, and that if they are in the process of developing a project similar to yours, it's a coincidence. You can find an example of a submission release form in the attached CD.

If the group decides to develop your project, get every detail in writing — an agreement between professionals is more resilient when it's detailed on paper. If you don't have a written contract, it is almost impossible to receive any kind of compensation. A traditional contract for a producer and a client specifies how much time you and they consider it will take to develop, write, shoot, and edit your project and how much that time is worth. In most cases, the client prepares the contract, and it is your responsibility to ask for explanations or changes.

As you consider drafting any contracts, agreements, deal memos, or releases, talk first with your entertainment lawyer or review similar agreements in relevant books or that you have been given by experienced producers. Find the format and wording that you can understand, adapt it to your specific project, and keep it short and to the point. Brevity can prevent misunderstandings.

> The ultimate goal of a contract is to articulate to the parties what the understanding is between them in such a way that you never have to look at it again. It's to describe the understanding between the parties. It's a very valuable process. What happens in drafting contracts is that I will write something down and send it to the client or to the other side, and very often they say, "I can't agree to that," so it's a very good thing that we wrote it down that way. So then we change it to what you can agree to or what you think you are agreeing to. It's the same with warrantees: when you sell something, you have to warrant to the guy that it is yours to sell and you are not actually selling somebody else's property. That is what a contract is.
> —J. Stephen Sheppard, *excerpt from interview in Chapter 11*

Here is a list of relevant contracts that you might encounter during various stages of producing. You can find specific examples of contract templates in the CD included in this book, such as cast and crew deal memos. For more in-depth information on other contract formats and templates and union regulations, research the listed reference texts and Web sites.

1. Most deals start off with a handshake or a verbal mutual agreement.

2. *Contract/written document*: This lists the details in your handshake deal, and is binding in a court of law.

3. *Actual contract*: Defines most fees, all screen credits, and assures indemnification; it is binding in a court of law.

4. *Deal memo*: A one- to three-page letter between two or more people that's signed by all parties involved and details the bare bones of the deal.

5. *Literary options*: A clearly defined outline of the assignment of any literary rights to the producer, the project, and its major participants.

6. *Writer employment*: This agreement is between the producer and the writer(s) and outlines the writing and/or revising of a final script for a specific project. It usually follows the WGA formats.

7. *Director's contract*: The terms of the director's employment through DGA are outlined.

8. *Pay or play contract*: A statement that the director or actor or other participant will get paid even if she or he is taken off the project or the project is cancelled.

9. *Art director/production designer contracts*: Legally sets out the status of employment and payroll details.

10. *Long form contract*: A 20- to 70-page document, that might include private placement or distribution, that is signed upon completion of the picture.

A. Rights and Territories

Often a network gives the producer the full budget amount needed to complete a project and bring it to broadcast. The producer negotiates a license fee with the network that outlines how much the network will pay, how many runs they get, and so forth. If there is not enough money to make the project, or if the network is only contributing a percentage of the budget, it's up to the producer to find the remaining money.

Coproduction financing is an example of one funding source. Though this doesn't apply to all projects, the producer sometimes grants the license for specified rights to the network to broadcast the project in the United States, over a certain time period, and in clearly defined territories. The producer owns the project and retains all the rights connected to it, other than those granted to the American network, and he or she can then negotiate with broadcasters in other countries for additional monies to fill the budget gap. This gives the broadcasters the rights to air the project, but for a specific time in defined territories. Coproduction financing can be a complicated process. Everyone involved wants as much as possible out of the deal like home video rights, extensions of territory and broadcast time periods, and net profit splits. This is another area where an entertainment lawyer is an essential component of the producer's team.

B. Insurance Coverage and Policies

Producing for television is an expensive proposition. When a producer controls a budget (regardless of the size), insurance is always included in the costs. As the producer, you want the protection for yourself and your production. For more information on insurance coverage and policies, review the information in Chapter 4. *Completion bonds* are a form of insurance sometimes required in television production. They guarantee that you can complete the job and that you will fulfill all the requirements of delivery. This is in addition to workers' compensation and liability insurance, as well as extra insurance that might cover a variety of contingencies. Although this is more common in filmmaking, some networks or distributors require this extra protection.

Bond holders can also take over much of a project's control. They can fire the crew and do whatever else they feel will bring the project back on track. The budget line for the completion bond runs around 3%. After the producer sends the shooting script, the budget, shooting schedule, the financing plan, and the bios of key production personnel, the bond company reviews them and meets with the producer and director to discuss ways the project will be produced. The primary requirement by the completion bond company is that the producer and the team bring the project in, on, or under budget and on time.

C. Fees and Compensation

Financial compensation for the producer, especially the independent producer or production company, is obviously an important issue to consider. The range of financing can be considerable; for example, a major network pays more money than a premium cable station, which pays more than a standard cable channel. Is your project a single documentary, a multipart reality series, or a sitcom? Each example has its own budgetary parameters. Compensation depends on costs like foreign locations, big stars, complicated rights clearances, and animation, which are then balanced against any revenue that could be generated through ancillary opportunities. There is no set fee structure, and each deal is on a per-project basis.

D. Contracts for Television versus Films

In signing a contract for a film project, the producer makes a commitment to work on that one project. When the film is completed, so is the contract. By contrast, television contracts usually require a commitment to the entire run of a series unless your project is a one-shot program, which is often the case with pilots. You may start a TV project with a short deal memo that details the essentials of your deal like compensation, screen credits, the duration of the project and so on. A more in-depth, long-form agreement may follow.

IV. Double-Check It

Reviewing and checking each important document is a vital part of the producer's job. Some documents require extensive research and thought by an entertainment attorney, although the majority of contracts, releases, and clearances are standardized forms that are preprinted or available on software program templates. Make sure these forms are current with legal rulings, relevant to your specific needs, and written in language that you can follow.

- *Find the right attorney.* You want an experienced attorney who is reputable and knowledgeable, and respected within the television industry. Using a lawyer simply because he or she is inexpensive can cost you in the long run. Face any legal challenges in the beginning of the process, rather than ignoring them until it is too late.

- *Review releases, clearances, and permissions.* If you haven't gotten a signed release from an on-camera talent or a signed location agreement, or have neglected to obtain permission to use a film clip that your program depends on, your project could be terminated or eligible for a lawsuit. It is the producer's responsibility to cover all these bases, whether you are an independent producer or on a work-for-hire contract with a network. You can find examples of talent and extras release forms in the attached CD.

A. Production Contracts

Each specific job requires a new set of contracts. Double-check the details in an often wordy contract between the producer and the production company, network, or buyer before it's finalized. Make sure that it is accurate, and that it mirrors the deal you think you have agreed on.

B. Agreements with Television Unions

If you are producing a show with a production company that is a *signatory* to any of the unions, this means that you have agreed to only use dues-paying members of that union in your project. It also means that you can't use *creatives* — writers, actors, directors or other union members — who are not members of that union. Unions are the bargaining agents for the on- and off-screen talent in television. The major TV unions are:

- The Screen Actors Guild (SAG)

- The Directors Guild of America (DGA)

- The Writers Guild of America (WGA)

- The National Association of Broadcast Employees and Technicians — Communication Workers of America (NABET-CWA)

- The American Federation of Television and Radio Artists (AFTRA)

- The American Federation of Musicians (AFM)

- The Producers Guild of America (PGA)

- IATSE

As you'll see in Chapter 7, negotiating with unions and drafting and signing various agreements that outline the terms of the project, job descriptions, fees, and schedules are just a few of the details the producer focuses on. Know the union rules — and follow them. When you're hiring, be very clear about your status as either a signatory company or a nonunion shop.

C. On-Screen Credits

Virtually all contracts and deal memos outline the specific screen credits at the opening and/or closing of the show. Most union contracts are also clear about what they demand for their members. Negotiation for proper screen credit might include how the credit is phrased, how long it stays on the screen, the size of the font, or whether the person's name is by itself or part of a group of names. This also applies to any advertising like posters, promos, and so forth. Networks and cable companies have their own rules that cover most, if not all, of these areas.

Most programs give screen credits that might include: produced by, film by, directed by, story by, written by, and composed by, as well as credits to executive producer(s), and associate producer(s). There may also be extra attention to the opening logo(s) of the production companies, the presentation credits, the executive producer(s), and a "special thanks" section that gives courtesy credits to people and companies who have contributed goods or services. As many people as possible who took part in the project should also be given a screen credit as a courtesy. This shows your appreciation for their work. You can see examples of a credits list by watching programs similar to yours or by checking specific union-related Web sites.

D. Ancillary Revenues

The producer seldom gets rich from ancillary revenues, partially because the formulas used to make the overall calculations vary with the network or client, and because the producer's financial participation is usually based on net profits — a tricky area that can be difficult to pin down or audit. Although there are exceptions to this "formula," here is how it works in most cases:

- First, the network adds up all revenues from the project and any extra sources of income that total the net profits. Networks, like everyone else, are experts at "creative accounting" so net profits are seldom profitable to anyone but the network. The producer is wise to get as much money as possible up front; whatever extra comes at the back end is icing on the cake.

- Then, they deduct a distribution fee from this net profits total. This fee is paid to itself or an outside distributor for home video, foreign sales, and other ancillary licensing. All production costs, which could include each phase of production, insurance, overhead, services, overhead, costs for promotion, and more, are also deducted.

- Finally, the network divides any profit that might still be left between the producer and themselves. The producer usually receives a much smaller percentage than the network, but over time and with experience, producers can negotiate deals that benefit them as well as the network.

E. Making the Deal

- Get it in writing. Protect yourself with ample documentation and take notes.

- Don't make the first offer. See what the other side has to offer.

- Keep each promise you make. If you can't keep it, don't make it.

- Don't be afraid of negotiation. In most cases, it is expected.

- Always try for a win-win situation where everyone is happy, and no one will sue.

On a human level . . .

The necessities of making sure that everything is legal and fair can create a detachment from the people with whom you are making the deal. Stay conscious of this — being a good producer requires objectivity as well as being empathetic and emotionally balanced with everyone involved.

> A memorandum is written not to inform the reader but to protect the writer.
>
> —Dean Acheson

V. Summary

The legal aspect of producing is as important as the creative, technical, or budgetary needs of your project. In many ways, it could the *most* important part. We live in a litigious society, and a small overlooked detail can lead to production delays and often to lawsuits. You can't be expected to know everything, especially in the beginning. It is worth the investment to have an entertainment lawyer on your side. With all the legal aspects taken care of, you can move more freely into pitching and selling your idea. We will explore this in Chapter 6.

VI. Chapter Review Questions

1. Why is legal documentation important to a producer?

2. What are the responsibilities of an entertainment attorney?

3. What are three areas of intellectual property?

4. What's the difference between a copyright and a trademark?

5. How can you legally protect your project idea?

6. What are the steps you'd need to take if you wanted to use a top ten single as music for your project?

7. Pose an imaginary situation in which a favored nation clause would benefit your project.

8. Name three primary types of production insurance.

9. What's the difference between a contract for television and a film contract?

10. Why are screen credits included in a contract?

CHAPTER 6

Pitching and Selling the Project

This Chapter's Talking Points

I. Pitching and Selling: The Big Picture of Television

Selling your project can be a real challenge. Getting the green light can depend entirely on the quality and content of your pitch, so the pitch process can be stressful for even the most seasoned producers. Yet giving a pitch is simply about making a sales offer — you are appealing to someone in a position of power who can approve your project and who stands to benefit from its success. In most cases, a pitch has two parts:

1. **A written pitch** — also called a proposal, prospectus, or pitch on paper (POP), it also may include a business plan

2. **A verbal pitch** — a face-to-face, in-person meeting where you get a chance to share your idea, your confidence, and your ability to produce it

Before you translate your project to paper and rehearse your pitch, take a moment to explore the bigger picture of the television industry.

A. TV Is All about Business

Television offers a wealth of creative rewards and opportunities for the producer, yet TV is also about commerce, and profit is the bottom line — whether it comes from advertisers, a subscription base, or from an expanding range of other revenue streams. In theory, your project can be a business opportunity — for other people as well as for you — especially if it can generate high ratings, advertising dollars, critical acclaim, ancillary markets, and international sales.

B. Know the Market

When pitching your project, you want to be certain that the network, cable channel, production company, or client is the right venue for your project. Watch the channel you're pitching to and research its current programming, their history, what they pay for shows, and other details that are pertinent to your project. Be professionally aware of who they are.

You can keep in touch with current projects that producers have sold — and to whom — by reading publications that target the television and entertainment industry such as *Variety, Applause, The Ross Report, Entertainment Weekly, Creative Directory*, and *The Hollywood Reporter*. You may feel overwhelmed at first by the sheer number of names, companies, broadcasters, and production companies, but you'll soon recognize names and companies that appear across many of these publications. You can also surf Web sites that focus on the TV business, join television chat rooms and blogs, and ask questions about resources and contacts.

Don't ignore the rest of the world. There is a huge world outside the United States that historically consumes American programming. Some American shows that do only moderate business in this country can generate significant profit from international markets. Although the trend is moving toward more programming being locally produced in these markets, American shows continue to sell. Watch programs in other languages, and research the global marketplace — it's a potential gold mine for your project.

II. Research Your Pitch

Writer Dashiell Hammett once advised another writer, Raymond Chandler, to "make it sound fresh." As a producer, your job is to make your sure that your project is unique and has a hook — a newness that appeals to viewers. Even if it bears some similarities to an existing show, you want your idea to have its own voice and to offer a solid business opportunity.

Know that when you finally do give your pitch, the development executives or clients are paying attention to your idea, and they are also looking closely at you as its producer. They want to see elements of your professionalism, your passion, and your potential to follow through on the project you're pitching. Do they want to spend two or three years with you as they develop your project? Do you reflect the confidence and enthusiasm that creates a real foundation for your project? Or could you be a loose cannon who is not capable of collaboration or taking critiques on your work? You want to project an image of a professional, flexible producer who can be both passionate and pragmatic.

A. Pitch Your Project to the Right Place

Your project should have a comfortable fit with the buyer's branding, public image, vision, and programming. You wouldn't, for example, pitch a children's cartoon show to a documentary channel, or a sports show to a classic-movie channel. Do your research before you go into a pitch meeting. You should know their brand, their logo, their mission statement, the demographics of their audience, their primary advertisers or subscribers, and their budget range, as well as the shows currently airing.

> I think the most important thing for young television producers is to understand that you can take the same pitch to about nine different places, but you need to alter that pitch for each place. When people come up with ideas, it's really helpful to

> know to whom you're pitching. Know which networks serve what audience. Is there
> a way to change certain aspects of your pitch so it appeals to different networks?
> —Brett Morgen, *excerpt from interview in Chapter 11*

B. Get Your Pitch in the Door

After you have researched the channel, production company, or client for your project, the next step is to find the right person to listen to your pitch. There are no rules or protocol that apply to who will and won't take a pitch. Some people take a pitch based on your written material, and will ask to see a *demo reel* of your work, or a brief video portfolio of your previous work. Other buyers might accept a faxed paper pitch, and if they like what they see, they'll call you for follow-up material. Development executives will usually only take a pitch meeting if your lawyer or agent has first paved the way, and they know you have representation. Generally, you may be asked to sign a *submission release* (see an example in the attached CD) before they will read the pitch or meet with you. Newer, younger channels or buyers are more open to taking a "cold" pitch if your material excites them.

Make a list of the people you know — or the people they might know — who could connect you to an insider for a pitch meeting, or an investor who might help fund your project or its initial development. This list might include:

1. Family and relatives

2. Fellow and former students

3. Actors

4. Writers

5. Directors

6. Producers

7. Lawyers

8. Agents

9. Managers

10. Investment Brokers

11. Professors

12. Other professional and creative people

Perhaps your proposal was rejected by the person you thought could be the right buyer, or you may live in an area that makes it difficult to set up a meeting with the right people. In both cases, you have options. For example, you can approach an independent production company that has produced projects similar to yours that air on the channel you have targeted. If the company likes your idea, it may agree to act as an "engine" for your project, pulling your project along with the working relationship they have with that channel. You can find the names of these production companies in the opening and/or closing credits of a program.

There are other potential markets, listed below, for your project, and each has its advantages and its drawbacks. As a producer, your job demands ongoing self-education; finding in-depth information; researching books and articles; talking to producers, professors, and international producers; and going on the Internet as well as taking advantage of television classes, conferences, and seminars. There is a potential buyer for every good project.

C. Potential Markets

1. *Motion Picture Studios*

Every major film studio produces television programming, and some also own their own networks such as Fox, Warner Brother's WB, and UPN from Paramount. Ideas for programming might start with the studio's executives, or come from independent producers or production companies. A network pays a *license fee* to the studio for producing the series for them, and gets the exclusive rights to broadcast the *first run* of the series along with limited *reruns*. The studio traditionally retains ownership of the property and can eventually sell it to cable, syndication, or to other markets. Often, a studio and a network, such as Sony and F/X, will coproduce a project with an independent production company.

2. *Major Broadcast Networks*

By selling your idea to a network, such as NBC, CBS, ABC, or Fox, you are likely to be well paid because your program reaches an audience of millions. But networks are under pressure by advertisers to adhere to certain constraints and formulas, so each network has a Standards and Practices Department with strict guidelines that dictate parameters for a program's themes and creative risk-taking.

3. *Premium Cable Channel*

Creative control is a key benefit for the producer. You're more likely to get some semblance of control from premium cable channels like HBO and Showtime. Although their budgets tend to be lower than what the networks pay, their subscriber base removes the pressure of offending advertisers, and ratings aren't as big a concern as they are for the networks. There are few boundaries on adult content or complex themes, and a series like *The Sopranos* can attract a large audience base that stays loyal to the channel.

4. *Cable Channels*

Cable channels such as Discovery, The History Channel, or MTV tend to have lower production budgets, although they generally give greater creative leeway to the producer. Ratings play an important role, but they are measured in much smaller increments than those of the networks. Advertisers are also essential, and can voice objections or withdraw ad sales if they disagree with programming content.

5. *Public Television*

The traditional role of public television has been to air educational and entertaining programming via independent, noncommercial, local and national public television stations. Public television is funded by individual memberships, private corporations, and grants, as well as city, state, and/or federal funding. A station can acquire programs that have been independently produced, or it can partially or fully fund a project. Budgets are generally medium-to-low, and each station adheres to specific standards for the programs they broadcast. Many producers find that if their project is aired on a local station, it could subsequently be picked up by other local or national stations.

6. *Production Companies*

In addition to having their own "in-house" production arm — such as NBC-Universal's NBC Studios — most networks and broadcasters also work closely with independent production companies. who produce programming for them. These recognized suppliers are trusted by their clients, and act as the engines for smaller production companies and independent producers.

They can usher your project into the network with their experience and staffed facilities after you have mutually agreed on your involvement, credits, payments, and ongoing interaction with the project. Production companies might be small, local companies, or larger businesses that are listed in the opening and/or closing credits of a television show, the Internet, or in *Variety* or *The Hollywood Reporter*.

7. Local Television

Though most local television stations have limited budgets, they often produce their own programming, such as children's television shows, daytime programs that deal with women's interests, social issues, news and information, or home-shopping shows. A producer can often find funding from local advertisers that pays for the entire cost of production; this adds an extra appeal to any smaller station to consider your idea more positively. Check in the phone book or online for television stations in your area.

8. Syndication

Most programs in syndication have already been broadcast on the networks and now air on local stations. Frequently sold in five-day-a-week *strips* by syndicators, they are usually classic favorites such as *Friends* and *I Love Lucy*. Shows can also be designed and produced for the syndicated market that can air on local stations in whatever time slot the station chooses. Occasionally, a show starts in syndication and is popular enough to get picked up by a network or cable channel. Budgets for syndicated shows vary considerably, as do the sources of funding.

9. Home Video

Some programs might first air on a network or cable station, have a second or third run, and then go into reruns or syndication. Some hit shows are repackaged and sold on VHS or in DVD packaged sets, such as all the episodes in each season of *Friends* and *Sex in the City*. Each of these phases of a program's potential revenue stream is spelled out in the contract between the producer and the buyer. Some independent producers create projects specifically designed to be sold to a home video distributor who then markets and sells directly to home video markets like video stores and online sites.

10. Direct Mail

This is a growing market for producers who have raised enough money to produce their project through grants, private investors, or other sources but cannot find a broadcast venue. The project may be too politically inflammatory, or it has an adult theme or a specific niche market like home improvement or exercise. Look for distribution companies that specialize in selling specific projects and genres to clearly defined markets that can help you sell your project.

11. The Internet

The options available on the Internet are rapidly increasing, and on it, you can find new venues for exposing your projects as well as getting ideas for creating, marketing, distributing, promoting, and even raising funds for it. However, there is no assurance that what you find online is legitimate, legal, or beneficial in the long run. If you aren't sure of the source of the data or information, research a "second opinion."

12. Self-Distribution

By far the most ambitious option for selling your project involves distributing it yourself. It can be time-consuming, and it requires not only an entrepreneurial mindset but also an initial startup fund, research, and infinite belief in your project. But if you can navigate the duplication, marketing, mailing lists, and networking, along with the packing and shipping, accounting, and phone calls, you could conceivably see a profit. It always helps to explore successful models of self-distribution before you take the plunge.

D. Understand the International Marketplace

A solid project has the potential for two rounds of audience exposure and income. The first round begins with domestic broadcast or market, and the second extends to the global marketplace. Europe, Latin America, Japan, and Australia are a few of the larger markets who regularly license or buy American episodic drama, children's TV, family shows, and a range of documentaries and reality shows. These markets can include broadcast, festivals, video stores, and the Internet, and are generally managed by specialty distributors.

However, there has been a shift in this traditional international market over the last few years. Advances in technology and the programming demands made by a more sophisticated international audience are attracting local producers and investors to create programming for their specific needs. Smaller countries, for example, Indonesia or Morocco, that may have previously acquired programs from the United States or the UK are now creating and producing their own versions of American and European hit shows that are packaged and sold as formats. In some cases, local broadcasters might buy the rights to franchise a specific show, or may "borrow" key elements as they produce their own version. They create a loyal audience base with shows produced in their own language that are entertaining and reflect local cultural and social issues.

Some American producers choose to shoot their projects in other countries such as Canada, where they offer tax incentives and strong currency exchange rates. Several television movies and series use the excellent facilities and experienced crew in places like Prague and New Zealand. Animated shows routinely send their complicated illustration work to Korea and China. The phrase, *runaway production*, describes the cost-cutting approach taken by American productions to go outside the country for shoots and locations, production personnel, services, and facilities.

The international marketplace continues to fluctuate. The merging of large companies; the chaos around digital, cable, and satellite; the effect of the Internet; the mercurial environments of advertising and sponsorship; political shifts; economic downturns; and a wave of other factors can all impact the sale of your project to the foreign market. With research and time, and by consulting experts in this field, you can evaluate the global market and ways your project can succeed within it.

III. Create the Pitch

The professional written pitch that follows industry standards is basic and direct. It avoids over-using fancy fonts and complex graphics, and instead, follows the "three font rule" by using no more than three fonts throughout. Any graphics are limited to illustrating an important character or theme, and the pages are bound by a spiral or stapled.

A. The Cover Letter

The written pitch is generally introduced by a cover letter, sometimes known as a *query letter*, that accompanies your proposal. The cover letter gives the reader a first impression of you and your project, and it plays a strategic role in enticing a potential buyer to consider your proposal.

In some cases, the cover letter acts as a stand-alone sales vehicle, persuading a client, a development executive, an independent producer, or an investor to read your proposal. It might excite them enough to take a pitch meeting with you, prior to seeing anything fully developed in writing. Anyone to whom you might send a proposal probably receives dozens of similar pitches every week, so you want your cover letter to stand out from the others. A well-crafted cover letter can reveal several things about you and your project:

- It sets a tone for the proposal that accompanies the letter.

- It tells a potential buyer why he or she should be interested both financially and creatively.

- It creates enough interest for the reader to read your attached proposal.

- It gives selected "highlights" of the proposal.

- It reflects you — your personality and your voice.

A cover letter reflects your professionalism, and to a degree, your own personality. It also conveys the impression of a confident producer. Below are a few simple guidelines:

- If you have gotten a referral from someone important or known to the reader, state in your opening sentence that he or she was kind enough to recommend you.

- Make your first paragraph an attention-grabber just like a good novel.

- Reduce your complex ideas into simple, brief sentences. Each word counts.

- Keep the letter to one page. Avoid distracting fonts or graphics.

- Use good paper that is of professional letterhead quality.

- Use a high-quality printer for your copies.

- Allow for margins and white space, avoid crowded spacing, and make it visually easy to read. Use 12-point Times New Roman or another simple font.

- Make sure you have spelled the person's name correctly. Confirm his or her title if you're using it in your letter.

> *Carefully check your spelling and grammar, and don't rely on a spell-check. Ask a trustworthy colleague to double-check it. Potential buyers will see your mistakes.*

Creating the cover letter itself can be easier and more effective when you write it after you have finished the proposal. By then you've gotten comfortable with the material in the pitch and can summarize it more objectively in your cover letter. Here is a sample cover letter.

```
Your letterhead
Date
Ms./Mr. Development Exec (Buyer, investor, etc.)
Title
Company
Address
Dear Mr./Ms. ___,
At the suggestion of So-and-So, I'm enclosing a proposal for my
television show called (title), a program about (the show's log line).
```

```
The story centers around (very brief synopsis). (Optional: Emphasize
any key people with name value attached to your project such as stars,
writer, director, etc.)
Your network (production company, studio) is the ideal venue for my
project because (it has a track record with similar projects, etc.)
As the producer (writer and/or director) of this project, my background
compliments the project because (your brief bio or connection with the
story).
I appreciate your taking the time to consider my project. I look forward
to hearing from you at your convenience (and/or to having an opportunity
to pitch you in person).
Sincerely (cordially, respectfully, best regards),
Name
Address
Phone, email, fax
```

B. The Written Pitch

Your proposal is a direct reflection of your project, as well as the "voice" of your idea. Also called a prospectus or the pitch on paper (POP), it can attract a possible buyer. Most important, a good prospectus gives an investor (or buyer or network) a reason to trust you with their money.

Like the cover letter, a strong prospectus demands the reader's attention and reflects your professionalism. It uses simple fonts and limited tasteful graphics; plenty of white space on the page; attention to spelling, grammar, punctuation; and the right choice of words. However, unlike the cover letter, don't personalize your written pitch. Avoid using the phrases "I think" or "I want to accomplish." Write it in the present tense, for example, "the project is an exciting exploration of college life." Some producers print their proposals in the landscape format, rather than in portrait. This is an approach that is easier to hold if you want to show your proposal while you're pitching it. Look for creative ways of infusing the pitch with your ideas, vision, and passion without overworking it.

Most producers integrate the following components into their written proposals, adding their own individual styles:

Title page — On this first page, the title is centered in a font that is no larger than 28 points. Your name (or that of a representative) and contact information is flush right on the bottom of the page, and the copyright notice (and/or WGA registration notice) is on the bottom left. Any artwork or graphics should be subtle and used only to emphasize a specific element of the project, such as a drawing of the main characters in a cartoon show or a logo of a show's title.

The title — A good title can create a distinct impression about the genre and tone of your project. Program titles like "Survivor" and "Six Feet Under" are short, memorable, they set a tone and often tell a story.

Genre and format — Is it a sitcom? Reality show? Episodic drama? Is it a half-hour or one-hour series, or a self-contained *one-off* that airs just once? The page that follows the title page repeats the title at the top, and quickly moves to genre, format, and log line.

The log line (one-liner or tag line) — Your log line can be an enticing and snappy appetizer that grabs the reader's immediate interest. *TV Guide* is an excellent source of good examples as are movie and TV ads, promos, and movie trailers.

Star value — If a well-known star, director, writer, or producer has shown an interest or a real commitment to your project, highlight that fact in your proposal. If you own exclusive rights to a book, or have rare access to a story, this is also valuable information to include as an extra attraction. Your project could also be right for a specific actor who may have his or her own production company. Research this information and approach the company with your proposal.

The synopsis — A well-crafted synopsis is easily read and understood. It also confirms that a good story is at the core of your project. As you explored in Chapter 3, most story ideas for any kind of show can be viewed as a basic three-act format.

- *Act One*: Sets up the story and the main characters, their current situation, where it takes place, sources of conflict, and provides the turning point to Act Two.

- *Act Two*: The main action. It explores the challenges the characters face.

- *Act Three*: The resolution or climax. The synopsis may leave the resolution up to the reader's imagination.

In your synopsis, you're telling your story in one or two short narrative paragraphs. Even if it is reality-based, there is a story with characters who come to life with carefully chosen words. Let's say the main character is a cop. Is he or she a tough cop, a crooked cop, or sensitive, gay, old, or respected? The right word can flesh out a character and lend depth.

After you have refined your synopsis, this is a good time to think ahead to your verbal pitch by shortening the synopsis into a few sentences in which you lay out the main character, the primary story line, important back stories and secondary stories, the journey and the conflicts. This ability to succinctly tell a story without losing its overall tone is a valuable skill for a producer to develop.

Structure — The effect of your synopsis depends on its structure. You want the elements of the story to be organized, and to flow smoothly from segment to the next.

Comparisons — Producers often like to compare their project idea to hit shows such as *Friends* meets *ER* meets *Scrubs*. But what does this set of comparison really say about the uniqueness of your project? There are too many existing images in the way to create a new impression. Give your idea its own identity, and simply imply a resemblance; for example, "in the spirit or the tradition of the timeless classic . . .." Your idea should speak for itself.

Style — Use the tools at your disposal to emphasize your project with a unique stamp. These could include production design, the lighting, ways in which the actors or talent are directed, integrating photography or graphics, the editing pacing, or your sound design. All combine to make your project more saleable and desirable.

History of the project — If pertinent, include the evolution of your project. It may have its genesis in a book, stage play, or a newspaper article. Or it may have grown out of your personal involvement in the story; for example, you once worked for the FBI and now you want to create a series based on your own stories and experiences from that job.

The cast list — This is especially relevant if you plan to use well-known talent who lend credibility and quality to your project, as well as increase its value in the international markets in which the talent is popular.

Research — It is important for a potential investor to understand if your project is reality-based, a documentary, or requires extensive research, especially if there are any rights involved or if it is based on a real story or event.

Production schedule — Provide a short breakdown of your production schedule. Discuss the proposed number of days or weeks needed for preproduction, production, and post-production; how and where you'll shoot; locations and/or constructed sets; and a general project overview.

Creative team — Devote a brief paragraph to each key person involved in making your project come to life. As the producer, your own bio should reflect your experience, jobs, awards, professional affiliations, travel experiences, and people who can be contacted as references. If you are a student with limited experience, mention any experience you may have had in television, film, or other media, as well as your course of study, pertinent classes, internships, study abroad programs, and independent studies that have added to your skills as a producer. Mention other areas that make you more unique, such as fluency in other languages, computer skills, athletic abilities, and travel experience.

Demographics and market description — Create a need for your show. Look for projects like yours that are already on the air and making money, or conversely, show evidence that there *isn't* anything like your project out there, and provide convincing arguments for why there should be. Use industry publications, newspapers, and the Internet to find credible resources that back up your line of reasoning.

Global markets — International sales can be impressive and provide an important piece of a project's potential sales. Does your project appeal to other cultures with contrasting customs, views, and traditions? Can it be dubbed and/or subtitled in other languages? Audiences in every country have their own personality and tastes. Research the markets that routinely buy American product as well as the show genre you are pitching.

Budget top sheet — The top sheet, or *budget summary,* represents a brief overview of your more detailed, estimated budget, and gives a potential buyer or investor a general idea of what your project could cost to produce. Neither the top sheet nor the budget should be included in the proposal unless it has been specifically requested; many buyers will rework your initial budget to suit their company's financial parameters.

The financial benefits — Though the financials aren't always included in a proposal for a television show, they can be vital when seeking investors. They could include a distribution plan, an in-depth financial statement, any tax breaks, projected profits, and the means of transferring funds from an investor to the production account. This area is best handled by an attorney and/or an accountant.

Each pitch is unique and has its own approach. Weave the components listed above through your proposal. There is no single template that is used by everyone, so without going too far outside the professional box, make your pitch reflect the voice and tone of your project.

Now for the pitch itself. We're big fans of not sending materials ahead of time and instead showing up with a simple, but well art-directed pitch book that takes the reader through the concept. We'll usually talk through the pitch and refer to the book as we go. Occasionally we'll use a piece of video or still photos to capture the essence of what we're presenting. The power of a pitch book shouldn't be underestimated. Basically, until your show is produced, the pitch book **is** the show. Everything from the overall look and feel, to the writing, to the design should be reflected in the book. It becomes a great presentational tool and a great way to solidify your own vision of the project.
—Justin Wilkes, *excerpt from interview in Chapter 11*

C. The Demo Reel Pitch

Producers generally have a short video *demo reel* that is a composite of their best work. When short clips and excerpts are skillfully edited together into a demo reel, it helps a potential buyer form an overall impression of a producer's ability, experience, and creative approach. Most demo reels don't exceed five minutes, ten at the very most, and the first one to two minutes should be compelling enough to keep the viewer from fast-forwarding or hitting the stop button.

> *Produce a mini-version of your project as a sales pitch. Shoot one pivotal scene from your script or produce a five-minute "trailer" that could effectively engage a potential buyer or investor. The caveat? It must be good enough to showcase your creative vision and technical abilities. Don't expect people to use their imagination and look for something that just isn't there.*

D. Next Steps with Your Pitch

After you have polished and finished your written proposal, legally protect it. Although a document is protected by copyright the moment it is written, you also want to protect that copyright by filing the proper forms from the U.S. Copyright office. You can also register your treatment or script at WGA, either online or by mail. You can review how to best protect your work in Chapter 5.

Even though you may have legally protected the ownership of your project, most studio or network development executives will still insist that you sign a submission release form, especially if you aren't represented by an agent or a laywer, before they agree to read your proposal. It protects them from any plagiarism charges you may bring against them later. Other executives only accept proposals from your agent or entertainment attorney, though a few may take unsolicited material that is mailed or hand-delivered. Having an "inside contact" is also an effective way to by-pass the usual requirements.

IV. Pitch the Pitch

Without good project ideas, executives and potential buyers have no product to sell. They stand to gain as much as you do if they can buy, develop, and sell your project. So your goal is to prove to them that your project is viable, and that, as its producer, you are competent, focused, and passionate. Even a beginner can inspire confidence in the buyers.

Experienced producers know that today's secretary can be tomorrow's television executive. The people who answer the phone can frequently make decisions for the boss, field calls, give feedback, and review incoming proposals. How you treat these people now can get you work later when they've got their boss's job. They can also make sure you never get another chance if you haven't treated them with respect.

Your sense of timing is important. Certain times of the year are death for getting a pitch meeting, or an answer to your query letter. Winter holidays, the summer months, and religious holidays can be dead zones for an aspiring producer to try scheduling a pitch. Instead, ask the assistants or secretaries what times and dates they suggest. They know their boss's schedule and moods better than anyone.

A. The Verbal Pitch

The written proposal is only half of the producer's sales job. The verbal pitch is the other half and is just as important. The verbal pitch can effectively convey your passion, your professional skills, and your ability to handle the project.

The average pitch meeting is short and sweet, with only a few minutes for you to make your sale. The most effective pitches immediately grab the attention of the person or group you're pitching. If they like it, you may be asked to give a longer version that expands on the short pitch or to answer specific questions. However, not every producer is comfortable giving a verbal pitch; this skill is a unique gift, but it's one that can be developed. So what are a few ways that you can approach the fine art of pitching?

B. The Elevator Pitch

The elevator pitch is a metaphor for your ability to "own" your project so thoroughly that you can pitch it convincingly and easily any time and any place. Let's say that you are attending a seminar on television programming, and you find yourself alone in an elevator with a development executive for a major network that you think is the perfect home for your project. The elevator is moving toward its destination, and you've got just seconds to pitch your idea. You are fully prepared. Your pitch is a clear and compelling synopsis that isn't complicated by the characters' back stories, ideals, or irrelevant quirks. A good elevator pitch excites the executive, and by the time the elevator door opens, he or she is asking for more.

C. Energize the Pitch

People in a position to green light a project have heard dozens, even hundreds, of pitches so you want your pitch to shine. You want to capture their attention with your idea and with your presentation. As you work on developing your verbal pitch, concentrate on your eye contact, and find a balance of enthusiasm and calm in your voice. Keep your body language loose and relaxed — even if that's not how you feel. Speak clearly and memorize the pitch so you can give it without notes. Using a timer as you practice also helps you to keep it short and sweet. Your genuine enthusiasm and confidence can control the meeting when people are as comfortable with you as they are with your project. Forget about yourself, and think about the people who are listening to you as fellow human beings.

There are several approaches you can use in the actual pitch meeting. You might act out a short scene, put on a storyboard presentation, screen a short demo piece, or even use a few well-chosen props. Or, you can simply, deliver the pitch in a straightforward and direct manner, without gimmicks. However you choose to deliver your pitch, do what fits the project and your personality.

> *Ask your friends to pretend to be potential buyers or network executives as they listen to your pitch. Have them put up barriers as you practice, like wandering attention, yawning, impatience, answering the phone, gazing out the window, or simply being rude.*

D. Work with a Partner

If you are pitching your project with a partner, practice who will be doing and saying what. Don't come to the pitch meeting with a Las Vegas routine, for example, unless the act is genuinely relevant to your project. Rehearse your roles before the meeting, and come in with an attitude that is relaxed, respectful, and enthusiastic.

You may have come to the pitch meeting with only one project idea, but sometimes the people to whom you are pitching may not like your original idea, or they're already in development on a similar program. Have one or two ideas ready to pitch, just in case. And you can always entertain the possibility that they might also be interested in you as a producer for other projects.

E. The Follow Up

If you do succeed in getting a pitch meeting, or even a courtesy phone call from someone in power, e-mail or send a brief thank you note for their time and any thoughtful feedback you got from the meeting. In following up, you want to be assertive, but not aggressive. Avoid calling every other day, people in positions of power are genuinely busy and you don't want to be regarded as a pest. If your calls go unreturned, take the hint and move on to the next potential buyer.

V. Keep Pitching

After the meeting, you may get feedback about what was good or what didn't work. The people you pitched to know what they're looking for, and their suggestions are valuable; they could improve your idea or propel it toward a possible development deal. They can also help you sharpen your pitching skills, or give you valuable references to other buyers.

If the people you've pitched to continue to say no, they usually mean it. Even if they initially seem to be receptive, don't get too excited — this could also change. If you haven't heard from someone who expressed interest, let a few days pass before you call to check in. Some producers let a week or two go by. It isn't personal. These are busy people who are swamped with work and are considering other producers' pitches and ideas.

Every show on television represents a deal that was agreed on by a buyer and a seller. The producer may have taken the first deal that was offered, or pitched the project to several other places before finding the right one. The negotiations may have been straightforward or highly complex. The producer is often tempted to hold out for a better offer, believing that one should never accept the first offer or that a sweeter deal could be waiting in the wings. How do you know that the first offer isn't the best? Ask other producers, your attorney, or an accountant. But act on the offer, one way or another, while it is still active and fresh in a buyer's mind.

A. Networking and Connections

In most situations, success depends on *who* you know. *What* you know follows. Most producers get jobs or projects, or find their financing, through connections, colleagues, friends, or friends of friends. You may be smart, creative, and motivated, but you're hindered if you don't have contacts. Get to know people who are in the position to help you through as many avenues as possible. As you'll find in Chapter 10, there are several directions you can take to expand your sphere of connections as well as your experience:

- Work on student films or independent projects
- Find internships or apprenticeships
- Surf the Internet for ideas
- Watch television for an overview of what shows air on what channels
- Attend television and film festivals; go to panel discussion and social mixers
- Continue learning about the television industry
- Join TV-related organizations
- Subscribe to industry journals and publications

- Keep creating projects on paper and on video

- Make your own projects. Buying or renting a quality video camera as well as desktop editing systems is now inexpensive and accessible.

> I really have to be in love with each and every show, and I think that's one of the reasons that I've been successful is because that's what I look for. I look for something that I'm going to love and something I'm going to laugh at after eighteen months of the same jokes that I laughed at to begin with. It's a really hard business because you burn out. You're expected to work one day for eight hours and the next day is fourteen, and to keep your energy and enthusiasm up day after day, year after year.
> —Valerie Walsh, *excerpt from interview in Chapter 11*

On a Human Level . . .

Selling your project is a lot like selling yourself, and it can be easy to confuse the two. Expect to encounter rejection along the way. You have a responsibility to yourself, and to your project, not to take rejection personally. Each time you hear "we've decided to pass on your idea" should motivate you to try even harder.

> Nothing in this world can take the place of persistence. Talent will not; nothing is more common than unsuccessful people with talent. Genius will not; unrewarded genius is almost a proverb. Education will not; the world is full of educated derelicts. Persistence and determination alone are omnipotent. The slogan "press on" has solved and always will solve the problems of the human race.
> —Calvin Coolidge

VI. Summary

Pitching your project is a necessary part of the producing process. There are countless stories of producers whose pitch won enthusiastic kudos from development executives — and then went nowhere. Yet every time you turn on your television set, it is clear that hundreds of shows did get made. After your project does sell, the next step is the preproduction stage. This will be explored in the following chapter.

VII. Chapter Review Questions

1. Define "the pitch." What are its two necessary components?

2. Why is it important to research the network, cable channel, or production company to whom you are pitching your idea?

3. List five potential venues to whom you could pitch one specific idea. How are they similar? Different?

4. Discuss the benefits of the global marketplace.

5. What is a query letter? Why do you need to write one?

6. Describe the synopsis element of a POP. Write a brief example, using an existing script or your own project idea.

7. What is a demo reel? What are some of the ways it can benefit a producer?

8. Define an elevator pitch. Why is it advantageous to have one ready?

9. List five possible venues that can help you increase your breadth of networking connections in the television industry.

The producer is like the conductor of an orchestra. Maybe he can't play every instrument, but he knows what every instrument should sound like.

—Richard Zanuck

Preproduction: The Plan

This Chapter's Talking Points

I. The Script

The many details of preproduction come together to form the big picture — like pixels on a TV screen. These details are the essence of production, and in the preproduction stage, they add dimensions and texture to your project. When you devote attention to the script — researching, double-checking, making dozens of careful decisions — you can often save costly mistakes. Planning ahead is easier than looking back.

If you are shooting a narrative script and must be faithful to it — as in a dramatic series or sitcom — make sure it has been fully written and reviewed before you begin principle photography. The late delivery of shooting scripts can limit the director's preparation time or drastically slow down the production itself. You do *not* want to wait until you're shooting that an essential story element just isn't there, requiring a last minute rewrite.

Maybe your project is an episodic drama, with a full script that can act as a blueprint for preproduction planning. Or perhaps your project is reality-based and you've only got an outline for who and what you hope to shoot. Both extremes, and every kind of project in between, require preproduction strategies.

TOP TEN

The Top Ten Things a Producer of Documentaries Should Know:
1. There's no substitute for a good story
2. Working with great people is better than working with a lot of money
3. How to write
4. How to use as much of your production gear as possible (just in case)
5. How to budget (and stay within it)
6. If you're traveling with equipment, show up really early at the airport
7. If you're going on location somewhere, it's best to have someone local on the crew
8. It's never going to be the way you expect it to be
9. It's okay to ask for advice
10. Everything takes longer than you think it will

—Michael Bonfiglio, *excerpt from interview in Chapter 11*

A. Script Breakdowns

Chapter 4 explored the budget ramifications of your project by breaking the script down into specific categories. This same breakdown process now applies to preproduction planning. A breakdown sheet is a valuable tool to help you organize and categorize the crew, locations and sets, props, wardrobe, stunts, explosives, and on-camera talent; you can find a sample breakdown sheet form in Chapter 4 as well as in the attached CD. It helps you to delineate the elements in the script boards that you plan to shoot. Each scene has its own breakdown sheet that includes any or all of the following components:

- The scene number and name

- The date of the breakdown sheet

- The project title

- The page number of the script

- Location: A constructed set or a real location

- Interior or exterior: Shooting inside or outside

- Day or night

- Brief scene description

- Cast with speaking parts

- Extras: Any nonspeaking people in the scene or background

- Special effects: From explosions to blood packs to extra lighting

- Props: Anything handled by a character in the scene, like a telephone or pencil

- Set dressing or furnishings: Items on the set not handled by the character

- Wardrobe: Any details that are pertinent to a scene, like a torn shirt

- Make-up and hair: Special effects, like wounds or aging, wigs or facial hair

- Special equipment: Jibs, cranes, a dolly, Steadicams

- Stunts: Falls, fights, explosions, and may include a stunt coordinator

- Vehicles: Cars or other vehicles used by characters in the scene or as background

- Animals: Any animal that appears in the scene will come with a trainer, or wrangler, who takes charge of the animal during production

- Sound effects and/or music: Anything played back on set, like a phone ringing, music for lip-syncing, or music the actor is reacting to

- Additional production notes

B. Production Book

All productions involve details — hundreds of them. As you saw in Chapter 4, organizing these details is easier when the producer uses a *production book*. The traditional production book is kept in a three-ring loose-leaf binder, with dividers for each section. Often a production assistant (PA) or production coordinator is put in charge of making multiple copies of production books for the staff so that everyone has the same updated information. A production book is divided into sections of information. It includes most, if not all, of the following categories:

- Contact list: Names and phone numbers for talent, crew members, and other essential contact information

- The script, or pages to be shot

- Shooting schedules (refer to Chapter 8 for more information)

- Breakdown pages (an example can be found in Chapter 4)

- Storyboards (see the attached CD for a storyboard format)

- Cast list

- Props and furnishings

- Wardrobe

- Transportation details

- Meals and craft service plans

- Location agreements and shooting permits (Chapter 8 goes into more detail)

- Releases and clearances for talent and other areas (see the CD for examples of each)

- Deal memos with crew (see the CD for examples)

- Insurance information (Chapter 4 goes into more detail)

- Budget (usually confidential and not distributed)

C. The Look and Feel of Your Project

After you have organized these components, you can begin to explore the more aesthetic dimensions of your project.

Your *visual approach* provides important clues to the viewer. A narrative drama may reflect a moody noir texture, while sitcoms are brighter and use more color. One show might be shot with three or four handheld cameras, while another show uses only a single camera or takes a standard three-camera approach. Elements like lighting, camera angles, wardrobe, make-up, props, and set design contribute to the overall aesthetics.

Shooting original footage is not your only option. Producers of all genres make clever use of components such as stock footage, still photos, archival or historical footage, text, documents, or graphics in post-production to either augment or replace original footage. These elements can add visual and audio effects and textures to the overall look.

The *audio impressions* you create are no less important. Sound is subtle, and even though viewers aren't always conscious of what they hear, they get an audio impression from it. The clarity of dialogue and the ambient background sounds, such as birds, traffic, conversations around the actors, and even the tone in the room, all combine to tell a story. The many elements of sound can be designed and enhanced in post-production. Although music can contribute to your essential story beats, it can be distracting if it's not used with descretion.

D. Storyboarding and Floor Plans

The next step is to plan out the camera *coverage* you want to get from each scene. A scene, for example, might call for one long shot, or it might require master shots, individual close-ups, pans, 2-shots, or cutaways. In more involved productions, the producer might rely on storyboards or floor plans to get a clearer picture of these elements and to set up these shots in advance of the actual shoot.

Storyboards are either hand-drawn simple, cartoon-like sketches or computer-generated renditions of each scene in a script. Each numbered box has a drawing that depicts a scene or shot number from the script (see the storyboard form example on the attached CD). When the image or camera angle changes, so does the content of the box.

Prior to shooting, the producer and/or the director review(s) the script, making a rough sketch of each scene (often using a *storyboard artist* or storyboarding software) that details every camera setup in that scene. Most storyboards are minimal black-and-white line drawings, although they can be in full-color illustrations, photography, or even animated. They save time and money by providing a visual synopsis of the scenes to be shot, the look and the feel of the set or location, the location of one character to another and their actions, and even the colors, textures, and mood of a scene.

All these aspects are essential to an art director, production designer, director, producer, the director of photography (DP), and others involved in production. However, not all projects can be storyboarded; many reality-based shows are shot with little or no advance knowledge of the shooting circumstances. And in the case of many dramatic television shows, the camera coverage can't be planned until the scene is blocked for the camera on the actual day of shooting.

Storyboards can also be an effective way to sell an idea or project. Often producers pitch and sell their project by using creative storyboards as persuasive selling tools.

Floor plans provide an overhead view of what you plan to shoot, as well as the space around it. In complex, highly detailed projects, a floor plan can augment or replace the storyboard; floor plans can provide details for the director, the DP, lighting director (LD), camera and audio operators, and the various department heads about what is needed for that scene like props, furnishings, and set design. Because a floor plan shows the camera placements and shooting angles, it helps the DP plan the blocking for the actors. Floor plans and storyboards illustrate the shoot and make it easier for everyone involved to visualize the producer's ideas.

E. Shot List

By carefully studying the storyboards, the producer can compile a shot list, which details each shot needed to create a specific sequence or scene. Most shot lists are made on set after blocking rehearsal, although when time allows, they are drawn up prior to the day of the shoot. The shot list is distributed to the camera and audio crew, as well as to other crew members who are directly involved in the shoot. This list uses a specific language that everyone understands to describe the shot that is needed:

- ECU: Extreme close up (eyes or mouth, or part of an object)

- CU: Close-up (the whole face or entire object)

- MS: Medium shot (an upper torso or an object in part of its surroundings)

- MWS: Medium wide shot (most or all of a body or group of objects) that's framed between a medium shot and wide shot

- WS: Wide shot (an entire body or larger grouping of objects)

- EWS: Extreme wide shot (many bodies or shots of horizons, buildings, sky lines, etc.)

F. Production Meetings

The producer promotes collaboration during the production, and schedules regular daily or weekly production meetings toward that goal. Production meetings generally include the key people such as the producer(s), director, line producer, and production manager. Prior to the meeting, the producer may create an agenda and makes copies of documents or plans to be discussed, including the script or shooting schedule. As each person gives notes or comments, the producer stays focused, sets priorities, delegates jobs, and after the meeting, sends out memos outlining what was said and agreed upon. Production meetings can be an excellent forum for complimenting those people who are doing their job well in front of everyone else. If, on the other hand, you have a problem with a specific person, the production meeting is not the place for discussion — do that later, in private.

> I love bringing talented people together. There's no greater feeling than standing on a shoot, sitting in an edit session, or watching the final product on TV, knowing that you as the producer pulled together an incredible, hard working group of people to create it.
>
> —Justin Wilkes, *excerpt from interview in Chapter 11*

II. The Talent

The concept of *talent* covers a broad range of descriptions. Your talent can be highly professional actors or on-camera hosts, or they might be real-life subjects in a documentary who have never been on camera before. Talent can also include children, animals, and extras. Regardless of the category, talent plays an essential role in telling a story and can give your project credibility and energy, providing a genuine connection with a viewer.

A. Casting Talent

Listed below are some of the components a producer considers during the *casting* process.

1. *Casting Directors and Agencies*

Specialized talent agencies and *casting directors* work with producers and directors to help them find the right face, voice, or special skill for a project. Some casting people work only with actors, while others specialize in casting "real people" or extras for a crowd scene or atmosphere. Casting directors keep actors' resumes and headshots, and they're familiar with their skills, other roles they've played, and their work ethic. A good casting director maintains solid relationships with talent agents and managers and can often help in setting talent fees and negotiations. The producer first contacts the agency or casting director and spells out the project's needs. Then the casting director calls agents, places ads, or posts notices for a *casting call* where auditions are held in a rehearsal or casting space. During the audition, the producer may shoot video and/or stills of the talent and go over them later while making casting decisions.

You may not have a casting director at your disposal or the money to hire one. For low-budget projects, producers can post their own notices and hold casting auditions in spaces that are inexpensive or free. So how and where can you find good talent?

- Advertise your casting calls in local newspapers and community penny savers.

- Attend local theaters, high school and college plays, churches or synagogues, or youth groups that put on plays. Look for talented actors who stand out.

- Post an audition call with local film or television schools or classes.

- Many towns and cities have Web sites with cultural links. Surf these sites for possible venues to post your audition notice or to find talent.

- If you want "real people," your local grocery stores, health clubs, block associations, PTAs, or hardware stores might have a bulletin board for posting your audition ad.

- Consult with other producers and directors who work regularly with talent.

2. Casting Calls

After you have attracted talent to an audition, the next step is casting the parts. You may be auditioning many people, so keep track of who shows up, and make sure they're comfortable while they wait. In an audition, you or your casting director will:

- *Schedule the audition*: Consolidate the auditions into as short a time as possible by scheduling each actor for a specific time. Build flexibility into your plan; working actors often have several auditions a day.

- *Find a comfortable space for auditions*: Check the room temperature, and make sure there's an ample waiting area outside the audition room. Assign a "people person" to the waiting area to keep the talent calm. Provide water and snacks.

- *Keep a log of those auditioning*: List their name, agent (if any), phone number, e-mail address, and the part they're auditioning for.

- *Make the script available*: Give the talent pages from the script (also called *sides*) in advance. This allows time for the talent to get comfortable with the audition material. Or ask them in advance to prepare a monologue for the audition.

- *Videotape the audition*: A taped audition gives you a chance to review a performance later, and to compare it with other actors' performances. Take close-ups of facial expressions and wide shots for the overall performance and body language.

- *Give yourself space*: The audition room should be quiet, and large enough to accommodate the talent, the producer, director, casting director, a camera and its operator, PAs, and often clients. If needed, set up extra lighting. Supply water and enough chairs. Assign someone other than the producer or director to read any additional parts with the actor.

- *Keep track of the talents' photographs (headshots) and their resumes.*

- *Allow enough time*: Schedule about 10 to 20 minutes for each audition. After each actor leaves, make notes and label each headshot to avoid confusion.

- *Be patient with children*: They can be a casting challenge, regardless of their age or professional experience. Children get tired, hungry, grumpy, and nervous. Keep the environment calm and provide games, crayons, and books.

- *Arrange for callbacks*: After the auditions, you may have found talent you want to see again; these repeat auditions are known as *callbacks*. It's not unusual to have an actor come back two or three times. The general rule — especially if the actor is a member of SAG — is to pay the actor a fee after three callbacks. Try to audition potential cast members together — the chemistry between actors can make or break a project. Any actors you have rejected deserve a polite phone call. They may not be right for this project, but could be perfect for another one in the future.

> *Stay focused. Auditions are repetitive for you, but they are new to each person who is auditioning. Make it comfortable for the talent. Introduce them to key people in the room. You'll encourage a better performance when you treat the talent with respect.*

B. Hiring and Working with Union and Nonunion Talent

The talent category is a broad one. It includes actors with major and minor parts, on-camera hosts, narrators, background extras, children, animals, magicians, stunt people, jugglers, as well as nonprofessionals and "real people." Many are members of a talent union, though not all good actors are members of a union, and not all union members are good actors. But most experienced and professional actors belong to unions like SAG, AFTRA, and Actors Equity that impose specific rules under which the actors work. The producer must honor them or risk hefty fines from the union. Many producers are limited by their budgets to work only with nonunion talent, avoiding the additional expenses, paperwork, and more regulated working conditions that talent unions require on a production. On the other hand, an independent producer, production company, network, or studio may take the steps necessary to become a union signatory, and agree to comply with the guidelines and regulations of the union.

Becoming a union signatory involves looking at the budget first. There must be enough money in the budget to cover union talents' wages as well as *fringe benefits* (payments after salary that include payroll taxes, pension, health, and other union and/or employee benefits). Though the statistics vary, nonunion fringe benefits are usually budgeted at around 18%, while union fringes can exceed 30%. In addition to extra benefit costs, you might factor in fees for studios or stages that only allow union members on the premises. Your project could rest heavily on hiring specific actors or on-camera personalities who are union members and not allowed to work for nonsignatory producers.

Each talent union has its own guidelines, but most will make special concessions for projects that include student productions, low-budget shows, and affirmative action contracts, as well as multimedia, new media, some educational, and Internet projects. The agreements generally include lowering the pay scales and allowing more flexibility in the overall working conditions. You can find in-depth information on this complex aspect of production in the Books and References section in the attached CD, as well as by going to the Web site of the specific union.

1. *Union Actors*

Talent unions' rules and wage scales are detailed on their Web sites, along with the producer's role in honoring their requirements. These include:

- *Rate of pay*: Daily, weekly, or picture rates

- *Per diem*: A daily allowance to cover meals, transportation, and other production-related expenses

- *Speaking lines*: All on-camera parts with or without lines have their own pay scale

- *Screen credit*: The actor's credit itself, its placement on the screen, the order of the name's appearance among other actors, and other union or contractual agreement

- *Turnaround time*: A 12-hour break of time between the end of one shooting day and the call time for the next day.

- *Meals and breaks*: Talent must have regularly scheduled breaks to eat and to relax

- *Wardrobe stipends*: A fee paid to actors who provide their own wardrobe

- *Specific requirements*: Child actors who work fewer hours than adults, if they are absent from school, specifically require a tutor, parent, or social worker to be with them at all times

- *Benefits*: Additional monies paid to an actor like P&W (pension and welfare) and worker's compensation

In some cases, there may be a "SAG representative" on the set. He or she is employed by the union to resolve any contract disputes or member complaints, and deals primarily with the producer on a day-to-day basis in this regard.

2. *Nonunion Talent*

Actors who are not members of an actors' union deserve the same respect — and base salary, when possible — as those protected by unions. Producers are not required to pay them union benefits, and there are fewer restrictions for on-set hours or turnaround time. Producers do have an ethical responsibility to treat everyone fairly, regardless of their union status.

3. *Stunt Actors*

Some actors do their own stunts, but most use a *stunt double* for dangerous action like a fall from a building or a blow to the head. If a stunt is dangerous or complicated, a stunt coordinator is hired to plan and oversee the stunt actor's work. Most experienced stuntmen and stuntwomen belong to stunt associations covered by SAG.

4. *Extras and Background*

Many productions involve people milling in the *background,* walking on a street, getting into buses, driving cars, etc. These *extras* add extra dimension and credibility to a shot. Depending on the scene, extras can be professionals in Screen Actors Guild (SAG) hired by casting agencies or nonprofessional locals — even friends and family can fill in as background. Extras are scheduled and rehearsed just like actors with larger parts.

5. *Actors' Staff*

An actor might bring his or her own people into a production. In certain situations, the production pays these salaries and provides accommodations and workspace. These extra personnel might include:

- *Hair and/or make-up*: Knows the cosmetic and emotional needs of the actor.

- *Wardrobe designer or stylist*: Maintains the talent's specific wardrobe "look," keeps track of clothing, and mends and cleans the clothing needed.

- *Wrangler*: Has expertise in training or managing talent, and might be a wrangler for an animal or a child actor.

- *Personal trainer*: Often a necessity when the part calls for an actor's overall health, sex appeal, or specific physical demands of a part.

- *Secretary or personal assistant*: Handles requests for personal appearances, correspondence, and phone calls, as well as production-related details.

C. Rehearsals

In actor-driven projects, rehearsal time helps the talent feel more comfortable with the script, the camera blocking, and fellow actors' individual styles and rhythms. Depending on the project, the producer either hires a director who works directly with the talent, or rehearses and/or directs the actor himself. Not all projects require talent rehearsals before shooting, although some documentaries, reality-based shows, talk shows, and sports events, for example, benefit from other kinds of rehearsals. For a documentary, a producer might find a location prior to shooting and rehearse camera moves. Many reality shows depend on special sets designed for TV production, such as Tribal Council on "Survivor," Trump's boardroom on "The Apprentice," or the house in "The Real World." The majority of reality programming has rehearsals with *stand-ins*. On "Survivor," producer Mark Burnett employs his "dream team" to run through all of the possible challenges they might encounter during the actual shoot. And in most talk shows, producers rehearse anything that's out of the ordinary, such as demonstration segments, musical performances, fashion shows, etc. Before the show begins taping, the producer does "look-sees" of every component of the show: "host entrance," "guest entrance," "desk cross," and other aspects of blocking and rehearsing.

In most narrative dramas or sitcoms, the director works with the actors during rehearsal. Some directors give actors the freedom to interpret their roles, while others prefer to "direct" the actors. Directors know precisely what they want in a performance, and it is their job to motivate actors to explore their character's back story, create a specific regional accent, or use distinctive body language to explore the range of their roles.

Once the action is determined, the next step is *blocking* the scene. Blocking is a process in which the scene is set up for the shoot. It involves the DP, director, camera operator, the lighting director (LD) and lighting crew, and usually the producer. Blocking looks at the camera's placement in relation to the actors (or their stand-ins) and their sequences of steps and actions — it's like choreographing a shot. Blocking considers furniture, props, or greenery in the scene, the relationship between one actor and another, and how the camera can capture it all. Blocking decides what the camera is shooting and from what angle, and is often marked with masking tape on the floor or wall as reminders.

III. The Crew

Finding and then hiring a full crew can be challenging to a novice producer. You may have had some experience working on productions and meeting crew professionals whose work you like. If not, look for creative options. Ask other producers or filmmakers for their recommendations. Contact local production crews or national crew-booking companies and ask for crew reels to screen; these reels reveal a video or audio approach that could be similar to your vision. Research television and film departments in universities that may have talented students who are eager for an opportunity to augment their experience.

> The essential point is that you have to try to gain the trust and the confidence of the client, and all the other parties — from all the audio people, from the staging people, the artist, all the parties involved in this event. You have to gain their trust, that you understand what their issues are, and bring them on board to be on the same team for the overall good of the project.
>
> —Stephen Reed, *excerpt from interview in Chapter 11*

Although the talent provides the on-screen charisma, the crew creates the behind-the-scenes magic. Your project may only require a small two-person crew, or you might need a large crew that includes several camera and audio operators, as well as lighting designers, DPs, set designers, and wardrobe and make-up specialists. Regardless of the size of your crew, each crew member has his or her own area of specialty. Over time, you'll build your own team of experienced, talented, and collaborative crew members who can be trusted and who share your vision.

A. The Key Production Department Heads

Whether your project is large and ambitious, or small and controlled, certain areas in every production need at least one person to cover them, or in lower budget projects, people who supervise several of these areas. They can be union or nonunion members. The key people the producer hires for every project are

- The director
- The director of photography
- The production manager
- The assistant director
- The production audio manager
- The production designer

1. *Director*

As discussed in other chapters, television is the realm of the producer. The TV producer can also be the director or will hire the director. In many genres of television, producer/directors map out the desired look and creative approaches of the production.

If a director is hired, she may fill the traditional director's role, working with actors, the crew and the producer in visualizing scenes. The director is a strong creative force in the production — supervising the writing, casting, and rehearsing of the actors, and crafting the overall aesthetic approach. Or, the director might be technical director (TD) who, in a studio setting, works out of the control room. The TD is generally assigned to multi-camera shoots, and among other responsibilities, directs each camera and "calls the shots" as they come into the control room, often creating a line-cut, or rough edit, in the process. Under the Directors Guild of America (DGA) guidelines, the director, the AD (see below), and the technical director each falls into a separate fee category and pay scales. Although each project is unique, it can only thrive when the producer and director cohesively and collaboratively work together.

2. *Director of Photography*

The DP is often the first key position to be filled. The DP brings the creative vision of the producer and/or director to life. Whether he actually operates the camera himself, or supervises the camera operator(s), he's mastered the essentials of lighting, formats of video and film, and the use of cranes and dollies. He can bring his own experienced people into the production and helps outline a shooting schedule. The DP often owns his own equipment or has relationships with equipment rental companies.

3. *Production Manager*

The role of the production manager (PM) or *unit production manager,* (UPM) varies in each project depending on its size and budget. Hired by the producer, the PM might be in charge of breaking down the script and creating a schedule and budget from that breakdown. She keeps track of costs and deals with paying the vendors. She might also negotiate with and hire crew members, arrange for equipment, and cover a range of essential details. Depending on the project, she monitors the daily cash flow; makes the arrangements for travel, housing, and meals; applies for shooting permits; oversees releases and clearances; and generally supervises the production activity. In a smaller or low-budget project, the producer or assistant producer doubles as the production manager.

4. *Assistant Director*

The *assistant director* (AD) is the on-set liaison between the director, the producer and/or production manager, the crew, and the actors. He typically plays "bad cop" to the director/producer's "good cop," helps to create the shooting schedule, and keeps the crew in sync with the day's schedule. The AD might also be responsible for timing shows or segments during taping.

5. *Production Audio Engineer*

The subtleties of sound design can get lost in preproduction planning, so a strong producer hires an audio engineer who can capture the clarity of dialogue, background sounds, special on-location audio (sirens, birds, traffic, muted conversations), and other ambient audio. She knows how to use microphones (mics) like booms, wireless, small clip-on microphones (lavs), and windscreens for minimizing wind, air conditioners, fluorescent lights, and other sounds that can cause interference. She either owns audio equipment or can lease what's needed for the project.

6. *Production Designer*

The aesthetic texture, design, and "look" of a production are essential elements in every project. From creating elaborate sets to simply rearranging set furniture, the *production designer* (sometimes called the set director or *art director*) works closely with the producer and director to create an environment for the action. He knows what camera shots and angles are planned, and he uses storyboards or sketches to design what will be seen in the camera's framing. As always, the budget has an impact on the choices, although a clever production designer can improvise and plan carefully. He may do all the jobs necessary or hire additional staff such as scenic designers, *prop masters,* and support crew.

7. *Post-Production Supervisor*

Whenever possible, a producer hires a *post-production supervisor* who consults with the producer in making early decisions about post-production details like the choice of editor and the editing facility, the sound designer and the audio mix facility, music, and other post-production elements. In some productions, the post-production supervisor comes onboard during production and sets up systems for screening the *dailies,* and organizing, labeling, and storing the footage. Her overall responsibility is to be well-prepared for the post-production stage.

The post-production supervisor thoroughly understands the professional standards for editing. This almost exclusively involves nonlinear editing (*NLE*) systems and the editors who are creatively and technically familiar with them. The primary NLE systems are Final Cut Pro, Avid, and Adobe Premiere; all involve similar principles. Each offers options for finishing and strong technical support. More post-production information can be found in Chapter 9.

B. The Support Crew

Depending on the size of the production, some or all of the following positions need to be filled in the preproduction phase. Others may extend into the production phase.

1. *The Writing Team*

Researcher — Most projects require some degree of research. An historical storyline, for example, involves details in architecture, costume, or speech mannerisms. A reality-based show may hire a researcher to unearth interesting ideas and real-life characters, a talk show may need a researcher to find guests, and a quiz show employs researchers to investigate subject areas for questions and correct answers. Researchers are valuable components in news or fact-based programs for double-checking sources or backgrounds. They might be professionals, academics, or consultants who specialize in specific areas of knowledge, or who are adept at problem solving. Researchers can also be production assistants or other administrative staff who are assigned to specific research needs.

Writers and revisions — During the writing process, the original script writer(s) might be teamed up with new writers, replaced because of "creative differences" with the producer or writer, or leave the project because of prior commitments. The initial concept of the project can change as part of the creative process, or the client or network makes demands the writer isn't willing to make. Script revisions are generally agreed on in the writer's contract, either following WGA guidelines or on a fee-per-revision basis.

2. *The Visual Team*

Storyboard artist — Working with the producer or director, and examining each scene of the script, the artist translates the visuals onto paper either by hand or using a software storyboarding program. These sketches are generally simple and cartoon-like, and easily illustrate what needs to be created by the production team.

Lighting director — In some productions, the LD works with or doubles as the DP. He designs the lighting for the production, plans where the equipment is best placed, and decides the best lights to use and their wattage. On set, the LD supervises the rigging of the pipes and the hanging of lights, and also recommends scrims, *gels,* and patches for various lights.

Camera operator — Either working with the DP, or doubling as the DP, the *camera operator* shoots the scenes, works with blocking and framing and lighting and lenses for each shot and coordinates with the audio engineer.

Assistant camera operator (AC) — In a larger production, the AC helps the camera operator, keeps camera batteries charged and available, changes and maintains lenses, and sets up and breaks down the camera equipment for each shot. The AC also slates each take, works closely with the script supervisor, and completes the camera reports for the editor. Some duties may be given to the 2nd AC if one is hired.

Still photographer—The photographer takes a number of still shots during rehearsal and behind the scenes, as well as on set, for purposes of providing publicity *stills* as well as creating a photographic journal of the production.

Gaffer — This lighting specialist works closely with the DP and cameras to set up lights, adjust them during the shoots, supervise and install various *gels* and *gobos*, and supervises the electric power sources or generators.

Best boy — An assistant to the gaffer, the best boy works specifically with electrical cables and ties them in to a power source or generator.

Key grip— This main grip works with the physical aspects of setting up the shoot, which includes rigging light stands and C-stands that hold up *silks* or *cycs* (hanging background fabric or paper); and installing special equipment like a *dolly* and dolly tracks, camera *jibs* and *cranes,* and more.

Grip — A *grip's* responsibilities include pushing the dolly, and setting up, adjusting, and taking down lights.

3. *The Audio Team*

Boom operator — In the audio department, the *boom operator* works with the camera operator and aims the *boom* (a long flexible pole with a microphone fixed to the end) at the audio source without getting into the camera's frame. Each camera has its own mic and boom operator. A boom can also be a large wheeled stand with a moveable arm from which the mic hangs.

Audio mixer — There are often several sources of audio in production. The *audio mixer* operates the console and separates each source onto a separate audio channel for post-production mixing. The mixer might also "live mix" the sound as it comes into the console; this can make the post-production audio mix easier or unnecessary.

Audio assistant — This member of the audio team keeps track of all audio equipment, changes and labels audio tapes, separates the microphone and audio cables from electrical cables, places mics on set or on talent, and often tapes the cables down to either hide them from the camera or to prevent people from tripping over them.

4. *The Production and Administrative Team*

Production secretary — As the liaison between the cast, the crew, the producer, and the UPM, the production secretary is often in charge of distributing paperwork such as *call sheets,* contacts sheets, schedules, paychecks, and other duties assigned per project. On smaller projects, the production secretary can also double as receptionist, PA, even catering.

Script supervisor — A vital asset to the director, the *script supervisor* checks that all the planned shots in the script have either been shot or deleted and also acts as a watchdog for *continuity*. For example, when an actor wears a red tie in one scene, he needs to be wearing the same red tie in another scene that will be edited to follow it. Taking continual notes during the shoot, the script supervisor describes each shot in each scene and keeps notes on all takes. The script supervisor also marks down gestures or movements (like a hand on someone's shoulder) that need to match another shot along with dialects and dialogue, wardrobe, hair and make-up (matching a bleeding wound from one shot to another), and what lens is used. The script notes provide important references and directions for the editor in post-production.

Location manager — As the liaison between the location and the producer, the location manager looks for and secures locations for the production, negotiates the location agreements, takes care of shooting permits, parking, on-location catering, and cleans up the location after the shoot has wrapped.

Catering manager — In charge of providing water, coffee, and tea, and snacks at all times, as well as providing a healthy hot meal at least every six hours, the catering manager sets up a table, cart, or vehicle for serving food as close to the action as possible.

Transportation manager — The transportation manager (or a key driver called the transportation captain) is in charge of moving the cast, crew, and equipment from one location to another. The production may require the transportation manager to rent the proper vehicles — mobile dressing rooms, *honey wagons* (portable bathrooms), trucks, or vans for equipment — as well as keeping them operational and ready to move.

2ⁿᵈ assistant director (2ⁿᵈ AD) — This crew member, when needed, assembles the call sheets, sets the call times for the cast and crew, and tells the cast and crew where to show up and at what time. The 2ⁿᵈ AD may also direct any action in the background involving extras.

3ʳᵈ AD — If a situation calls for traffic or crowd control, the 3ʳᵈ AD may be in charge. He also secures the set in whatever ways are necessary. The 3ʳᵈ AD works with the production secretary to coordinate the actors for their arrival on set.

Production assistant (PA) — A necessity in all departments, the PA can be a tremendous asset who contributes both physical labor and administrative help. Most productions have a pool of PA's, assigning them on set, in the office, on location, or where help is needed.

Interns — Often college or high school students can work for a semester on a production for school credit, while learning in the process. Few interns have worked in television production before; they require an intern supervisor to make sure they're doing their assigned tasks and are also getting a positive and organized learning experience. Interns are paying for their internships in school credits, and their energy is important to the production. Like PAs, they're assigned to areas where help is most needed.

TOP NINE

Important Tools for PAs and Interns

1. **The phone**: Use it as a good communication tool. Get everyone's cell and office number, so you can contact them in emergencies. Don't stay on the phone more than you need to.

2. **Meals**: Feeding people is important, and it makes them like you more.

3. **Driving**: You could drive for hours, on errands and runs. Have a current license, and know if your company covers you with their insurance. Avoid parking tickets, get to know the area you're driving in, and be comfortable with the vehicle.

4. **Paperwork**: Write everything down. Carry a notebook with you, and put everything down that you're told to do. Keep copies of everything to avoid problems later.

5. **Computers**: Several software programs are standards on a production, like Excel, Word, Final Draft, and Movie Magic, among others.

6. **The Internet**: Know how to search for things you need, like equipment, vehicles, venues, and a dozen other things you'll be asked to find out about. Refer to Lexis-Nexus, IMDb, and Google for great research.

7. **Attire**: Pockets in pants and jackets are important for holding phones, pens, stopwatches, and other things. Wear comfortable shoes when you're standing or walking a lot, and layer clothing because it gets really hot or very cold on set.

8. **Maps**: Get familiar with the city or location you're working in. Know the streets, public transportation, and how to get around in it easily and quickly.

9. **Production book**: Get as organized as you can. You'll have lots of information to deal with so when it's organized into one production book, it's all right there, in one place.

—Jonna McLaughlin and Becky Teitel, *production coordinators*

5. The Production Design Team

Set designer (construction coordinator) — Works with the production designer and creates blueprints for the set(s), hires the crew to construct it, and supervises the assembly of sets, floors, ceilings, or moveable set pieces.

Set dresser — Finds, transports, makes, or paints all furnishings, including tables, chairs, appliances, or other furnishings that are part of the action on a set or location. May require working in advance of the next day's shoot, and being on call during the shoot to fix any last minute problems.

Prop master — Supplies all props that are handled as part of the shoot, such as a paintbrush for a home makeover show or a tissue in a crying scene. He works closely with the script supervisor to maintain continuity.

Assistants — Depending on the project, each of the above may have one or more assistants working in various capacities.

Wardrobe designer or stylist — Designs the wardrobe "look," as well as coordinates all wardrobe needed for the shoot with the production designer, buys the wardrobe, measures and fits the talent, keeps all wardrobe elements in the order of the shooting schedule, and regularly cleans and repairs the clothing or costumes.

Dresser — Works with the wardrobe department to keep track of clothing. Helps the talent change clothing when needed. Some productions may require several dressers who often "swing" between wardrobe, make-up, and hair, unless they are members of a union with regulations that prohibit this multiple work load.

Hair stylist — On set during any scenes that involves talent. The hair stylist may create elaborate high-concept hair styles, design and maintain wigs, or simply be on hand for re-combs to maintain continuity from one scene to the next.

Make-up artist — Covers a range of needs from applying traditional cosmetic on-camera make-up to creating special effects like wounds, prosthetics, facial hair, and more. The call time for make-up precedes the shoot time and requires an on-set presence.

6. Additional Production Specialists

Your project might require the hiring of other specialists such as a stunt coordinator, a *choreographer,* crane and *Steadicam* operators, on-set tutors, animal wranglers, explosive experts, a *teleprompter* operator, florists and greens specialists, an on-set nurse, security personnel, and more. Many productions might also call for production support from an accountant, an entertainment lawyer, publicists, and marketing consultants.

The visual effects team — Your project might need a visual effects designer who can create extraordinary effects ranging from magical flying characters to subtle background enhancement. You might want animation or special graphic design for screen credits and a program title, or the illusion of a city blowing away in a tornado. As the producer, you'll make an assessment of your production needs, and then consult with the designers prior to the shoot.

I used to think that being a producer was being the brain because you have to have knowledge of what is going on in all of the other areas. Now I think it is a lot of different peoples' brains put together. But at times I have thought, am I the only one who is responsible for keeping track of this because it seemed like everyone was always coming to me. Then I realized that you do have to delegate. It will make your life so much easier, you know, find the right people who can take care of things for you.

—Valerie Walsh, *excerpt from interview in Chapter 11*

IV. Scheduling the Shoot

One aspect of preproduction is mapping out a *shooting schedule*. By using storyboards and a scheduling software program, the producer calculates what gets shot, when, and where. The end result is a concise, clear schedule that everyone involved can adhere to and understand. There is an example included in the book's CD.

The ideal shooting schedule allows scenes to be shot in the exact sequence as the script. This allows producers, directors, and actors to become familiar with the script, and the storyline can build with a more natural pace. Yet, shooting in sequence is a luxury that few producers can afford. Most projects are shot *out of sequence* and not shot in the order in which they appear in the script or in the final product. This approach saves time and money.

The size of your production crew depends on what you plan to shoot. A high-profile sitcom or multiple-location episodic requires a larger, more complex crew structure. A documentary or reality-based show, on the other hand, might only need a small compact crew that can move quickly and whose members can competently assume multiple duties.

Before you actually shoot, you'll revise your schedule often based on the following components that are factored into the production's overall structure.

A. Shooting Format

Current technology offers a provocative range of shooting formats. Most television shows are now shot in video, using either the more traditional Beta-SP analog videotape format or on digital video (DV), including *24P* and *high def* (high-definition television). Some big-budget episodic dramas are shot on 35-mm film, transferred to video, then downloaded into and edited with a nonlinear edit (NLE) system.

The question of shooting in digital versus analog seldom applies in today's video world. Outside of Betacam SP, all broadcast-quality cameras now shoot a digital signal. However, shooting on Betacam video continues to be a standard in television production. This is a good option because it can be fed into an NLE system via a component signal, or through a Digibeta with an analog board, which processes the analog images to a component digital path. More details of shooting and editing are discussed in Chapters 8 and 9.

The rapid expansion of technology in television production makes almost anything possible. You can shoot your footage in the digital domain, or you can shoot on film and transfer that to video for the edit. If you want to project your finished video piece onto a theatrical screen, the final master can be transferred to a film print. Yet, because this technology is continually evolving, some formats are not yet compatible with other systems while others may eventually become obsolete. Your DP or director is an integral part of the discussion about the right format for the project.

B. Sets, Soundstages, and Studios

A project could call for a complex set, built on a *soundstage* with backdrops, various room sets or exteriors, as well as enough space for set construction and painting areas, props, wardrobe, make-up, and production offices. Another project may only require a simple set on an inexpensive site. And increasingly, virtual sets are important components in television production as well as feature films; these virtual sets are designed and created on computers and then projected behind the action.

Control is the main advantage of shooting on a set. A set, for example, can be lit with leisure, it has a light grid that can be regulated, and electric power isn't an issue. Outside sounds are nonexistent, and there is enough space for talent, meals, equipment, production administration, and other production needs. A studio or soundstage may come empty or fully equipped with cameras, audio equipment, light grids, and crew. Studios have different policies and rate structures. Some may be rented by the half-day, whole day, weekly, or for the duration of the project.

Shooting in a soundstage can be expensive, and puts pressure on the production schedule. If your production calls for set design and construction, build in extra time for changes or mistakes as well as time for the lighting and electric crews to review the sets before the actual shoot.

C. Locations

Location shooting can add a specific look and mood to the production. It is generally less expensive than on a soundstage, especially if the location comes with furnishings, props, colors, and/or production space. The downside of location shooting is space limitations for shooting, production equipment, and areas for the cast and crew. Locations also involve legal agreements and fees. You can find an example of a standard location agreement form in the book's CD.

The goal of the production manager and/or producer is to group together all the shots needed in one location before moving the cast, crew, and equipment to the next location. This consolidation is called *shooting out* your location, saving time, money, and energy. The producer considers what time is needed to break down the equipment in one location, move it all to the next location, and set up in the new location. A production is generally shot in one or both of the following locations:

- A static location can be inside an existing home, an office space, a store, or an outside building, garage, baseball field, etc.

- A moving location can include a character on a busy street, shooting a day-in-the-life sequence, or *B-roll* (extra montage and background footage)

A *location scout* is a valuable component in location shooting. He or she is familiar with a range of locations: from a suburban home to an urban loft, from exteriors that match with a set on a soundstage to the right interior that suits the production's requirements. Some locations are free while others charge a fee. It is the job of the location scout or manager to find locations, negotiate the best price, and draw up location agreements. The location manager checks that:

- The locations are right for the project and reflect a look and texture. The location scout takes stills or video of the location to show the producer.

- A signed location agreement with the legal representative of the property is obtained. Some locations charge a fee, while others are free. Make sure that the production carries adequate liability insurance to cover any damages in the course of the production, which are negotiated with the location manager or producer. At the completion of the shoot, the property owner signs a release agreement.

- Whenever possible, the locations are close to one another.

- The location can supply adequate electrical power; if not, a generator must be brought in.

- There is enough space to accommodate crew, talent, and equipment.

- The necessary production equipment can fit into the location, and that there are elevators, ramps, and/or loading docks.

- The location can be lit adequately — either with natural light or supplied light.

- The audio in the location has minimal noise interference from traffic, neighbors, animals, conversations, machinery, air conditioning, schoolyards, or construction.

Shooting in a foreign location can lend additional depth or mood, or might be part of the script's direction. Foreign locations can be less expensive by offering professional support crews with lower pay scales, tax incentives, or a strong currency exchange rate. Locations like Canada, South America, Eastern Europe, Australia, Iceland, and New Zealand can help the producer stretch the budget as well as provide viable locations. In some countries, the weather patterns can also extend a shooting season.

1. *Exterior and Interior Shots*

Most producers prefer to shoot their *exteriors*, or outside shots, before they shoot anything else. An exterior may be a master shot of an apartment building, a park, or a crowd shot on a busy street. When these exteriors are shot, the production can move on to the *interior*, or inside shots, with more security.

Any number of factors can interfere with shooting exterior shots, such as bad weather, a fire in the neighborhood, or equipment failure. What's your backup plan? A cover set (an alternative interior location that has been prepped and dressed for shooting a back-up scene) can save time and money.

2. *Day and Night Shoots*

Shooting at night can reflect the storyline or create dramatic textures. It can also increase your budget and overall workload. Night shoots require specific lighting and equipment, and put a burden on scheduling crews because they often have to shoot at night as well as in the daytime. Below is a list of ways for the producer to ease this burden.

- The look of nighttime can be achieved by shooting during the day, and blacking out or relighting the windows to give the appearance of night behind the action.

- The producer can schedule all the night shoots consecutively, building in a break for the crew and talent before switching back to a daytime shooting schedule.

- A producer might also divide the day and night shooting into *splits*, a half-day and half-night schedule.

D. Actors and Talent

Because most actors' unions require that actors work no longer than a ten-hour day, the crew must set up the equipment before the shoot and then break it all down after the actors have finished their work. Crews are usually booked for 12-hour shifts to accommodate the talent, so scheduling talent and crew requires a review of the big picture — what needs to be shot and when, what union rules might govern certain decisions — and then balancing that with the crew and their needs. Other factors that deal with talent include:

- *Child actors*: Union rules require that children have a shorter working schedule, and a tutor, parent, or social worker with them at all times, especially if the talent is missing regularly scheduled school time.

- *Animals*: Using an animal in a shoot requires a special trainer who can prompt it to do tricks and stunts, and who supervises the animal between takes.

- *Extras and crowds*: The producer in charge of the extras auditions or locates them, then schedules times of arrival on set, arranges for a comfortable waiting area, gives them the proper release forms to fill out, and decides who needs wardrobe, hair, or make-up. While they wait for their scene, extras are provided with food, water, and bathroom facilities. When time permits, the extras are rehearsed before the shoot.

- *Stunts*: The stunt category can include tripping on the stairs, a car chase, explosions, gunshots, falls from buildings, and fistfights. An effective stunt requires careful design, test runs, and rehearsals, and is generally performed by professional stunt men and women. Stunt work translates into rehearsal time, fees, and additional insurance.

- *Convenience vehicles*: Some productions require mobile dressing rooms, portable bathrooms, and craft service trucks. The transportation captain is in charge of locating the vehicles, negotiating fees, and arranging for their call times on the production. If extra insurance is necessary, that information is given to the producer or PM.

- *Meals and craft services*: Provide snacks, coffee, tea, and water, and make them available at all times, close to the set or location. Give everyone a complete, healthy meal at least every six hours.

- *Security*: If local police are not involved, hire a private security company, or assign a strong-willed PA to keep the crowd at a reasonable distance. If any of the people milling around could be captured on camera, the person in charge posts a notice, stating that people may be on camera and they have a choice to stay or leave. You can find an example of a videotaping crowd notice on the attached CD.

- *Equipment*: Each member of the crew either gives an equipment request to the producer prior to the shoot, or provides the equipment as part of their contract. Special production equipment needs to be arranged in advance of the shoot, and might include a dolly and tracks, additional cranes and jibs for cameras, Steadicam mounts, explosive devices, HMI lights, camera cars, a video monitor for each camera, special mics, teleprompters, and more.

E. The Timing of the Shoot

All of the production elements listed above need to be choreographed into a seamless set of movements for each shooting day. The producer coordinates them, taking into consideration the time needed for the:

- *Art department*: Building and delivering sets, furnishings, and props

- *Transportation department*: Vans or trucks for loading and transporting equipment, sets and set dressings, the crew, and the talent

- *Setup*: Prelighting and camera blocking

- *Break down*: Disassembling equipment after the shoot is completed, and either taking it to the next location or returning it

As the producer, your objective is to accomplish what you have planned for each day's shoot, which is known as *making the day*. You want to keep the production on schedule, so always add extra time and money to the budget. This contingency safeguards the production if you should go over budget or need more time than you thought.

Some productions shoot a few script pages each day; others cover 10 to 15 pages. Compare this to a feature film that might only cover 2 to 5 pages a day. You want to shoot as much as possible in a short time, and still maintain quality. Unless you have a limited budget or time constraint, limit your production days to 12 hours, maximum. You don't want to burn out the talent or crew. Whenever possible, give everyone an occasional day off.

F. Call Sheet

A *call sheet* is like a blueprint for what shots are planned for the following day, and might be prepared by the producer, the line producer, or the 2nd AD. The call sheet lists what will be shot and who needs to be on the shoot, as well as call times for cast and crew, the locations, equipment, and scene numbers. The night before the next day's shoot, the call sheet is distributed to the producer(s), director, UPM, production coordinator, studio or network executives, and other people that the producer puts on the distribution list. An example of a call sheet can be found on the book's CD.

G. Production Report

At the end of the shooting day, a summary of what was shot is compiled in the production report (PR). It includes call times, scene numbers, deleted shots, setups, video and audio reel numbers, the crew members involved and the hours they worked, the locations, meals served, equipment and vehicles, and any delays or accidents on the shoot. It is often prepared by the same person who is responsible for the call sheet. Occasionally, the script is changed at the last minute, an actor is replaced, or the dailies show a mistake made during the shoot. A producer budgets these realities into the schedule to cover any possible reshoots. For every plan A that you schedule, have a plan B, and even a plan C as a backup.

As you plan your preproduction, double-check what you'll need by referring to the Preproduction Checklist in the book's CD. Look at each item. It may — or may not — be needed, depending on the genre of the project, the size of your crew, the budget, and needs of each department. You won't necessarily be doing every single thing — on larger productions, many of these areas are handled by the head of each department.

> A producer is a person who needs to be organized. Not everybody's system is the same. Let's put it this way, producers have their own systems. Whether or not they're organized or not, I guess is a subjective thing. But any producer has a system that works for her somehow.
>
> —Ann Kolbell, *excerpt from interview in Chapter 11*

On a Human Level . . .

Even the most experienced producers forget important details in the midst of the preproduction stage. As a producer, you are being asked a hundred questions, and you can't always know the answers. Yet each day you learn something new, and learning as much as possible is what a producer does to be successful.

> Luck is what happens when preparation meets opportunity.
>
> —Seneca

V. Summary

Your project can only be as good as the people on your team. They are the nuts and bolts of the project, and they are integral to the actualization of your vision. You want to work with people who believe in your vision, share your work ethic, and are compatible with other members of the technical and creative crew. This team can bring your project to life when the production stage begins, as you will see in Chapter 8.

VI. Chapter Review Questions

1. What are the primary elements included in a breakdown sheet?

2. How does a producer benefit by keeping a production book for each project?

3. What is the difference between a storyboard and a floor plan? How do they each augment a project?

4. What steps would you take to cast a project you're producing?

5. Who are the key production heads in most productions?

6. What does the location manager contribute to a production?

7. Name five support crew members who you might use in your production.

8. Describe options for shooting locations. Discuss the pros and cons of each.

9. What is the difference between working with child actors and adult actors?

10. Name ten areas of preproduction that are important to double-check.

Hell, there are no rules here — we're trying to accomplish something.

—Thomas Edison

CHAPTER 8

Production: The Shoot

This Chapter's Talking Points

I. The Producer's Role

As the producer, you have carefully developed each stage of your project and now, you're ready for the actual shoot. Your vision is about to become tangible. The production schedule might be ambitious, stretching over one or two weeks, or it's simple, small and compact with a two-day shoot. Regardless of its scope, the components are in place, and the writer, director, crew, and talent, are prepared to collaborate in making this project come alive. The actual shooting, called *principal photography*, can begin when everything is ready to go: the script has been finalized and distributed, the sets are built, the talent is prepared, the crew hired and the equipment is up to speed, all locations secured, and the dozens of details put in place.

Seventy percent of success in life is showing up.

—Woody Allen

A. The Producer's Team

The producer depends on — and is a part of — a team of individuals, each with his or her own style and personality. You want to respect their talents, skills, and moments of real genius.

Successful creative teams often have a history of working together; some producers formed their team as students or interns on a job.

The producer's team succeeds through mutual trust, respect, humor, and a shared vision. The difference between the "creative" and the "technical" teams is a nonissue. You want the people you work with to fit both descriptions, translating your ideas with their skills and the tools of their trade into a true synthesis of art and craft. The producer has the final word in decision making, though your decisions are based on many factors: the suggestions from everyone on the production team; the client's notes and requirements; and your own goals. Only after all these parts of the equation have been factored together do you make final decisions.

B. Production Protocol and Politics

In almost all television projects, the producer takes an active part in the production stage. If a director has been hired, the producer makes sure that all the elements are in place so the director can move ahead. The producer also keeps the action moving along, knows who is doing what job, stays on top of what needs to get done, and clearly communicates everyone's area of responsibility. As a producer, you work closely with your team by:

- Explaining your ideas and vision

- Agreeing on the vision and the creative directions

- Communicating frequently and openly with your team

- Listening to ideas and suggestions from your team

- Nourishing them with praise, food, and enthusiasm

- Providing a model of collaboration and mutual respect

> You have to know people's skills and respect them for their skills. I think that's one of my greatest strengths. As the executive producer, I've got 500–600 people working for me, like the technical team, the audio team, the camera team, the director, the stage manager, the PA, the events team, the crowd control, the security, the choreography, the dancers, the production department. And unless you can be a good collaborator and really communicate to the troops, everything can just fall short.
> —Salli Frattini, *excerpt from interview in Chapter 11*

II. On Set and on Location

At this point, you have chosen to shoot in one or more of these location options (discussed in Chapter 7):

- Studio

- Static location

- Moving location

- Virtual location

A. Virtual Locations

Locations can be costly. Sometimes a location can't be negotiated, is unavailable, is too expensive, or — it simply doesn't exist. An excellent alternative is that of virtual locations, designed and created on a computer by *computer graphics* (CG) that can contribute a range of creative images, such as a futuristic building, a landscape, or a battleground with thousands of warriors. Sets for news broadcasts, sports events, and current affairs programs use virtual backdrops for quick scene changes, as well as for advertising.

Building these virtual locations relies on a *blue screen* or a *green screen* background (chroma-key backdrop) that is placed behind the action you're shooting. These screens can be hundreds of feet long, or simply 8 × 8 feet mobile traveling screens. Let's say that the scene calls for an actor to fall into Niagara Falls. The actor plays out the scene in a studio in front of a special blue or green screen. Meanwhile, a camera crew shoots the actual waterfalls at an angle that will match up with the action of the actor in the studio, or the producer acquires stock footage of Niagara Falls (see Chapter 9 for more information on stock footage), and the two scenes are then layered together in the editing room. The result is a seamless edit that looks as though the actor really tumbled over Niagara Falls. It is highly effective, less expensive, and nobody gets hurt.

Other locations can be built entirely on the computer, and don't require the shooting of any footage, for example, a futuristic landscape or fantastical galaxies. Even an actual photograph; say, of an historical time period, can act as a backdrop for live action or computer-generated image (CGI) figures.

III. The Camera

Although the use of 16- and 35-mm film is still a presence in television programming, digital video technology is growing at such a rapid rate that the merging of film and video in television has essentially arrived. So, for the purposes of this text, video is the format of choice. The reader can consult additional sources and reference material for shooting and/or editing your production in film.

The camera operator — known informally as the *shooter* — and his or her camera form an intimate team that composes an image and tells a story. A good camera operator shoots compelling footage that not only looks good but can be can be easily cut together in the editing and mixing stage.

Today's video cameras can be sophisticated, inexpensive, and flexible. Most cameras offer creative options such as framings and angles, lenses, in-camera settings, varying shutter and shooting speeds, and built-in optical illusions. As you've seen in Chapter 2, a video image is like a matrix, with hundreds of horizontal lines that are comprised of thousands of vertical and horizontal pixels. American productions are generally shot and broadcast at 30 frames per second (fps) with 525 horizontal lines known as *NTSC video* (or standard definition) that adheres to broadcast standards set by the National Television Standards Committee. Film, in comparison, is shot at 24 fps. Other countries use systems with a higher resolution of 625 lines that run at 25 fps: phase alternating line (*PAL*) is used in the UK, Australia, China, and parts of Western Europe, while *SECAM* (Sequential Couleur a Memoire) is the standard in France, Russia, and Eastern Europe.

A. Component Video or Composite Video Formats

Think back to the Technicolor films from the 1930s and 1940s. In Technicolor, three neg-atives were shot, then processed into three separate red, green, and blue negatives. Ordinary film processing used only one negative with no color separation in the negatives, while the Technicolor prints made from the three-way process had vivid, memorable color and resonance.

In much the same way, a video camera separates the light that hits the lens into three components of color: red, green, and blue (RGB). Three-chip video cameras have three separate charge-coupled devices (*CCDs*) that can produce a sharper, higher quality color picture than the standard single-chip cameras with only one CCD. The image is processed as an electrical signal that can be recorded onto analog videotape, digital videotape, disk, computer card, hard drive, or eventually on other data storage options being developed. Each of these recording formats works, and each has its own creative, technical, and budgetary advantages — along with its limitations.

In the past, all video was recorded from a *composite* path. The entire video signal, with its luminance, chrominance, and horizontal and vertical synchronizing, was combined into one analog signal. Today, professional video is shot as *component* signals that keep luminance and chrominance signals separate. Component video retains sharper detail and color, and is a much cleaner way to edit and dub. Below is a list of several video formats.

- *Component video* is the superior format, producing sharper images with more color clarity and no loss of quality when it's dubbed down several generations. Examples of component video are Betacam SP and Betacam (both analog). They are shot as a composite signal but can be edited and dubbed as either component or composite. Digital Betacam, DCT, D1, and D2 are all digital formats.

- *Composite video* is often easier to shoot and broadcast, but it has a softer image clarity and loses quality quickly after one or two generations. Formats include $1''$, $\frac{3}{4}''$, U-Matic, and VHS (all analog) and digital formats of D2 and D3.

- *S-Video or Y/C* falls between component and composite video in quality, and uses two video cables — one for RGB and the other for brightness. The tape formats used in S-Video or Y/C are S-VHS and Hi-8, both analog.

You want your project to be shot with the best camera possible based on your budget and how you want your footage to look. Today's technology is changing so rapidly that cameras and their formats can upgrade or become obsolete in a matter of months. Some formats will survive as others disappear. Shoot your project professionally, in broadcast-quality video, and discuss the options with your DP or camera operator.

B. Shooting High-Definition Video

The technology of high-definition television (HDTV) has created an extraordinary leap in how we view and produce content and programming. HD has been heralded as a revolution because it can "see" better than the human eye with its depth of field, brilliance of color, and its image clarity. Often, HD can see *too* much — every blade of grass may be crystal clear, but so is every wrinkle on an actor's face and each poorly painted set that might have gone unnoticed in film or standard video.

HDTV promises to be the future of television, in both broadcast and nonbroadcast. The majority of prime time programming is regularly broadcast in HD, as are many sports specials and events, such as the Academy Awards. Compared to the current analog system that broadcasts NTSC programming in 525 horizontal lines, an HD image has either 720 or 1080 lines, depending on the specific HD format. This difference results in a higher resolution and a clearer picture.

Yet shooting in HD has taken years of development before it could be considered a feasible format for producers. In 1996, the FCC upset the television industry when it mandated that the traditional method of broadcast — the analog terrestrial TV transmission system — would be eliminated, and its replacement would be an all-digital system. According to the FCC, this system was to be completely in place by the end of 2006, provided that by that date, 85% of the country could receive digital television. The consequences of this ruling are considerable and involve complex and expensive issues like transmission standards, the costs for local and national networks to convert their equipment to all-digital, the glitches in the technology, the small number of consumers who can afford the expensive HD sets, the higher costs of production and editing, and the lack of HD programming.

The "85% rule" is problematic as well. As of mid-2005, almost 20% of the TV viewers in America still use rabbit ears, and only 12% of the television population has digital TV sets in their homes. Providing households with converter boxes that would allow viewers to get digital broadcasts could cost literally billions of dollars, and there is little assurance that those viewers without the boxes can still receive a signal. Yet as broadcasters wrestle with these issues, they're also developing HD content. In addition to the four major networks (NBC, ABC, CBS, and Fox), more cable and satellite services such as HBO, Showtime, Discovery, ESPN, and HDNet are offering HD channels.

Currently, HDTV has two formats. There are arguments for each, though HD sets display both formats equally well in its wide screen 16:9 format, also called *letterbox* or film-style. Compare the size of this screen to a standard TV set that's only 4:3.

- *720p*: A horizontal resolution of 1280 vertical lines × 720 pixels that works well for broadcast, though it's usually not recommended for a project that may be transferred to film or projected on a large screen.

- *1080i*: A resolution of 1920 × 1080, best used when the final product needs a "reality" aspect that looks as if the viewer is seeing it live, in sharp detail.

C. Shooting in 24P Video

When you shoot in 24P (24 fps, progressive scan), the process involves video that runs at 24 fps, with an intermittent flash of black in every frame cycle. Put simply, 24P has a look that is similar to film. It's softer, it has a film "flicker," the colors appear richer than real life, and because it can be both standard and high definition, it is becoming a favorite format for shooting, especially for producers who might want to transfer their project to 35-mm film for projection purposes. Television industry insiders agree that most projects should be finished in HD with a 24P 16:9 master. It is the best format for broadcasting, progressive streaming on the Web, creating PAL versions for broadcast in Europe, and for release on DVD.

D. Time Code

When shooting in video, a *time code* (TC) signal is "burned on" the videotape and assigns each frame a specific number. TC is equivalent in film to a sprocket hole and frame numbers. It is broken into four segments. Let's say that if the time code number is 07 02 45 17, then:

- 07 is the hour

- 02 is the minutes

- 45 is the seconds

- 17 is the fps (only valuable to the editor for frame accuracy and isn't necessary in taking notes)

Working with time code is an integral part of the editing process. It makes the editing frame-accurate and exact. TC is also a valuable tool for screening and logging footage prior to the edit session. As you'll see in Chapter 9, you can use these TC numbers to create a storyboard, or *paper cut*, that the editor uses as a "script" for the edit. In screening footage, it must first be dubbed to VHS or DVDs with the TC displayed visually on the top or bottom of the screen; this is known as *visible time code, VTC*, or *vizcode*. The TC is exactly the same as on your original footage. As you screen the dubs, you'll make notes. For example, a teenage boy opens the door at 03 04 15 on Tape 1. The close-up of his hand on the doorknob is on Tape 4 at 06 13 15. These two scenes come from different tapes but need to be edited together in the editing room.

As you screen each tape, take good notes of all the time code numbers. As you screen each tape from start to finish, log the TC that describes specific parts of the footage, such as a great cutaway shot, a move from one location to another, and so on. From these notes, you can create a paper cut (storyboard) for editing, with the TC numbers, scene descriptions, and tape numbers. It's a valuable time-saver.

On a shoot, there are two ways to set and record TC in the camera:

1. *A studio multi-camera shoot*: All the cameras are linked into the "house" TC generator. This sends out time-of-day time code (TC that records the actual time of day) to all cameras and tape machines, simultaneously. This way, the tapes from each camera can be "synced up" in the edit room. This system is helpful in organizing notes based on the chronology of events that occurred during the shoot. It also simplifies the editing, making it easier for the editor to match up each camera's footage simultaneously. Without this synchronization, the editor wastes time and money going back and forth to each tape and trying to stay in sync.

2. *A single-camera shoot*: An internal TC generator can be set inside the camera itself. Producers usually start Tape 1 at hour 1 (01 00 00 00), Tape 2 at hour 2 (02 00 00 00)), and so on. Because there are only 24 hours in a video day, TC numbers beyond 23 59 59 29 don't exist. However, Tape 24 can be set at 00 00 00 00 and Tape 25 at 01 00 00 00, and so on. This system helps in logging and screening footage for the edit session later.

E. Capturing the Image

The producer, director, and/or DP discuss the creative and technical options for the best way to shoot and capture an image. Their decisions direct the narrative flow, affect the style and pace of the program, and guide how a viewer sees a character. The perspective of a shot, for example, can convey dramatic tension or character motivation when the viewer knows from whose perspective the story is being told. This perspective is either objective or subjective.

- *Objective perspective*: Captures the viewpoint of an unseen narrator or storyteller who is an onlooker. The shot is usually a wider, more distant shot or a *two-shot*.

- *Subjective perspective*: Tells a story from a character's point of view, and the shot is closer or tighter, such as a close-up or an over-the-shoulder shot.

When planning a shot, the primary factors that play into capturing the image in the shoot include:

- Framing and composition

- Camera angles

- Camera moves

- Camera shot list

1. *Framing and Composition*

The primary concept of *framing* a shot involves shooting an image — usually a person or an object — with a particular size of the image in the frame, as well as everything that surrounds or affects them. An extreme close-up of a face gives one kind of narrative message, while an extreme long shot of the same person tells a different story altogether. Each option frames the image and composes the frame around it.

    Composition is the relationship of objects to each other in the frame, or to the shape of the subject being shot. Colors, lighting, scenery, props, and camera blocking all contribute to a scene's composition. This total effect is known as *mise-en-scene*, or the setting up of a scene.

2. *Camera Angles*

Each time the camera moves, and every angle at which the camera is placed relative to what it's shooting, creates a different effect both visually and thematically. A sitcom can be shot in a fixed frame, using a stationary or *locked down camera* on a tripod, and the actors move only within that framing. A gritty detective drama might use a *handheld* approach, moving fluidly in and out of the characters' faces and lives. Both the genre of your show and its content help determine how you'll shoot it. As you decide on camera angles and movement, keep two things in mind:

1. *Viewpoint*: The height of the camera's position determines the viewpoint of the character and gives the viewer a sense of theme and direction. When shot from below, for example, a character has the illusion of superiority, but a character shot from above may seem inferior or small. When an actor speaks directly into the camera, the dialogue is directed to the viewer; when the actor looks off to the right or the left of the camera's lens, it appears that he is speaking to another person.

2. *Eye-line*: The position of the camera needs to correspond to the character's eye-line, usually in the top third of the frame. The viewer should be able to follow from what the actor sees to the actor's eyes. This guarantees that the eye-lines from one character to another match up in editing.

3. *Camera Moves*

Your camera can be a fluid and flexible tool for capturing an image or the action. These are traditional camera moves from which a camera operator can choose:

- *The tilt*: A camera can maintain the same eye-line, and tilt down (giving the impression of the subject looking toward the ground) or tilt up (suggesting that the subject is looking toward the sky). This tilt can also give an impression of a subject's inferiority or superiority to another character or to the viewer.

- *The Dutch angle*: Often used in reality shows and interviews, the camera is rotated so that the image itself appears at an angle, and creates a sense of intimacy or tension.

- *The pan*: The camera swivels on the tripod or on its axis to form an arc from right to left or left to right. A pan is smooth and even-paced. A *swish pan* moves faster and can be effective in action sequences or as transitions in editing.

- *The tracking shot*: Also known as a *traveling shot*, it pulls the viewer into the action by using a camera on a dolly that either moves on tracks or on special shock-resistant wheels alongside a moving subject. The same effect can be accomplished by mounting a camera mounted on a *crane* or a *jib* that swoops above, into, or away from the action in a scene. Another effective approach is a camera rig (such as Steadicam, Glidecam, and the DVRigPro) that's worn by the camera operator for shooting smoothly in any direction.

- *The zoom*: The camera lens moves smoothly into a close up of a person or object.

- *Extending the frame*: The camera is stationary and steady, and holds on an object or scenery for a few beats, possibly with off-screen sound effects — a ringing phone, a closing door — before the character enters the frame from right or left.

Another area of discussion with your DP is that of lenses for the shoot. In some cases, a wide-angle lens might add to a more spacious feeling to a shot, while a fish-eye lens creates a subtle distortion that can be interesting when shooting buildings or interiors that are otherwise mediocre.

4. Camera Shot List

Prior to the shoot itself, or on set, a *shot list* (an inventory of each shot needed to be shot for a specific sequence or scene) is distributed. It uses specific terms for each camera angle, such as ECU for extreme close up, and so forth. The list is discussed in Chapter 7.

F. Video Camera Options

Historically, the camera has been considered the most important factor in shooting. Now, the computerization of the editing process is changing the standard approach to shooting in video. Whether you decide to shoot in analog or digital video, each option provides a "data gatherer" for recording and storing the data or images on your footage. Yet certain cameras do stand out as distinct technological advances in shooting.

In addition to professional quality cameras that record onto Betacam or Digibeta, independent producers and networks are depending on professional camcorders for shooting broadcast-quality productions. Although the current advances in camera technology provide a glimpse into revolutionary cameras and equipment available in the near future, the current favorites of most video camera operators and DPs include:

- *Panasonic AG-DVX-100*: It is rapidly climbing the top ten list of favorite cameras. It's inexpensive and offers the choice between shooting in standard NTSC 480i/60 or in two HD modes: 24 fps/480p and 30 fps/480p. This 3-CCD DVX-100 has a variety of add-ons, like lenses, matte boxes, long-life batteries, and more. The footage is easy to edit and composite, and its images are richer, with less of the "DV look." Some filmmakers are using the DVX-100 to integrate 24P with 35-mm film or are shooting entirely in 24P.

- *Sony PD 150 and 170*: Both are established DV camcorders with broadcast quality and field endurance in documentaries, reality-based shows, and sports. Both systems offer regularly updated add-ons.

- *Sony XDCAM*: Uses blue laser light to store images onto a data disk. This camera can be assigned its own IP address and connected with an Ethernet cord, with the data instantly transmitted to any workstation, server, or editor with compatible software. This concept potentially eliminates satellite trucks, making footage available anywhere in seconds. The XDCAM has few moving parts and instant playback with no rewind. It can shoot in either 24 or 30 frames, and the disk can be fed to a server or uploaded in the edit room.

- *Studio cameras*: When shooting a talk show or news broadcast, for example, larger DigiBeta cameras are generally used. They are often mounted on moving pedestals that keep the camera stationary; these pedestals can glide smoothly around a limited set, and they can tilt the camera up or down. Most studio-based productions require three to six pedestal cameras, as well as one or two cameras mounted on a swooping jib, or crane, that can fly over the audience and onto the set. Some productions might augment the DigiBeta cameras with a handheld camera as well. Microphones are hung at regular distances over the audience for reactions, like laughter and applause.

In a multi-camera studio shoot, the footage from each camera, as well as the audio from the talent and audience microphones, are all fed into a central control room that is close to the set (or fed to a mobile truck with its own control room). In the central control room the director, producers, technical director, audio mixer, graphics person, etc., watch each incoming camera feed on its designated monitor. As the crew in the control room records the footage, it is generally edited live. This process is called "live to tape," and it's how most studio shows are produced. Any additional editing changes can be made later. Ultimately, producers talk with the DP and director, and often the editor, about the camera options that are best for your particular project.

IV. Lighting

Lighting is an essential tool for painting the video image. The subtle use of light creates atmosphere and mood, dimension, and texture. It can convey a plot line, enhance key elements such as set color or skin tone, and signals the difference between comedy and drama and reality and fantasy.

A. Hard versus Soft

Artificial lighting is either "hard" with sharp and distinct shadows, or "soft" with less defined, softer shadows and fewer background images. The intensity and clarity of the bulb, or its diffusion, combine with placement to design a shooting environment.

- *Hard light*: Aimed directly on its subject, with a brighter single-source illumination. The sun is one example. Other hard light is incandescent, ellipsoidal, and quartz.

- *Soft light*: Diffused, created with less intense lamps that reflect or bounce light off a reflector, a ceiling, or another part of the set. Soft lighting effects are enhanced with scrims, strips, scoops, and banks.

Production lighting includes three major lights and their positions in relation to each other (three-point lighting):

1. *Key light*: Powerful, bright light that illuminates a primary, or *key,* person or object, creating a deep shadow. It is positioned above and at an angle to the subject being shot.

2. *Fill light(s)*: Softer light placed at an angle to "fill" any unwanted shadows created by the key light.

3. *Back light(s)*: Lamp that is positioned behind and above the primary subject being shot. This helps to create an illusion of depth behind the main subject and brings it forward from the background.

Most TV talk shows, sitcoms, variety shows, musicals, and family entertainment use *high-key* lighting — a high ratio of key light to fill light. *Low-key* lighting creates a more dramatic, moody, and textured effect.

B. Hot and Cold

All lights have a color temperature that influences what the camera records.

* *Daylight (outdoor)*: The most powerful and brightest light. Daylight is hot and produces a blue tone on video.

* *Artificial (indoor)*: Considered cold. Creates a reddish yellow cast.

C. Interior and Exterior

* *Exterior lighting*: As you consider shooting an exterior (outdoor) scene, you may want the spectacular intensity of the sun at high noon or the moody waning light after sunset, known as the *magic hour* — each has its own effect on an exterior scene. However, outdoor shooting can pose real challenges. Along with the sun's continual movement, its degrees of brightness can fluctuate dramatically through the shooting day. When the sun is your key light, it might need to be partially blocked out or augmented by fill lights or back lights. An exterior set can be shot at night but lit to look like daylight or vice versa.

* *Interior lighting*: Shooting interior (indoor) scenes poses fewer challenges as video cameras and shooting formats become more advanced. A camera's iris, for example, can play with light and color and go from automatic to manual. This avoids the camera's normal tendency to focus on the best-lit object in the scene.

Both interior and exterior lighting can be altered by using *reflectors* or bounce cards. These are glossy, white light-weight cards in varying sizes that reflect light onto an object or actor. Large *silks* (squares of translucent material) can be strategically hung and positioned to filter the sunlight and maintain lighting consistency.

When shooting in video, there are certain colors or patterns to avoid:

* *Stripes*: A striped shirt, for instance, can create a wavy effect on the video, known as a *moiré* pattern.

* *Red*: Certain bright shades of red can "bleed" and morph into other objects nearby.

* *White*: Too much white can overpower a scene and "blow it out."

* *Blues and greens*: Some shades can blend together and become invisible. Blue or green screens are used as backgrounds to shoot special effects.

V. Audio

Sound design is a highly creative art. The careful recording of audio during production, as well as in post-production, can make a visceral impact on the project. What the viewer *hears* has a definitive influence on what the viewer *sees*. Sound design is a genuine collaboration between the audio recorded on a location and the extra layers of sound that are added and enhanced in post-production.

A. Sound Design

An overall choreography of recorded sounds is known as sound design and usually includes:

* *Dialogue*: Conversation between the main characters in a scene

- *Background or ambience*: Muted conversations of extras in the background, barking dogs, sirens, playing children

- *Sound effects*: Narrative information, like a ringing phone or an angry shout

- *Added audio*: More thematic information, like a musical theme or a "sting"

If you could draw an audio storyboard, you would "see" audio everywhere: the dialogue, conversations in the room, the clatter of plates, and the tip tap of walking shoes, as well as outside noises like background traffic, singing birds, children playing, sirens, a parade, and planes flying overhead. These all might be part of the scene, forming an essential layer of ambience. However, these extraneous noises can also be a major interference.

B. Four Major Elements of Sound Recording

- The microphone, or *mic*

- Acoustics in the location

- The recording medium and its sensitivity to audio

- The perspective of the audio

1. *Microphones*

Microphones fall into several categories:

- *Directional mic*: Aimed directly at its subject. Captures only the subject's audio with as little other background sounds as possible. This mic is a *cardioid* microphone (so named because of its heart shape) and records dialogue clearly.

- *Shotgun mic*: Mounted directly on the camera at the end of a boom (a long rigid pole that can extend as much as 18 feet) or mounted in a pistol-grip rig. It has a selective pick-up pattern that primarily records the sound in front of the mic. It can be as far as five feet away from the source of the sound and still get clean audio. A valuable add-on is a fuzzy windscreen around the mic that reduces most wind or breeze interferences.

- *Lavalier* (lav): Clips onto a shirt collar and picks up dialogue close to the speaker's mouth, isolating it from other audio. A lav also solves the problem of seeing a boom or its shadow in the frame. It can either be hard-wired and connected by cable to the camera or sound recording device, or it can be wireless and powered by a bodypack transmitter worn under clothing in the small of the back.

- *Omnidirectional mic*: Sensitive to sound from any direction and source. It records dialogue and also captures all background sounds. This mic works best for recording man-on-the-street interviews and for dialogue where any ambient sound is required.

- *Handheld mic*: In interview situations, it's the most dependable mic because it only requires sound pressure from the person who's speaking into it. A handheld mic can be either directional or omni and can be hard-wired or wireless.

- *Prop mic*: When it isn't feasible to use a boom or lav, the audio crew conceals a microphone in a prop or on a set furnishing to hide it from the camera. A mic can disappear inside a plant or a book that's close to the dialogue, be taped under a table, or draped inside a curtain.

> The essential point is that you have to try to gain the trust and the confidence of the client, and all the other parties – from all the audio people, from the staging people, the artists, all the parties involved in this event. You have to gain their trust, showing that you understand what their issues are and bring them on board to be on the same team for the overall good of the project.
>
> —Stephen Reed, *excerpt from interview in Chapter 11*

2. *The Acoustics of the Location*

Audio engineers often refer to the sounds they hear in visual terms. Sounds can be warm, bright, and round, hard or soft, fat, or thin. The quality of the recorded sound is controlled to some extent by the microphones used to capture them. Another important factor of recording sound is the location acoustics. Sound waves are impressive and fluid. They can be muffled by surfaces that are soft and spongy such as rugs, furniture, clothing, curtains, and even human bodies. On the other hand, surfaces that are hard and reflective, like glass, tile or vinyl floors, mirrors, and low ceilings, can deflect and bounce sound waves creating echoes or distortion.

Some locations can pose a real challenge to an audio engineer. A location might look just great, but it's got challenging audio problems like loud air conditioners, the buzz of fluorescent lights in the ceiling, ticking clocks, or public address systems. As the producer you might want the controlled environment of a soundstage or studio, avoiding unwanted noises. Say, for example, a scene calls for a young couple to have a romantic conversation as they dance across a crowded dance floor with a band and other dancers in the background. On a controlled set, everyone can play their part, but only the couple's dialogue is actually recorded — no one else is talking and the band isn't really playing. All the other sounds, such as the dancers' conversations in the background, body movements, and the music the band is playing are added later in post-production. Often, the couple's dialogue is also rerecorded for added clarity. This process is called automatic dialogue replacement (*ADR*) and it involves mixing and layering all these additional sounds together to create the final product. You'll find more details in Chapter 9 about ADR.

3. *Audio Recording Formats*

While shooting most formats of video, the audio goes through a *single system*. This means that the sound is recorded directly onto the videotape, disk, or hard drive. In the case of a multi-camera shoot, the audio from each camera is fed directly to a videotape recorder (VTR) and monitored by an audio mixer who is continually balancing the levels and sound from each microphone onto separate channels for mixing later in post-production.

Because you want professional, broadcast-quality sound, most videotape formats come with four separate audio tracks or *channels*. It is possible to assign microphones to each channel. Now you've got the capacity for stereo recording, with two channels on the left and two on the right. These channels can be expanded later in the audio mix.

HDTV broadcasting features the additional capability for 5.1 surround sound, which is found on DVDs and digital television broadcast. HD camcorder systems can record audio directly onto HD videotape with at least two tracks of audio. Sometimes in addition to recording onto videotape, a *double system* is useful in recording the audio onto an independent recording device — DAT, DA88, or another system listed below — in which the frame rate can be set to match that in the camera.

Sometimes the audio needs to be recorded separately and mixed with other audio elements in post-production. Professional digital formats for recording isolated audio continue to be improved, though currently each must be compatible with both the video equipment and the editing system. The most popular digital audio recording formats include:

- *DAT (digital audio tape) recorder:* Currently the most widely used method, DAT records clear audio with no hum or hiss. A DAT recorder's speed control is extremely accurate, it has TC capability, and there is no loss when it's digitally duplicated. The cassettes are small and easily stored or shipped.

- *Disk recorder:* Takes the audio onto either a hard drive or a computer tape data drive.

- *Chip-based recorder:* Audio is recorded onto computer memory cards that have no moving parts.

- *MiniDisc:* Recording audio onto magneto-optical disks.

When shooting in DV, the audio engineer cautiously monitors any digital distortion caused by audio that may be recorded too hot on the meter, because it's generally unfixable and useless. Loud sounds or dialogue can peak the meter in the camera or the digital recording device, so whenever possible the audio engineer tests the audio before the shoot and won't allow the meter setting go over "zero." He or she usually sets the audio at -12 dB and even -20 dB, and is careful to never let the audio levels hit the top of the meter.

4. *The Audio Perspective*

In the same way that an image is shot from a visual perspective, dialogue and ambient sound is recorded with an audio perspective in mind. For example, dialogue spoken by an actor in a close-up shot sounds clear, intimate, and appears to be coming from the immediate foreground. Dialogue yelled from across a busy street in a wide shot has a different perspective, coming from the background of the shot, as the distance blends with the ambient sounds from traffic.

It's not always possible to record sound that has the same perspective as the footage. A visual might be a long shot, for example, of two mountain climbers as they reach the summit. The only way to record their dialogue is by using a concealed wireless mic, but this will sound like audio for a close-up, not a long shot. It can be altered during post-production with added sounds like blowing wind and crunching snow, or recorded in ADR after the shoot has wrapped.

C. Recording Production Sound

Audio that is recorded during production on a sound stage or at a location is known as *production sound* and refers to all scripted dialogue, ambient sound, and background noise. If an unwanted sound creeps in, or the dialogue changes after the footage has been shot, most production sound can be rerecorded later in the post-production stage. This is explored in greater detail in Chapter 9.

1. *The Challenges of Recording Sound*

Whether you're recording audio on a soundproof set or outside on location, there are situations to be aware of and situations to prevent.

- *Obstructions:* Jewelry or clothing can rub or click against a clip-on lav.

- *Lights:* Neon or fluorescent lights that are barely audible to the ear can cause a buzz or hum on the audio.

- *Appliances:* Certain set pieces or existing appliances on location create their own sounds like a refrigerator or an air conditioner.

- *Motors*: Your location might be near a busy street or under an air traffic pattern.

- *Weather*: The rustling of wind, even a faint breeze, can be a detriment in recording clean dialogue.

- *Neighbors*: A school playground, a lumberyard, an auto repair shop, or a house with a lawnmower can create interfering noises.

- *Construction*: Incessant reverberations from jackhammers or saws can travel into a location or a studio, even from a distance.

- *Batteries*: If the battery power on a mic's body pack goes out, you've lost your sound. Plan ahead with an adequate supply of charged batteries.

Most of these problems can be avoided with foresight, thoughtful use of microphones, and sound mufflers like moving blankets and microphone windscreens. You don't want to depend on the post-production audio mix to fix your audio problems, but that's where you can often solve unavoidable audio dilemmas.

2. *Some Sound Advice*

Your ultimate objective is to record and mix your audio elements so seamlessly that when you listen to it with your eyes closed, you hear no audio cuts or drastic changes in levels. Any audio transitions from one scene to another should be equally smooth. Most every challenge in recording production sound has a solution, such as:

- *Record sound effects and ambience separately*: If two characters are walking and talking as they pass an outdoor café sound is everywhere around them: their dialogue, the clinking of glasses, conversations, church bells, and fluttering pigeons. Whenever possible, record each of these sounds separately. In the audio mix they're mixed together with the dialogue to create an overall audio impression.

- *Record room tone*: Room tone refers to the subtle, nearly inaudible sounds that are unique to each and every set or location. At either the beginning or end of each camera setup or at the completion of a scene, while the entire cast and crew and equipment is on set, the audio crew asks for complete silence and records 30 to 60 seconds of sound. In the audio mix, this room tone can fill in gaps in the dialogue or effects.

- *Keep continuity*: Just as a script supervisor maintains visual continuity in a shoot, there is a definite continuity in recording audio, too. The audio levels between actors in a scene, for example, need to be constant and unvarying in volume. Any background or ambient sound is measured for consistency of levels so they don't interfere with the dialogue. When a camera angle changes, its accompanying audio might also be different.

- *Rehearse and re-rehearse*: There is a real difference between setting up audio for one shot in which both actors are walking and talking on the street and a shot where they're sitting quietly on a couch on a set. Carefully consider how you can record the audio that fits with the visual camera angles and perspectives for each scene.

- *Keep an audio log*: One person on the audio production crew has the job of keeping track of what is recorded on a set or location, including dialogue, ambient sounds, and special effects. This *audio log*, or sound report, lists details that are pertinent to the audio mix in post-production such as the tape number with time code numbers (in and out points), the scene number, and the *take* number with a short description of what's been recorded.

> You have to be flexible. You have to be willing to roll with the punches. You have to believe in what you are doing, and believe you can do it. If someone is telling you something is impossible, it usually is not. Anything is possible. There are some things that are impossible for budgetary reasons, but there are always compromises and ways to make your vision come to life.
> —Tom Sellitti, *excerpt from interview in Chapter 11*

VI. The Actual Shoot

Before the actual shoot starts, the producer checks, and double-checks all the legal documents. Make sure you have signed deal memos with the crew, contracts with the talent, release forms from the extras, and that all location agreements are signed and negotiated. Below is a list of elements needed for a successful shoot.

A. Arrival of Cast and Crew

Based on their call times, crew members arrive on the set or location. Usually the transportation department arranges for their equipment, vehicles, set pieces, and other production materials to be delivered and unloaded early in the shooting day. The actors and talent arrive for wardrobe, hair and make-up, and any time-consuming special effects.

1. *Wardrobe, Hair, and Makeup*

Actors and talent (including minor parts, extras, background people, children, and animals) may need to go into hair, make-up, and/or wardrobe before they're ready to appear in their scene. They may need simple hair combs, minimal make-up, and little or no wardrobe or make-up could be more challenging like applying wound make-up, creating facial hair or designing wigs, or a complicated wardrobe such as an historical outfit or costume. The wardrobe, hair, and make-up people stay close to the set for any last-minute extra touch-ups such as a hair combing, powdering a sweaty nose, or adjusting clothing.

2. *Dressing the Set or Location*

The art director and his or her crew *dress*, or prepare, the set or location for the shoot. This can include finishing touches on the set pieces, adding furnishings, props, or greenery, and moving pieces around to accommodate the action or movements of the characters.

3. *Craft Services*

The *craft services* crew generally arrive at least a half hour before the overall call time, and set up a table for coffee, tea, water, and snacks for the cast and crew that is close to the shoot. They also serve at least one healthy meal a day or every six hours. Attention to craft services keeps everyone happier, more productive, and energized.

B. Blocking for the Camera

The producer, director, DP, and/or gaffer survey the set or location, review their storyboards, and map out the day's shoot. They plan the placement of the cameras, lights, and audio equipment — a process called *blocking* the scene. Any revisions or changes in the original plans are determined here because last-minute changes slow up production.

1. *Blocking for the Actors*

Once the camera movements are decided, the scene is rehearsed for the cameras and lights. Often a stand-in takes the place of an actor in the blocking. Any places for the actors are marked on the floor with masking tape.

2. *Lighting for the Set*

Lighting a set or location properly takes time. Depending on the size of the crew, the DP and the gaffer set the lights, replace bulbs, try different scrims and gels, and find various angles that work. If a stand-in doubles for an actor, the crew can experiment with the lights while the actual actor is in make-up or rehearsal.

3. *Audio Set Up*

All microphones and recording devices are set up, tested, and rehearsed. The audio may need muffling with heavy *sound blankets* or acoustical equipment. Any mic cables are kept away from electrical cables or wires to prevent interference. If a separate sound mixer is used, it's in an area where the audio engineer can watch the meter and ride the different levels coming from each microphone and keep them all in balance. Any boom shots can be rehearsed with the camera operator so the boom or mic shadows won't enter the camera's frame.

C. Rehearsing the Actors

Whenever feasible, the director or producer rehearses the actors on the set where they will be shooting. This on-set rehearsal gives the talent a chance to loosen up in the shooting environment, and get familiar with the script. Sometimes the rehearsal takes place in another area away from the set, which allows the actors to concentrate.

1. *Rehearsing and Blocking the Extras*

Any people in the background — called extras or atmosphere — must be rehearsed and blocked just like the main actors. A member of the crew, usually the AD, works closely with the extras in rehearsing movements such as crossing the set from one side to the other, chatting and laughing at tables, or walking behind the action. The extras are directed to not look into or at the camera, and generally only pretend to talk or laugh; in fact, they're moving their lips in complete silence. Their audio is added later during the mix.

2. *The Technical Run-Through*

This final rehearsal checks for technical details and their relation to the action being shot. Camera angles, lights, audio mics, dolly moves, the placement of furniture or props — all are essential steps in the choreography of production. If you're shooting on a location, cover anything that could be damaged with plastic tarps or moving blankets. Move valuable or breakable items — plants, furniture, china, glassware — that are part of the location. You, the location manager, or a PA can take notes as well as photographs of each object in its original place so they can be returned after the shoot. Leave each location in better condition than when you started.

3. *Shooting Publicity Stills*

Often, a still photographer is hired to take publicity stills that can be important to a publicity campaign as well as for archiving the production. The photos can be taken during the technical rehearsal, or, if the photographer uses a silent camera, during the shoot itself. Digital still cameras are preferred because of their excellent quality and their ability to erase shots that don't work, saving disc space and developing costs. A professional still photographer knows how to get great shots without being obtrusive.

D. Time for the Shoot

All the equipment, the crew, and the talent are in place and ready. Now, it's time for the shoot. The director calls for action and the camera operator and the audio engineer both confirm by saying "up to speed," or "speeding."

Slates — Some productions use a *slate*, or a *clapboard*, which is held in front of the camera each time it rolls. This slate gives relevant details such as the name of the producer and director, what camera(s) is in use, the scene number, take number, date, and the project's title. Other video productions might use a *smart slate*, which matches the camera's time code with the audio. However, because a professional video camera records the sound directly onto the videotape or disk, slates aren't always necessary.

Takes — With few exceptions, a scene is shot several times before it feels right to the producer or director; each attempt is called *a take*. You might run into technical problems like poor lighting, a boom in the shot, and a misread line, or a number of other challenges might occur as part of the process. Additional takes can cover these problems up. A seasoned producer calls for a final take for *safety* just in case. Each shot in each scene has been planned out with its own camera and lighting angle and often its own lens. Each shot is assigned a description and a specific number on the shot list and production schedule. For example, the close-up of the small child digging in the sandbox might be the third shot in scene 3. Every time the scene is shot, it is given a new take number.

Coverage —Every shot requires a new set up, usually with new lighting and different camera angles. Whenever possible, get your most important key shots first. Then, as time permits, work down your shot list for any remaining shots you still need. Depending on the style you're using to shoot your project, the general rule of production suggests that you cover one or more of the following shots:

- *Establishing shot*: Also called a master shot, it establishes the scene and what's going on in it. It is a wide shot of the whole scene that shows its action as well as the actors' movements and their relationships to each other. The master shot can be intercut with tighter angles like those listed below.

- *Close-up*: A tight shot, usually of an actor's face or an object. It is revealing and intimate, and shows more crucial detail.

- *Single*: A shot of one actor, in close-up, medium shot, or wide shot. When editing from one single shot to another, pay attention to continuity of eye-line.

- *Two-shot*: A scene with two actors in the frame. Three- and four-*shots* have three, and four, actors in the frame, and are useful for variation and cutaways.

- *Over-the-shoulder*: The camera is placed just behind the shoulder of one person and focuses on the person he or she is facing. That person's face is in the frame along with a portion of the listener's shoulder. This shot brings the audience closer to the characters and varies the cutting.

Video monitor — It is vital to have a video monitor on the set. Connected by cable to the camera(s), the monitor shows the DP, director, producer, and other technicians what the camera sees as it's being shot. It can also provide instant playback of what was just shot.

However, spending too much time reviewing each take in playback can slow down the production.

Continuity — The script supervisor — or a competent production assistant in a low-budget production — is a constant presence on the set, checking to make sure that each shot will match up with the shot that comes before it — and after it — in editing. If, for example, an actor puts his hand in his pocket in one shot, his hand must still be in his pocket in the shot that will follow it in editing. Because most projects are shot out of sequence, the script supervisor's notes are a major time-saver for the editor and audio mixer. Continuity notes generally include:

• The shot number and description

• The camera and lens used

• The length of the shot itself

• Comments on the action in the shot

• Comments or notes from the director, producer, and/or DP

Cover shots — Even the most experienced producers and directors get into the editing room, only to realize they're missing an important shot. During production, the script supervisor can avoid this problem by suggesting cover shots, or additional footage. For example, let's examine a dramatic scene in which a man reads a letter out loud to his wife:

• It might start with a wide shot, or master shot, of the whole scene with the two actors, their location, the set around them. Then, the following tighter shots will later match up with this wide shot in editing.

• The camera shoots a close-up of the letter, known as a *cutaway* shot.

• When the wife hears what's in the letter, the camera shoots a *reaction shot* as she listens in shock.

• The man angrily tosses the letter on the coffee table, and the woman reaches for it. Her reaching action is shot as an *insert shot*, with an angle that's lower and with action that is slower than in the original wider shot.

All of these shots are then cut together in the editing process to form a seamless sequence.

Audio pickups — Often there is additional audio that needs to be rerecorded, such as a line of dialogue that was muffled, ambient background noise, or other sound effects. It is easier in the long run to record it right away rather than wait. If you wait the actor may have left the project or the ambient sounds like heavy traffic or children at play may no longer exist.

When each shot on your list has been captured, all the gear is either moved or reset to shoot the next item on the shot list. The camera, lighting angles, and audio are also repositioned.

E. The Equipment Breakdown and Location Wrap

When everyone is happy with the footage, the crew *breaks down*, or disassembles, all the lights, cameras, audio equipment, and whatever else is not needed for the next day's shoot is packed away. On location shoots, the crew removes all tarps, protective coverings, and masking tape and puts items back in their original positions, thoroughly clearing up the location. With this done, the shooting day is over.

> The thing I really need is not more money, or food. It's five more hours in the day.
> —Valerie Walsh, *excerpt from interview in Chapter 11*

On a Human Level . . .

The producer is either the leader of the production team or an integral part of one. You set the model for clear communication, mutual respect, and for occasional human error. Mistakes get made — move past them and avoid making them again. You also must stay healthy. During the stress of production, it can be tempting to drink too much coffee, and forget to eat or sleep. But if you go down, so does the production. Find a balance and enjoy the process.

> Action springs not from thought, but from a readiness for responsibility.
> —Dietrich Bonhoffer

VII. Summary

No matter what your project entails, each shot and each scene is recorded and shot with post-production in mind. No matter how brilliant the scene is by itself, it must be edited with one shot that precedes it and another that follows. The shots must match visually, and the audio must have continuity. Together, they combine to create a narrative flow or story line — regardless of the show's genre. In the next chapter, the post-production process that brings the elements from production into a cohesive form is explored.

VIII. Chapter Review Questions

1. Name five leadership qualities a producer brings into the production process. Describe how each one impacts the project.

2. Discuss the advantages of using a virtual location over a soundstage or location. Create a brief story idea in which virtual locations and backdrops are a key feature.

3. Contrast composite video with component video. Discuss the pros and cons of each.

4. Describe the concept of matching eye-lines or draw an example.

5. What are the three key lights and their positions? Describe their functions, alone and combined, in lighting a scene.

6. Describe the microphone options available for recording production sound. Pose a situation in which each mic is put to its most efficient use.

7. What are the typical problems you might run into in recording useable audio in an exterior location? In a soundstage? How could you solve these problems?

8. What are the strategies you would find valuable to make the audio recording process easier?

9. Describe the role of the script supervisor and the importance of this job during production.

Everything you can imagine is real.

—Picasso

Post-Production: The Final Product

This Chapter's Talking Points

I. The Producer's Role

II. The Editor's Role

III. The Sound Designer's Role

IV. Delivering the Final Product

V. Summary

VI. Chapter Review Questions

I. The Producer's Role

Post-production can be the least understood aspect of the producer's domain. This is where the footage and audio are joined together to create a flowing coherent piece.

Before starting post-production, you want to know who to hire and you want to learn the shortcuts necessary to make post-production more creative and efficient in both the editing and the audio mix. The producer's job is to know as much as possible about everyone *else's* job — what they do, their working style, the tools of their trade, their fees, and the nuances of their art. You want to find the most talented and highly qualified people who can work within the limits of your budget. The more prepared you are when you begin post-production, the faster the process will go.

In producing for TV and video, the producer in most cases will oversee the project from beginning to end, including the entire post-production process. However, a more complex project might require a *post-production supervisor*, who is in essence the producer of post-production. He or she keeps track of all the footage that has been shot as well as all the reels, logs, locations, dubs, and log sheets. Stock footage, archival footage, animation, graphics, and all audio elements like dialogue, background audio, special effects, original and/or stock music, and cue sheets are also overseen by the post-production supervisor. This person works closely with the producer to maintain the vision of the project, and supervises all phases of post-production including editing, mixing, and delivery of the final master to the end user, client, or broadcaster. So whether you are hiring a post-production supervisor or you're the one in charge, the guidelines below can help you through the post-production process.

A. Guidelines

1. *Triple-Check Your Contracts*

The need to legally protect your project continues through post-production. As you compile the many components needed in the edit and mix, be sure that all clearances for music used in the mix, releases for stock footage, and other legal contracts are confirmed in writing.

> When I'm drafting contracts, after I'm finished, I will always go back over it, not just for each word, but I have a checklist, too: did I do this and did I do this? I make sure that I haven't left anything out.
> —J. Stephen Sheppard, *excerpt from interview in Chapter 11*

2. *Spend Money to Save Money*

Let's say that a good friend owns a computer with an editing system, and wants to help you edit your project for free. This sounds good, but you also want your project to act as a calling card and an example of your talents. The equipment may be free, but you may have to reedit if it's not done right the first time. In the long run, you can save both time and money by editing with a seasoned editor on a professional-quality system. Also, editing systems are so inexpensive that it can be cheaper to buy one rather than to rent.

You are looking for an editor who is familiar with the editing system's nuances, who has experience cutting broadcast-standard programs, and who has a keen eye for editing. Most editors and editing facilities have demo reels you can screen to look at editors' work, prior to meeting them in person and taking a tour of the editing facility. When possible, meet with the editor before you start shooting. Ask for ways to make the editing process easier. You will save money and time in post-production when you can:

- Organize your tapes and tape logs

- Screen and log your footage

- Organize editing elements

- Write a paper cut for the edit session

3. *Organizing the Components for the Edit*

A producer can shoot two hours, or twenty hours, of footage for a one-hour program, especially in reality shows or documentaries. This requires an organizational system during the actual shoot that keeps track of what footage exists on what tape numbers. It helps when you label each tape cassette and its box and include:

- The tape, number (Tape 1, Tape 2, etc.)

- The location where it was shot (Studio B, in Central Park, etc.)

- The date of the shoot

- The audio tracks (Track 1 is the lav, Track 2 the boom, etc.)

- The camera it was shot with (Camera 1, Camera 2, etc.) in multi-camera shoots

When labeling your tapes, design an easy system for naming each one. For instance, if you shot in Central Park and used nine tapes, you might label them as CP01, CP02, and so on to CP09. In a studio setting with several cameras, match the camera number with a tape number. Say you're shooting *The Jane Smith Show*. You use two cameras and change the tapes three times. Your first two tapes can be labeled JS0101 (Jane Smith Tape 1, Camera 1), JS0102 (Jane Smith Tape 1, Camera 2), and JS0201 (Jane Smith Tape 2, Camera 1), and so on through the subsequent tapes.

4. *Tape Log*

The producer keeps track of the tapes that have been shot in a *tape log* so that when the time comes to edit, you know where everything you've shot is located. During the editing, for example, you may find that you're missing a shot. The tape log provides a way to find footage and save time. You can find an example of a tape log on the attached CD.

5. *Film-to-Tape*

Any footage shot on film (Super 8, Super 16, 16- or 35-mm) must first be transferred to video before it can be edited in a nonlinear editing (NLE) system. Film-to-tape transfer is a complicated and costly procedure in which the film is converted to video via a *telecine*, also called a *film chain*, that scans each frame and converts them all to a video signal. The production sound is transferred, and the film is color-corrected during the process of transferring it to video. Some producers color-correct all their footage as they transfer it, while other producers prefer to wait until the rough cut is approved, and only correct the footage in the final edit. Possible complications can arise from the difference in frame rates between film (24 fps) and video (30 fps) as well as in audio syncing. If you plan to shoot in film and transfer it to video, discuss the *film-to-tape* process with the editor, and research the resources available on the subject.

6. *Tape-to-Film*

You may have a project that is perfect for a festival, but it only accepts film submissions, not DVD or video. Or you may have produced a documentary or feature, and you're looking for theatrical distribution. Both of these situations require a 35-mm film print of your project. Regardless of whether you shot it in video or film, if you have edited and mixed it in an NLE system, your master can be transferred to a 35-mm film print. However, this process is expensive and could equal your entire post-production budget, so research it carefully. More festivals are now screening with video projection, and the Cineplex down the street is not far behind.

7. *Stock Footage*

Using high-quality stock footage not only saves money, but also adds nuance and production value to your vision. Say, for example, you want an opening establishing shot of a glittering Manhattan nighttime skyline from an airplane. By the time you hire the airplane and pilot, book a camera and operator, pay for the stock, arrange the shooting permits, and pray for good weather, you've spent a small fortune. For considerably less money, you can buy the exact shot you want. Hundreds of stock footage houses around the country license acquired footage shot all over the globe by professional cameramen and -women, and sell the clearance rights to producers. This footage is high-quality and is often shot on either 35-mm film and transferred to video, or on digital or high definition video. The choices of shots seem limitless, covering almost any scene description ranging from field workers in Viet Nam to time-lapse footage of Tokyo at night.

Finding stock footage is relatively simple. Begin by surfing the net for stock footage houses, some examples of which are listed in the attached CD under Web sites. You can view what they offer online or speak with them on the phone. After giving them a list of the footage you want, they will refer you to an online search or send you a sample reel. Then pick the footage you want and negotiate a fee for the rights to use it in your project. The fee depends on several factors. Using the Manhattan skyline footage as an example, if you plan to use this stock footage in a program that will be broadcast by a major network or cable channel, the fee is higher than if you're using it for an educational piece with limited distribution. If it is part of a one-time, nonbroadcast project — a training film for an organization, for example, or an industrial — that fee is more negotiable and usually lower. If you are buying the exclusive rights, the cost is even higher. Other factors that influence the license fee are

• The amount of time (from two years to perpetuity) you want the rights

• The territories (United States or worldwide)

• Any special advertising or promotional uses

• The total number of runs (broadcasts)

You also want to clear any copyrights and trademarks. For example, if you want to feature the Hollywood sign, it is trademarked and must be cleared before it can be used. Stock footage may also require you to obtain releases from any talent or people on screen. Music or narration that is mixed into footage also needs to be researched. You can find more information on legal clearances in Chapter 5.

8. Archival Footage

There are dozens of excellent archival footage houses that research, gather, and distribute footage that has an historical context. Let's say that you're doing a documentary on the history of the Manhattan skyline, and you want to contrast the modern skyline footage you found through a stock footage house with the New York skyline of one hundred years ago. An archival researcher can provide old photographs, etchings, and a range of images shot in 35- or 16-mm film. They can also provide you with still photographs, magazine covers, newsreels, and a range of in-depth material that adds extra texture to your project. The process of finding and buying rights to this historical footage follows a similar process as stock footage, and the pricing scales are negotiated with the same considerations. Often the rights for the images may be available, but the rights for the music under the footage need to be negotiated separately.

9. Public Domain Footage

When the copyright has elapsed on specific footage, it isn't owned by anyone, and it can be used without paying for clearances or royalty fees. This footage is in the *public domain* (PD) and you can use it freely. Many private companies find and resell PD footage, and will charge you fees for research and duplication. If the footage has been shot by the U.S. government, using taxpayers' money, it can also be used without clearances or royalty payments. NASA, for example, offers a collection of libraries available to the public; the only costs are for duplication. The Department of Health and Human Resources and the FBI offer similar libraries.

10. Screen and Log Your Footage

Over the last few years, the use of nonlinear editing systems has revolutionized the post-production process. This is good news for producers who want to be creative while staying within their budget. Because of the ease of NLE, it can be tempting for producers to bring all their tapes into the editing room and screen them as they download, rather than screening them prior to the edit session. This turns the creative process into an expensive administrative swamp that can be time-consuming as well as frustrating for the editor. It can also be expensive to buy or rent the memory storage for all this footage.

A more cost-effective method of preparing for editing is to screen and log your footage before the edit session. From these log notes, you can construct a *paper cut*, or editing storyboard. It's like a shooting script for editing, and it gives your editor a clear outline of what scenes appear in what order, and where each shot can be found on specific tapes. The paper cut lists time code (TC) locations and descriptions of selected edits, as well as notes about graphics and audio, and the order in which footage appears in the script. You'll find a storyboard template in the CD.

Ideally, you want to transfer your footage for screening to VHS or DVD with *matching time code*. This means that the TC on your original footage is exactly the same on your screening cassette. It's called visible time code, also vizcode, or VTC, and it is displayed in a small box on the bottom or top of the screen. As you saw in Chapter 8, TC has eight numbers. For example, 01 03 16 22 is the same as one hour, three minutes, 16 seconds, and 22 frames.

As you screen the footage, you can *log* it by taking notes of each pertinent shot and its TC number. Let's say that you're screening Tape 1. You like a specific shot where the actor picks up a cup of coffee, sees a note on the table, reads it, then angrily throws his cup against a wall. The action starts at 01 03 16 (one hour, three minutes, 16 seconds) and ends ten seconds later (at 01 03 26). Your log notes on this scene might look something like this:

Tape #	TC in	Scene description	TC out
Tape 1	01 03 16 MS	Tom picks up cup, reads note, throws cup	01 03 26

Your tape log details the tape number, the TC numbers for the in-point and the out-point of the scene, the shot's angle (CU, etc.), and a brief description. If you're logging dialogue, either scripted or unscripted, you might type each word verbatim for an exact transcription. Or you can type key words and mark irrelevant sections with an ellipsis (. . .). Often, the tapes are transcribed by a professional transcriber who makes a note of the TC at regular intervals, usually every 30 to 60 seconds.

A number of logging software programs are available such as *The Executive Producer* and *MediaFiler*, along with free programs from Avid and Final Cut Pro. These programs cut down your screening time and provide notes for the editor during the digitizing process, saving download time and easily transferring your logging notes to the NLE along with the footage. Another choice is to screen and log by hand using the simple forms found on the CD such as the Tape Screening Log or the Storyboard.

Footage is just one of several elements in your project. Other elements include the audio, animation, music, and graphics. As you did with your footage, you'll keep a log for every element on a *tape log*, and distribute copies to anyone involved in post-production, such as the post-production supervisor, production assistants, the editor, and the sound designer. Your log sheet might include any of these elements:

1. Studio or location footage (tape numbers, dates, locations, etc.)

2. Stock footage (footage that's been professionally shot for resale, like helicopter shots or time lapse photography)

3. Archival footage (historical footage or photographs)

4. Graphics (opening titles, closing credits, lower thirds)

5. Animation (animated insert segments)

6. Audio tracks (anything recorded separately from the tracks on the footage)

7. Additional audio components (music, stings, needle drops, special effects, ADR)

11. *Write a Paper Cut*

As you develop your skills as a producer, you use a visual and aural vocabulary with its own terminology:

- *Shot*: A single uninterrupted taped segment that is the primary element of a scene.

- *Scene*: A dramatic or comedic piece consisting of one or more shots. Generally, a scene takes place in one time period, involves the same characters, and is in the same setting.

- *Sequence*: A progression of one or more scenes that share the narrative momentum and energy connected by an emotional and narrative energy.

Not every producer has the ability to "visualize" what footage cuts well with other footage. But they know what the primary scenes are and their sequence in the script. Because you have most likely shot your footage out of sequence, include all the reel numbers and TCs onto your paper cut in the order in which they will appear in the final edited product.

The scene earlier in which Tom picks up his coffee cup, sees the note, reads it, and angrily hurls the cup against a wall is paper cut like this:

- The first shot on Tape 1 is a medium shot (MS) of the whole scene — except you will cut out of the scene before Tom throws the cup.

- Cut to a close-up (CU) of the note.

- Cut to his CU reaction shot.

- Cut back into the original MS as he throws the cup.

Although the footage was shot at different times, on different tapes, and maybe at different locations, they all cut together as one smooth sequence. The finished paper cut might look like this:

Tape #	TC in	Scene description	TC out
Tape 1	01 03 16	MS — Tom picks up cup, reads note	01 03 20
Tape 2	03 10 04	CU — the note	03 10 08
Tape 3	02 20 25	CU — Tom's reaction to note	02 20 30
Tape 4	01 03 21	MS — Tom throws coffee cup	01 03 26
Transition (cut, dissolve, wipe, etc.) to next scene			

The ideal editing storyboard could be called an *80/20 paper cut*. This means that you're coming into the edit room with a paper cut that provides notes and details for roughly 80% of your key scenes, cutaways, and the sequence in which they'll appear in the final edited product. The paper cut also includes tape numbers, TC, and descriptions. The extra 20% represents the creative leeway for the editor to take creative and technical chances that enhance the piece.

After you've transferred your footage to VHS or DVD for screening, have screened and logged it, and written a paper cut, you will have new areas on which to focus to prepare for editing and mixing your project.

II. The Editor's Role

An *editor* can be a magician, a consultant, and an effective arbiter of what works and what doesn't. Each editor has his or her own strengths and styles of cutting. One editor might have the perfect style for MTV, while another is adept at cutting a documentary for PBS. One editor might specialize in sports or news, sitcoms, or movies-of-the-week. And then there are those few editors who can cut almost anything.

An experienced editor can take disparate shots and elements and weave them together in a seamless flow. As a creative artist, he or she can "paint" a mood with pacing, place a perspective on the action, and signal conflict or comedy. Technically, the editor can design special effects or transitions between scenes, color-correct the footage, and make sure your project conforms to broadcast standards. Often, the editor can "fix it in post," covering up mistakes or finding solutions to seemingly impossible problems that inevitably pop-up in everyone's project.

A. Working with an Editor

Producers come into an editing room with varying levels of experience in post-production. One producer may have spent hundreds of hours editing and mixing, while another may have only limited exposure or expertise. Some producers don't have the luxury of extra time or the foresight to screen their footage before the edit session, and will give hours of their unscreened footage to the editor, and expect him or her to work miracles without direction.

The producer's role with the editor is highly collaborative. You want to give the editor specific targets for the project, and you also want to create an environment in which the work can get done. For example, when you're in the edit room the editor needs to concentrate, so keep phone calls and distracting conversations to a minimum and discourage people from crowding into the editor's space. When you have creative leeway or enough time, encourage the editor to try new ideas. A simple "thank you" can be augmented with plenty of water, coffee, and food during the edit sessions. The editor is one of the most valuable players on your team.

> One of an editor's golden assets in an edit room is that they were never part of the production process. They weren't shooting the film for four weeks and feeling the "magic" of that process. The war stories the crew told about shooting in the midst of a hurricane or when half the staff came down with food poisoning — they mean nothing to the editor. Editors only see the dailies, and the only "magic" they feel is what comes out of those dailies. If a shot works, they will use it, but if it doesn't, they can easily let it go. The pain, the love, or the cost of any one element means nothing if it doesn't work in the edit. No one thing is more important than the whole of the film.
> —Jeffrey McLaughlin, *excerpt from interview in Chapter 11*

Using today's user-friendly and inexpensive NLE systems, an entire project can be edited on a laptop. You can now build a functional edit room in your bedroom or edit on an airplane. Yet not every producer has the technical or creative skills to be a good editor. You want your project to reflect your vision, and to adhere to all broadcast standards so it can be aired on television and have the technical capacity to be dubbed with no loss of *generations*, or quality. So, how do you find an editor who can satisfy these objectives?

- There are dozens of Web sites and directories that list professional editors, unions, and editing facilities in various regions and cities. You can also look for editing facilities in your local phone book. Visit their Web sites or make an appointment to go to their facility. Meet them, screen the editor's reel, and discuss what you need in editing your project.

- Talk to other producers, directors, and writers about editors they've worked with.

- Call your local television stations who often "hire out" their editors and facilities for outside work. If not, ask if they can recommend local freelance editors.

- Check with local high schools and colleges that have editing equipment for their students. Often, their student editors can be hired for low-budget projects.

B. Working with New Technology

The rapid evolution of post-production technology over the last few years is virtually unprecedented. As it steps into the digital domain, the advances in digital editing and sound design equipment have expanded the producer's horizons. From prime time broadcast to art gallery installations, from educational teaching tools to high-end commercials, today's digital tools are limitless.

Yet the learning curve can be steep, and the many choices, confusing terminology, and conflicting advice can be frustrating for any producer. Every six months new equipment is introduced to the marketplace; a system that is state-of-the-art this year is either upgraded or replaced next year. But there are consistencies in these systems. As you research the right editor for your project, explore the range of digital nonlinear edit (NLE) systems that conform to professional, broadcast-quality standards. These systems work on the same basic principle as editing on film, but with an NLE, pieces of footage can be digitally "spliced" together out of order.

Film editing has always been nonlinear, done with tape and scissors, and its pieces cut and pasted together by hand. Before nonlinear editing, video editing was linear — electronically edited in an "always moving forward" direction. An editor could only start at the beginning and work toward the end because of the nature of electronic recording. The traditional way of editing video has been to edit in the chronological or *lineal order* that shots appeared in the piece.

Now, editing with digital equipment is done in a cut-and-paste mode, just as with film, except it's edited electronically rather than manually. The popular NLE systems like Final Cut Pro, Avid Xpress, Premier Pro, Media Composer, and iMovie all work on similar principles. When you can learn one system, it's simply a matter of nuance and finding the right buttons in the right place on a similar system. Final Cut Pro and Avid are the systems currently used by most professionals. They offer high-quality options for finishing, are consistently updated, and support more plug-ins. Because these systems are now the pervasive editing modes, we'll be concentrating only on this method of editing and its technology.

If there is one downside to editing on NLE systems, it is the tendency to shoot more footage than is really needed, and to make decisions about your footage in the edit room. This one factor can result in spending valuable time deciding between Take 3 and Take 14 in the editing room, rather than prescreening it. This often translates to spending more money than you budgeted.

> I first ask producers for notes and scripts. If I'm lucky, they'll have those, but more and more producers seem to think that editors wave a magic wand over hours worth of stuff, and only the good stuff comes up. I remind them that if we first need to screen, log, and digest the material, and then make an insightful and coherent movie, it's going to take time. For every one hour of footage, it takes at least two or three hours to view, log, and highlight every hour of film. You then need to knock this down into a script with some kind of theme, and only then can you start to edit.
> —Jeffrey McLaughlin, *excerpt from interview in Chapter 11*

1. *Digital versus Analog*

Once a subject for lively debate, the "digital vs. analog" topic is seldom pertinent in today's video world. Outside of BetaCam SP and Hi8, all professional-quality cameras now shoot a digital signal. Many producers still shoot in Beta, because it is a tried-and-true standard. It is also easy to edit; it can be downloaded into an NLE via a component signal, or through a Digibeta with an analog board that can process the analog signal to a component digital path. But not all digital is alike, and Beta can be as efficient as DV. Talk with your DP and editor about your shooting options and how they translate into the editing process.

2. *Compression*

Compression relates to digital video, and simply means that the video signal is compressed to reduce storage and transmission space and costs. Compression techniques involve removing redundant data or data that is less critical to the viewer's eye. The more the digital signal is compressed, the more distorted the image's details. You can see this effect in pirated copies of DVDs when the picture dissolves or fades to black — the sharpness of image disintegrates and the pixels become larger. You can see this same effect on your NLE at a low resolution (low rez).

At what compression rate do you load your video into your NLE? Compression in editing is a decision that depends on the number of hours you have shot and the disk space you have available. You can start at the lowest rate of 1–1, which results in the highest resolution (best quality picture). You can also load in at a low resolution, up to 40–1 (the poorest quality picture). This decision is based on how much storage you have and how much material you're working with. Downloading at 40–1 gets you 40 times more dailies and footage you can access, but the quality suffers. If you download at 1–1 or 2–1, your footage is high resolution (high rez), and doesn't need to be reedited later.

3. *Drop Frame versus Nondrop Frame*

During the shoot, the DP or camera operator might ask if the footage needs to be shot with a TC setting that's either *drop frame* (DF) or *nondrop frame* (NDF) This means that because video runs at 29.97 fps and not 30 fps, *nondrop frame* footage has a .03 frame discrepancy. By the end of a one-hour show, there are several extra seconds to account for. Broadcasters demand an exact program length, so a 60-minute program is usually delivered in DF, because it's exactly 60 minutes long and the show's timings are in real time.

Why work in NDF? If your show doesn't have to be frame-accurate or an exact length for broadcast, it's easier for the editor to work with graphics and match edits in NDF because every frame has a sequential number. Some edit systems encounter problems in dealing with both DF and NDF simultaneously, though with the advent of HD and its different frame rates, most NLE systems can now easily make the necessary adjustments.

C. The Steps in Editing

There are several steps to follow if you are using an NLE system to edit a project.

1. *Download and Store Footage*

Before you begin editing, the footage has to first be transferred, or *downloaded*, into the NLE and *digitized*. The downloaded tapes are digitized in *real time*. For example, it takes 8 hours to digitize 8 hours of footage, so build digitizing time and costs into your budget. As it's being digitized, the editor categorizes the footage with recognizable information — tape numbers and scene descriptions — and stores everything in folders or *bins*. Producers often designate only certain segments or portions of tapes to digitize so as not to waste valuable storage space for footage they won't use. This is an area in which a good logging program is an invaluable tool.

The amount of storage in the NLE is a real consideration if you're dealing with excessive footage, complicated audio components, animation, or graphics. Only a few years ago, a 1 Gigabyte (one billion bytes) hard drive cost $10,000 so it made sense for producers to download their projects in low resolution (low rez), which was poorer quality but needed less storage space, and then *conform* it (the final cut, reedited with high rez footage) later. Now, a similar drive costs under $300, so editors don't always need to edit in low resolution to make their creative decisions. Based on the amount of footage you've shot and the amount of disk space at your disposal, you might not be limited to low rez at all. You can load everything in at high resolution (high rez) and avoid the conform process.

2. FireWire

Initiated by Apple Computer, this process is also called known as IEEE-1394 and is a standard communications protocol for high-speed, short-distance data transfer. Think of it as a transfer pipe that receives and stores data in its native compression/decompression scheme, or *codec*. FireWire theoretically presents itself as the only "lossless" way to digitize footage directly into an NLE. It's considered the most efficient way to load editing components into an NLE. Avid uses this protocol in its Adrenaline series, and Sony has implemented a similar brand, called I LINK. Though FireWire initially worked only with DV, it is now capable of working with uncompressed standard definition video, and with data transfer as high as 65 mps. FireWire allows you to transfer video to and from your hard drive without paying the higher costs of JPEG compression, or buying heavy duty NLE software or banks of RAID-striped hard drives. It also deals well with artifacts.

3. The Rough Cut

After all the footage, audio, and graphic elements have been loaded into the NLE, the editor puts together the first *rough cut*. It forms the core of your finished piece, and reflects all the basic editing decisions. The rough cut changes and evolves over time, but this first cut shapes the project.

Some editors refer to the rough cut as a *radio edit* or an *A-roll edit*. This describes the process of first laying down all the sound bites and making sense of the project's narrative viewpoint. The next step is to make it visually interesting by editing in all the video footage. But each project is unique, and it dictates its own approach to the rough cut. In a music video, the editor first lays the music down and then cuts the footage to synchronize with the musical beats. In some programs, the narration is laid down before the footage is edited in that fits the narration. If the narration hasn't been finalized, you can record whatever script you have on a *scratch track*. This is a preliminary track of narration, read by you or someone else, that helps set the timings and beats for your rough cut. It is replaced later by a professional narration. Regardless of what your particular project calls for, your rough cut shows what works and what doesn't, what shots cut well with other shots, and the total running time (TRT) of this first pass.

4. The Rough Mix

Throughout editing, the editor also works with the audio tracks: separating them, balancing out levels, and keeping track of where everything is in the computer. The editor might do all the rough audio mixes and the final mix, or may only do a rough mix and then give all the tracks to an audio designer in an audio facility for the final mix.

5. The Final Cut

Most projects take time to edit, and the editing process usually requires several rough cuts before they are finalized. When everyone agrees that the final version is ready, the editor makes an *edit decision list (EDL)* that provides exact notes of all the reel numbers, time codes, cuts, and transitions in the rough cut. Finally, the editor reedits or *conforms* the rough cut by matching the original footage in high rez, using the EDL. The final cut is the result of all these decisions that come from fine-tuning, tweaking, shortening or lengthening the piece in editing.

This online finishing stage, also called the *conform*, concentrates on adding any high-end graphics, color corrections, and audio leveling that your project needs. The entire process is known as going from *off-line to online*, and is a system that many seasoned producers follow to save money and maintain their vision.

Editors go into their NLE at 1–1 compression and output the project, saving them hours of redigitizing and conforming. They can also digitize at 2–1, getting twice as much storage space. This works fine in the standard definition world, but with the advent of high definition, editors can use several terabytes (one trillion bytes) of storage to work in a high-rez quality. So for now, the off-line to online process has become the norm in HD editing. However, as disk space gets cheaper and computers speed up, this final conform stage may eventually be phased out.

D. Editing High Definition TV

NLE technology is also expanding rapidly in the areas of editing in high definition. It's a still a work-in-progress, however, and the producer needs to plan ahead to make it a successful process.

The first step is to know what *downconversion* format you want to use. This means that the HD footage is converted to an NTSC (standard definition) tape that can be downloaded into your NLE system. (For example, when your 24P project is downconverted, the video changes from 23.98 fps to 59.94, and the TC changes from 24 to 30 frames.)

Shooting 24 frames in HD can occasionally complicate the editing process. Some producers downconvert the 24 frames to 30-frame DVCam, and then rely on a conversion program to reconvert the 30 frames back to 24 frames for the conform session. Other producers stay in 24 frames, feeding the 24 frames directly into the NLE. Both systems work, yet both come with pros and cons, so talk the process over with your editor before you start the edit process.

Because a mistake can be costly down the line, professionals recommend that projects shot in 1080i and 24P projects be edited in the NTSC video format; it's easier and cheaper at the moment. The standard downconversion formats are DVCam, DVCPro, and Digital Betacam. They all share similar high-quality images, digital audio, and TC capabilities. Other formats like MiniDV and DV aren't recommended because of the problems with embedding TC that exactly matches those of the field tapes. The Beta SP and $\frac{3}{4}''$ formats both have analog audio tracks and lower image quality.

Next, the downconverted footage is digitized into the NLE system. Before you download, clearly mark each reel with a name or number that can be easily read by the computer. Ideally, limit it to 4 to 6 characters so the computer can easily read and distinguish each name. For example, Tape 1 shot in Griffith Park could be named GP01. Also make sure that the TC from your original field tapes is properly downconverted with an exact match.

Although it's easy to import animation, graphics, and computer generated imagery (CGI) into an NLE system, taking these elements into an online session can be tricky. You can either have them created in the final HD resolution, or you can bring them into the online session, render them out to frames, and transfer these to an HD tape. These are then downconverted and treated like all the other elements in your edit.

After you've completed your NLE off-line edit, the editor can export an EDL with all the information needed to conform in the online session. First make a digital cut of your show; send its EDL and the digital cut to the online editing facility in advance of your actual session. Come prepared to the online session with all your original camera reels, graphics files, CGI and effects reels, and any titling or credits information that may be added to your cut. The online editor then assembles the show using the EDL information. Your presence in this phase of editing is critical — the editor isn't familiar with your project and the EDL is only an impersonal list of numbers that may not include transitions, wipes, dissolves, and other important creative details.

You don't have to be an expert in post-production, especially at the beginning. If you're unsure of how to edit your a project, you should feel free to consult the editor who has actually taken a project from start to finish.

E. Styles of Editing

What *is* editing? Essentially, shots and scenes take on specific meanings when they are juxtaposed with other shots. This juxtaposition is editing. It can manipulate time and create drama, tension, action, and comedy. Without editing, you'd only have disconnected pieces of an idea floating in isolation, looking for a connection.

Editing for television follows most of the classic editing guidelines for film that were established by American director D. W. Griffith and Russian directors V. I. Pudovkin and Sergei Eisenstein. They realized a century ago that film possessed its own language and had its own rules for "speaking" that language. They set the standards for editing that are used by virtually all editors today in both television and film.

During the production phase, the producer and director shoot their footage with camera angles and movements that tell a story from a certain vantage point. The editor then takes this footage and — consulting with the producer, editor, and/or the post-production supervisor — makes artistic decisions about how to cut the footage together. Some styles of editing include:

- *Parallel editing*: Two separate yet related events appear to be happening at the same time, as the editor intercuts sequences in which the camera shifts back and forth between one scene and another. Let's say that the story involves a man on death row who is being taken to the execution chamber, while the governor of the state is frantically trying to call the prison warden to save the condemned man. Parallel editing might also reveal a story element of which characters in the preceding shot are unaware. It adds excitement and tension to action.

- *Montage editing*: In this process, footage is cut together using short shots or sequences to represent action, ideas, or to condense a series of events. The montage usually relies on close-ups, dissolves, frequent cuts, and even jump cuts to suggest a specific idea. For example, a single mother moves to a small town with her child. A montage might show them happily moving into their new home, shopping for groceries, unpacking boxes, hanging clothes in the closet, and snuggling in bed on their first night together — all this in about a minute. This montage effect gives the viewer a lot of information in minimal screen time.

- *Seamless editing*: This style of editing is used in many dramatic series, some sitcoms, and in feature films. The viewer is unaware of the editing because it is unobtrusive except for special dramatic shots. It supports the narrative and doesn't distract with effects. The characters are the focus, and the cuts are motivated by the story's events. Seamless editing motivates the realism of the story, and traditionally uses longer takes, match cuts rather than jump cuts, and sound that can act as a bridge between scenes.

- *Quick cut editing*: This relatively new form of editing is highly effective in music videos, promos, commercials, childrens' television, and in programs on fashion, lifestyle, and youth culture. It uses lots of fast cuts, jump cuts, montages, and special effects.

F. Techniques in Editing

An editor looks at the footage with the producer and strings the shots together to form the piece using a variety of techniques to get from one shot to the next. These techniques include:

- *Cut*: A quick change of one shot — with one viewpoint or location — to another. There is always a reason to use a cut rather than a slower transition like a dissolve or wipe. On most TV shows there is a cut every 5 to 9 seconds. A cut can compress time, change the scene or point of view, or emphasize an image or an idea. Most cuts are usually made on an action, like a door slamming or a slap to the face.

- *Match cut*: A cut between two different angles of the same movement or action in which the change appears to be one smooth action.

- *Jump cut*: Two similar angles of the same picture cut together, such as two close-up shots of the same actor. This style of editing can make a dramatic point, but it can also signal poor editing and continuity.

- *Cutaway*: A shot that is edited to act as a bridge between two other shots of the same action. For example, an actor may look off to the distance; a cutaway shows what the actor sees. A cutaway also helps to avoid awkward jumps in time, place, or viewpoint, and can shorten the passing of time.

- *Reaction shot*: A shot in which an actor responds to something that has just occurred.

- *Insert shot*: A close-up shot that is edited into the larger context and provides an important detail of the scene. An actor, for example, reads a sign on the door. An insert of a close-up on the sign itself is then inserted into the edit.

G. Editing Pace and Rhythm

The genre of your show and the footage you have shot both dictate the editing pace and rhythm. For example, an editor can start with longer cuts, then make more frequent cuts that surprise the viewer or build suspense. This rhythm can create excitement, romance, and even comedy.

H. Editing to Manipulate Time

Few television shows are broadcast in real time. What the viewer sees is known as *screen time*, a period of time in which events are happening on screen: an hour, a day, or a much longer time span. There are several devices that an editor can use to give the viewer an impression of compressed time or time that has passed or is passing.

- *Compressed time*: The condensing of long periods of time, is traditionally achieved by using long dissolves or fades, as well as cuts to close-ups, reaction shots, cutaways, montages, and parallel situations. Our experiences as a viewer can then fill in gaps of time.

- *Simultaneous time*: Parallel editing, or *cross-cutting*, shifts the viewer's attention to two or more events that are happening at the same time. The editor can build split screens with several images on the screen at once, or can simply cut back and forth from one event to another. When the stories eventually converge, the passage of time stops.

- *Long take*: This one uninterrupted shot lasts for a longer period of time than usual. The lack of any editing interruptions gives a scene the feeling of time passing more slowly.

- *Slow motion (slo-mo)*: A shot that is moving at a normal speed and then slowed down. This can emphasize a dramatic moment, make an action easier to see at slower speed, or create an effect that is strange or eerie.

- *Fast motion*: A shot that is taking place at a normal speed that the editor speeds up. This effect can add a layer of humor to familiar action or can create the thrill of speed.

- *Reverse motion*: By taking the action and running it backwards, the editor creates a sense of comedy or magic. Reverse motion can also help to explain action in a scene or act as a flashback in time or action.

- *Instant replay*: Most commonly used in sports or news, a specific play from the game or news event is repeated and replayed, usually in slo-mo.

- *Freeze-frame*: The editor finds a specific frame from the video and holds on it or freezes it. This effect abruptly halts the action for specific narrative effects. A freeze frame can also create the look of a still photo.

- *Flashback*: A break in the story in which the viewer is taken back in time. The flashback is usually indicated by a dissolve or when the camera intentionally loses focus.

> I usually go a little crazy in the edit room. But crazy in a good way. I like a lot of frenetic editing — a lot of music — a lot of cuts. I grew up watching MTV, so I'm used to seeing things at that pace. But many other news programs and producers don't see the need for it. It's a judgment call. What's important is the content. Jane Pauley once told me, "too much whipped cream spoils the cake."
> —Matthew Lombardi, *excerpt from interview on Chapter 11*

I. Editing Transitions

A simple cut is a transition from one shot to the next — it's abrupt and quick. Some storylines require another kind of transition from one shot or scene to another that signals the movement of going from one idea to another, moving from one location to the next, or one action that changes to another. These transitions can be achieved in the editing by using any of the following transition devices:

- *Dissolve*: When one image begins to disappear gradually and another image appears and overlaps it. Dissolves can be quick (5 frames, or $\frac{1}{6}$ of a second), or they can be slow and deliberate (20 to 60 frames). Both signal a change in mood or action.

- *Fade outs and fade ins*: There are two kinds of fades. A fade out is when an image fades slowly *out* into a blank black frame signaling either a gradual transition or an ending. A fade in is when an image fades *in* from a black frame introducing a scene. A fade out or fade in can also be effective from a white blank frame rather than a black one; like a dissolve, this editing transition also works to show time passing or to create a special "look."

- *Wipe*: An optical effect that marks the transition from one shot or one scene to another one that *wipes* it off the screen. There are dozens of wipes available in editing systems, though a professional editor uses only a few of them, judiciously. Examples of wipes include a page wipe, a circle wipe, sliding an image from right to left or vice versa, and breaking an image into thousands of tiny pixels. A wipe can be very effective, or it can be an awkward distraction. Because a viewer's attention is drawn to wipes, they're used sparingly; overuse of wipes can be the mark of an amateur.

- *Split screen*: The screen is divided into boxes or parts each has its own shot and action that connect the story. The boxes might also show different angles of the same image, or can contrast one action with another. It works as a kind of montage, telling a story more quickly.

The split-screen device can be done cleverly, though too many moving images can also strain the viewer's attention span.

- *Overlays*: Two or more images superimposed over one another, creating a variety of effects that can work as a transition from one idea to the next.

J. Graphics, Animation, and Plug-Ins

Most programs include graphic elements of some kind. These graphics can be a simple show title and closing credits, or they can be complicated animation sequences and special effects within the program itself. Graphics can be generated in the edit session with programs like After Effects and Photoshop, or might be created by artistic designers in a graphics design facility. Graphics, however, can be expensive, and usually require extra consideration in your budget. Below are a few examples of graphics you might use in your project:

- *Text*: Almost every show has opening titles (including the name of the show) and a limited list of the crew (such as the producer, writer, director, etc.) that are known as *opening credits*. Titles that appear at the end of the show are called *closing credits*, and they list the names and roles or positions on the production as well as other detailed production information. Words that slide under someone on screen and spell out a name, location, or profession are called *lower thirds* because they're generally inserted in the lower-third portion of the screen.

  The electronic text is known generically as *chyron*, originally the name of a company that for years was the only professional system that could output high-resolution graphics. Now, chyron can be generated by most editing software programs. The overall impression that the text conveys is determined by its size, color, font, and general style. The text can be digitally imported onto the picture with various speed, rhythms, and movement and from any angle — say, from one side of the screen to another. The graphics give the viewer an impression of the tone and pace of the show, and when combined with music, text can create a unique style for your piece.

  Opening and closing credits might be superimposed over a scene from the show, or on top of stills, background animation, or simple black. Some projects require subtitles for foreign languages or close captioning for the hearing-impaired. As the producer, you're responsible for double-checking all names, spellings, and legal or contractual information for the lower-thirds and final end credits

- *Animation*: Simple animation can be created easily and cheaply by using software like Flash and After Effects. More complex animation is created by an animation designer who uses storyboards and narration, and manages an impressive crew of people who draw, color, and edit animated sequences.

- *Motion control camera*: Special computer-controlled cameras that shoot a variety of flat art like old newspapers, artwork, and photos. They are sometimes called *title cameras*. They are designed to pinpoint detail and to create a sense of motion for otherwise static material with zooms, pans, and other camera moves.

- *Design elements*: Some project genres — documentaries, news shows, commercials, educational, and corporate industrials — depend on the use of various design elements to add depth and information to the content. These elements include logos, maps, diagrams, charts, and graphs, as well as historical photographs, still shots, and illustrations.

- *The look of film*: Falling loosely into the graphics realm, Filmlook is a post-production process that gives video the appearance of film. It closely mirrors the color levels, contrasts, saturation, and grain patterns of film at a fraction of the cost and time of film.

- *Color-correction*: The process of reducing or boosting color or brightness levels. This can be done by using color-correcting tools like the Flame or After Effects.

- *Retouching*: This plug-in process offers a gamut of tricks that can enhance an image, like "erasing" a boom dangling into the shot or a wire holding up a prop. However, if it's complex, it can be costly.

- *Compositing*: Two or more images are combined, layered, or superimposed in the composite plug-in process.

- *Rotoscoping*: Frame-by-frame manipulation of an image, either adding or removing a graphic component. Human action can be rotoscoped or a blemish erased from a celebrity's face with this plug-in process.

The editing process is vital to the ultimate success of your project. It is aesthetic, intuitive, and technically challenging. But visuals are only one half of the picture. The second half is the audio with its layers of nuance and possibilities.

> That's all the technical stuff. But the most important thing is that you really have to have a feel for the music and the artist, and what's going on, and creatively pull all this stuff together. The creative part is really why I'm hired and what you need from the head person pulling this all together [though] as a producer, you also have to be aware of all this technical stuff.
>
> —Stephen Reed, *excerpt from interview in Chapter 11*

III. The Sound Designer's Role

The sound designer, like the editor, can perform small miracles by manipulating audio to create an impact on the viewer. The sound designer adds another dimension to your vision by raising or lowering levels of dialogue or ambient sounds, removing distracting background hums, and adding the right musical elements. His expertise lends a higher production quality to your finished project.

In a less complex project, the video editor can deal with all the audio requirements and components in the edit session. However, some projects have more complicated audio elements and needs an audio facility for additional work and refining. Here, the *audio mixer*, sometimes called the sound editor or sound designer, takes over. An audio facility might be a simple, room-sized studio with one or two sound editors who work on audio equipment that synchronizes TC and computers and charge $100 to 200 an hour. It could also be an elaborate, theater-sized studio with several audio mixers and assistants, extensive equipment, and a set up that could cost up to $3,000 an hour. So before you book time in an audio facility, discuss your project's audio needs and their possible costs.

The sound designer works with two contrasting "qualities" of sound (direct and studio), and approaches them differently, both aesthetically and technically:

- *Direct sound*: Live sound. This is recorded on location, and sounds fresh, spontaneous, and authentic, though it may not be acoustically ideal.

- *Studio sound*: Sound recorded in the studio. This method improves the sound quality, and eliminates unwanted background noise, or *ambient sound*, and can then be mixed with live sound.

A. Working with the Sound Designer

As the producer, you want to work closely with the sound designer. Supply the necessary audio elements and logs, then discuss the final cut of your piece. Offer your ideas and ask for suggestions. In the first stages of an audio mix session, you and the audio crew sit in a *spotting session* during which you rewind and review each area of your project that needs music and effects for dramatic or comedic tension. In this session you're listening for variations in sound levels, for hums and hisses, and anything else that wasn't caught in the rough mix. The sound designer can mix tracks, smooth out dialogue, equalize levels and intensity of sound, and add and layer other elements like music and effects that all contribute depth to the project.

The spotting process takes time. So does the mixing, or *sweetening*. You're paying for each minute, so discuss with the audio facility how much time you will need to book. Often, an audio facility is willing to negotiate a flat fee for the whole job. You may have only booked six hours but the actual mix ran ten; it not only cost you more money but it placed a real strain on the facility — they may have booked the studio for another job after your estimated six hours was scheduled to end.

Working with the sound editor is much more effective if you can:

- *Be prepared*: When possible, send a rough cut of the project to the sound editor before the mix session. Come prepared to the mix with a show run-down that lists important audio-related details like transitions and music. Provide a *music cue sheet* that lists all the music selections' titles, the names of the composers and performing rights society affiliation, names of the recording artists, the length and timing of each cue, the name and address of the copyright owner(s) for each sound recording and musical composition, and the name and address of the publisher and company controlling the recording. You'll find an example of this on the CD included in this book.

- *Be patient*: At the beginning of the mix, the sound editor needs to do several things before the actual mix can begin, including separating the audio elements, patching them into the console, adjusting the gear, and finally, carefully listening to everything. Be patient during this stage and don't put pressure on the process.

- *Be quiet*: Although you may have worked with these audio tracks for days in the editing room, it is the first time the sound editor has heard them. Keep your conversations, phone calls, and interruptions to a minimum.

- *Be realistic*: Your mix may have a strong clarity in the audio mixing room because the speakers are professional quality, balanced, and the acoustics are ideal. But most television and video projects end up being played on TV sets or VHS monitors with mediocre speakers. Many of the subtler sound effects you could spend hours mixing may never be heard, so listen to the mix on small speakers that simulate the sound that the end user will hear.

B. The Technology Behind Mixing the Audio

The digital revolution has provided a wealth of creative and technical opportunities for the producer. Images and sound can interact in new and dynamic ways that were previously difficult to achieve — if not impossible. Digital sound offers an unparalleled clarity of sound. There is no loss of quality when dubbed, and because digital requires less storage space than video, it doesn't need compression. By editing sound in the NLE domain, the audio mixer can work freely with sound in the same way an editor can play with visuals: sound elements can be cut, copied, pasted, looped, or altered. Digital audio is easily labeled and stored, making it more efficient to keep audio in sync and to slide it around when needed. Most sound tracks are now prepared on a multitrack digital storage system. The popular professional options include:

- DA88: A digital 8-track tape

- DAW (digital audio workstation): Programs such as Pro Tools.

- Digital multitracks: Programs include DASH 3324 or 3348.

- Analog multitracks: 24-track Dolby SR or A.

Often the editor can handle the entire audio mix in the NLE system. In other situations where the mix is more complex, the picture is first *locked*, or finalized, and then the audio tracks are exported, usually to a *DAW*. The tracks are either married to the video or are separate. In the DAW, for example, the sound designer uses software such as Pro Tools and digital storage techniques to focus on specific tracks; clean up audio problems; and record and add narration, music and special effects (*M&E*), and dialogue. This process gives the sound editor an impressive range of options: moving the tracks forward and backward, looping music, and extending dialogue and effects. Finally, when everyone's satisfied with the audio, the track is ready for a *layback* where the final audio mix track is married to the picture using TC. The piece can be delivered in stereo, mono, 5.1, or in all versions.

In high-definition or DVD projects, the audio can work well for a 5.1 audio system sound mix. This gives you five full channels — left, center, right, right rear, and left rear — plus one low frequency effects channel. The result is an impressive clarity and fullness of sound, which is one of the many distinctions that 5.1 audio lends to a final product.

C. Components in Sound Design

Just as visual components are edited together, audio elements are mixed together to create new layers of sound. In larger, more complicated audio mixes, each component listed below might be supervised by an expert who specializes in that specific area. The sound designer works with any or all of these components.

- Dialogue (DX)

- Sound effects (SFX)

- Automatic dialogue replacement (ADR)

- Voice-over (VO) or narration

- Foley

- Music

1. Dialogue

Words spoken between characters or actors is called dialogue. Sometimes it's recorded with background ambient sound, although it is usually recorded in isolation from other audio. Dialogue is usually the main audio element.

2. Sound Effects

On a set or on location, any background sounds that surround the dialogue are recorded separately on another mic. These include blowing wind, singing birds, insects or tree frogs, water lapping on shore, traffic, children playing, glasses clinking, and so on. These existing effects are known as *wild sounds*, or recorded sounds that will later be synchronized to the footage. If the sounds don't exist on that location, the sound editor can search through the range of prerecorded sound effects available from a sound effects library. These options range from a door slam to the howl of a monkey. Producers often buy libraries of sound effects and stock music that offer thousands of options and are usually royalty-free.

3. *Automatic Dialogue Replacement (ADR) or Dubbed Dialogue*

After all the scenes have been shot, actors often need to rerecord lines of dialogue or add a line written after the shoot. In the recording studio, actors read their lines, keeping them in sync with their on-screen lip movements. Another option is to record new lines that will be mixed into the program later, either over a cutaway or in a long shot if their lips don't match the new lines. Actors might also read a script in a different language that is later dubbed over the original track. Often, a *loop group* of people is brought into an ADR session to create crowd sounds like background conversations, laughter, mumblings, or yelling that will be mixed into the dialogue. This area of ADR is called *wallah*, which is intentionally unintelligible so audible words won't intrude on the dialogue.

4. *Voice-Over (Narration)*

The narrator who reads a script or commentary adds another layer to the audio. *Narration* can introduce a theme or link elements of a story together. It adds extra information with an air of authority, and helps interpret ideas or images for the viewer. Often, an on-camera character speaks over the picture in the first person as though she is directly speaking to the viewer. A minor character can tell the story in the third person, or an unidentified narrator who is not on camera can distance the viewer from the image by adding an objective voice to the story. Narration is generally recorded in a separate audio session and mixed in later over the picture. *Voice-over* can be dialogue that is originally shot on-camera and later played over another picture. For instance, we see a two-shot of a mother who is reading aloud to her child. That shot cuts to a CU of the child's face while the mother's audio continues over the picture. Her audio is the voice-over; on a script, it is written as 'VO.'

5. *Foley*

Usually *Foley* is described as the sounds of an actor's movements — hands clapping, rustling clothing, a kiss, quiet footsteps, or a fistfight. All these sounds can be created by the Foley artist who uses audio props, tools, hands and feet, and other objects and devices to create the right sound effect. They're recorded separately in an audio facility, often in sync with the action, and then mixed with other sound elements.

6. *Music*

Original — Original music is composed specifically for a project, and includes themes for the opening and closing, and/or for the body of the show; its emotional direction can highlight the action, characters, and their relationships. The composer is familiar with the creative and technical process, and either hires the musicians or creates the music alone or with a partner. A composer can use computer language known as musical instrument digital interface (MIDI). It is capable of simulating a range of music from a single guitar to an entire orchestra. The final score can go straight from the computer into the mix.

Stock — This is music that has been specifically composed and recorded to be available for multiple uses. The composers use audio sampling and composition software and sophisticated equipment to create vast libraries of engaging and effective music that is both versatile and inexpensive. Stock music is a creative alternative used in every genre from corporate videos, documentaries, news, and commercials, to talk shows, sitcoms, and even drama. It's less expensive then hiring a composer, and the negotiated rights can be either exclusive or shared, depending on your budget and the end use. Stock music houses can be researched and located by an online search, and many now offer samplings that can be downloaded via the Internet.

Prerecorded — The source of this music could range from a popular song to an obscure CD, but a strong sound track adds an extra appeal to your project. Regardless of the source, you'll first need to clear all music rights, a time-consuming and expensive process that is reviewed in Chapter 5.

7. *Music Cue Sheet*

Regardless of where your music comes from, you'll make a *music cue sheet* that lists every piece of music, its source, its length, and who holds the rights to it. An example of a cue sheet can be found on the CD.

> Simple silence in the right place can be as effective as music or effects. Contrasting an image with silence heightens suspense, freezes time, pulls the viewer into a character's reality, and alters the viewer's expectations.

D. Stylistic Uses of Sound

In addition to creating a clear audio audible track for your project, manipulation of sound can create stylistic impressions for the viewer. Here are a few classic examples.

- *Sound bridge*: Audio elements — dialogue, sound effects, music, and narration — can act as a transition between one shot (or scene) to the next.

- *Selective sound*: Lowering some sounds in a scene, and raising others, can focus the viewer on an aspect of the story, such as heavy breathing or quiet footsteps.

- *Overlapped dialogue*: In natural speech patterns, people tend to speak over one another and interrupt. Yet dialogue is usually recorded on separate tracks without this overlap. The sound editor can re-create this authentic-sounding effect in the mix, and can also separate dialogue tracks that are too close together. Conversations between several people, like those in two different groups, are often recorded on separate tracks so they can be woven together in the mix for a natural sound.

E. The Steps in Mixing Audio

During your video edit session, the editor separates the dialogue, music, effects, and other audio elements onto various tracks or channels. Depending on the complexity of your project, either the video editor has already mixed the project, or the mix needs to be completed in a special audio facility. During the mixing all the separate audio elements are blended together into a final mix track that is then "married" to the picture and locked in.

F. The Final Cut

Before the audio mix begins, be sure that all the video and audio edits have been agreed upon and won't require any further changes. Revisions after the picture is locked can mean costly remixes. Sound editors take varying routes in mixing, and each has a unique style of approaching the process. Depending on the complexity and genre of the project, any or all of the following components are part of an audio mix.

- *Dialogue*: All dialogue is cleaned up and extra sound effects or extraneous noise are either deleted or moved to separate effects tracks. Any ADR, narration, or voice-overs are also laid onto their own tracks.

- *Special effects*: Any special effects tracks — wild sound, ambience, prerecorded effects, and Foley — are separated, cleaned up, and each put onto its own channel. Ideally, there is room tone from each location that can fill in any gaps in the audio.

- *Music tracks*: The music is generally the last element that is mixed into the audio. All the musical tracks are separated and divided into two categories: *source music* (music the characters or actors hear on screen, like a car radio) or *underscore music* (music that only the audience hears, like an opening theme).

- *5.1 audio*: 5.1 refers to the positions in a five-speaker set up in which each speaker is placed to the right, center, left, right rear, and left rear of the TV set. This kind of mixing is also called AC3 and Dolby Digital, and is prominent in DVDs, theatrically released films using SDDS and DTS systems, and in some TV broadcasts. 5.1 audio requires a specially equipped television set to hear it at home. To achieve a full 5.1 sound mix, the audio is synchronized and laid off onto the field tapes that have been downconverted to 29.97, taken into editing, and then transferred as open media format (OMF) files into the audio mix. Here, the elements are synced up, mixed, and sweetened to a downconvert of the assembled HD master that can be used for HD distribution or converted to standard definition. However, because each of the five channels delivers sound to a specific spatial position, extra time is needed in the audio sessions to deliver a multichannel mix that works in this medium.

IV. Delivering the Final Product

As the producer, you want to deliver a project with the highest quality possible. It may be broadcast on a network, sold to a distributor, or used for training and education purposes. All of these venues require broadcast-quality work that adheres to certain technical standards, which make it possible to dub, copy, and transfer to DVD or other formats without losing quality. Most clients are very specific about what they expect as a *deliverable*, or final product. Deliverables are generally part of your overall contract with a client, so you want to find out exactly what their expectations and specifications are. Ask for them in writing so there are no mistakes. The most common requirements for deliverables include:

- *Video format*: If your project is being broadcast, it is usually evaluated by a station engineer to make sure it meets broadcast standards. Acceptable video formats for air include most projects in DV, DigiBeta, Beta SP, $\frac{3}{4}''$, $1''$, and D-3. If it's being dubbed, the dub house has technical specifications, too. You may be asked to also provide a *clean* copy of the show that has no text superimposed on it.

- *Audio format*: This might include separate mono mixes and stereo mixes, or a 5.1 mix, an M&E mix, special tracking, levels that are constant or undipped, and even one mix in English and another in a different language.

- *Length*: The required program length can be quite specific. For example, some public television stations set a standard half-hour length at 26:46 minutes, and a one-hour show at 56:46 minutes. PBS show lengths are 6 seconds less to accommodate a PBS logo. Commercial stations may require a half-hour show to be 22 minutes, while premium and cable channels are less demanding. Most nonbroadcast projects are more flexible.

- *Dubbing*: Depending on the client's requirements, you may be responsible for making *protection copies*, which are exact copies of your final master. These serve as backups in case of damages or loss in shipping. You might also need to provide VHS or DVD copies of the project to the client. The amount of copies and their format should be spelled out in your contract, as should any special labeling or packaging and related shipping costs.

- *Abridged versions*: You may need to provide an edited version of your project in which any nudity, violence, or offensive language has been removed or "bleeped out." This version can be required by airlines, certain broadcasters, and foreign distributors.

- *Subtitling*: Written text under a picture that translates only those words being spoken on screen from one language into another; for example, the French translation of an American production. However, song lyrics or sounds are seldom subtitled.

- *Closed captioning*: Also called *close captions*, this method of supplying visible text under a broadcast picture is mandated by law to be built into all American TV sets sold after 1993. These sets are designed with a special decoding chip that translates all the audio on the screen into text, such as spoken dialogue and unseen sounds like a dog bark or a knock at the door. Especially designed for the hearing impaired, closed captioning is also useful in loud public places, when learning a language, and when the dialogue isn't clear. The text usually appears in white letters in a black box at the bottom or top of the screen. It is decoded in the TV set or with a special decoder box attached to the set.

All of the above deliverables are those most commonly required in television programs or video projects. They should be clearly stated in all contract negotiations and included in your post-production budget.

> Be in control, but allow for creativity and open up your budget for that extra time. As a producer, your golden rule is to always be prepared. You are in a creative business, so sometimes even the best preparation is not enough. At that point look to the future and learn from your mistakes.
>
> —Jeffrey McLaughlin, *excerpt from interview in Chapter 11*

On a Human Level . . .

Finishing the post-production process is a kind of triumph in its own right, signaling the project's completion and the collaboration of everyone involved.

> There are no passengers on spaceship earth. We are all crew.
>
> —Marshall McLuhan

V. Summary

At this stage, you may well have a tangible product you can see on the screen. You have delivered all the final dubs to the client, and said goodbye to the editor and audio mixer. But your project isn't finished. As you'll see in Chapter 10, there are more details to wrap up, as well as guidelines for getting exposure for your project, and for yourself.

VI. Chapter Review Questions

1. What is the producer's role in post-production? How is it different from that of the post-production supervisor?

2. Name four important legal documents that are essential to check prior to the post-production process.

3. Why is time code so important in the editing and mixing of a project?

4. Describe the uses and the differences between stock footage, archival footage, and footage that is public domain.

5. What can you do as a producer to prepare for the edit session? For the audio mix?

6. What would you look for in hiring an editor? How could you find one in your area?

7. Compare an NLE system with linear film editing.

8. What audio elements are needed in mixing most projects?

9. Briefly describe the audio mixing process.

10. Name three deliverables that are required in most contracts.

Life shrinks or expands in proportion to one's courage.

—Anais Nin

CHAPTER 10

It's a Wrap!
Then, Next Steps

This Chapter's Talking Points

I. It's a Wrap!

II. Professional Next Steps

III. Festivals

IV. Grants

V. Publicity

VI. Starting Your Own Production Company

VII. Summary

VIII. Chapter Review Questions

I. It's a Wrap!

After all the stages of post-production have been completed, your next step is to *wrap the project* and tie up all the loose ends. There are dozens of details to clear up. Some can be fun, many are tedious, but they all add up to a list of finalized elements that help your project succeed as well as mark you as a producer who gets things done. These steps can include any or all of the following:

- *Final budget and billings*: When all the final bills have come in, you want to review each one for accuracy. Clients can make mistakes, and when they do, it's usually in their favor. Check your bills against your purchase orders and budget, and compare your original estimated budget with what you have actually spent on the project. As discussed in Chapter 4, the estimates can be different from the actuals.

- *Petty cash and receipts*: This area of expenses is often underestimated, throwing your budget off target. If, for example, you've doled out $1,000 of petty cash, you want to have $1,000 worth of matching receipts.

- *The wrap party*: Your entire team has dedicated considerable time and energy to your project. You can say thank you by throwing them a great wrap party. Usually it's informal,

167

and only the cast and crew is invited. It can be held at a restaurant, a bar, on set, you can have it elegantly catered, or serve beer and pizza. Whatever you choose, it is money well spent when you can show your team how valuable they are.

- *Complimentary copies*: A surprising number of professionals seldom see their finished work or their name in the credits. It shows professional courtesy when you send copies of the final product to the cast and crew. If it is a drain on your budget, make sure that at least the key department heads and primary talent each receives a personal copy.

- *A screening party*: Unlike a wrap party, this event is more formal and carefully planned. It is a premiere of your project for the press, clients, top talent, and potential investors, buyers, or distributors. Generally, you rent a screening room or theater and distribute a press kit (see Section II) to attendees. The project may be introduced by you or another project representative and then screened. Usually wine and cheese is served afterward. A screening party can be a great opportunity to mingle with the press and potential buyers.

- *Thank-you notes*: Other than money, nothing goes farther than a personal "thank you." Send thank-you notes to the cast and crew, and the client or investors, as well as editing and audio facilities, locations, and others who may have helped you in the project.

- *Dubs*: In addition to making complimentary copies, you might want to have additional dubs made of your project on VHS or DVD to send to clients, or to potential buyers, distributors, or investors. Dubs can be expensive because they require copying, labeling, packing, and shipping. Your editing facility may be equipped to make dubs for you, or in some cases, you can burn DVD copies in your computer. Keep a log of who has been sent a dub and the date it was shipped so that you can follow up later.

- *Tape storage*: After the project has wrapped, all the elements need to be stored. Your original footage and masters, the graphics, music elements, dubs, and other material must be organized and delivered to a storage area that is safe and dry. Your editing facility may have library space to rent, or check into local storage warehouses.

- *Update your production book*: The binder in which you've kept all your notes is a valuable tool for future projects. As you are wrapping the project, go through your production book (refer back to Chapter 4) and update any notes, contact information, contracts, and budgets while they are fresh in your mind.

II. Professional Next Steps

Seasoned and experienced producers are no different from a motivated first-timer — they all take advantage of a few simple tricks of the trade to build and expand their careers. They also realize that no matter what project they are working on now, it will eventually be over, and they'll be looking for their next job. As a producer of any kind of TV or video project, you want people to know about you and the quality of your work. Listed below are just a few directions you can take to reach these objectives:

A. Create a Resume

There are dozens of resume formats and templates that you can use for your own resume. One resume might be a formal academic curriculum vitae (CV), while another might have a more casual and personal approach. Whatever style you choose, your resume ultimately reflects you both professionally and personally. In the television industry, "real-world" experiences are a plus, so include any internships, jobs, and production work you've done in television, no matter how insignificant it seems to you. Mention skills such as fluency in a foreign language, your talents in computer graphics, skateboarding, or singing — aspects of your uniqueness that make you stand out can often be valuable to a potential employer.

You want your resume to look professional. Use a simple 12-point font, allow for white space so the information isn't crowded, print it with a good printer, and use quality, non-colored $8\frac{1}{2} \times 11$ paper. Print only on one side. Be brief and use action verbs for impact. Limit any personal information, don't include your salary history or requirements, and mention that you have references available if needed. Most software word processing programs feature templates for resumes, and the Internet offers hundreds of sites that offer examples and constructive advice.

B. Build a Demo Reel

The purpose of a demo reel is to reflect your professional abilities, your creativity, and your technical know-how. Each producer's demo reel is unique, because it reflects his or her specific vision and talent. The demo reel contains short clips and excerpts of your best work. They can be edited to a music track with quick cuts, or clips strung together with special effects and wipes. Because most people won't view more than 3 to 4 minutes, put your best work at the beginning and at the end. Be objective about your choices. A demo reel should open and close with graphics that include your name and contact information.

C. Make a Short

Your long-range goal may be to produce a dramatic series or a two-hour documentary special, but in the meantime start by producing a short. Usually 5 to 30 minutes long, a short is easier to conceptualize and produce, to raise funds for, and to enlist people's help for production and post-production. A good short can be an excellent calling card that can be entered in festivals, shown to potential clients, or broadcast on channels that showcase shorts in their programming. Some of the premium channels, like HBO and Showtime, often air short pieces called *interstitials* in between their regularly scheduled programs to fill the time gaps.

TOP TEN

Top Ten Helpful Hints for Creating a Short Film in Both Narrative and Unscripted Formats:

1. Avoid the overuse of voice-over narration to carry your vision. Think about narration as a means to introduce your story, or express salient points, but do not allow the focus of your project to be the voice-over.
2. The first few minutes of your project are integral in creating the tone. Think about your opening very carefully, and stay away from traditional and oversaturated openings, such as "alarm-goes-off-character-wakes-up" or "pan-across-a-mantle-of-photographs," for example.
3. Consider the running time of your project while it is still in the concept stage and have a clear idea of content versus running time. The longer your project, the stronger your story should be. Remember, it's all about the story, regardless of whether it is narrative or documentary.

4. Particularly with documentary projects, think about your story progression. You still should have an idea where the film is "going." Twenty minutes of talking heads interspersed with archive footage does not a documentary make. What is your viewer going to learn/experience by the end of the film and how do we get there?

5. Montage sequences serve a very specific purpose — to move the story ahead in an expedient manner. Regurgitating previously viewed shots simply for the sake of putting them to music is not in your best interest, and detracts from the overall impact of the film.

6. Speaking of music, the use of songs should not undermine the visuals, but enhance them. Too many filmmakers who grew up as part of the MTV generation cavalierly use song lyrics to express their vision. This is not a music video.

7. Your main credit sequence should not imitate a feature film. A ten-minute short with a two-minute main credit sequence is unnecessary. Give "credit where credit is due" in the end credits! If you produce a lavish opening credit sequence, make sure it matches the style of the film, and does not jar the viewer when it goes from credits to first shot.

8. The one-character documentary has its own set of challenges. A producer may think someone's life is unique by the hurdles he/she has overcome or something in his/her life that warrants capturing the experience, but others should as well. Before you produce a film about a friend or relative, keep your audience (and objectivity) in mind. Is this person interesting enough on-camera to sustain a viewer's attention for ten, twenty, or thirty minutes?

9. One of the most exhilarating aspects of short-form filmmaking is that "there are no rules." Don't feel confined by the structure imposed by features. Programmers are looking for creativity, new voices, and a captivating story supported by visual imagery.

10. Finally, be aware that you're not going to get rich from a short film. Your goal should be to produce a project that accurately reflects your talent and the ability to create and complete a vision. A common and accurate descriptive is that a short film is your "calling card."

—Sharon Badal, *excerpt from interview in Chapter 11*

D. Network

Agents and managers can be helpful, but most producers find work opportunities from people they know. You want to meet people at the top of the ladder, or who are on their way up. You can find them in TV and film industry organizations, on Web sites and blogs, in classes, internships, and at festivals. If there are no festivals in your area, start one — create a festival theme and focus, find a local movie theater or screening facility, get a couple of like-minded people to help you, study models of successful festivals, and throw a fund-raising event to get you started.

E. Find a Mentor

A mentor or advisor is a valuable asset to a beginning producer. He or she has worked hard to achieve success, and understands the importance of giving back to people who are on their way up. Mentors can be found in the workplace, in film and television organizations, and in the classroom. You may also be aware of a person whose work impresses you and who models success in ways you admire. Take a chance, request a meeting. Because you've already carefully thought about how this particular mentor can be of benefit to you, you can explain your position and how you would like to be mentored. Do you want to work alongside the mentor? Can he or she give you valuable advice, internships, or contacts? Be respectful of time and keep the first meeting brief.

F. Internships

A good internship can give you invaluable learning experience — and contacts. Most producers in television started their careers as an intern or production assistant. Whether you're doing an internship for school credit or simply for the experience, keep in mind that an intern who regularly shows up on set or in the production offices becomes a steady, dependable presence. Producers and directors start to depend on the intern, and over time, they give him or her more work and more responsibility. Often a valued intern is offered employment after a few months or when an entry-level job opens up. An intern can ask for a letter of recommendation or a referral to another internship.

As an intern you're a valuable asset to the project. You're giving them your energy, education, and unique skills. You want to be punctual, keep your word, and anticipate what needs to be done before you're told. Your behavior in the workplace is appropriate, and you're respectful of everyone around you. You may only be photocopying dozens of full-length scripts, but do it with a smile. In return for your time they can expose you to learning experiences like on-set duties or sitting in on meetings. And, unlike a full-time job, you can leave an internship guilt-free if it isn't a good match.

In some cases, the internships aren't well organized, and you can feel as though your time isn't being fully utilized. Look for areas in which you can be helpful; often, that initiative is really appreciated.

G. Get Experience

You may not want to commit to a formal internship, but you do want real-world experience. Most cities and towns have local video production companies and TV stations where you can volunteer your services in exchange for a chance to be part of the action and learn in the process. Often colleges and universities with TV and film departments have bulletin boards on which students can post notices about their up-coming projects that you might be able to work on for more experience. You can also post your own notice, offering your services.

H. Take a Course

Depending on your location, you might find TV courses, seminars, or programs that can expand your knowledge. You may not be interested in directing or editing, for example, but the more you know about how these jobs are performed, the better producer you can be. The course instructor may be actively involved in the profession that he or she is teaching, and can hook you up with internships, jobs, and networking opportunities. Your classmates, too, could be valuable members of your future production team. Look into classes for business writing, public speaking, marketing and sales, computer skills, and even foreign languages. Each of these areas improves your overall skills, and your marketability as a producer.

> In television producing, it's important to not be in a vacuum. An educational environment provides ways of seeing how other people interpret and how they do it — and ways of seeing how other people interpret their work after it's done. So it is a kind of a laboratory setting where you're getting feedback
> —Sheril Antonio, *excerpt from interview in Chapter 11*

I. Keep Up-to-Date

By subscribing to publications that report on the television industry, you can familiarize yourself with trends — financial, technological, and creative directions. Most top-notch magazines and journals can be accessed online either by subscription or for free. Although the sheer amount of information and names can be overwhelming at first, you'll eventually connect the dots. The attached CD features more information in the Publications and Trade Journals and Web site sections.

J. Get a Job

Producers often started off as interns, production assistants, personal assistants, or secretaries. Other producers came from careers as lawyers, writers, accountants, and even actors. If you're starting out in the business, look for an entry-level job in a network, production company, entertainment law firm, or other areas of the television industry that can help you build up your producing skills and contacts. If you've got strong office skills, you can find temporary jobs in entertainment and communications companies. In larger cities, temp agencies specialize in providing staff for short-term jobs like receptionist, secretary, assistant, and so on. If you like the people at the company and they like you, they'll keep you in mind when a job opens up. If it isn't promising, you can simply go back to the temp agency and ask for a different job.

TOP TEN

Ten Ways to Be a Great PA — and Keep Moving Up

1. Be prepared to work for little if any money at first. You'll make it eventually.
2. Be willing to work long, long hours.
3. Always keep a smile on your face, as hard as it may be.
4. Work hard! Go above and beyond your duties.
5. Know everyone's name and their position on the production.
6. Never complain. No task is too small.
7. Remember that everyone has been where you are, even if they act like they haven't.
8. Ask questions and show a genuine interest in the business. Most people like to talk about what they do for a living.
9. Listen carefully, and know that watching is a learning experience.
10. When you have a choice, work for the right people. Your gut instinct usually lets you know if they're a good fit or not.

—Becky Teitel and Jonna McLaughlin *(former PAs)*

III. Festivals

Your goal may be to produce a prime time series for a major network. It is certainly a reasonable goal, and one you could well achieve one day. But in the meantime, you want to hone your producing skills by raising funds, producing small but meaningful projects, and making sure that people see your work. You also want to promote yourself as an effective producer who can tackle other projects. Understanding the festival circuit, researching grant sources, and knowing more about publicity can help you take these steps with more confidence.

The number of television and film festivals, both domestically and internationally, has tripled in the last few years. Festivals are a valuable venue in which to screen your project and get candid visceral reactions from a real audience. At a festival you'll meet other producers and filmmakers, network with potential clients, and maybe sell your project to a network or distributor who has seen it during a screening. In addition to the information below, refer to the Television and Film Festival section in the book's CD.

> There's not much you can do about what other people are creating, but there's almost always something you can do about what *you* are doing.
> —Michael Bonfiglio, *excerpt from interview in Chapter 11*

A. Package Your Project

Press kits may vary in content and graphic approach, but a good press kit reflects the unique tone of your project. A compelling press kit is a primary piece of the festival circuit and includes these elements:

- A good title
- A story synopsis that's compelling, brief, and hooks the reader
- Copies of any newspaper or magazine articles and positive reviews
- Bios on key personnel and the cast and crew
- If pertinent, background on the genesis of your project
- Production notes and photographs
- Still photographs that are high-quality representations of the project's images
- Graphics and artwork, like posters and handouts
- A DVD of selected scenes, promos, or trailer that can be used in TV news
- Contact information including name, address, phone, fax, and e-mail
- A DVD or VHS screener of the project itself that might be sent only to specific people

B. Submissions to Festivals

In the United States, a one-hour slot on commercial television is actually 42 to 48 minutes of programming; internationally, the TV hour is 50 to 60 minutes long. Because representatives from networks, cable channels, and distribution companies come to festivals to shop for programming, your project has a better chance of appealing to them if it fits comfortably within their programming framework; keep these parameters in mind when you submit material to festivals.

As the producer, you want to research those festivals that are best suited for your specific project. There are literally hundreds of festivals around the world, and most are "branded" — they focus on specific genres like narrative features, documentaries, gay and lesbian, human rights, African American, Jewish, and experimental. Although most film festivals show programming that could be bought for television broadcast, there are specific festivals, like Banff, Real Screen Summit, and IFP Market that are geared to the television market. They tend to attract professionals and generally don't have audience participation. Research TV and film festivals, then target those that are right for your specific project and genre. Enter at least ten festivals, more if you can afford the submission fees and the time. Start with the top tier festivals, then work your way down to the lesser known festivals. Keep a careful log of where each tape or DVD of your project has been sent.

There are Web sites such as www.withoutabox.com that provide excellent information on these festivals. These sites are easily navigated and inexpensive to join. Details about these festivals can be accessed online, and many accept online submissions. Regardless of the festivals you enter, your log line, compelling synopsis, good reviews, and the information in the festival's catalogue page can help jurors consider your project for their festival.

For every project that is submitted to a festival, there is at least one festival juror who screens it and makes the decision to either reject your project or will recommend it for further consideration. Jurors screen hundreds of submissions, usually on VHS or DVD; few watch each one from start to finish. If they're not engaged within the first 4 to 5 minutes, they will either fast-forward through it or hit the eject button.

C. Acceptance to a Festival

1. Publicists and Representatives

If your project has been accepted by a major festival — Cannes, Berlin, Sundance, and Toronto — it's going to generate a significant buzz and you're wise to hire an experienced publicist who can help you navigate the media frenzy that is part of the high-profile festivals. Publicists charge a fee for their work, and you'll also pay for various publicity materials and expenses. If you can't afford a publicist, you can contact the press office of the festival that has accepted your piece and talk to their publicists about promotional ideas. And, as you'll see in Section V, you have quite a few options for creating a publicity campaign yourself.

Festivals attract buyers and distributors; they attend many screenings in a short time, primarily based on advanced word of mouth. A producer's "rep" is experienced in convincing these potential buyers to screen your project. He or she designs a strategy for the initial introduction of a program into the marketplace, creates a buzz, and knows how to talk directly to buyers in their own language. Generally, the producer's rep works on a percentage basis, which you want to discuss prior to further negotiations.

2. Festival "Premieres"

The fierce competition in the festival world requires most projects to be deemed "premieres," or first-time festival screenings. This term can be somewhat ambiguous, however. A premiere in Boston can be considered to be the Massachusetts premiere by one festival or the American premiere in another. Carefully read each festival's guidelines — many festivals won't accept your piece if it has been screened or broadcast somewhere else first.

3. Attending the Festivals

Not many festivals can afford to pay finalists' expenses to come to the festival — most costs are up to the producer. But it could be worth the money to experience sitting in the midst of a real audience and watching their reactions to your project. Your festival acceptance speaks to your skills as a producer for future projects; if you're available after the screening, the audience and interested buyers can meet you while their experience is still fresh.

Festivals are a fertile ground for networking. You'll meet other producers, filmmakers, writers, directors, attorneys, agents — any of whom are potential collaborators in future projects. Fellow producers can be your allies and spread valuable word-of-mouth about your work, so attend their screenings and get to know them. Go to panels, attend the social mixers and events, and introduce yourself. Be sure to bring plenty of your business cards.

At a festival you can use creative tricks to grab people's attention. For example, you can hand out promotional mini-posters, about the size of a post card, with the name of your piece and the location, date, and time of the screening. Other attention-getters include, mugs, T-shirts, key chains, notepads, pens, hats, or other useful or fun items that advertise your project. You can throw a party with a theme, or host a unique event. Ask other producers how they have generated interest for their films or video projects.

If your project features a well-known actor, writer, and/or director, they should also attend the festival. Their presence on panels or at a question and answer (Q&A) session after the screening can add extra credibility and weight to your work. If your project is nonnarrative, bring the subjects of the piece for the Q&A.

4. *Making a Deal*

You could find yourself chatting with a buyer or broadcaster at a festival event and they might ask if you have other finished projects or story ideas to pitch. Be mentally prepared to pitch new ideas when an opportunity arises.

Deals for distribution or foreign sales are occasionally negotiated and secured on the spot in the festival lobby, but not always. Unless your project has triumphed at Toronto, Sundance, or another high-profile festival, potential buyers may hold back and won't make immediate decisions. They know that a project can elicit a great response at the festival, but might not find a broader audience in the real world. You might get a call weeks after the festival from an interested buyer — or it may never come — don't expect instant results.

Regardless of the festivals that accepted your project, you still may not be offered a network deal for your comedy or distribution for your documentary or educational project. Still, as you learned in Chapters 3 and 6, you do have other options, like straight-to-cable, direct-to-video, or a broadcast by a lesser-known cable channel.

IV. Grants

Why do you need grant money? You might be looking for money to edit and mix the footage you have already shot but can't afford to finish. You could want an entire project to be funded, or you simply need the donation of services, like tape stock or legal advice. Most private funding is awarded to nonprofit organizations with a 501(c)(3) status, so you as an individual grant-seeker can usually apply for grants through an umbrella organization that has the required nonprofit status. If you qualify, you might be able to establish your own company with 501(c)(3) status. The Internet offers a range of sites that can give you more information on this process.

Funders and grant makers are an important resource for you as a producer. They have gone to considerable lengths to set up their foundations, define their goals, and make money or services available to the public. Each granting foundation establishes very specific goals, objectives, and guidelines that include these elements:

- *General purposes*: The history and background of the foundation, and the primary purposes of establishing the grant.

- *Current program interests*: The themes, subject matter, and shared assumptions of the projects that the foundation seeks to promote and encourage through its funding, as well as specific eligibility components.

- *Grant-making policies*: Specific restrictions, limitations, and parameters regarding the conditions for which funds, services, and endowments are awarded.

- *Application process*: Components required by the foundation, such as a letter of inquiry, a detailed proposal, the grant-seeker's qualifications, a project budget and the amount being requested, proof of nonprofit status, and other aspects of future accountability.

Most foundations insist that you stick closely to their required proposal format; their guidelines outline all the requirements, so study them closely.

Grant writing is a highly valuable skill, acquired with time and practice. You want to focus your energies on targeting the right funding sources, and writing the grant itself. You can explore the process through foundation centers, Web sites, and specialized directories and publications. Refer to the CD in the Grants and Funding Sources and Web site sections for more information.

A. Preparing and Writing a Grant

The grant-writing process can truly challenge the patience of a first-time grant writer. It can be time-consuming, it requires you to maintain an uncomfortable objectivity toward your own work, and it involves copious paperwork. Each grant has its own specific guidelines and objectives that require intensive research. But when you find the rhythm of the process and explore the many grants for which you qualify, it could be worth your efforts.

After you have researched and targeted the specific grant makers who might be responsive to your proposal, you'll follow these basic steps to write and apply for a grant:

1. Describe your project.

    - Write a brief mission or vision statement that clarifies the goals of the project.

    - Assign the project a specific genre, discipline, and/or geographic area.

    - Clarify the project's goals and how the funding can promote those goals.

    - Draw up a grant-writing schedule that includes the planning, proposal writing, submissions, and anticipated start date for the project.

2. Find and contact the funders.

    - Consider applying to many funders, not limiting the search to just one or two.

    - Carefully review the objectives and priorities of each funder.

    - Determine what amounts the funder awards, and what funds they have previously issued and to whom.

    - Ask the funding organization for their proposal guidelines and application specifics.

    - Locate a project officer at the granting organization who can answer questions, such as how the proposal review process is conducted, and if there might be any budgetary limitations or requirements that aren't outlined in the guidelines.

3. Review the guidelines for the proposal.

    - Look carefully at the guidelines for details that include eligibility qualifications, timetables, deadlines, budget information, and the specifics for formatting the proposal.

- If not outlined in the guidelines, inquire about the goals of the funder, the various award levels, and any contact names and addresses for submission. Ask about the notification process and the date of the notice.

4. Write the proposal.

- Structure the format for the proposal by following the guidelines provided by each funder. Often a slight deviation from the guidelines can disqualify a proposal.

A proposal traditionally includes a narrative, an estimated budget, an appendix of supporting material, and an authorized signature of the grant-seeker.

The narrative — This opens the proposal and states what is needed and how it can be approached. Provide your goals and objectives, and reasons why the funder should support your proposal. Delineate your approach for setting and meeting these goals, an outline of the process, and the personnel needed to accomplish the goal. The narrative also provides a schedule of activities, work flow, and projected results, as well as pertinent information about the grant-seeker that assures the funder that you can assume all responsibilities.

As with any professional project, you want to make sure that the narrative is well-written and reflects the tone of the project as well as your own ability to carry it through. Any grammatical mistakes or spelling errors can cast doubt on this ability.

The project budget — A carefully planned budget reflects the goals and sensibilities of the grant-seeker, and gives the funder an indication of how well a project might be managed. The budget needs to be detailed and consistent with realistic prices and rates. It should request a specific amount needed to get the job done. Often, funders supply a budget form that you must fill out in order to meet their specifications.

Supporting materials — A funder often requests a compilation of supporting materials that is organized into an appendix. This could include sponsoring agencies or institutions, advisory committees, charts and tables, biographies on key personnel, letters of recommendation, any pertinent newspaper articles and positive reviews, endorsements, and validating certification that can lend credibility to the grant-seeker. Most foundations also require proof of your tax-exempt status.

Authorized signature — Funders require the signature of the grant-seeker who may be awarded the grant and who is responsible for the funds.

5. Follow through.

- Keep a log of the funders that you have contacted, when they were contacted, and their deadlines for submitting grant applications.

- Keep track of their notification dates; know when to expect a letter of either rejection or acceptance from each funder.

- If possible, ask for feedback on the proposal and ways you might improve it for a follow-up submission if it's not accepted.

- Request recommendations for other funding sources that might be better suited to your project.

These five steps address the basics of grant writing, though each grant has its own unique guidelines and expectations. Take advantage of courses and seminars on grant writing, and read examples of grant proposals that have been awarded with funding. You can also consult the Grants and Funding section on the CD.

V. Publicity

You want people to see your project. You want it to win festival awards, secure distribution or broadcast, and to attract the attention of potential buyers. As the producer, you are the liaison between the program and the network, distributor, or festival, and it's important that you make people aware of your work. This is where publicity comes into the picture. Hiring a publicist can be expensive, and you can often do just as good a job as a professional for free. Below are a few tips for getting the word out about you and your project.

Define your audience — It's easier to focus your publicity when you know your audience. If, for example, you're promoting a children's television program. you want children and their parents and teachers to know about it. So target your publicity to parenting magazines, PTAs, teachers unions' publications, school fairs, family festivals and events, and other child-oriented possibilities. Every genre of programming has an audience — find them and tell them about your project.

Write a press release — A good press release can make your project newsworthy. Its purpose is to provide information that is interesting enough to be repurposed for news sources like local or national newspapers, local TV news stations, magazines, Web sites, or other audiences. A press release is simple, direct, and brief — a few well-written lines are more effective than a long-winded description. And a well-written press release makes a newspaper editor's job a lot easier.

You might want to issue a press release about your project, your new production company, or even your latest festival nomination. A finished press release is folded in thirds so that it can be opened and read more easily. Whether mailing or e-mailing a press release, give the recipient time to respond before you follow up. These are the brief elements that are included in a press release:

Your letterhead

FOR IMMEDIATE RELEASE: This is standard wording, in all caps, that appears in the upper left-hand margin under your letterhead.

Contact information: Skip two lines, then list the name(s) and title(s), e-mail, and telephone and fax numbers of the primary contact person.

Headline: Skip two more lines, use a boldface type, and briefly describe your news in a headline language that grabs the reader's attention.

Dateline: This gives the name of the city and state from where you've issued your press release, and the date of its mailing.

Lead paragraph: The first 10 to 15 words of your opening paragraph are crucial in a press release. They determine whether the reader keeps reading, or rejects it. Like any compelling narrative, you're writing the information using clear language, action verbs, and few adjectives. You're presenting highlights rather than useless details.

Supporting text: Ideally, you can fit your information into one paragraph. If not, you'll further develop your news in a follow-up paragraph.

Recap: You can restate your news in the lower left-hand corner of the last page. For example, you might include the date a program is airing, the festival screening, a release date for your DVD, or the location of your new production company.

End of release: Three number symbols (# # #) follow the last paragraph, centered, and indicate that the press release has ended.

A press release generally includes the following formatting components:

- *Paper*: Use $8\frac{1}{2} \times 11$ high-quality, white or cream, printed on only one side.

- *Typeface*: Use 12-point Times New Roman or Courier, in upper- and lower-case font, except in the IMMEDIATE RELEASE line that written in all capital letters.

- *Margins*: All sides of each page have $1\frac{1}{2}$-inch margins.

- *Headlines*: Use a bold typeface to draw attention.

- *Continuation*: Finish the paragraph on one page, rather than carrying it over to the next page. When the word "more" between two dashes (— more —) is centered at the bottom of the page, it lets the reader know that another page follows.

Contact your local newspapers — Your project may have a human-interest story behind it — how you originated the idea, the use of local talent, interesting locations — and most local newspapers, magazines, and business publications gravitate toward a good story that is compelling to their readers. Research these publications and look for an angle in your project that could interest them. Call first to determine who should get a letter of inquiry in which you can briefly outline your idea.

Look for a star attachment — If your project has garnered praise in a newspaper review or won a festival award, consider taking it to a well-known actor, producer, or director who would be willing to sign on as an executive producer. This lends it extra credibility for publicity and investors.

Ignore your own hype — It can be tempting to believe that you are as good as the PR you've generated about yourself. Keep an objective frame of mind as you do your job and maintain a focus on your own emotional anchor.

Know when to move on — You may have to face the candid truth that a reasonable amount of time has passed, but your project still hasn't sold, or the deal you were offered wasn't nearly what you had hoped for. Chalk it up to experience, and give yourself validation for having learned so much. You are a creative and motivated person, and you've got new projects ahead of you, so take a deep breath and move on.

> You have to be flexible. Not all producers are flexible, but *good* producers are.
> —Ann Kolbell, *excerpt from interview in Chapter 11*

VI. Starting Your Own Production Company

Some producers prefer working within the structure of an existing network or production company, and others are more comfortable working for themselves. You may have considered starting your own production company, with the creative and financial freedom of being your own boss. You may have found the perfect partner with whom you can coproduce your ideas. You may want to form a company solely to produce one specific project, or you may want your company to develop and produce ongoing content or programming.

By starting up a production company, you're theoretically adding another large chunk of work to your already overbooked life. The many details of running a production company can fall between the cracks during production, so before you rush into what can be a demanding challenge, ask yourself these questions:

1. *Do you have the right personality?* Some people are happiest when they can work within the comfortable structure of an existing company. Others like to set their own deadlines and goals. Examine your own personality traits, and ask yourself if you've honestly got the motivation and energy to be self-employed. Consider taking on a partner whose strengths and character work well with yours, or who is adept in areas you're not, like administration or pitching or budgeting. Sometimes a partner can come in with funds and specific abilities, but if there isn't a positive chemistry between the two of you, it's seldom worth the trade-off.

2. *Can you support the business for a period of time?* A start-off company needs money to cover initial costs like office space and furniture, phones, computers, faxes, utility bills and deposits, and printing stationery and business cards. If you're hiring other people, they need to be paid while you look for clients and jobs. You have your own personal rent and expenses to cover, too. Explore these realities by creating a spreadsheet that lists your realistic income potential and weigh them against your planned expenses. Come into a business with enough money to cover your expenses for at least six months to a year.

3. *What investors could you bring into the business?* You may not have a large cache of personal funds with which to start your business, so look for friends, family, colleagues, and private investors who might invest in your business. You can consult with an attorney and/or accountant to help prepare an *investment offering* that details your cash flow projections and notes, how the funds will be used, tax consequences, and a projection of returns on the investment. This document also includes information about the producer's team, the manager of the project, and other details. You can grow your business from these investments without giving up ownership and personal control. If you have a good credit rating, can prove your business integrity and expertise, and have compiled a strong business plan, you may qualify for funds from a lending institution. In order to receive these funds you'll also need to offer up some form of security like a home, a boat, or land.

4. *What do you bring to the business?* Take an objective look at yourself to see if you've got the skills, personality, experience, and endurance to run a business. Just like a good story needs a hook to capture our imagination, you want to identify your own hook or "brand" and then build on it. Maybe you are an excellent administrator who can spot good talent or you are a hyphenate — a producer - director or writer-producer. These are attributes that you can use to market yourself or your business.

5. *Who is your competition?* As clever and energetic as you may be, there are other companies out there competing for the same clients. You want to be really confident that you can maintain an advantage over other businesses by delivering better services, reasonable rates, and star treatment.

6. *Can you create a demand for your services?* Promoting your business is as important as marketing your creative projects. Get the word out about your new company. This requires advertising, press releases, making a lot of cold sales calls, talking to all your friends and business acquaintances, and thinking of clever approaches to connect with potential clients.

If you've objectively answered these questions and still want to forge ahead, here is a mini checklist of the many components and personnel that might play a part in creating and forming your production company:

- A dependable and reputable entertainment attorney
- An accounting service or a good spreadsheet program for doing your own accounting, payroll, taxes, and production expenses

- An insurance policy that covers liability and other production-related coverage

- The legal structure of your company, such as general partnership, incorporation, sole-proprietorship, limited liability company (LLC), etc.

- The location for your office space involves parking, proximity to a freeway or public transportation, adequate utilities, and a creative neighborhood; look into zoning requirements, local taxes, rents and lease options

- Renting office space that only covers rental for the production period or extends to cover the space for an ongoing business

- Office furniture and equipment like phones, computers, faxes, printers, etc.

- Deciding on a name for your company

- Designing and setting up a company Web site

Study the winners. Look closely at successful companies who are doing what you hope to be doing eventually. Read their promotional material, research their client list, and see how they solve their clients' problems. You don't want to copy them, but you do want to see what has helped them succeed.

Keep it legal. You don't want to ignore the legal issues involved in starting a business. Meet with an accountant and/or attorney before officially opening your doors for business. Depending on where and how you plan to set up a business, there are several elements you'll need to carefully research first:

- *Business license*: Most towns and cities, counties, and/or states require a license to operate a business within their boundaries.

- *Business organization*: Options include general partnership, limited partnership, sole proprietorship, limited liability company (LLC), or incorporation, and each choice affects issues like taxes and liability.

- *Certificate of Occupancy (C of O)*: Some city or county zoning departments require this document if you plan on moving your business into a new or used building.

- *Business name*: When a company's name is different than the name of the owner, this fictitious name needs to be registered with the county. It doesn't apply to a corporation doing business under its corporate name.

- *Taxes*: Depending on the company's structure, its owner could be responsible for withholding money from an employee's wages for state and federal income taxes and Social Security insurance, known as FICA. If you're self-employed, you pay your own FICA. Businesses are required by the state to pay unemployment insurance in some cases, as well as state and federal income taxes — and in some cases, city income taxes — on their company's earnings. If a business employs three or more people, it must provide workers' compensation insurance to cover accidents incurred on the job.

- *Business insurance*: Coverage for a business is essential. Insurance coverage might include protection against fire, theft, and areas of liability, as well as additional insurance that covers property, automobile, interruption of business, or a home office. In some cases, insurance is obtained to cover an officer or director of a corporation who could be held personally liable on behalf of the company.

- *Federal Employer Identification Number (EIN)*: A one-of-a-kind number that the IRS assigns to a business by which it is identified and accessed. More information can be found at the IRS Web site, www.irs.org.

A. Dealing with Clients

The term "client" casts a wide net — a client can be a major network, or your brother-in-law with an ample bank account. A client pays the bills, gives you creative direction, and has demands that must be met. No matter how independent a producer you might want to be, there is always a client. And the client is always right.

1. Keep Your Clients Happy

Getting clients is hard enough, but keeping them can be even more challenging. The television and video industry is a competitive business and most clients can get a better deal somewhere else. Find ways to make your clients feel valued. How do they like their coffee? Are the chairs comfortable? What's their favorite take-out restaurant in the neighborhood? Thank them for their continuing business by treating them well.

2. Negotiate

If you've got a client who can provide you with steady business, consider bringing your rates down and negotiating a long-term deal. However, if a client tries to consistently nickel-and-dime you, the price of your sanity may not be enough of a trade-off. There is a subtle difference between the two. Your intuition is usually right when you listen to it.

3. Ask Questions

Often a client has great ideas and directives, but they aren't clearly stated. Don't hold back — ask for clarification. Take notes and then write a memo to the client after the meeting, detailing what you think was said. This way, if there is still confusion, changes can be made by both you and the client.

4. Keep It Simple

Whenever possible, subcontract your work rather than hire full-time employees. Technology has made it feasible for a producer to run a successful home-based business with just a cell phone, e-mail, a PDA, and a fast computer. On a larger project, consider working out of a turnkey office space that you can rent on a monthly basis. For each project, hire the most experienced freelancers you can find who charge reasonable rates. When the project is over, you can move on to your next job.

> You try to get across that "We've got certain things we have to accomplish, we understand that you have certain things you have to accomplish, let's work together to see how we can do as much of that as possible" and find ways where we can compromise as necessary. It's as much about personal relationships and schmoozing as it is about, technically, how you're going to achieve whatever it is that you need to do.
> —Stephen Reed, *excerpt from interview in Chapter 11*

On a Human Level . . .

The elements involved in producing for TV and video never really end. They continue through current projects and onto the next productions in your future. For those of you who enjoy the never-ending realm of possibilities that are inherent in producing, each new phase is a journey. You may well have found a profession that is rich in potential and tailor-made for your unique range of skills.

> Today's wind is one of spectacle. It may not be of our making. Its origins may not be the pure lands of the Enlightenment but instead the commercial barrens of advertising and entertainment. But use it we must, for without the wind, we are becalmed, stuck, going nowhere.
>
> —Andrew Boyd and Stephen Duncombe,
> *The Manufacture of Dissent: What the Left Can Learn from Las Vegas.*

VII. Summary

Over the last ten chapters, you have explored the hundreds of elements that play an integral part in taking a project from beginning to end. Each chapter offered a range of details pertinent to the TV producer, from current information to interpersonal skills, that are part of the process called "producing." The final chapter of this book is designed to give you yet another perspective. In Chapter 11 you will be introduced to the diverse ideas, advice, and experiences of experienced television producers and industry professionals who actively produce in television and video. Each contributor talks about his or her area of television producing, and each conversation provides its own unique lens — a good producer learns from the best.

VIII. Chapter Review Questions

1. Name three key aspects of wrapping a project. Why are they important?

2. Create your own resume. Ask two people to critique it for you.

3. What are the steps you might take to promote your project? To promote yourself as a producer?

4. What are the benefits of entering a project in a festival? What are the drawbacks?

5. Discuss the compelling elements in an effective press kit.

6. Research the foundations that award funds and services to projects produced in video. Single one out and write a brief report on the organization's requirements.

7. What three areas of publicizing your project are you most comfortable doing? Why?

8. Write a sample press release announcing an imaginary news item you want to promote.

9. List the pros and cons of starting your own production company.

10. Outline what your professional next steps might be.

PART II

When you follow your bliss . . . doors will open where you would not have thought there would be doors; and where there wouldn't be a door for anyone else.

—Joseph Campbell

CHAPTER 11

Producing in the Real World: Conversations with the Pros

This Chapter's Talking Points

I.   Chapter Review Questions

In this chapter, an impressive array of seasoned television producers and industry professionals share their professional practices and personal odysseys. Through sit-down interviews, e-mails, faxes, and transcontinental phone calls, each person's unique story, insight, and solid advice has added dimension to this entire text. Their collective interviews form a body of work that is so rich it has become a chapter all its own. Excerpts from the following interviews are scattered throughout the preceding chapters.

The contributing producers, academics, and industry professionals are

- Sheril Antonio — New York University, Associate Dean

- Sharon Badal — Tribeca Film Festival, programmer for Shorts Program

- Veronique Bernard — Executive producer/producer, nonfiction and documentary

- Michael Bonfiglio — Executive producer/producer, nonfiction and documentary

- Salli Frattini — Executive producer, MTV

- Barbara Gaines — Executive producer, *Late Night with David Letterman*

- Ann Kolbell and Matthew Lombardi — Producers, NBC

- Jeffrey McLaughlin — Post-production director and senior editor

- Brett Morgen — Producer/Director, theatrical and television documentaries

- Stephen Reed — Executive producer/producer, live music events

- John Rosas — Producer, promotional and added value content

- Tom Sellitti — Coproducer, *Rescue Me* and *Shorties Watchin' Shorties*

- J. Stephen Sheppard — Entertainment lawyer and former producer

- Valerie Walsh — Executive producer, cocreator, *Dora the Explorer*

- Justin Wilkes — Executive Producer/producer, TV series, features, documentaries

Sheril Antonio

Associate Dean, Tisch School of the Arts, New York University

Q: *Let's address the classic argument: Is television an art form or merely a craft? What is it about television that creates such controversy?*

A: I think it's because it is mundane. It's like a kitchen appliance that we use. We seem to control it, it's in everyone's life. It seems to do what we want it to do when we want it to do. Especially now, with TiVo, and the six hundred channels, getting something that meets your own feeling, your own needs. So I think because there's this false sense of it belonging to each and every one of us individually. It goes back to the old network days where it was ABC, NBC, CBS and everything was geared toward *Texaco Star Theater*. It was all very limited. Everyone came to this preexisting well.

And now, there's every genre you want. Places like HBO are trying to be smorgasbords to get something going for everybody. It's become so accessible to people's individual needs. There are just certain physical and psychological reasons why people think it's so everyday. It's become mundane and maybe even innocuous. As opposed to film, where you have to have clothes on. You have to have shoes on. You have to pay money. You'll be with all these other people. As someone once said to me, "the spectacle of film, staring up in awe and being totally focused." With television, you might be ironing, doing other kinds of stuff. And I think so many people feel exactly this way about television.

Every night I flip through the channels just for fun — before I go to bed — no matter how tired I am, I just go through all the channels. The fact that television is a place where films that don't do well can go is also great. I love television! I have a great deal of respect for television and there are certain people who watch television very selectively. I have friends who watch the News Hour on PBS and BBC News, and for them it's a very high-brow and intellectual engagement. That's because it's how they choose to use television. I also watch commercials. I love commercials. I think they are fantastic storytelling vehicles. One day I actually went up to the 600s on my TV, where there was music, and I saw the Chinese channel. It's just amazing. The Bulgarian news. I like to go to a different country, and watch MTV, and the BBC, or just flick on the television to see what other people are watching.

In terms of answering the question of why don't people see it as an art form? Because it is so many things. Maybe you'll see one particular piece of it as an art form. *Angels in America*. Amazing. Amazing. It blew my mind. But television is so many things at once — some is art, some is commerce, some is paid programming, it is hard to see it as one thing.

Q: *There was a time, not all that long ago, when film and radio and television each had a separate domain. Now they're merging, not only technologically but creatively.*

A: Now, there's no delineation. You know if you make a movie, it'll appear on television. Now people are signing contracts for video distribution. Certain things go straight to video, which will show up on television.

Q: *As you said before, TV is like a family member. You can argue with it, you can disagree with it, you can even turn it off, but it's part of our daily life.*

A: And for a lot of people, it's company. I used to listen to the radio for the weather report, but now I can turn on New York 1 for the weather. You want to watch something highbrow, let me see what IFC (the Independent Film Channel) is doing. It's like when you go to your refrigerator or your closet. It's about choice.

Q: *What should a student of producing look for in getting an education?*

A: I think education should be about education, not education at a specific place. Reading and writing and 'rithmetic should be taught the same throughout the whole country, maybe even the world. I think there's a level that education has to reach, no matter what the institution is. If you're a producer, it means you're making a marriage between somebody who can come up with something that has some sort of value in entertainment that can be given to the larger world. To me, a producer could be producing any kind of commodity: food, clothing — you are making something that is interesting, comfortable, exciting, new, comforting for a market.

In television producing, it's important to not be in a vacuum. An educational environment provides ways of seeing how other people interpret and how they do it — and ways of seeing how other people interpret after it's done. So it's a kind of a laboratory setting where you're getting feedback. That's number one.

Number two is that everyone will admit that there's a target audience age. If you're in a university setting, you're engaging with that target age. So one could certainly take the money one uses for tuition and make films. But how will you get the history, the way it's been done before now? Here's how the world looks. This is how TV intersects with all the other art forms. Look at one assignment, and how everybody has taken this one simple assignment and interpreted it so differently. Look at how you produced something, thinking you would get THAT, look at how you got THIS instead, and how differently everybody reacted to it. Where else but in an educational environment could that happen?

If you do that out in the real world, you know when you're going to find out something is amiss? When you try to sell it to somebody. They'll say "what is this?" Or, "do you realize how this is going to read?" Or, "I'm not going to get advertisers to buy a spot on that." There's a price out there — and there's a big price in educational institutions, but look what you're getting for it. And there are other things than the history of just image making. You are in this kind of petri dish of activity so that you can gauge and contextualize certain things. That's a part of the education that no one ever focuses on, but to me that's the value of education. That's the value of being here, and in terms of NYU specifically, the value of being in a big place. The benefit of being in an educational environment is not being by yourself. There are limitations to our knowledge, our own history, our understanding of how things interpret. Who's going to help us unearth these things? When you do a production, your classmates are going to interpret it, critique it. You're having this exchange. That's the true value of education, no matter where you are.

Q: *How valuable are internships?*

A: Critical! The value of internship is the difference between the dream and the reality. I do believe educational institutions are sites for people, no matter how old you are, to grow quickly in something you think you're interested in. It is a compressed learning environment. And you are learning and growing and maturing. So that's the dream that I think institutions have to be a part of perpetuating, and they have to be different than the reality. Internship is the transition into that so-called reality. You're in a *real* environment in a safe sort of bubble or pocket, observing and seeing before you get out to the real thing. That's what the value of an internship is. It's being in the real world, without the penalty, without getting fired, which is why it's so critical to the education.

I thought I wanted to be a television producer. When I was in school, I was a television major when television was very separate, and you never studied film, and when I got out and saw this world, I thought: "No way." In TV, it was life or death every day. And then you did it again the next day, and I'm thinking: "You wake up one day, you're born, you grow up, you die that night, then you do it again." It was too intense for me.

Q: *In your experience working with students who are on a producing track, do you notice any shared traits or commonalities?*

A: What I have noticed is that the personality of a producer is someone who not only can tolerate but who loves doing a lot of things at the same time, engaging with a lot of people at the same time. It's like juggling with no level of frustration. You like to keep a certain pace. You almost have to like problem solving, and it has to be second nature. You have to be very good at predicting problems and having plans B and C in the back of your mind. So you're kind of a puzzle maker. Not just a puzzle solver but a puzzle maker, because as you see something, you're making a puzzle out of it. You have to be sort of a Type A personality, you have to have a little OCD. And you have to be a fantastic therapist, and well-organized in your head. A producer facilitates. You're an enabler. You're enabling all these other people, you're the one person on the production that has to keep everything in their head. You've got to know what's good from a story, to who is the best editor for that story. It's really sort of your baby.

In television, it still is a producer's world, really. In film, it's not. It's a director's world. So you have to be in touch with everybody: audiences, advertisers, networks or cable stations. You have to be sort of crazy. And you have to know you're crazy to like it. And you can't be lukewarm. You've got to want to produce more than you want to do anything else. There is nothing you're going to like to do more.

Q: *How important is it for a television producer to have a backdrop of television history?*

A: Critical! Urgent! "An unexamined life is not worth living." If you are interested in developing an art form and you consider yourself to be in an art form, you must, must, *must* know what came before you. How things work, what the traditions were. The people who are the most informed are people who can take the most risks and be successful. The people who aren't aware of the history are the very safe ones who don't change things because they are not building on what's been done before.

Where does one place television in the larger world? In times of emergencies, in times of war, how is television responding? In times of election, where is television? For me, the most critical aspect of television is that it always exists as a place where one gets information, where one gets history in the real sense. How good is television at being in moments when history is being created? That's where I want my TV to be. There, it's like a lifeline. I think television is probably better with the past than the future. You know, Biography, the History Channel — but what about today? What about now? I'm talking about shows like *The L Word, The Sopranos, Six Feet Under, Desperate Housewives, Wife Swap, The Apprentice, Law and Order* — it's all like wow, wow! What's going on today? Where are we today? It's about Now. Give me NOW!

Q: *Here's the classic question: Does television reflect our culture, or is our culture shaped by television — or do we care?*

A: Yes, we do care. I just showed a clip to my class from *Hollywood Chronicles* where they talked about *Birth of a Nation*. And the question was: Does television reflect or shape? After *Birth of a Nation,* both lynchings and clan membership went up. It is when it's shaping *without* consciousness that concerns me. What scares me about television — whether it's shaping or reflecting — is this notion of things being presented as if we've all agreed. What if I *don't* agree with it? If you reflect something that exists, you're actually magnifying it. And if you're magnifying it, it's almost like a wake-up call to the people who are out there, not actively doing that or thinking that, and so that reflection becomes a shaping. So if you look at the clan thing with *Birth of a Nation,* they were reflecting something that existed but they reflected it so much, to so many people, that it shaped it because more and more people got interested and agreed that it was OK.

Q: *How important is the choice of schools for a producing student?*

A: Film schools like Chapman, USC, UCLA, Columbia, Chicago — people call them competitors but to me, they're sister schools. If you teach image making and you teach consciousness of images, I don't care whether it's film, television, photographs, or the Internet, it's the same principle being applied. It's just about giving the history of the images, how images have affected people and being conscious about consuming them, and then of course the skill of making them. Everybody's trying to peg a film school. Everybody's trying to say Columbia does mostly writing, NYU is mostly production, the LA schools are more commercial. No. We've all got people coming to us who want to make images. Period.

Q: *What are the essential points that you would emphasize to your students about producing for television?*

A: Well, I would emphasize being a conscious spectator, whatever sort of creative output that one wants to engage in. For any artist, spectatorship is something they should keep in mind all the time. If they can be conscious of their own role in spectatorship, they can be conscious of other spectatorship. Look at the cutting-edge producers. I would ask students to do case studies in any genre that they feel really speaks to them. Do case studies about these producers and what was it that they accomplished. What was so familiar yet so new about the work? Try to dissect it by watching it over and over and over again. Pick three producers throughout the course of the term and let's see what they do. What was the first thing they produced? What was the last thing?

Q: *What other advice would you give to a beginning producer in television?*

A: Watch television. Look at it in terms of the time slot. What time slots are the advertisers' picks? Let's say that one channel has the Academy Awards — how does another network program? What goes on opposite big sports games? How does a particular network or cable station change its programming through the hours of the day? Who goes twenty-four hours? Who sells to paid programming, to advertising? And again, it's just like school. People come here liking a certain director and a certain kind of film and our job is to educate them on the whole. That's what I would try to do in terms of television. How hard or how easy is it to break a mold?

Q: *How important is ethics in a producer's job description?*

A: It has, I think, levels of real importance. It's sort of like you have to know narrative before you can know experimental. You have to know the ethics of the network, the ethics of the time, the ethics of broadcasters, and then you can put your show on television. Have you seen the Production Code from 1934? I used it in my African-American cinema class. The code forbids miscegenation on the screen, and forbids any depiction of reduced moral standards. It's a brilliant document. When I talk about ethics, I ask the question, "How do you know what society thinks? Where do you look for those ethical values?" And you have to find them — not just in the law and not just in the company that you're working for, but in what the culture says, as well.

Q: *What other thoughts can you share about this vast subject of producing for television?*

A: I'm just intrigued that somebody's talking about television. No one ever does. You know, television is a huge cultural tool. One of the most important historical films for me, coming from my own background in African-American cinema, is Marlin Riggs' *Color Adjustment* made in 1991. He explores how black people have been represented in television — from the beginning of television, up through the late 1980s. Television is a huge social and cultural tool that is overlooked. Coming from African-American cinema, coming from the point of view of a black woman, I think that TV wants to tell me what I should weigh, tries to sell me stuff I shouldn't eat, and it tells me what the American dream is.

Q: *What is your sense of the technical advances that are exploding in television and media now?*

A: I think of television now the way I think of my computer. It is a square thing that I look at and get information from. Five years ago, even ten years ago, I never thought that. It's now merged for me into a whole bunch of other things. TV is now on airplanes. At the dentist's office. On cell phones — they're putting television on cell phones. They're going to have it in cars, on beaches. I was watching something on *60 Minutes* where a sheik was in a tent somewhere, and he was watching four television screens at once.

I can imagine that with the technology becoming more like a cell phone or a computer, television is going to be much more of a vehicle of access. I think it's already close to being like what a telephone was in the early days. Think back to when we used to have only six channels, then seven channels, then eleven channels, and no remotes, so we had to get up and change the channel and the volume. A lot has changed. This medium of television is becoming much more portable.

Sharon Badal

Tribeca Film Festival/Short Films programmer, and NYU Professor/Producing for Film.

For most new producers, entering a project into the film festival circuit represents their first foray into the "real world" of the entertainment industry. They are navigating the film festival labyrinth. Most of these initial projects involve the short film format, that is less than forty minutes. As the Short Film Programmer for the Tribeca Film Festival, I have watched literally thousands of short film submissions over the past several years, in addition to the shorts I watch from my students at New York University where I am a full-time faculty member of the Tisch School of the Arts Undergraduate Department of Film and Television.

With my eyesight still intact, I offer the following:

> **TOP TEN**
>
> **Top Ten Helpful Hints for Creating a Short Film in Both Narrative and Unscripted Formats:**
>
> 1. Avoid the overuse of voice-over narration to carry your vision. Think about narration as a means to introduce your story, or express salient points, but do not allow the focus of your project to be the voice-over.
> 2. The first few minutes of your project are integral in creating the tone. Think about your opening very carefully, and stay away from traditional and over-saturated openings, such as "alarm-goes-off-character-wakes-up" or "pan-across-a-mantle-of-photographs," for example.
> 3. Consider the running time of your project while it is still in the concept stage and have a clear idea of content versus running time. The longer your project, the stronger your story should be. Remember, it's all about the story, regardless of whether it is narrative or documentary.
> 4. Particularly with documentary projects, think about your story progression. You still should have an idea where the film is "going." Twenty minutes of talking heads interspersed with archive footage does not a documentary make. What is your viewer going to learn/experience by the end of the film and how do we get there?

5. Montage sequences serve a very specific purpose — to move the story ahead in an expedient manner. Regurgitating previously viewed shots simply for the sake of putting them to music is not in your best interest, and detracts from the overall impact of the film.

6. Speaking of music, the use of songs should not undermine the visuals, but enhance them. Too many filmmakers who grew up as part of the MTV generation cavalierly use song lyrics to express their vision. This is not a music video.

7. Your main credit sequence should not imitate a feature film. A ten-minute short with a two-minute main credit sequence is unnecessary. Give "credit where credit is due" in the end credits! If you produce a lavish opening credit sequence, make sure it matches the style of the film, and does not jar the viewer when it goes from credits to the first shot.

8. The one-character documentary has its own set of challenges. A producer may think someone's life is unique by the hurdles he or she has overcome, or that something in his or her life warrants capturing the experience, but others should see it as well. Before you produce a film about a friend or relative, keep your audience (and objectivity) in mind. Is this person interesting enough on-camera to sustain a viewer's attention for ten, twenty, or thirty minutes?

9. One of the most exhilarating aspects of short-form filmmaking is that "there are no rules." Don't feel confined by the structure imposed by features. Programmers are looking for creativity, new voices, and a captivating story supported by visual imagery.

10. Finally, be aware that you're not going to get rich from a short film. Your goal should be to produce a project that accurately reflects your talent and the ability to create and complete a vision. A common and accurate descriptive is that a short film is your "calling card."

As a producer, you are the ultimate creator and decision maker on the project. Make certain that the decisions you make result in the best film that you can create.

Veronique Bernard

Executive producer and producer, nonfiction and documentary

Q: *You've covered a lot of ground in your producing career. What are some of the highlights for you?*

A: My most recent job is as Director of Program Development for New York Times Television, the *New York Times'* production company, specializing in journalistic documentaries and other nonfiction programming for its own channel, Discovery Times, for other cable outlets, and for PBS "Frontline" and "Nova." Before that, I was producing for the Sundance Channel's *DocDay* and *Anatomy of a Scene* strands. Another highlight was being Head of Production at SBS Television, a national pubcaster in Australia.

Q: *Yet you didn't start out as a producer, did you?*

A: My career path began with acting. I was an actress, and moved into directing in London, then Australia. I've worked as a teacher, reporter, director, producer, executive producer, and production executive in Sydney, Australia. In New York, where I live now, I'm a professor at NYU and also work as a development consultant and executive producer or senior producer, depending on the project. My path has been an unusual one for a producer, in that I've straddled the fiction and nonfiction worlds of television.

Q: *You work primarily as a nonfiction producer, including documentary. What are some of the historical precursors that you see in your field?*

A: In documentaries, I'd highlight some genres in particular. For an observational approach, there's Michael Apted's *Seven Up* and Fred Wiseman's *High School*, and for reenactments, I would certainly refer back to *Nanook of the North* by Robert Flaherty. More recently, in reality shows, *Real World* could be a precursor for *Survivor, Blind Date* could be somewhat of a model for *Temptation Island,* and the English program, *Jim'll Fix It* is an early version of *The Swan.* The original "docusoap" was *American Family* in the 1970s, followed by *Sylvania Waters* shot in Australia for the BBC. They paved the way for shows like *Growing up Gotti* and *The Osbournes.*

Q: *Do you believe that "a producer is a producer is a producer," meaning that most producing skills can be applied to different areas of television?*

A: To a certain extent. The skills are the same but you do need to know about your special field. For example, producing for dramatic series, sitcoms, or soaps requires special knowledge of the genres and their respective processes, which are very different from producing news, magazines, or sports programs. I think the industry is divided between fiction and nonfiction. Some directors cross over, but producers mostly travel across mediums in the same field (e.g., narrative/drama versus documentary/nonfiction whether it's TV, film, or theater and video art).

Q: *How do you keep a balance between your professional and personal lives?*

A: Everything is compartmentalized. Although producing is all-consuming and may be taking up a lot of my waking brain time, I make sure I carve out time each day, week, month, for other life categories like family, socializing, entertainment, and personal relaxation. When you can, employ hired help for those jobs you really don't have time to do so you can concentrate on quality time for the things you prioritize in your nonwork life.

Q: *What are your speculations on the future of television?*

A: It's an ongoing conversation. Having moved away from broadcasting to narrow casting with the advent of cable and the multichannel environment, the next stage is even more niche programming where everyone can program their own channel and personal viewing schedules. The growth of video-on-demand (VOD) is apparently the next big thing in television. This will individualize TV viewing even more and move it further away from the communal experience of its origins. Advertisers will have to rethink their strategies to reach their target audiences, and the very nature of TV advertising will change drastically.

Q: *As a producer with a lot of experience in so many areas of the television industry, what would be on your Top Ten List of what a producer of nonfiction television should know?*

TOP TEN

Top Ten List of What a Producer of Nonfiction Television Should Know

1. Who is your target audience?
2. What is new/unique about this program?
3. How much is it going to cost or what is the budget?
4. Who is paying for it and what are their expectations?
5. Hire the best people you can afford.
6. Try not to cut corners on anything that is going on the screen.
7. It's all about the story.

> 8. It's all about the casting.
> 9. Ideas are easy, getting them made is hard.
> 10. You're only as good as your last production.

Q: *What do you wish someone had told you when you first started producing?*

A: I wish someone had told me how fickle the market is, and that basically nobody knows anything.

Q: *When you teach your classes on television production and producing, what do you want to impress on your students?*

A: Know when to be passionate and when to be cynical, but always have something to say.

Michael Bonfiglio

Producer, including *Metallica: Some Kind of Monster*

Q: *As a producer, what areas do you work in primarily? And what do you do?*

A: I work as a documentary producer, primarily in cinema verite films. I work for @radical.media, a multifaceted international production company that specializes in television commercials, but includes divisions that create a variety of other forms of media. I've been working in documentaries for about nine years, having worked my way up as an intern for directors Joe Berlinger and Bruce Sinofsky (*Metallica: Some Kind of Monster, Paradise Lost, Brother's Keeper*), whom I now produce for. Working with Joe and Bruce is my main job within the larger umbrella of @radical.media. As Joe and Bruce's producer, I am responsible for a wide and varying set of tasks, which really run the gamut between coordinating and line producing, to generating ideas for new projects, getting projects financed, and helping shape the films creatively. I've also been involved in PR and distribution for some of our projects.

We usually operate with a skeleton crew, so I wear a lot of hats. Every project with us is different, so I am very fortunate in that my role is constantly changing and evolving, and I have a certain level of freedom that I really enjoy. The flipside is that because our projects are not terribly heavily financed, on any given day I also find myself doing work that would probably be considered the duties of a PA. That said, working with filmmakers of Joe and Bruce's caliber ensures that I very rarely find myself working on things that bore me or that I am not happy to be involved in.

Q: *The demands of your job, of any producer's job, are quite incredible. How do you juggle your work pressures and still keep a perspective on your personal life?*

A: This is a fantastic question, and one that really should be part of the larger cultural debate, not just in regards to producing for television. I'm a working guy in the relatively low-paying documentary field, not some big Hollywood producer who buys properties and gets them set up. So work for me literally means making the money to pay my rent and hopefully start chipping away at my debt — it's not some glamorous situation. The "entertainment business" (which is such a regrettable term for the unfortunate reality) is, however, a pretty cutthroat field. It's also somewhat capricious and you're constantly at the whim of networks, studios, or whomever it is you've convinced that your project is the best, or, in the case of an assignment, that you're going to do the job better than anyone else.

A guy I know says, "You're only as good as your last project," which is also a reality that creates a great deal of pressure, though this is often self-imposed, too. I do think this is a good thing in many ways, because it forces you to always push yourself to make everything you do better than the last thing you did. That said, you make choices. I often find myself neglecting my personal life and my personal projects in order to do the best that I can at my job. My girlfriend is always saying, "When you're on your deathbed, are you *really* going to regret not going in to the office/making that phone call/writing that e-mail, etc.?" And she's right. I don't usually listen though, largely due to the tenuous nature of my work, but also because of a personal need to do my best work.

Back to my initial point, though, I don't think that this quality is specific to producing. Cell phones, e-mail, and other technological advances have made it nearly impossible to get away from work, and corporate downsizing and our out-of-control consumer culture (and in New York City, skyrocketing rents that are pricing regular people out of town) have made it almost a necessity to work harder and more often than ever before just to make ends meet (well, maybe not *harder* — I wouldn't make that argument to a dairy farmer, say, or the immigrants who built the railroads). But this is really true in most fields — my father works for the phone company and was rarely home when I was growing up because he was always working. There are tons of people like him who probably regret those decisions who I could learn from, but the need to keep one's career together is really a necessity, not completely a choice. It certainly is true in producing, but it's far from exclusive to it. It hasn't always been that way, and it's not like that everywhere in the world, which is why I wish it were part of our larger social discourse.

Q: *What, and who, are the historical counterparts to your area of producing?*

A: The clearest historical counterparts to the kinds of work that I do are the cinema verite films of the 1960s by people like Pennebaker, Leacock, Robert Drew, Albert and David Maysles, Chris Marker, and Frederick Wiseman. On any given project, though, I've taken inspiration from all kinds of places — feature films, television shows, paintings, photographs, books, and life experiences — though it may not be obvious to anyone but me.

Q: *In addition to being a producer yourself, you also work with other producers. Do see a predominant "producer's personality"?*

A: I don't really think there is a "producer's personality," but I think there are many qualities that a good producer should have, if he or she wants to do his job well and also be able to sleep at night. Despite the clichés of what a producer acts like (sharp-dressed, fast-talking, megalomaniacs), I think that honesty is very important. Anything else will eventually come out anyway, so aside from basic ethics, there's really no point in making things up to cover your bases, or to convince someone of something that isn't true, just so you can get out of them what you want.

Being adaptable is also very important. Nothing ever works out exactly the way you expect it to, so you have to be able to adapt to situations that are in flux. I think that a lot of good producers are also very anal and a bit obsessive — I'm not really this way, but I sometimes wish I were (in my work). Working well with people is also very important. The people you are working with are so important in a field that is so collaborative, so if you get the opportunity to work with great people (as I've been lucky enough to do), you'd better get along well with them so they'll want to work with you again.

Q: *It's clear that the future of television is highly speculative, depending on who one talks to. What are your own speculations on this intriguing new world?*

A: I have positive and negative feelings about the future of television. With every step forward, there seems to be a step backward. As media consolidation puts control into the hands of fewer and fewer corporations, there have been some alarming trends. The bottom line is all that matters at most networks, to the detriment of the viewing public.

The perceived power of right-wing groups who try to censor voices on television is also pretty terrifying. The prospect of "branded entertainment" is a bit unseemly, as well. For someone whose livelihood hinges upon working in the field, the decreases in production budgets for documentaries is also a bummer. However, these decreases are largely due to the greater number of programming outlets that are fighting for the same number of viewers, which is a good thing. There are now more places where you can make things, and that has opened up the field to some truly original voices. Before the rise of cable, shows like *South Park*, *The Daily Show with Jon Stewart*, *The Sopranos*, and pretty much anything on the Cartoon Network's *Adult Swim* never would have made it to the air. The increased need for content has also allowed for an expansion in the industry that has allowed more people to actually have jobs in it, and advances in technology have made it easier and cheaper to create things of good production value. So the type of person who can get his or her voice heard is no longer an archetype. So I guess I am cautiously optimistic about the future.

Q: *What do you wish someone had told you early in your career?*

A: That there's no secret formula. I didn't actually set out to do this, and it's far from the career goals I am still hoping and working to achieve, but here I am doing it. It's not rocket science — you just have to learn from your mistakes, rise to the challenges in front of you, and be willing to ask someone who knows better than you when you need to. And there's *always* someone who knows better than you.

Q: *What is your personal Top Ten List of what a producer should know?*

> **TOP TEN**
>
> ## My Own Top Ten List of Things a Producer of Documentaries Should Know
> 1. There's no substitute for a good story
> 2. Working with great people is better than working with a lot of money
> 3. How to write
> 4. How to use as much of your production gear as possible (just in case)
> 5. How to budget (and stay within it)
> 6. If you're traveling with equipment, show up really early at the airport
> 7. If you're going on location somewhere, it's best to have someone local on the crew
> 8. It's never going to be the way you expect it to be
> 9. It's okay to ask for advice
> 10. Everything takes longer than you think it will

Q: *If you were to give a guest lecture in a producing for television class, what would you tell the students?*

A: Don't do this work if you want to get rich and/or famous or you think it's a glamorous, cool-sounding job. Chances are, it won't work out that way anyway, but if that's the reason you want to do this work, please don't. As corny as it sounds, it really is a privilege to create and help create mass media, and there is a responsibility inherent in that, not only to the people who are seeing your work, but to your own soul. There's not much you can do about what other people are creating, but there's almost always something you can do about what *you* are doing.

Salli Frattini

Executive producer, MTV, including Super Bowl Half Time and MTV's *VMA*

Q: *You started off in the television business at a young age. What inspired you?*

A: I really do think my inspiration was Mary Tyler Moore because she was the woman in the newsroom surrounded by all these men. She seemed to be really organized and she was the woman in the room telling all the guys what to do. She was compassionate, she was organized, and she was sweet, she was pretty, and she was single.

I grew up in an Irish-Italian Catholic household, having two older brothers, being child number four, having two parents who were really not college educated — my dad was a painter, my mom was a nurse — and somehow I became one of the organizers of the house. I was very organized, very conscious, and among my friends, I was always the one you could count on to drive. But I was also wild. I had that crazy side to me, which always surprises people. So I think that starting when you're young and having those kind of traits, being somebody who was compassionate and organized with leadership qualities, living in a house with five kids and parents, you've got to know how to speak and you've got to know how to get what you need. You learn how to multitask, and you learn how to think on your own two feet.

The skills for producing for me started really at a young age. Throughout the years, I was really inspired by the Olympics. I thought the Olympics were the best thing ever — I looked forward to them every four years. Parades, too, I've always liked big events. I used to like to watch them on TV and that was, of course, when there were three TV channels. I loved watching Jerry Lewis' telethon every September. So I was a lucky person who started out at a young age really intrigued by television. I knew what I wanted to do by the time I got to college, which was to work in television.

I was always a hard worker. The work ethic started young because I didn't really have a choice and needed to make money, and I don't mind hard work. Some of my jobs included having a paper route, babysitting, and cleaning houses after school. I knew a lot about the money we didn't have. I was good in math and I guess people sensed that I had some sort of business skill or common sense. My strengths were being street smart and having common sense. Unfortunately, I was never book smart. I was never a straight A student until my TV courses in college. I didn't go to school on a scholarship, I received college loans and student aid, and worked hard.

Q: *While you were in college, how did you learn about the "real world" of television?*

A: I knew that I liked TV, and my organizational skills and people skills lent themselves to this business. And I think for me it was so much about hard work, like getting internships. In college, I had four internships that were just so valuable to me. I learned so much. I met many mentors and friends who are still close to me today. These internships gave me the experience and confidence to be able to say — give me a few minutes and I'll figure it out with the help of professionals. Not freaking out. Not acting like an idiot. Knowing how to be composed on the phone. You're like a sponge at that age.

Q: *How did you get involved in the live events and music aspect of television?*

A: The first time I had done a music event was in Boston in 1982. We taped a Windham Hill concert. I just thought this was the greatest thing. Now mind you, I grew up in a house without a stereo. We had a radio in our house and that was it. So I wasn't a concert-goer and music really wasn't my thing, but when I first did this concert, it was like — this really is cool. I was learning how to cable a camera and how to set up the audio control system. I was carrying in equipment cases, I was schlepping equipment — nowadays PA's don't schlepp the amount of equipment they used to do. I also learned post-production. So that's kind of when the bug started for me.

My first job was with John Sullivan Associates in Boston as the office manager. They had a small mobile truck — actually, I was booking the truck, and when you start booking equipment and booking facilities, you understand what it takes. You start pricing things. I did billings, I did accounts payable and accounts receivable for the company. And while I was working at Sullivan, I was still waitressing part-time.

Q: *Should students of producing look to a network or a production company for job opportunities?*

A: A lot of people who come here thinking that the network is the place to start forget that starting in a production company or in a smaller company — making commercials, videos, sales, or the corporate side of it — is a way that you can learn so much more because you're hands on. I don't see that as much now, that trend.

Q: *Do you think there is a producer's personality?*

A: I do. I think you have to know how to understand people. I meet a lot of producers who are a Type A personality. They're anal, they're organized, they're detailed, they're compulsive, they're control freaks. I think that there are some really, really good producers who are great storytellers, but they may not be great organizers. They may be really great at telling a story and conceptualizing a story, but they're not organized in the sense of how to put it all together. Those are the kind of producers who always seem to have a partner who balances that. But I definitely think there's a producer personality. I meet people who aren't even producers: You look at them and you go, you could be a producer! You have the creative and organizational skills.

Q: *How are women as producers?*

A: I think women have a little more compassion due to our natural maternal instincts, which are so important. A good executive producer is someone who knows how to put together the best team and gets respect by giving it. As you're young, you kind of grow and get yourself in the system. In the world of MTV, I'm surrounded by such incredibly talented women, and they all have their own story, which is really inspiring. There are so many more women in this organization than there are in many others. You know, we breed that kind of environment, whereas in some other networks, you just don't get that. Look at the Olympics and tell me how many female producers there are.

Q: *Yet you eventually became one of these female Olympic producers. How did you make that happen?*

A: When I left Boston, I came to New York. *Entertainment Tonight* hired me while I was freelancing to do a two-week, on-the-road shoot with them, and I was the production manager. My skills led me more to production manager possibilities. I remember walking into NBC for my first interview for the Olympics after calling and calling and calling, just being persistent. I don't know if this was the truth or not, but I swear it had something to do with the fact that I had an Italian last name. I finally got in and I think personality-wise, we hit it off. There was something charming about the interview. They asked me, "Have you ever done anything like this?" It was no, but I said, "I can do it." It was just hard work. It was working fifteen hours a day. It was learning to do everything. We didn't have a staff of twelve people to delegate things to.

Q: *Did you have people showing you what to do?*

A: I just figured it out by myself, and by taking on so much, you learn so many different roles. Some of the producers who come up the ranks now come from different places. I came up through technical, production management, and eventually line producing that led to producing, then to executive producing — that was kind of my pattern. Some producers will come up the writing path, or from interning, as a PA, an AP, to executive producer, or producer. They may not always learn that logistical side, or they learn it when they're finally there and have to figure it out.

Q: *What was your job on the Olympics?*

A: They put me on rowing and canoeing venues, and I had the best time of my life. I had such a good experience and I made so many friends. The other part of it all was networking, knowing the right people, humbling myself, asking a lot of questions, making people feel good about their jobs, and showing an interest in what they do and then establishing that relationship with them.

In 1992, they called me back to the Olympics. "I want you to come back, but this time, I want to put you in the A venue to do opening and closing ceremonies and track and field. So I went from the C venue as the junior broadcast manager, working rowing and canoeing, to four years later having the A venue. That was one of the coolest things I had ever done. And that was the year of the Dream Team and Michael Jordan and Shaquille O'Neal. I remember the Dream Team didn't want to walk into the stadium for opening ceremonies with everybody else, so they were coming to our compound. I actually walked the Dream Team in the back door into the opening ceremonies. For a child who always wanted to work on the Olympics, and then actually be seeing or doing opening ceremonies, it was an amazing moment.

Q: *The very nature of a producer is a collaborative one, isn't it?*

A: Yes. You have to know people's skills and respect them for their skills. I think that's one of my greatest strengths. Now, as the executive producer, I've got 500 to 600 people working for me, like the technical team, the audio team, the camera team, the director, the stage manager, the PA, the events team, the crowd control, the security, the choreography, the dancers, and the production department. And unless you can be a good collaborator and really communicate to the troops, everything can just fall short.

Now when you think about a television show as large as the *VMAs,* making one small change has a domino effect on the entire production. With the *VMA* this year, Will Smith starts the show, seventy feet high on a stage that drops in. There's J-Lo who introduces Usher, then Usher, then Will — all these things have to be choreographed. If you changed the running order of the show, you personally had to walk up to every department head and say "did you hear what we just did? Did you know we changed the format?" "Oh no, I hadn't heard that yet." So communications, to me, is so important, being able to understand the skills of others. All those years of watching, learning, and asking all those questions have enabled me as a producer to have confidence.

Q: *What are some of the steps you take in setting up these large events?*

A: A lot of things happen simultaneously. One of my job responsibilities is finding the venue and the city to host the event. The creative drives the venue choice. We also look at the year in music, and where the trends will lead us. So starting with the city bid process, you basically put together a bid letter that outlines what the show requirements are: the size of the venue, city support which includes police, city services, traffic, department of transportation, sanitation, etc. I need hotels that can accommodate twenty-five hundred people including staff, talent, and visitors. We work with the visitors' and convention bureau to secure hotel and airport needs.

In addition to the show itself, there are all the ancillary events that go on around the city to promote the event; also, we need to know where to hold the preshow, where the red carpet arrivals are, all the other parts that go along with that.

The right venue is crucial. It also inspires you creatively. That's all part of the process. One of the first things we do is have a large meeting with all the department heads and we'll say: "This is what we decided. We're going to the city, here are the plans and the maps, here's our creative vision; this is why we chose this city and this particular venue. The city puts together a host meeting for us, where we can all spawn off to individual people, like the promotions people, the airport travel manager people, the creative people, and so forth.

Then there's the whole music marketing part of the bid. This includes our on-the-ground promotions since there are music events every single day — everything from street banners to airport signage to park signage, grass roots marketing, all sorts of local promotions. We see what the city has to offer as far as cultural events, diversity, and music events that might exist in the city. So, the basic standard letter went out to seven different cities that we identified that could be a good market for us, musically. And musical talent will go everywhere, as long as we take good care of them. Celebrity talent mainly comes from New York or Los Angeles, so sometimes it's more difficult for them to travel.

We follow the letter with a site visit to the appropriate cities. After the tour of available venues, we generally meet with the mayor's office to discuss our multiple needs.

The next step is to prepare a financial analysis. Each city has a deadline to respond to our inquiries, and we look at what each city has to offer. The city process goes on and on and on. Each city has its challenges to evaluate, and you have to give your best analysis of creative choices. Safety is the chief concern and you must have confidence in the city and the venue security. Creatively, does this venue work for what we're trying to do? Will the talent go there? In the meantime, you're coming back and meeting with all these individual departments because you have to take into consideration all the departmental needs. Then, we make a final presentation to the executive team with our production recommendations.

Q: *Do each of these cities know who they're in competition with?*

A: Actually, I don't typically reveal that until the very, very end. Some cities do their own research and find out. You know, I have learned a lot about politics, which is a big part of my job now. In many ways, it is no different than understanding life in a big city or at a large university. It all comes around . . .

Q: *How do you organize your staff and delegate tasks back at home base?*

A: The *VMAs,* as one example, involve a year-long production, and the staff works on it all year. We constantly discuss the creative elements, we're developing a logo, and the advertisers look for integrated marketing ideas. They have promotional campaigns that have already started. Each department has staff dedicated to making the best of this event.

Q: *You seldom say "I," you say "we." Everything you've talked about seems to involve teamwork.*

A: We are team people. We try to look after the big picture and then it just all gets communicated to the various departments. If I made a list of departments that go into this show — I don't think I've ever really done that, and I probably should — it's probably thirty different departments of people. We really are the only awards show that's produced from within — we don't hire an outside production company. When this all comes together, there is a great sense of accomplishment for all of us. I just happen to be one of the lucky people who leads the troops.

Barbara Gaines

Executive producer, *The Late Show with David Letterman*

Q: *As an Executive Producer on* The Late Show with David Letterman, *what is it that you do?*

A: This is a question my mother went to her grave asking. "What exactly do you do? Did you talk to any celebrities? What can I tell my friends?" There are actually nine "Emmy-eligible" producers, and four of us are executive producers.

Q: *What does each of you do, and how do you divide responsibilities among you?*

A: Rob Burnett is the CEO/President of Worldwide Pants, Dave Letterman's production company. The company's shows include our namesake program, *The Late Show with David Letterman, Everybody Loves Raymond,* and *The Late Late Show with Craig Ferguson.* Maria Pope is in charge of the talent department, Jude Brennan is our liaison with the network (CBS), the press, the world. And me, Barbara Gaines — what is it I do? Let's see. I routine the show (order and times), I oversee all of production. I'm really what we used to call a floor producer. Beginning in July of 2002, now I man the podium — I think Dave would probably say out of the five people who have had this job I'm not the best, I'm not the worst.

Q: *And your day-to-day job? What does that look like?*

A: First thing in the morning, I send an intern for coffee. I have a Starbucks and cereal for breakfast. Then I participate in a production meeting where the staff discusses the bones of the show and I make determinations about how much time things will take. I ask for a certain number of segment questions/acts of comedy accordingly. Back in my office, I "discuss" or write notes to Dave about the bones of the show and make adjustments according to his desires. I go over the jokes for the Act One comedy segments and pitch/cut jokes accordingly, and "discuss" with the head writers how to change the comedy to suit Dave's needs. Throughout that process I answer budget questions, personnel questions, and listen to people complain about their coworkers.

Around 1:00, I revise the official rundown for the day's rehearsal, with all of the elements to be rehearsed or pretaped filled in. Then I read and answer voluminous e-mail from the talent executive about future bookings and have a nice lunch. Around 2:30 I go down to the stage for rehearsal where I watch the tapes the writers have cut, see the graphics married to the jokes for the first time, or listen to the stage manager stand-in for Dave. While I'm in rehearsal, I try to get more answers from Dave about how he feels about the show. Then I come up to my office. I read and answer even more e-mail about booking, budget, and personnel problems. I make a revised rundown as a guide for the pitches in Dave's dressing room. I may have a light snack.

Around 4:30 I go to Dave's dressing room and continue to discuss the elements of that night's show. I discuss guest segment notes/questions. Around 4:45 I participate with the head writers/producers in pitching the comedy to Dave. Then I make a list of suggestions from those pitches and choose a running order for the comedy in Act One. Dave looks at it, asks for changes, and I make adjustments. Then I go down to the show and set the desk and stand at the podium onstage so that I can produce the show. I talk to the control room about segment orders and running times and make decisions on the spot about when to do the next segment. I try to tell Dave what is happening in the commercial breaks and try to take care of problems that may arise during the taping. Then I come upstairs and start to choose edits for the show. I tell the edit room what to do and show the edits to Dave and discuss with him their merits and make changes according to his desires.

Afterwards, I eat a nice dinner at my desk. I may also listen to staffers complain again, and read and answer yet more e-mail with questions and concerns about bookings, budgets, and staff issues. And also get the information from the writers about what they plan to do the next day and make a rundown for the production meeting. Then I put the show to bed and remain vaguely nauseous at the thought that someone may (and half the time will) call me between 11:35 and the end of the show (12:37) to tell me about things that were wrong (which I'll then fix for West Coast feeds).

Q: *People think of the show as a late-night talk show, but you think of it as a variety show. What's the difference?*

A: I would most certainly call the show a variety show (not a talk show). A talk show is one that is built around talk — we always felt our show was built around comedy. I would call *SCTV* and *Saturday Night Live* sketch shows. And for that matter, I would not call Dave Letterman a talk-show host, I would call him a broadcaster. *Donahue, Oprah, The View* — they're talk shows.

And while there are a hundred syndicated and local talk shows, the variety show is not as easy. Just ask Joey Bishop, Jerry Lewis, Chevy Chase, and Arsenio Hall. I think the idea of a "talk show" came in the early 1960s when I suppose shows began to drop the sketches and the jugglers and just talk to people. In some way I suppose after the years went by, the talk shows started to add back music, comics, and then with us, the sketch as well. Carson, the greatest of them all, did comedy bits, but not to our extent.

Q: *In 2002, the show won an Emmy and you went on stage to accept it on behalf of the producers' team. Can you remember what you said?*

A: It went like this . . . "I started as the receptionist on Dave's morning show over twenty-two years ago. We've all worked for Dave forever (*turned to other producers*) which I think shows what kind of man Dave is, that he inspires that kind of loyalty. Dave always says, 'All credit to the team.' We're just a very small part of that team. And we, of course, say all credit to Dave. This (*held up the Emmy Award*) is all Dave. We want to thank our very wonderful staff and crew; they are the hardest working group of men and women in the world. They're up there (*pointed to the balcony*). And we'd like to thank the Academy for thinking that after twenty years on the air, we still put on a quality show. On behalf of The Late Show, thank you very much."

Q: *What do see happening in the future of television?*

A: In the future, people are going to spend more time on the Internet. They will use their televisions simply as monitors for their computer. I think the Internet/monitor will make things more interactive. No longer will you just sit on the couch and watch.

Q: *This interview wouldn't be complete without asking the obvious question: What are the top ten things that an executive producer needs to know?*

TOP TEN

The Top 10 Things You Need to Be a Good Executive Producer:
1. Snappy dresser
2. Good listening skills
3. Pick your battles
4. Learn to take a joke
5. Ability to make a split-second decision
6. Organizational ability
7. Attention to detail

> 8. A small ego
> 9. A long fuse
> 10. Loyalty to the host and show that borders on insanity

Ann Kolbell

Coordinating Producer for NBC News Productions

Matthew Lombardi

Segment Producer for *Dateline*

Q: *You've both kindly agreed to be interviewed together because your career paths have intersected for years. Let's go back to the beginning. Who would like to talk first?*

Ann: I'll start because I got here first. For me, it started many years ago, when I interviewed Jane Pauley for a radio show I was doing in Ann Arbor, Michigan, where I was living at the time. I created the opportunity to interview her because I was looking to move from my job then into a producing job.

Q: *And you knew what producing was, as an actual job description?*

Ann: Yes, I did. I was doing a series on women in broadcasting that created a chance to meet women in the industry, and I took advantage of the opportunity. I wrote to Jane, researched her backwards and forwards, came to New York, and did a great interview because I was well prepared. As I was leaving I pitched myself to Jane — I said I was looking to leave my present job, and then described a job function and how my skills could be useful to her. The timing was not right, she said, but please keep in touch. At that time Jane had been the *Today Show* anchor for two-and-a-half years. So I kept in touch — and six months later we began what would be a twenty-five year partnership lasting until she left NBC News.

In that case, I identified what I thought was a need, and then I showed how I felt I could fill that need. I had read an article about Barbara Walters and her assistant producer who was described as her right-hand. The article listed a number of things this person did of a substantive editorial nature, and I figured Jane Pauley was probably a little too young to have formed a relationship like that with somebody. At that time I had been working seven years and had a resume and experience of my own to offer. And as it turned out, I was right.

Q: *What were you hoping you would be doing with Jane? What did you propose?*

Ann: I was interested in content . . . specifically, news content. I knew how to organize things, I was smart, and I knew how to research. I think those were some of the things I talked about.

Q: *Did you start off as a producer?*

Ann: I started off as her assistant, which was not what I had pitched. She had an assistant at the time, and the then-executive producer approved my hiring. So Jane would have had an assistant and me, and I would have been her research producer. Then as happens in network television, within two months, the guy who approved my hiring was replaced by a new executive producer who said she could have only one person working with her, so she brought me in as her assistant.

Q: *Now it's your turn, Matt. How did you start as a producer?*

Matt: I carried my tape recorder with me everywhere as a kid. I had this odd fascination with recording things and playing them back. I taped everything. As I got into school, I brought my video camera to school. It was this odd fascination with wanting to play things back for some reason. By the time I was old enough to try and figure out what I was supposed to do for a living, all I really knew was I wanted to continue this process of recording something and making it into something. So film school was sort of a logical step, because I was working in a movie theater at the time. So naively, I decided, "This is how you go to Hollywood, you work in a movie theater and go to film school." Except I found out if you really want to go to Hollywood, you go to NYU. I went to The School of Visual Arts instead. While I was there, my parents were sort of kicking me in the butt saying "You really ought to have some plan after school" and I had none. They suggested I get an internship somewhere. So meanwhile, at the same time I'm at the movie theater and I'm now the manager hiring box office cashiers. One of them said "I can't work on Fridays because I have an internship at NBC." I said, "That's interesting. I'm actually looking for an internship, how do you get one?" She said, "It's easy, they'll hire anyone for free."

So I got an internship at NBC, but I was late getting to the party. I think this was late August, where the internships for the fall are already taken. So they said, "We've got one left, and it's at the *Today Show,* have you ever watched it?" I said no. And they said, "It's yours if you want it. Take it or leave it." So I took it. Right around that time, around my first week starting at the *Today Show,* I met someone named Ann Kolbell — who is my partner in this interview — who was working for Jane Pauley. But within a week of my starting, Jane announced she was leaving the *Today Show* after 13 years.

Q: *How did you and Ann begin working together back then?*

Matt: This was in October of 1989. Talk about identifying a need! Ann identified a need for someone to answer the phones, which were going crazy because Jane's just made this announcement and the mail is pouring in, literally by the buckets full, everyday. It was impossible for anybody to keep up. So I was the intern and I met Ann and she basically brought me into Jane's office and gave me five buckets full of mail and said, "Please sort these." The real breakthrough was three months later when Jane was actually going to leave the show. Ann hurt her back, and couldn't be in the office for Jane's last week. And she said, "I'm going to be this way for at least a month. I know you have school and two jobs, but if you can be 'me' for the next month and extend your internship into the next semester, you will have a job when you graduate from school." She guaranteed it. So there you go. I graduated on a Friday and started on the payroll at NBC on the following Monday.

Q: *So now we fast-forward to 2005. What are your jobs now?*

Matt: I sort of liken my job to making movies because your role is very much like that of the director. Producing for TV and producing for film are very different. A lot of people say they're the same, I think they're very different. Especially in news. What's unique about producing for news is you are responsible for the product from the time it's budgeted, to the time its shot, to the time it's written and, ultimately, to the time it's edited and aired. From conception to it being broadcast, you're really responsible in, some way, for every bit of it. So, at least in terms of what I do specifically, I'm usually assigned a particular story and I am responsible from that moment — the moment it's assigned — to conceptualizing it, trying to figure out what is the story, and hopefully being open to it changing if that's editorially what should happen, and paying for it responsibly, then getting it on the air.

Q: *And Ann, you've worked for NBC for most of your professional life. What are you doing these days with the network?*

Ann: I am the Coordinating Producer for NBC News Productions. We are a unit within NBC News that repackages current NBC programming, and produces new programming that we sell to different venues, mostly in cable. For example, we produce A&E Biographies. We sell to Discovery, National Geographic, Court TV, among others. We do things for MSNBC and CNBC. Since NBC recently merged with Universal, we provide extra content on Universal movie DVDs.

Basically, we're for hire. We're a profit center. We produce a half-hour syndicated program called *Your Total Health* which airs in 95% of the country hosted by Hoda Kotb, a *Dateline* correspondent. It's produced by NBC Productions and distributed by NBC Enterprises. We've done a couple of pilots for Bravo, one of them was a comedy show, and we just did a two-hour year ender for A&E, a two-hour bio show. We produce for Good Housekeeping, VH1, and Spike TV. We're hooking up with books. It's a very eclectic portfolio. I am the Coordinating Producer for the unit, which means it's my job to keep track of everything that's going on. I'm dealing with lawyers, finance people, producers, marketing. On *Your Total Health* I'm the coordinating producer, and a segment producer. I am involved in editorial, in programming the show. We're a small group, so we all do a lot on it.

Q: *Matt, what is your particular producer's title? And what responsibilities does it cover?*

Matt: Producer is kind of a broad term. What does it mean? Usually, I refer to myself as a "segment producer for *Dateline*." It's funny, if you call someone who's not in the business and you say, "I'm a producer for *Dateline*" very often they think, "Oh, he's *the* producer of *Dateline NBC*," which is not the case. So, a segment producer is probably a better way to put it.

Q: *How similar is the TV producer's job to the film producer's?*

Matt: Between film and TV? Well, I've never been fortunate enough to follow my dream of producing for film, but from what I understand, producers for film have limited control over the film produced in that, at a certain point, the director is the person who really controls the editorial content of the film. He controls the editing and the shooting; specifically "the look" of each shot. A list of duties for a film producer can be anywhere from the budget, to scouting the locations, to hiring the crew and casting the film. But ultimately, at some point, the producer is going "Well okay Mr. Director, we brought you all this wonderful stuff, now go make a film out of it." With producing for TV, the final product is, ultimately, your whole responsibility. The producer's cap is a big one because, ultimately, you have responsibility for the entire thing, which is more fun, I think.

Q: *You are both producers. You've worked with one another for years, and you work with dozens of other producers from all areas of film and television. What traits or personalities do they share, if any?*

Ann: A producer is a person who needs to be organized. Not everybody's system is the same. Let's put it this way, producers have their own systems. Whether or not they're organized or not, I guess is a subjective thing. But any producer has a system that works for her somehow. She or he is probably detail oriented.

Matt: To produce anything, I think you need to have some communication skills because you end up turning over a lot of work to other people. When you go out on location, you're entrusting a cameraman and a soundman. You're not actually working a camera. You're turning it over to them, and hoping that what you have asked this crew to capture is what will ultimately wind up on the tape. You're putting your faith in those people. It happens to be unique to news where the producers have to turn over the editing of the piece to another person. In this case, an editor. Graphics, once again, you're not physically designing the graphics. Someone else is designing the graphics. So you need to be able to communicate an idea to a series of individuals who, hopefully, will be able to interpret your vision or whatever it is and translate it onto tape.

Even in the research stage, it's almost impossible to do all the research yourself; so at some point, you have other individuals who are pulling research for you. You have to be able to trust that those people are finding the information that you want. I think all producers are control freaks and the irony of that is that you really don't have control over any of it. The entire thing at some point is turned over to different people and you're hoping and praying that it comes back to you in the way you envisioned it.

And even when it goes on the air, you've turned it over to some more people in a control room somewhere. You have to pray that the settings are right, that the vector scope is the way it's supposed to be, and that the luminescence level is where it's supposed to be. You go home and watch it on the air and you cringe sometimes because you realize that something was way off. It's weird stuff like that you really have no control over.

Ann: Plus, keep in mind all this is taking place in a network environment. Obviously, at a local station, you are doing a lot of these things yourself so you're not turning it over. I think that's important to remember.

Q: *Because you are both quite familiar with* Dateline, *what and who could be considered its historical predecessor?*

Matt: *60 Minutes . . .*

Ann: Dateline *was the 18th effort by NBC to create a strong news magazine.*

Matt: If you look at *60 Minutes* now, the style of the way they tell stories is almost identical to the way it was thirty years ago. The biggest change is they went to shooting it on film to video, which I think was a big leap for them. I mean this technically. Visually, the show looks exactly the same. I approach editing differently. I usually go a little crazy in the edit room. But crazy in a good way. I like a lot of frenetic editing — a lot of music — a lot of cuts. I grew up watching MTV, so I'm used to seeing things at that pace. But many other news programs and producers don't see the need for it. It's a judgment call. What's important is the content. Jane Pauley once told me, "too much whipped cream spoils the cake."

Q: *You've both talked to hundreds of students in producing for television classes. What insights and advice have you shared with these students?*

Ann: You have to be flexible. Not all producers are flexible, but good producers are flexible. The best producers are good writers. And, you have to be creative. Take initiative.

Matt: Willingness to collaborate. And, definitely the ability to tell a story. At the end of the day, you're telling stories. You have to be able to structure a story so that someone knows what you're talking about. One of the functions of a news producer is to write a story in collaboration with the on-air talent. If you don't have the writing skills to write a story and collaborate with someone who may have a different vision for that story, you're not going to be very happy.

Jeffrey McLaughlin

Director of Post-Production and Senior Editor, All Mobile Video

Q: *What are the main qualities in an editor that a producer should look for?*

A: Editors are all different. In terms of "a style," most editors fall into one of these three categories, and from those categories, there are countless combinations and degrees.

Category 1 is the storyteller — This is a classic editor who is able to take footage and script and tell a story. He or she is "an author of images." If you need someone who can sit through hours of footage and come up with a cohesive story with a good pace, this is your candidate.

Category 2 is the graphic artist — This category did not exist a few years ago. An editor always edited, and a graphic artist always designed. Now, that line between these two is fading. An editor's style has as much to do with their look as their pacing. Editing is not always story-telling as much as it's the layering of images and graphics. This editor doesn't see story as much but sees energy and image. A classic director like Eisenstein would never be able to hold a job at MTV because he couldn't think beyond one layer of image. I was critical of this nonnarrative style for years, but have grown to appreciate it when it is done well.

Category 3 is the technical editor — This is an editor who isn't always the go-to person for creativity, yet is often the one every producer should worship. They are important in the preproduction stage as well as the post-production stage. No matter how creative you may be, the final look of your project better be technically solid. Directors like George Lucas and all of Madison Avenue look to these "pocket protector" editors with a great deal of respect.

Q: *So how can a producer make the right decision in finding the right editor?*

A: First, look at the project, then look at your own skills. How creative are you in making editing decisions? Are you organized? Do you have the time or the budget to experiment? What "type" of editing style will benefit your vision? The obvious choice would be an editor who possesses all skills equally, but that's not always possible. Plus, each project is different and each project needs a different style. Look at your project and your skills, and keep these three categories in mind when you're interviewing editors.

Another factor in choosing your editor is based on organization. If you and your project are totally unorganized, make your first priority an editor who is obsessive compulsive. If you do have an organized work style, look for someone who is looser and less predictable, and probably more creative.

Communication skills are a must. After your marriage, your relationship with your editor is going to be the most stressful relationship of your life. Think about it: You and this editor will be sitting in a room together for ten to twelve hours a day, six or seven days a week, till the project has been completed. You are going to be sharing your dreams with this editor, and he or she is going to disagree with almost everything you want to do. It can get rough in an edit room, but like a marriage, it's all about trust. Make sure your editor trusts your vision, and vice versa. The final result always looks better when there's peace in the house. The TV and video business is a collaborative world. Listen to your vision and follow that vision but look to the editor for outside help. You can get so engrossed in your idea that you may need a new voice.

Q: *What was your career path in editing?*

A: I have been editing since 1976. I started by editing in film, on a flatbed. Now, I have continued to edit in video, on whatever tools come my way that can make editing better, easier, and cheaper. I became an editor because I felt that it was the single most important step of the whole filmmaking process. I don't prefer one software or one product over another. I found out through the years that the process is always getting better. To adopt one edit system over another works for individual projects but not for career decisions. Editing is always changing and there is always a newer software program out there that could benefit a project.

Q: *What do producers need to know when they come into the post-production facility?*

A: Walking into the final stage of your project without any preparation for that stage is a mistake many producers make. Planning the budget, the script, and the shoot are obvious to every producer, but planning, or at least being aware of some issues you will face in post-production is just as important. No matter how good your budget is going along, or how good the script is, or how magical the shooting may have felt — you eventually have to put all the pieces together and make it work. You can blow a good film in the edit room, or you can save a bad one.

One of an editor's golden assets in an edit room is that they were never part of the production process. They weren't shooting the film for four weeks and feeling the "magic" of that process. The war stories the crew told about shooting in the midst of a hurricane or when half the staff came down with food poisoning — they mean nothing to the editor. Editors only see the dailies, and the only magic they feel is what comes out of those dailies. If a shot works, they will use it, but if it doesn't, they can easily let it go. The pain, the love, or the cost of any one element means nothing if it doesn't work in the edit. No one thing is more important than the whole of the film.

Q: *When you were a student studying filmmaking and editing, what were some of the lessons that have stuck with you?*

A: While you are talking about a producer's unique skills, it's really important to understand the unique vocabulary of television and film. As you develop your skills as a producer, be aware of the medium that you are working in and the visual and audio vocabulary that is part of the process. The history of editing has always fascinated me. Many years ago in the 1900s, a Russian intellectual named V. I. Pudovkin and his friend, a Russian filmmaker named Lev Kuleshov realized that film possessed its own language and its own grammatical rules for that language. They conducted an experiment where they showed a sequence of film. They started with the same neutral expression close-up of an actor. They then intercut this same shot with scenes of a bowl of soup, with a shot of a coffin being lowered into the ground, and a shot of a little girl playing.

They showed these sequences to audiences and asked them to comment on the actor's performance. The responses of the audiences revealed that the actor's face showed hunger, sorrow, and happiness, respectively. The neutral expression had been altered by its juxtaposition with other shots. The conclusion of this experiment was that film has its own language. The juxtaposition of images creates a meaning. Editing creates the meaning. The audience feels the emotions through the relationship between shots. I read about this experiment at 21 and it changed my life. I saw the power of editing and realized what it could do. It is a 20th century tool with endless potential if you understand how to use it.

Q: *How important is editing in telling the truth versus manipulating it with clever editing choices?*

A: Whether you're a producer of documentaries, a narrative filmmaker, or a TV commercial producer, you have the power to make up the truth. For example, most Americans think of the Civil War as it was portrayed in *Gone with the Wind*. The facts of John F. Kennedy's assassination are now deeply rooted in Oliver Stone's film, *JFK*. Fox TV and Bill O'Reilly show the "truth" every day and they inform a large audience, while Michael Moore shows another truth that is equally convincing. What are your responsibilities to the truth? If you are searching for truth, you have to tell the truth. It is easy to slant your side. If you are interpreting the truth, you are making propaganda. History paints this picture of the German filmmaker, Leni Riefensthal, as the master of evil propaganda. Her films portrayed Hitler and the Nazis as heroes. She was able to do this because she understood editing. She only showed what she wanted you to see. A "well-edited" documentary can make any war seem justified or evil. TV commercials can make beer and high-fat hamburgers seem like something we have to eat. As a producer, you can take a stand, and be aware of your power and the different rules that TV images and their juxtaposition can follow.

Q: *When you start a project with a producer or team of producers, what is involved in that process?*

A: I try to meet with producers prior to the edit, but often I come into the project after it has been completely shot. I usually meet the producers on the first day of editing when they show up with a suitcase of tapes. They tell me how much time they've booked to edit the piece, yet usually they don't realize how much footage they have shot. Sometimes they have roughly a hundred hours worth of film that they want to cut in the next two weeks.

I first ask them for notes and scripts. If I'm lucky, they'll have those, but more and more producers seem to think that editors wave a magic wand over hours worth of stuff, and only the good stuff comes up. I remind them that if we first need to screen, log, and digest the material, and then make an insightful and coherent movie, it's going to take time. For every one hour of footage, it takes at least two or three hours to view, log, and highlight every hour of film. You then need to knock this down into a script with some kind of theme, and only then can you start to edit.

Many producers don't get this, especially if they're new at the job, or there's a time dead-line. So often, I just fast-forward through the tapes, grab some sound bites that work, and randomly view the material. I basically edit whatever appears in front of me and make a story of this random material. When the producer sees what has been done, they are happy that there is a story and theme, but they may think something is missing. Then, if they remember anything specific, we go back, find other shots, fill them in, and fine-tune the piece. If nothing else, the piece is done. There could still be hours of unviewed tape, but the deadline has been met.

Sometimes, I might feel that I have cheated the project. But, if a producer takes no part in the process — like screening it, logging it, coming up with some notes before the edit — the editor can't be expected to take over, and become the producer, writer, and director for a project that's been dropped on their lap in the eleventh hour.

Q: *The budgeting process for post-production is usually an area that the producer gets very nervous about — even the most experienced producer can get bogged down.*

A: Budgets can be real, but they fall apart when producers lose control of the project. They have to find a fine line, for example, between allowing some experimentation — but not too much. A producer wants to give the client and/or editor the control they demand, and also knows how to convince the client and/or editor to let their project grow a bit. How do you play the middle? Know your clients, know your post-production people. Be in control, but allow creativity and open up your budget for that extra time. As a producer, your golden rule is to always be prepared. You are in a creative business, so sometimes even the best preparation is not enough. At that point look to the future and learn from your mistakes.

Q: *Regardless of the budget or the time or the people involved, a good story is always at the core of editing a project. How do you tell that story as an editor?*

A: I'll give you an example. One of my favorite films of all times was made by Steven Spielberg when he was twenty-one. It was called *Duel*. It's a story of a man driving his car who is being followed by a giant black tractor trailer — this goes on for ninety minutes. The entire plot is a mere nineteen words, yet it is a great ninety minutes of nonstop tension and action. The guy in his car is played by Dennis Weaver, and his entire motivation is to escape from this truck on his tail. That's it. But the editing created conflict, tension, split-second timing, and so on, and made this a classic.

Q: *You work with producers all the time. What advice would you give a producer who is starting out in the business?*

A: The easiest way to become a great producer is to work harder than any other producer. Try some writing, try directing and, definitely, try to learn more about editing. A good producer will try to walk in every one's shoes. Sit behind an edit console and edit for twenty-hour days for a couple of weeks and you will learn as much about how to produce and shoot your next project as you will about editing. Know the process, you don't have to necessarily master it. In the end it gives you more freedom and control over your project. And as with any job in TV, don't look at producing as a job. Look at it as part of your life.

Q: *Are there favorite producers and not so favorite producers?*

A: I like anyone who respects me and laughs at my jokes. There are many producers out there who lack creative talent. That's not necessarily a problem. It only becomes a problem when this lack of creativity turns into attitude. An example of this are the producers who have no idea of what they want, or any idea how to take their footage and make it into a coherent idea. Sometimes, these producers try to mask the fact that they are essentially clueless, creatively, or don't understand much if anything, about editing. So they'll give you no guidance and no real concept, meaning you must start from scratch and make something out of it all. You learn to accept this, it's part of the job. Except at this point many "clueless" producers now step it up. Yesterday, they had no idea of where to begin. Today, now that they've seen your first rough cut, they totally discredit it.

Editors should handle criticism but not from the person whose project they are trying to save. If, as a producer, for whatever reason like a time crunch or limited budget, you have to walk into an edit room totally unprepared, admit it up front. Seek advice from the creatives around you and give them a semi-solution, or some direction, just don't give them attitude.

Q: *What are some examples of excellent editing?*

A: My favorite examples — I've got a few that I really like. Films like *Day for Night, Duel,* and of course, *Jaws* —-especially the scene where everyone is told it's safe to go back in the water. There's also the Odessa Steps sequence in *Potemkin,* there's *Hearts and Minds* that I think is a classic example of a documentary that slants the facts by manipulating the sequences. A great example of parallel editing is at the end of *Silence of the Lambs,* where Jodie Foster is meeting the criminal that the audience thinks is being arrested at another location. But it's important to look at the editing in anything you're watching — TV, films, content on the Internet. They're all examples of editing — good editing, not-so-good editing, and the kind of editing that is really bad. When you can consciously study editing as the art form that it is, you can learn to prepare for editing, and you can learn what and how to shoot for editing. My final thought about editing? Think of it a Zen experience. It's a process that continues to ask questions and come up with solutions. It can be the ultimate journey.

Brett Morgen

Executive producer, producer, and producer/director, including *The Kid Stays in the Picture*

Q: *Do you approach a project differently for television than for theatrical distribution?*

A: Sometimes you don't know when you start a show if it's going to end up on television or go theatrical. Often, people set out to do it for television, and the story takes on a sort of life of its own and you finish the piece and say, "Hey, this has theatrical potential." Most of the time, though, you know if it's intended for television or for theater when you start a production, and you need to be aware because the transition from TV to theater is so expensive. For example, if you're doing a television production, for an hour-long show, you'll do a one-day or two-day sound mix, tops! And a five-day sound mix is almost unheard of. I'll spend six weeks to three months doing a sound edit or a sound mix on a theatrical. In television, the bandwidth is so small that very few sounds cut through so it's a waste of time to even try a complex mix.

On television, your work is being seen by more people. I remember when *The Kid Stays in the Picture* went into theatrical release, we did 1.5 million dollars which at the time was, I think, the fifteenth highest earning theatrical documentary. But when it premiered on HBO, we had 1.6 million people watching it that first night, which was five times the amount of people who actually saw it in theaters. Then in subsequent viewings, we added it all up and it's probably now thirty, forty times the people who saw it in the theaters.

When you have a message you're trying to get across, you're much better off being on television than being in a movie theater, especially with a smaller type movie, say, about Romanian street children. You know people aren't going to pay to see it in a movie theater. If you're into activism and your point is to get a message across, you're much better off doing it on television. Ultimately, however, if you're trying to get your message across, you're better off doing it as a fiction film anyway. Take a movie like *Hotel Rwanda*. Far more people will see *Hotel Rwanda* than will ever see a documentary about Rwanda.

I do think there are a lot of creative advantages to television — the immediacy, the amount of financing, funding — making it vastly superior to film, particularly now in cable television.

Q: *If you were to come up with a project and you wanted to see it broadcast, would it be on HBO — or would you approach another venue?*

A: I think more people still watch the networks than anywhere else. In terms of sheer eyeballs, networks are the best, but getting a project on the networks is very challenging if not impossible. In terms of documentary — cable, premium, or PBS — I think it's a toss-up between HBO and PBS. I think HBO appeals more to our egos as filmmakers. It's sexier. However, PBS is available in every household in America. They're getting three million people watching per night, whereas HBO may get a million, a million plus. Their viewers are different in terms of social activism. On PBS you'll reach the grassroots; you'll reach your core audience a lot easier than on HBO. But then again, HBO is an easier exercise. If they're into your project, they'll finance it and there you go. I think a lot of filmmakers have qualms about PBS in terms of their national distribution and promotion. I did a series for PBS that ran at a different time on a different day in every city, and it was a nightmare to promote.

I think the most important thing for young producers, for television producers, is to understand that you can take the same pitch to about nine different places, but you need to alter that pitch for each place. So I think a lot of times when people come up with ideas, it's really helpful to know to whom you're pitching. Know which networks serve what audience and is there a way to change certain aspects of your pitch so it appeals to different networks.

Q: *Say you're pitching a show called* Public Defenders. *How would you adapt your pitch for Court TV? Or to Lifetime?*

A: On Lifetime, it features all women public defenders, *Defenders* with more feel-good stories, no rape, no sex abuse, no incest. Now, for Court TV, they might say, "All right, we need more men in the show, because our demographics lean toward men, so the women need to be good-looking, make it a little sexier and a little more hard-hitting." Take it to HBO, and either it becomes a family of public defenders or it's dealing with some of the most hard-core crimes around. And you take that same show to VH1 and it's former celebrities who are now lawyers. Then, you take that to NBC and it's a reality show for a search for the world's greatest lawyer. The winner gets a contract working with Alan Dershowitz and they're going to compete against each other in an eight-week survival challenge. Guess what? It doesn't stop there. You can do a cartoon series for the Cartoon Network about a bunch of public defenders.

Up until the late nineties, television documentary was all about PBS. When you asked someone who they were working for everyone would say, "PBS." Then I started realizing that PBS only has *POV*, *American Experience*, and *American Masters*. So, people were producing work thinking "Oh, it's for PBS," but if it doesn't go on PBS, where is it going?

You've really got to know your audience. A lot of us are elitists. A lot of people in our industry don't watch television. A lot of academics and intellectuals, particularly on the documentary side, would rather read a book than watch television. I watch a LOT of television and I'm not embarrassed to admit it. I watch probably three hours of television a night. I think it makes me a better producer. My wife will sometimes walk into the room and she'll turn to the television and say, "What are you doing?" and I'll say, "I'm working," and she'll say, "You're watching *The Apprentice*." But the show has great production values. I remember the first time I saw *Survivor* — everyone in America might have been talking about how amazing these personality conflicts were, but I was obsessed with the way they were doing sound and their coverage of these scenes. This is the slickest, prettiest, nonfiction work I have ever seen. And so you can learn that way, but more importantly, you need to learn and understand the networks. You need to know what those networks are developing, and how they're growing. For example, TLC is a different network today than it was four or five years ago.

You can't just watch television for three months every ten years. Spike TV has changed dramatically. Bravo has changed dramatically. Every cable station with the exception of MTV has completely shifted their programming in the last five years. And even MTV has shifted more, to celebrity rather than reality series with younger icons. VH1, which was all about *Behind the Music*, is now all about celebrities in reality shows. They ALL are constantly evolving and we need to evolve with them. And when you go in to talk with the networks, it helps when you walk in and say, "I've loved *Housewreckers*, and it's my favorite show. You guys are doing such a good job."

Q: *Do you think of yourself more as a producer or a director, or both?*

A: Well, in television I'm more of a producer because as a member of the Director's Guild, it's very difficult for me to work in nonfiction on television and basic cable. It's almost impossible. Economically, what I'll do now is come up with ideas for shows and hire them out for people to do. I'm not even a showrunner anymore. I basically am a creator at this point.

Q: *Can you talk more about that?*

A: I would hire what is called the "showrunner," someone who is basically going to take the project over. At the end of the day, the show would probably say, "Created by Brett Morgen," and then I would be one of a number of executive producers. My job is to then find the right people to run that show who can implement and protect my vision for the program. My job then becomes to put that in motion — make sure the script is tight, oversee the casting, and oversee the editing. The showrunner is technically the director and I'm the executive producer.

Q: *Then how do you make money doing that?*

A: You can't start a series and then bail-out after the first season and think you're going to get rich by taking some sort of royalty — unless it's *The Osbournes* or some mind-blowing exception to the rule. Cable budgets are between $75,000 and $200,000 for a half-hour reality show. You can't take $50,000 off the top just because you came up with an idea. If I didn't direct commercials, then I would be the showrunner. I'd come up with an idea and I'd be the showrunner and I would make my living that way. At the end of the day, I'm just a guy who likes to watch television. I feel that there are certain programs that aren't on the air that I'd like to see so I try to push those through.

Q: *As a producer, how involved are you in the budget, not only creating it but the day-to-day supervision of it?*

A: I'm very involved in creating the budget. I work with the line producer in shaping the original budget. Once the budget is approved, I want to know that we're on budget, and if we're not on budget, why are we not on budget and how can we get back on track. But the line producer is dealing with all financial issues. I like to keep my role, at that point, more administrative and creative, dealing with the network, answering questions that the line-producer might have. But I don't want to know about the day-to-day.

Q: *Do you tend to hire the same people from production to production? Do you have a team?*

A: You know, if they're good, if they're talented, often they don't want to be hired to do the same job. I find that anyone I work with, whether they're associate producers, line producers, editors — unless they're directors or executive producers — everyone wants to be in the cat-bird seat, everybody wants to be in the position of power. If it's a theatrical movie, it's the director or producer and if it's a television show, it's the executive producer. So everyone else, for the most part, is working to get to those places, so if you have someone that's really talented — if it's the line producer on one project — chances are that on the next project, they're not going to want to take a line producer credit, they're going to want full producer credit, and you've got to decide if you want to go there or not. So I find it really hard to maintain. I just lost my editor that I've been working with for four years because he's now becoming a director, and my old line producers are now producers. But it's incredibly helpful to have a team around that you trust and respect.

Q: *Do you think there is a producer's personality?*

A: There are so many different types of producers. In television, there are people who are really brash and confident and charismatic. Then there's soft-spoken but talented producers. The key is to exude confidence. When you ask someone to give you more than one million dollars, they need to share your confidence, understand that you're professional and trustworthy. Most producers who work in television tend to be very authoritative, very strong personalities who are generals with their team. Editors tend to be a little more introverted, a little quieter, a little noncharismatic. You sort of have to be selfless if you're an editor on television because you don't get the credit or the money and yet you're doing most of the work.

Q: *How much do you think that "people skills" connect with producing?*

A: I think a really good producer is someone who knows how to sweet-talk people to get what they want. And I think, just as in life — if you treat people with respect, they give it back. Some people work better under threat and intimidation, and some people do their best work feeling valued all along — so it's tough to say. I know one television producer, this guy could sell anyone anything. He's a showman. And then there are people who are just very quiet and soft-spoken who happen to do really good work.

Q: *What advice do you give to beginning producers?*

A: Something I said earlier — know your audience. When you come up with an idea, know the answer to "Who is this for?" You have to have a certain sense of responsibility with money. TV is a business and therefore you don't want to pitch a show that's going to cost $300,000 and sell it for $300,000. There's no profit in it. Try to keep costs down.

The most important thing is to know your audience, and also know that probably any idea you have, there are a hundred other people with that same idea and you'd better have something unique and special about your particular take on it. There is not an original idea — there hasn't been since I've been around. There are just reinterpretations of things, and particularly non-fiction, where you can't copyright an idea. I'm doing a film about the Chicago Seven, from the 1960s, right now. I can't prevent anyone else from doing a film about the Chicago Seven. What's going to make my film different from the next person is my take on the events from back then, and my package that I put together. I have a very unique spin to my movie and so therefore if somebody else happens to do a film on the Chicago Seven, I'm not really going to be too bothered by it. When you go to pitch chances are they've already heard it — unless you've got something very specific about a very specific person, they've heard the pitch. So why are they going to hire you? You have to make sure to give them a reason.

Q: *What is your sense of the direction television is taking?*

A: Two words: branded entertainment. When TV first started, each program was sponsored, like *General Electric Theater*. I think we're going back to that now as a result of TiVo, which is going to open a lot of doors for producers. So, in my show about high school basketball in Michigan, I'm going to start thinking about that in terms of what products exist in that world. Are they basketball players? They need shoes, so I might think Nike. They play with a Wilson basketball. Can I go to Wilson and get a sponsorship from them? Can I go to Nike and get a sponsorship from them?

Q: *If you have to think about showing a sponsor's product or logo, as well as all the other details in the shoot, doesn't that get in the way?*

A: It may. But I think commercials are far more intrusive. You cut away from the action for three minutes and it's totally intrusive. Often times you can deal with some of these companies. It's not product shots they're asking for as much as lifestyles and attitude that they want to embrace and endorse.

Q: *You don't feel you're being preached to?*

A: Someone has to pay for it, so unless the audience is willing to shell out $5.00 every time they turn on the television, which no one wants to do, we're going to live with it. Does it compromise the integrity of the program? It depends on the project. It depends on how it's incorporated.

Q: *Do you see any sort of technical or creative kind of curves that might be followed in the future, based on what you see now?*

A: Yeah, we all know we're heading toward an HD world. If I want to sell a program five years from now, it's going to be a whole lot easier if I shoot it in high-def now, rather than standard def. Everything goes in cycles, though. I don't know what the next one is going to be.

Stephen Reed

Executive producer, producer, and producer/director, including The Newport Jazz Festival

Q: *Because you produce in so many different genres, what kind of producer do you usually think of yourself as being?*

A: I overlap between executive producer and producer these days. In the past, I've been a line producer, and an executive in charge of production. One is often a more glorified term for the other.

Q: *What area of producing, what genre, are you most comfortable working in?*

A: The things I like doing best are these big music productions of live events. Sometimes we do them as live broadcasts, and sometimes we do them live-to-tape for a quick delivery. Sometimes they're heavily edited. At The Newport Jazz Festival this year, we shot about ten hours of music and twenty hours, maybe, of B-roll, and interviews. And all this gets condensed. The ten hours of music is actually five or six cameras, for each hour. So you're dealing with a huge amount of material to cull down to a one-hour program.

There are two challenges in this: capturing everything well in the first place, and then an enormous post-production editing process to bring it down to a one-hour finished program.

I've also produced a few commercials, I've done music videos, and I've done some documentaries, as well as live satellite feeds, award shows. We even did boxing this year. We did Golden Gloves boxing over several days, many hours of live broadcast boxing. And then we cut that down to four to six hours, as another program for an HD channel.

Q: *These larger, live events must pose certain challenges to a producer. What are the challenges they present for you?*

A: I guess the challenge is understanding what the event is, and who our client is, and, is that client the same person that's putting on the event? Which is sometimes the case. Is the client a broadcast partner in an event that someone else is putting on? And what is the relationship there? Often, I'll produce the event specifically for television, and then I produce the television coverage as well. That's the ideal situation because you plan the whole event in the way it's going to run, in the venue, in the available camera positions, set design, lighting.

The ideal situation is designing the whole event for television, because all of those things are taken into account, right from the beginning. It's clear that television is the priority. The live audience, while you want to accommodate them, is not the priority. The other extreme is when you're brought in to cover an event that's already planned and is going to be happening anyway, and we have to cover it for television. Sometimes we have a really cooperative relationship with the producer or promoter of a live event. And sometimes we don't. So you've got to be sensitive to that relationship and that audience.

Q: *How do you avoid feeling pinned against the wall in some of these high-pressure situations?*

A: You try not to come up against the wall. You try to avoid that part right from the beginning by going in and meeting with the people who are running the event — understanding what their priorities are and what their necessities are, letting them know that you understand what those are, and trying to debunk their preconceptions about what it means to have a television crew come in and disrupt everything to cover their event.

I've found that many times the perception going in is that these television guys are a "pain in the butt" and they think they're going to control everything and run everything, and that it's all about them and they run roughshod, and they're not very nice about it. Maybe it's just my personality, or maybe because I do a lot of music and have done a lot of music, but I'm aware of that preconception and I do my best to go in the opposite direction so that people feel comfortable. You try to get across that "we've got certain things we have to accomplish, we understand that you have certain things you have to accomplish, let's work together to see how we can do as much of that as possible" and find ways where we can compromise as necessary. It's as much about personal relationships and schmoozing as it is about, technically, how you're going to achieve whatever it is that you need to do.

Q: *Let's take the Newport Jazz Festival as a working example. How do you set up an event that is so massive? Are you essentially the director as well as the producer?*

A: Yeah, I'm essentially the director. I don't do the multi-camera live directing in the truck. But I have all the other responsibilities of the director. I do all the interview stuff. I direct, generally, all the B-roll shots, knowing where that's going. I do the host stuff, I write the voice-over as needed. So, I usually have a concept of how we're going to pull the show together a little bit and try do it differently each year, although I never know what kind of music I'm going to get.

So you want to have a loose plan in mind. We usually know how many artists we're going to shoot, but we don't know how well their sets are going to turn out and how we're going to juggle that whole balance. All of the direction of that show from the start to the finish, with the exception of calling the cameras live, is what I do. Even to the point of once we've selected a song, we go back and take out all of the isolated shots, and recut the entire show anyway. So we don't even use the line cut.

I think the question you were talking about before is working with the venue. In that case, we're hired by Festival Productions, who puts on the jazz festival, to produce a show for PBS and also for their corporate underwriter, JVC. Festival Productions, since 1954, has been producing live events, primarily multiple-day festival events all over the country and all over the world. Their complete focus is on live events, not on television, which has been a big challenge for us because when we try to make changes big or small for the advantage of television, they usually understandably resist it.

A couple of examples: If you want to put a jib in the audience to get some nice big sweeping shots, that's uniformly rejected because the jib could, conceivably, interfere with someone in the audience's view of the stage. So they won't allow that. We had a heck of a time trying to clean up the stage at little bit at the festival. There are a lot of hangers-on around the stage area. Which leads to a lot of clutter in the background of the shots, which detracts from what you're trying to do in focusing on the artist. So we've tried to clean up the stage with design elements, with keeping more people off the stage . . . things like that.

There are only twenty minutes between sets. An entire band is taken off stage, a new band is put on stage, people are scurrying around putting microphones in place, and so on. We also have only twenty minutes to get set up between each artist. We don't have any influence on how microphones are positioned, for example. Sometimes we can position a mike so that it's still just as effective to capture the music from an instrument or a singer, but it's not in the way of the camera angles that you're able to get.

The more cameras you have, the more positions you have, and the more flexibility with moving the cameras around, the more you can compensate for those things. But then again, we're getting into "are we interfering with the audience's appreciation of the show by distracting their eye or their focus, or actually being in front of them?" Those kinds of issues we juggle back and forth, and we compromise and try to still come out with as good a show as we possibly can.

The essential point is that you have to try to gain the trust and the confidence of the client, and all the other parties — from all the audio people, from the staging people, the artists, all the parties involved in this event. You have to gain their trust, showing that you understand what their issues are and bringing them on board to be on the same team for the overall good of the project.

Q: *On a live music event, clearly, the audio is a huge challenge.*

A: Here's how it works. There are a lot of different audio requirements for putting on a concert. First of all, the musicians on the stage have their own monitors that allow them to hear their own music being played back to them. Every single person on the stage has to have a mix so that they can hear themselves, know if they're in tune, and hear the rest of the musicians clearly and plainly, despite where they may be located on the stage. The microphones all go to a central place and it's divided up into different purposes.

But our primary objective is to do an adequate mix for the musicians on the stage. That's the stage mix. Then there's a split of that audio that goes out to the center of the house where somebody else is mixing the sound for the audience. There you want a much more full, balanced mix then you would for the individual musicians on the stage. The singer primarily wants to hear himself or herself louder than they would in a normal mix, but that's not an appropriate mix for the house. So you've got five or six different mixes — depending on how many musicians you have on stage. Each one wants their own kind of mix featuring themselves. The house gets a different kind of mix.

The third split goes to the television truck, where we mix. Here, we do two things: The number one priority in the Newport show, which is a heavily posted show, is to get the multitrack recording done properly. It's usually 24 or 32, sometimes as much as 48 individual tracks that we're recording. That's the number one priority there. The number two priority of our TV truck mix is to get a rough mix, for reference purposes, that goes on the videotapes that we use for post-production to decide what goes into the show and to cut the whole show together. Only at the very end do we go back to those multitracks, and mix the music that ends up being the show. That's how the ultimate audio ends up getting done. But right now, with the way I've described it to you, you have three splits.

My audio guy says every year, "Hey, don't use anybody's first song if you can possibly avoid it" because he's always trying to figure out where everything is and get his tracking down. We have no opportunity to do a sound check ahead of time, so the first song is always the sound check. The trouble is that the artist usually wants to start with a bang and capture everyone's attention. Frequently, the coolest song is the first one, and you want to use it.

It's all so second nature to me that I kind of forget not everyone knows all these things. But it also relates to your point that a producer is a producer is a producer. Which is true in many ways. But there are so many nuances for different kinds of things, like getting the crew there, getting the facilities, thinking to the punt. That's transferable. But things like this, if you haven't done these kind of shows multiple times, you're not even going to be aware of what the issues are — let alone how to handle them. So in some ways, that producer, producer thing is accurate. But there are a lot of exceptions.

Q: *What were the pros and cons of shooting in a hi-def situation?*

A: This is our sixth year in shooting it in HD. It's a lot more expensive, of course. It's easier, in that there are more trucks, more facilities, people are more experienced with it, cameras are smaller and lighter for the handheld people, and you have more lensing opportunity, variability, and options. From all those points of view, it's gotten a lot better. From an editing point of view, you have to shoot all this stuff in HD, then convert it to an NTSC format for editing. So there's a time-consuming and extensive transfer process that takes place — that's the biggest hassle. Then you have to marry everything back together later.

Q: *What's involved in the post-production part of shooting in hi def?*

A: We do an off-line nonlinear edit using this NTSC stuff. When it's all done, we send the edit decision list and a tape of the finished off-line to the audio house for their mixing purposes, then they marry it back, according to the edit decision list (EDL). And then the EDL also goes to the online facility and there we start to, in theory, auto-conform the show based on the EDL. Then we fly in the audio track, which is now all done, and then throw in the graphics.

All of that stuff has to really be designed ahead of time. The coordination of how it flows together and how it's going to look, and the sweetening, and smoothly going from artist to artist and artist to interview, and all that kind of stuff has to be planned pretty carefully between a number of different parties to make it work well.

That's all the technical stuff. But the most important thing is that you really have to have a feel for the music and the artist, and what's going on, and creatively pull all this stuff together. The creative part is really why I'm hired and what you need from the head person pulling this all together. That's why I'm the producer-director I am, but as a producer, you also have to be aware of all this technical stuff.

John Rosas

Producer, promotional and "added value" material on DVDs

Q: *What exactly does a Promotional Producer do?*

A: I'm a DVD Producer. At one time I did promotional marketing, producing press kits, electronic press kits, corporate image, stuff like that, but for the past five years, it's been strictly "added value" for DVDs.

Q: *What is "added value"?*

A: Different studios call it different things, like special features, behind the scenes, added value, but it's all the special things that go on a DVD beside or along with the movie. For the first couple of years, all that went on the DVD was the movie. Now, every studio has their own DVD division with their own department that deals only with these added features. And then you have the menu content, and the people who do the marketing, and the graphics people who decide what the menus look like.

Q: *That's more of a graphics area, isn't it?*

A: Yeah, but it all has to interlace. You know, it's all about the look. You want to produce something that matches the overall look of the project. What we do is specialized. We're shooting the behind-the-scenes, we're doing the featurettes, editing the deleted scenes, taking thirty hours of footage previously shot on a set, maybe all the deleted comedic scenes, and either making it into an edited piece that makes some sense, or is in some cases, simply eye candy.

Q: *Who makes those decisions about what goes on the DVD with the film?*

A: It depends on the studio. They may say, "This is what we have." We're told that, "We have thirty-seven reels of mini-DVs that someone shot on the set. And apparently they got some good stuff so we'd like to do something with this. We'd like to get a featurette out of it." Then we come in and say, "We'll tell you what you have." You may have someone who walked around just shooting people's feet — you just don't know. What we normally do is tell them is, "Send us everything you have, be it trailers, deleted scenes, whatever. Let us go through all the footage and we'll come back to you with a proposal for what we can do."

For *Party of Five*, for example, ten years after the series, they wanted to put out Season I, Season II, and Season III. So we said, "Let us go interview whoever wants to be interviewed, and let's see what we get." We interviewed the creators of the series, and came away with enough footage that we could have easily cut a two-hour piece from. Well, that's a bit of overkill for the subject matter. What we did was just about an hour, a cohesive hour, going between the different people and footage behind the scenes and then we cut it into segments. We cut it into a twenty-minute piece and a ten-minute piece because it all made sense. It could all be played together.

I like to keep going back to something like the movie *Wilde*, which was the Oscar Wilde film. It was wonderful. It was a really well-done film about someone bigger than life. We produced a one-hour documentary, going back and revisiting the subject with the creators, the writers, the directors, the producers, and Stephen Fry who was the star. So when the movie comes out, a six-year-old movie maybe, it's released with a brand new documentary about what makes the film and its subject relevant today.

Q: *So you would write, and you would produce?*

A: Well, we don't write in the traditional way. It's not a narrative or voice-over thing. Most everything we produce tells its own story.

Q: *But you still have to be able to tell the story. How do you do that?*

A: From your interviews. What's interesting is that if you know what you're going after before you start, you can talk to people and say, "Look, truthfully we need some strong sound bites. So I'm not going to sit down with you for an hour and interview you about things that I know aren't going to be on the DVD or aren't going to be part of this."

Often, I'll do much more extensive interviews. For example, I interviewed Paul Mazursky about everything — his style of shooting, his style of writing, about making movies in the 1960s, his approach to comedy, how he works, because he has a forty-year track record of making films. My feeling is that I have Paul Mazursky here. I better sit down while he's here and talk to him about all of this. About the 1950s and John Cassavettes and *Blackboard Jungle* and working on *Harry and Tonto*. Luckily he wrote a book that helps me talk to him for hours and focus on the film, and then interlace his opinions on this, his styles, knowing Fellini and directing him in a film. I can talk to him about working with Woody Allen, about writing for Woody Allen and Peter Sellers. Later, you screen it and map out what you have, then go to the editor and say, "I've got three hours of Paul Mazursky talking, let's see how we can cut this up."

Q: *So research is important?*

A: Oh yeah. You've got to be familiar with the films, you want to know the person, and I think you've got to be excited. You go into something like that the way you would go in if someone said, "Hey, you've got an opportunity to interview Spielberg, what are you going to do with it?" How much time do I have? If I only have an hour, I'm not going to just talk about his latest film, I'm going to try and get inside his head a little bit. And let them know ahead of time you're going to touch on different topics.

Q: *Ultimately, you're still dictated to by your client. What happens when you may want to do something one way but the client has other ideas?*

A: It's how you position it. Usually they don't dictate because they don't know what we're going to get in the way of footage or interviews. So I say, "It will be great." You have to understand that the people who fund these are going to look at the packaging and say, "Wow, there's a half-hour interview Paul Mazursky." They're buying the film because it's a Paul Mazursky film so to get Paul Mazursky talking about his craft, that's an added value that is a very special feature.

Q: *How much does the budget determine your creative directions?*

A: You have to know what things cost because you have to know when you can say yes and when you can say no. We've got $30K to do this, and $30K seems like a lot but then you realize that $30K covers your travel, your crew, three days of shooting, your transfers. You have to know what is in the budget. What is allocated for what portion, and realistically, can it be done?

When you're young, you want the work, so when someone says "Can you do this?," you say "sure" and then you get there and find out that your crew costs X. Now all of a sudden, a third of the budget is gone, and then soon it's another third, and then you're screwed. You can't ask people who work for $3,000 a day to work for $500 a day. You can crew it with the person that makes $500 a day, but you're not going to get the skill. You're as good as your shooter, you're as good as your sound person. You can have the best footage in the world but if the audio's crap, well, you know what happens then. So you get what you pay for. After a certain amount of time, you've established those relationships so when you need to pull in a favor, you can get what you need for less.

Q: *How do you go about finding the right people to work with?*

A: That takes time. That's why when you're starting out, it's important to, again, surround yourself with the best people. Listen to what they say, watch them. Try to learn not only what they do, but how they do it. If you don't like the way they do it, remember that, too.

Q: *What resources do you rely on when you're researching how much a project is going to cost?*

A: Make phone calls. You can call a production company and say, "I'm thinking about putting together a shoot for so and so. I've got an opportunity to do this project but I have to know a budget. Can you take a few minutes and sketch one out for me?" Cold calls. I've called PR firms and other production companies earlier in my years because I didn't know what something would cost. Talk to people. Go into that production company on West 48th Street, or in Santa Monica, and talk to them.

You don't want to lie, but it's okay to call and say I'm working for this company and they've asked me to get some prices, or I'm thinking about doing a mini-doc and I'm trying to figure out what I can do. Can you tell me what a three-piece video DigiBeta crew will cost for this project? Call transfer houses to find what tape transfers will cost. Call duplication houses. These people are legitimate business people and they don't know if you're calling for a production house or you have an uncle who is a billionaire and wants to shoot his life story.

Q: *Because you have to work with talent all the time, how do you maneuver around their public relations people who can be very protective?*

A: You let them know that you have their client's best interest in mind. We are here to make the client look good. It's kind of loaded in my favor because I usually know the talent wants to do the project. After all, it is promoting them and their project. It depends on the situation, but you let the PR people know that it is *their* client who told the studio they wanted to do something. *Their* client asked us to call him or her to arrange it.

Recently we were getting responses from a PR person, saying "Well, she's so busy promoting this new movie that she can't possibly do the interview until blah, blah, blah." And I say, "Okay, by that date, I'll have missed my deadline and it won't get on the DVD. That's really weird because she was talking to the creator of the show, saying she wanted to do this. It's weird she would actually say she didn't want to do it. I guess it'll all wash out." The next thing you know, the PR person is calling you back and saying, "Oh, she can do the interview next Tuesday." It's about occasionally playing some games to get what you need.

Q: *Do you ever find yourself dealing with celebrities' agents or lawyers?*

A: Often. It doesn't hurt to find out who the manager is and go through them to get what you need. You always have to be aware that you need to put something in writing. You have to be able to present it in a few paragraphs very succinctly; what you want, what's expected, how long, what you'll do, where it's going to be used, how it's going to be used, and so on. It's in their best interest. Plus, remember that everyone on camera has to sign a release. Very important.

Tom Sellitti

Coproducer, *Rescue Me*, and executive producer, *Shorties Watchin' Shorties*

Q: *On your series,* Rescue Me, *you are the coproducer and part of a tight producing team. How do you and the other producers divide the responsibilities?*

A: We all kind of do the same work. Jim (Serpico) and I work very closely together. Jim is the EP, so all decisions that come from him are final in terms of production. We weigh in with Peter (Tolan) and Denis (Leary) on a lot of things, but they leave the physical producing to us. I play a role in everything. When the scripts are written, I read the scripts and give notes to Denis and Peter after they've written them. I participate in phone calls with the network (FX) and the studio, Sony.

Q: *How much involvement do FX and Sony have in the show, on a day-to-day basis?*

A: They read scripts and tell us what concerns them and what things they would like to change. Basically, they give us notes on the script. So when we hear those notes, we take into account what they said and we talk among ourselves afterwards, creatively, and decide what we want to do. Is this a note from the network that we should listen to and go ahead with it? FX is great to work for — the notes they give are helpful. They don't give notes just for the sake of giving notes. They have a good eye for story and production, so for us, it is usually a note that we try to give them. But sometimes, there is a creative difference and we may feel that even though they feel we should do something, they usually give us the creative license to agree or to disagree. We would then go back to them afterward and say, "Here are the fifteen notes that you gave us, and these are the ones we are going to make changes with, and these are the ones we want to keep the way they are." And then from there, we just move on to the next stage and the shoot.

Q: *How is working with the studio, Sony, different than with the network?*

A: They do give you numbers that obviously you have to comply with. FX weighs in as well, but Sony is watching us more than that.

Q: *How involved are you with the budgets?*

A: I have no involvement with that. Kerry (Orent) is our line producer, and he is in charge of the budget, day to day. Jim works closely on it, too.

Q: *Your producing role seems to have more to do with the creative process of the show. What's your involvement in this part of producing?*

A: Once we have scripts and we know what we're shooting, I'm involved with the casting. I will sit in on casting session sometimes, depending on what needs to be done. I may be in a session, I may not be in one. I'm involved in the scouting for locations that we may need, and

I will sit in on production meetings for production design, and decide what kind of sets that we need to build. It's just really across the board, creatively and production-wise. For most of our prep, I'm mostly involved in casting and location scouting.

Q: *Locations are an integral part of the show. How do you find them?*

A: We have a location manager, and he has people in his department, so when we get the scripts, the scripts are broken down with a list of locations that are needed. Usually the scene description will tell you what we are looking for, and then usually the scout will go out and do the scout and bring back choices, not only to us but to the director as well. The director has a lot of input on that. Often, we will defer to him unless it is completely wrong. Once we have a few selections, they bring back photos and then we will narrow it down to a couple that we want see. Then, we'll set up some scouts to go and check them out. The scouts will include the producers, the director, the locations people, the production designer, the DP (cinematographer), and the 1st AD. And those aren't the big scouts. Those are the scouts when we are trying to figure out what locations we can select.

Q: *What are you each looking for in a location?*

A: The locations people are looking at what the area is, where the trucks can go, what the hours are in the building. They will fill us in on that stuff. The production designer is basically looking for the look and feel of the scene. The director is trying to find out the way that the room looks, and he and the DP are trying to figure out how they will shoot it, where they will put the cameras for the scenes they want to shoot. And we are there, just basically overseeing it.

Q: *With* Rescue Me, *what is the ratio of locations to built sets?*

A: We probably shoot about 60% on location.

Q: *How many people are usually on your crew?*

A: How big is our crew? About a hundred people, more or less.

Q: *You are shooting the show in 24P. How is that working out?*

A: Very good. It looks like film. It's easy to shoot, because it's tape. It's less expensive than film. The cameras are a little bit bigger if you use the cameras that we use, but the operators who handle the cameras have gotten used to working with them and do a really good job. For us, it is a very efficient way to shoot the show.

Q: *You use an approach called "cross-boarding" when you shoot. How does that work?*

A: What we do is take two scripts together and we shoot it like a film. It's just a more efficient way to shoot, especially when you go on location as much as we do. We'll take two scripts — and one director directs two episodes — so that one director will do both of them. We will schedule them so that when we have a scene that takes place in a particular location, then we'll shoot everything that takes place in that location for both scripts. Consecutively. So if we have a day's worth of shots in the two scripts at one location, we'll do it all in one day. We'll have the actors' change clothes from whatever particular scenes are for whatever episodes. When we did the show, *The Job*, we used to cross-board four episodes at a time and that would get a little confusing. But this isn't so bad. It's just a matter of keeping continuity correct. A lot of that falls on the script supervisor, at least production-wise, but the actors seem to handle it, no problem.

Q: *How involved do you get in post-production?*

A: I am involved in that I will see rough cuts and give notes on it. I'll make suggestions on scenes we should add or lose, lines that we should add or lose.

Q: *Do you find that by shooting in video, you tend to overshoot?*

A: Most of the time that is something that we will talk to the directors about. We shoot our rehearsals, but we try to keep our takes limited. For example, Denis likes to work in his own way, doing as few takes as possible, so we will work with the directors and make sure they know about that ahead of time. Most of them do.

Q: *Where does your job overlap with the directors' jobs? How much of a support system do you try to give them?*

A: Well, they kind of do their thing and we go with them, but we don't really get into their job. We may talk about how they will shoot certain scenes, that's about it. We usually have four different directors a season. We all get used to each other's personalities.

Q: *Speaking of personalities, is there a producer personality? Do you have one?*

A: I don't think that I have the typical producer's personality. I guess there is one, it's someone who makes things happens, so I guess I do that. But I think everyone is different. Every producer I meet is different. Some of them are crazy Type A personalities, some are very laid back, others can be jerks. It has a lot to do with the way a person handles pressure and stress. Me, myself? I am pretty laid back.

Q: *You must like the pressure and stress, or else you don't view it as pressure and stress.*

A: To us, it's something we want to do, and we are of the mind-set that we can do whatever needs to be done, at least creatively, and we find a way to do it. Whatever it takes — there is always a way to compromise, and get what you need. We hire good people to work on our shows because they like to work on our shows. We treat them well and that plays a big part in it, too.

Q: *You have also created and co-executive produced shows for Comedy Central?*

A: For Comedy Central, we do a lot of things. We have an animated show called *Shorties Watchin' Shorties*. We do *Comedy Central Roast*, and we had a series called *Contest Searchlight* that's a parody of the show, *Project Greenlight*.

Q: *So you're obviously involved in creating new ideas on an ongoing basis.*

A: Yeah, I've probably got twenty other projects in different stages of development. Whether it is the script development stage or being edited, we have several things that are in some form of production.

Q: *Who is the "we" in this case?*

A: Apostle. This is Denis' production company with Jim Serpico and me. Creatively, we produce to the project but we pretty much work as producers the same way, all the time.

Q: *You've been doing this for a while now. Looking back, what do you wish someone had told you back then?*

A: I wish someone told me it's not as easy as it sounds. And that there are some things that you need to know that are helpful.

Q: *Like what?*

A: That you have to be flexible. You have to be willing to roll with the punches. You have to believe in what you are doing, and believe you can do it. If someone is telling you something is impossible, it usually is not. Anything is possible. There are some things that are impossible for budgetary reasons, but there are always compromises and ways to make your vision come to life. I think you need to treat the people around you right.

The way that we work, most people don't think of us as difficult producers (when I say us, I mean Jim and Denis and Apostle). For one of the other shows that we are doing, I was going to a sound mix and when I got there, the production supervisor was laughing. She was talking to the sound mixer and she said one of the producers was coming over to listen to the mix and he said, "Oh, the suits" and she said, "No, these guys are not the suits, it's the last thing we would call them." We are pretty down to earth and just normal — we like to have fun while we work. We pretty much see ourselves as just like everyone else on the crew.

Q: *Do you lead a normal life? Can you find some balance in your life with the kind of schedule you must have?*

A: I try. My wife says I don't . . . but I do. I do a lot of stuff. I have a wife, I have a little baby. I box. I play hockey. When we are not in production, we come to work at 10 o'clock and stay until 7 or 8. And the rest of the time, we try to do normal things, like go out on the weekends. But when we're shooting, it is harder. On the other hand, some of our projects are easier. We have an animated show, and it's not like you have to stand on the set for that. With *Rescue Me*, you're on the set for anywhere from 12 to 14 hours a day. And you have your travel time, and it becomes a 16- to 17-hour day or whatever it may be. So you do lose a little bit of your life during the week. But we shoot five days and we don't shoot on the weekends, so you get your time on the weekend.

Q: *So you have created some semblance of balance.*

A: We try. Sometimes it feels like it is not balanced, but we know the work that has to go into it to make it successful, and how to put out a good product and make things run properly. We try to be responsible. It would be easy to say I want to do this, and I am not going to go to work. But I wouldn't get anything done that way.

Q: *How important is the original vision? How do you keep that vision intact?*

A: The vision of the show is Peter and Denis. Really, we just try and facilitate what their vision is. With Denis, he is the one who really always has it on the tip of his mind — what he puts on the page, what he tells us in our conversations about what he's thinking or what he wants to do. We just help to bring it to life as much as we can. And we will tell him if we think something is not working, or if we feel there is some inconsistency in something. We will bring it up and say, "Hey, you want to do this but is it supposed to be this way?" and we bring it up for discussion.

Q: *You're producing for television now. Where do you think TV is going, and where do you think you'll fit into the equation?*

A: It's funny, because after the Super Bowl incident with Janet Jackson, every network seemed to be afraid to do anything that was considered risqué or edgy, at least in the development stages for projects that we were trying to develop. It seems like everyone was trying to button up a little bit. But now I think there has been some success recently with shows like *Desperate Housewives* where they're finally loosening up a bit.

I always think that maybe television is going back toward more scripted shows and less reality, and then new reality shows pop up. One thing is for sure: It always turns out to be cyclical. After awhile, things may go out of style and then they come back into style again. Pretty soon, everyone will want their *Seinfeld* again. Things will circle around and before you know it, they'll want Westerns back next.

J. Stephen Sheppard

Entertainment lawyer/partner Cowan DeBaets Abraham and Sheppard

Q: *Would you please talk about your decision to become an entertainment lawyer?*

A: I always wanted to be in the entertainment business and I didn't have any talent to do anything else. Seriously, I'm not a writer, I'm not a director, and I'm certainly not an actor. Publishing, television, movies, and theater always interested me. Law was the thing that I could do well to be in that world.

Q: *Were you not also a producer for a while?*

A: I've been lots of things. I finished law school and I worked as a lawyer, then I left that and was an agent for 5 or 6 years. Then, I was in the producing business, the feature motion picture business, for 3 or 4 years, and went back into the agency business. Finally, I migrated back to this desk.

Q: *Does your experience being a producer work for or against you in the business?*

A: I think it works for me, I think it works for the clients. I'd like to think that the whole is greater than the sum of the parts. I've seen this business from various perspectives, from the agent's perspective, from the producer's perspective. I think it all helps. When I come into a project on behalf of the producer, I'm seeing it as a lawyer, in terms of the issues that need to be attended to, where the problems may be, or how to solve this problem, or write a contract for that. But I also look at it from the producer's perspective who is much less interested in the piece of paper I write and much more interested in getting it on film. So, I think I bring a pragmatic view.

Q: *The majority of your clients fall into what category?*

A: The nice thing about my practice is that it's really varied — I represent a lot of producers, I represent a cable television network for its original movies of the week, but I also represent literary estates, in the protection and exploitation of deceased authors' works, and I represent an advertising agency.

Q: *What does an entertainment lawyer do?*

A: I can tell you what *I* do. Different entertainment lawyers do things differently. One of my partners is an entertainment lawyer, for instance, and functions in a mixed bag of semi-agenting, and semi-producing, and semi-deal-making business affairs, and what I call opportunity creating — introducing one party to another party. A lot of entertainment lawyers function that way, and I do a certain amount of that.

My practice tends to be a little more traditional lawyering. I negotiate and draft contracts, which is itself kind of unusual. Many senior lawyers have other people do the drafting and then they fix it. I don't like to do that. The value lies in getting it said right, and I believe that

I need to do most of that myself, and I am good at it. I negotiate, I draft, I review materials for libel and privacy issues, mainly for documentaries. I work with insurance brokers to get insurance for films. I also negotiate contracts between producers and distributors, networks or distribution companies.

Where I can, if I have a relationship that is useful, I can make an introduction. I'll call a network and say, "you should take a look at this project," or "I've got this client who is making this great movie," so that is sort of a little agenting. I never like to hold myself out as that; it's not my principal job as I see it. I also do some business counseling — what is the smartest, best way to come at this project? I'm often regarded by my clients as their "smart friend." It is business counseling, it's strategizing.

Q: *How much involvement do you take? Do you simply make the introduction or do you follow it through to the distribution deal?*

A: It really depends on the client and the project. I had a new client in yesterday with a new project, really interesting project, at square one. It's beyond the idea stage, they've already made good progress in terms of creating access to the subject, but that is as far as we've gotten. We talked about what steps were necessary, and what kind of documents were necessary to get the project started, and what their ideas were for what the project should be. They saw it as a documentary series. I suggested this project should go to such and such a network. I pointed out that they should be prepared to think about this as a one-off single special because, though we may be very intrigued about the subject, I wasn't sure that it could support a series.

When other clients come to me, this advice is not what they are looking for. Or the deal is already done and it's just doing a contract or production legal work, and doing every release for network nonfiction. Production legal work can involve making distribution contracts, acquiring rights and life rights — it really is driven by what the client needs and what the project needs.

Q: *At what point in the development of a project do people usually go to a lawyer?*

A: Certainly, at some point in the course of the life of a project, when you have to start dealing with third parties, with other people. If a book, for example, is going to be the basis of a movie, or if there is somebody's story, somebody's life rights, or if you need to get particular access to a building — these are all obvious triggers for a conversation with a lawyer. When you start dealing with third parties, you have to make arrangements with them, and you have to get certain rights or permissions or clearances from them. That's when it probably makes sense to start talking to a lawyer and make sure that you are getting what you need — and that you are not getting more than you need, and not overpaying for what you need.

Q: *Are there any times when a producer wouldn't want to bring in a lawyer?*

A: That is an interesting point, I hear it all the time and it pains me to hear it — this notion that bringing in a lawyer is a hostile, aggressive, negative thing to do. It is not, it doesn't have to be, and it certainly shouldn't be. Anyone starting off as a producer really needs to get over that. A lawyer who knows what he or she is doing, and is good at it, is there to effect a simple agreement that is really fair to both people.

I always tell clients that the best deals are deals where both sides are just a little unhappy. As long as both sides are just a little unhappy, then neither one got every single thing they wanted, which means there was compromise and that it is probably a fair deal. That's the way a good lawyer should come at this. You are here to get it done. You as a producer, and whomever you are dealing with, are going to be better off in the long run if you have done it right in the beginning.

You asked the question, "can any contract can be undone?" And the answer is "probably," if someone is inventive or hostile enough to do it. Let's say that you make an oral handshake deal with Jane Doe to do a movie about her. You don't want to bring in a lawyer, because that feels like a hostile thing to do, so you both agree that that is just fine and you make the movie and you've spent time, money, and energy and you've made the movie. Then, Jane Doe says, "I've changed my mind, I don't want you to do this, and I don't like it." You are stuck. Whereas if you have a simple agreement up front, it is harder for the other person to do that. Is it impossible? No, it's just harder because then, you are both relying on this agreement.

Q: *How does a producer know how and where to find a good lawyer?*

A: It's not black magic. You meet with somebody and you get a sense of what kind of person they are, if they understand you and they get what you're talking about, and see how you want to come at this. I have people who haven't retained me, because they want some kind of red meat killer who grabs the other guy by the throat. That is not the way I function, but if that is what the client wants, then he is in the wrong place and he knows that. I am not offended when somebody says, "you're not mean enough for me." For a young/new producer, there is an organization here in New York, and I think it exists in many cities, called Volunteer Lawyers for the Arts (VLA). That is exactly what they do. They make legal services available to people in the arts who can't afford to pay for them; whether they are young producers, or authors, or dancers, or whatever. They are all volunteers, they're very good young lawyers who work in big law firms and make their services available on a *pro bono* basis. Law schools very often have programs. It's great experience for the students, and it creates some kind of access to lawyering.

Q: *What do you consider the primary legal areas that producers should know about?*

A: In any business or project, there are a certain number of hot button issues that need to be paid attention to. An obvious example is rights. If you are dealing with existing material, you have to get the rights. If you are dealing with a person, you have to have a release and get permission to tell his or her story. Another hot button issue is collaboration; if you have a partner, look at the terms on which that partnership is supposed to operate — who is in charge, how are the decisions made, how does the money get split up, who get what kinds of credit? What happens if it doesn't work out? At what point do you walk away, and who gets to walk away with what? At that point there will have been time, money, and talent invested in coming up with a treatment, a demo, a something.

Insurance is a big item. Sometimes it's as simple as calling your neighborhood broker, someone who knows what they are doing. It may be as simple as calling and saying, "I need an insurance package for this project," and you'll get one. There are other instances where it may be more complicated than that but insurance is a big area. There is a bundle of insurance coverage that a picture needs. It needs liability insurance, it needs property insurance, general liability if you smash your camera through someone's plate glass window, or if someone trips over a cable, or if you've rented a car and have an accident during production Then, there is producers' liability, or errors and omissions, that protects against claims arising out of the content and copyright trademark, and libel and privacy claims.

If you are doing a larger picture, there are union issues and guild issues. It's not so much a function of the size of the project, it is more about the people involved. I am involved now with a project of relatively modest budget, a television project, but it needs to be done with guilds, so there are WGA issues, and DGA issues, and SAG and AFTRA issues, which then throw off another bundle of residuals and pension and welfare issues.

Q: *What about financing? What does a producer need to know about financial markets and financing?*

A: A producer needs to know a good lawyer or a good financial advisor, in all areas of financing independent film. It is a very highly specialized area. I've done a fair amount of work on a network that is producing pictures in Canada. This is its own whole universe; there are very specific rules and requirements that you have to comply with in Canada for the benefits which are all sorts of really good subsidies and tax credits. For a general-purpose discussion like this, that is almost too complicated. It really depends very much on the project, the producer, and the producer's access to money and ability to raise money. There are law firms that have built an entire business on financing independent films, and done very well at it. They function more as producers' reps and take executive producer credit on pictures more than lawyering.

Q: *What is a producer's rep and what do they do?*

A: They serve a variety of functions. I think they can be helpful with securing financing, and they can help find distributors. They sell the film to distributors; they will get it into festivals.

Q: *Does a producer's rep come in after the product is finished rather than helping it get produced?*

A: More often than not, that is when a producer's rep will come in. They can function earlier on in the process to find coproduction financing and presales, obviously before it has been shot.

Q: *From your viewpoint as a producer's lawyer, what skills should a producer have?*

A: I'll tell you what I respond to in a client: someone who asks the right questions. I get calls from clients who say, "I'm doing so and so and am I really okay to do that?" Having some common sense about the questions to ask is enormously valuable because if there's a problem, and nobody thought to ask the question and I never had the kind of information that I would need in order to think about the question myself, then you find yourself trying to solve the problem after it happens — and that can be really difficult.

So that quality in a producer is enormously valuable to him or her. It is in a producer's best interest to do that. It is very unusual for me to say, "no, you can't do that." My job isn't to say "no, you can't." It is to say, "here is how," or "let's solve this problem." But very often, all I can do is say, "here are the risks and you have to make the decision, this is a business decision, it's not a legal decision."

Very often, the decision is a business call: here is what I think, here are the legal issues, now you make the call. In that situation, having a client, a producer, who listens and is thoughtful and makes a decision, is pretty good for both of us.

Q: *What is a copyright?*

A: When someone writes a book or writes a play or makes a movie, or paints a painting, the law creates a certain rights that it calls "copyright," for this purpose. This says that the creator of the material is the only person that can do anything with it. He/she/it (if it is a company) is the only person who can sell it, can make copies of it, can do anything with it, so anybody else who wants to do anything with that thing needs the permission of the author/the creator to make copies of it, to make different versions of it, to translate it, to do anything.

And that right, that control, is called "intellectual property" and it applies to the proceeds of somebody's work that gets manifested into some content. And that intellectual property is an intangible. You can own that book, that is tangible, but you have no right to do anything with the contents of it. You can't make a xeroxed copy of it, you can't make a movie of it, you can't do anything with the content of the book unless you buy it from my client.

Q: *How can producers protect their work?*

A: You secure copyright. Securing copyright is very easy. You put a copyright notice on it, a little c in the circle and the year date and your name, and you put it on the film or script or whatever. That tells the world that somebody owns it. So, if anybody else wants to do anything with it, you have to get the permission of the guy whose name is on the copyright. You take a couple copies of it and you fill in a form that has about eight questions on it. You send it to the Library of Congress with whatever the filling fee is, thirty dollars, and it gets registered. Then, everybody in the world who looks at the copyright registry knows that it's yours.

Q: *Can you protect your work by mailing it to yourself?*

A: Before 1976, that was a useful devise because of the way that the copyright law was structured, but now it is not at all meaningful. The only reason it has any meaning is if it is important to identify a specific date in which something was created. That is a very simple method — mail it to yourself and get a mail receipt.

Q: *Is the dispute about who had an idea first very common?*

A: You're never protecting ideas. You can't protect an idea; you can only protect the expression of an idea. So, the business of mailing something to yourself is of really limited use. The Writers Guild Registration has certain value within the Writers Guild, but mostly it's from the perspective of identifying a date. If you are sending a treatment or script to the Writers Guild, you are going to put a copyright notice on it anyway. It's the copyright notice that really gets you what you want.

Before 1976, under the old copyright law, there were two stages of copyright. One was called "common law copyright." When you write something, as soon as you write it, it is protected by common law copyright. If you published it, which was a highly technical term, it was a term of art. If it was published in order to secure and maintain copyright, then you had to have a copyright notice on it. The trade-off was that under common law copyright, it was protected forever. As soon as you published it, however, it either went into public domain or you secured statutory copyright with a notice, and the notice had a term. It used to be 28 years and you could renew it for 28 years.

There was an enormous amount of litigation over the life of that whole law, as to whether or not something was published, since publication was the magic moment which took it from one form of copyright to the other, or left it unprotected in the public domain. If it was published, then it had to be published with notice in order to secure copyright. There were always disputes over whether such and such action constituted publication, or not. That concept of publication is of no consequence now because under the new law, you get statutory copyright as soon as the thing is written or it appears on a piece of paper or on film. As soon as it is in some sort of tangible form, you're entitled to copyright and you get it by putting a notice on it, and it doesn't matter if it's published or not.

Q: *What is fair use?*

A: Fair use was a concept that the courts developed under the pre-1976 law. The way I think and talk about it is as a concept of a "permitted infringement." You are using somebody's copyrighted material without his or her permission. Under certain circumstances, the court said that they were going to allow that, that fair use is a defense to what would otherwise be a copyright infringement. The things that the courts look at to see if something qualifies for this fair use defense are: How much footage or material did you take? What was the purpose for which it was taken? Was it scholarship and review, or educational, or was it commercial? Does the use in any way supplant or interfere with the sale of the original? In 1976 when Congress passed the law, they built fair use into the statute, into the copyright law. So there is a provision in the copyright law that lays out four or five tests for fair use. They made it clear from the language that these tests were not the only tests; there may be other factors that one might look to determine of something is fair use. It looks at the quantity of the use, relative to the whole, and the purpose of the use.

If you are writing a book review, you can quote big chunks of the book, which might look like you are taking a lot of the book except that relative to the whole, it is not so much, and that it is a review. Parody is another element of fair use. Parody is a whole world onto itself. The parody defense is sort of like fair use except that usually if there is a parody, you are taking the whole thing. If it is a song parody, you are going to use the whole song, it's not like you are taking just eight bars. That is a whole different set of tests.

Q: *Are copyright laws the same in all countries?*

A: There are differences, but there are international conventions that help to smooth out these differences. When the copyright law changed here in America in 1976, one of the big reasons for the change was that we were the only country, among those that paid attention to copyright, that measured the term of copyright by years from that mysterious moment of publication. Everywhere else in the copyright world, they measured the term of copyright by the life of the author plus 50 years. When we changed the copyright law, we got rid of the whole term of years with renewals, and we went to the life of the authors — plus, the number of years keeps changing.

Q: *Some filmmakers will go to Russian composers because they might freely use their music.*

A: It's not so much that they don't have copyright laws. Most countries, certainly in Europe, have some version of copyright law. Russia now recognizes copyright law, and most countries are party to one or another of these international conventions and treaties. For all intents and purposes, if you're covered in one, then you are covered in all of them. It's not so much that the countries have copyright law; it's more about who is going to know?

Q: *What does Right of Publicity mean?*

A: Right of Publicity exists in some states, but not all states. Some states recognize what is called the Right of Privacy. It is variously defined in various places, but basically it means the right to be left alone. You have the right not to have your name and face and your stories told without your permission, to a certain extent. It depends on who you are, on the circumstances, if it's a public event. In New York, for example, the Right of Privacy is fairly limited. It implies almost exclusively to somebody's name and likeness in advertising. The Right of Privacy is what is called a personal right — once you die, it's gone. There is no such thing as the invasion of privacy or libel of a dead person; when somebody dies, they are fair game.

The Right of Publicity is a relatively new extension of the Right of Privacy that doesn't exist in New York. It exists in a number of states, most notably in California. It is a property right as opposed to a personal right. It has to do with using a person's identity for commercial purposes to sell goods, so that it was created in California largely to protect celebrities. And because it's a property right, it carries over after the death of the person and, in that way, protects dead celebrities. The key is that the name has to have value and has to have been exploited commercially during the person's life.

Q: *What is the ultimate goal of a contract?*

A: The ultimate goal of a contract is to articulate to the parties what the understanding is between them in such a way that you never have to look at it again. It's to describe the understanding between the parties. It's a very valuable process. What happens in drafting contracts is that I will write something down and send it to the client, or to the other side, and very often they say, "I can't agree to that," so it's a very good thing that we wrote it down that way. So then we change it to what you can agree to or what you think you are agreeing to. It's the same with warranties: When you sell something, you have to warrant to the guy that it is yours to sell and you are not actually selling somebody else's property.

Q: *Do producers really need a lawyer?*

A: Do you really need a lawyer? If you are making a $15,000 movie as a thesis project, then maybe not. But if you have any notion of ever doing anything with it beyond showing it to the department, then you probably will need to get a lawyer involved at some point because nobody will distribute it unless they know that you have all the rights that you need, or all the clearances that you need, and that there won't be a bunch of claims flying in as soon as this thing ends up on television somewhere.

Q: *If you were making a film right out of college, when would you bring in a lawyer if you wanted to shop it around to festivals?*

A: Earlier rather than later. I recognize the financial implications of that bit of advice, but that is the truth — that's when you should do it.

Q: *How do lawyers get paid for their services?*

A: Variously. Some lawyers charge by the hour. Sometimes with a production, with a producer, the lawyer will be a budget item; there will be a line item in the budget that covers legal services. Lawyers may get a percentage, almost like a commission on some of the afterlife uses, so when you are finished with the production, the line item will cover the production legal services. But it very well might be that once the picture is shot, and there is a distributor and the lawyer is making a distribution deal, he may get some sort of percentage of what the producer gets.

Q: *Is an oral agreement legally binding?*

A: Sometimes. Samuel Goldwyn once said an oral agreement isn't worth the paper it's written on. Yes, oral agreements can be binding, they can be enforceable, but they are harder to enforce because if there is any dispute as to what the understanding was, there is no piece of paper. With an oral agreement, one person says, "I agreed to this" and the other guy said, "well, I only agreed to that." There is something called the statute of frauds, which requires that certain kinds of contracts must be in writing. Copyright licenses must be in writing; any license of intellectual property must also be in writing.

Q: *How do you handle pressure? How do you know when you are making the right decisions?*

A: It is a lot of trust. I've been doing this for a long time. For the most part, when you have been doing this for a while, you know what you are looking for and what you need to pay attention to. When I look at a contract, I actually read them, and I pay a lot of attention to them, but I know what I am looking for. I know with respect to any given project where the problems might be, what won't be a problem, or what I know may be a problem but nobody is going to be able to do anything about it anyway.

I have been doing this for longer than 20 minutes, so I bring a body of judgment to it that is mostly pretty good, most of the time. Do I worry about missing stuff? Sometimes. When I'm drafting contracts, after I'm finished, I will always go back over it, not just for each word, but I have a checklist: Did I do this and did I do this? I make sure that I haven't left anything out. Do I ever make mistakes: I'm sure that I do. Not bad ones, but I do. I'm not always calm, sometimes I yell, but I know that I'm really good at this and I'm good at it because I've been doing this a long time and I have pretty decent judgment, and not just about the specific words in a contract but about people and their relationships to people and the business they do. You just sort of develop a feel for it.

Q: *What resources can you could recommend?*

A: We have an office in California and one of the partners is a man named Michael Donaldson who just put out the 2nd edition of a book called *Copyrights and Clearances*. It's good. It's broken down by subject matter with text and forms. There is another book that I use, called *This Business of Music*, that's a useful handy guide to music issues.

Valerie Walsh

Cocreator and executive producer, *Dora the Explorer*

Q: *How can someone become a better producer?*

A: You need to study, and I think that that is something that everyone can benefit from. Look at TV in a critical way. In going into this industry, you can't be too snobby about it and say, "I don't watch TV." You should be able to study TV and watch it with a critical eye and think about the shots that they use. You can just watch a game show, for instance: how they cut a game show together is very different from how they cut a soap opera, or how they cut an animated cartoon. For a while, I was very removed from what was going on. This year, I watched *The Apprentice*, one show a week, knowing that everybody was watching. And that's the power of TV. It's available to everyone. I think it's something like 99.8% of households have TVs and that is the power of TV.

Q: *How would you define a good television producer?*

A: I think that one of the best traits for a producer is to be able to anticipate problems, so that they can hopefully avoid them, and if not, then they've got a number of solutions ready. They are always thinking one step ahead. It's not that you necessarily have the worst-case scenario in mind all the time. You're just a realist.

Q: *How do you develop the characters in your shows?*

A: OK, let's take cousin Diego. He's a real guy and he's an animal rescuer. The show is set in the rain forest and we're using real animals, very exotic animals, stuff that I've never heard about before, but we do research on them and we write stories about them. Part of being a producer is doing research, so we actually went down to Peru, to the Amazon, and to Costa Rica to an animal rescue center. Those trips, just a few days, are in forming a hundred episodes. From them, you know the backgrounds you are going to use, the animals that you find, the foliage, even what they eat. How do they use their medical supplies? How do they fix a broken wing of a macaw? A lot of people from the rest of the crew said, "Do you really need to go down to the Amazon?" like it was a vacation. Yet, it was very serious research. You have to do this research, and certainly when you do nonfiction subjects, you would always be expected to be that thorough.

Q: *How do you deal with the educational aspect of a show for children?*

A: I see our show as the best kind of kids' TV you can have. Because it is full of education, we have a curriculum, and yet for most kids, they're taking away the learning, but as far as they're concerned, it was just a fun show. We counted and we said a Spanish word but for them, it's just part of the story.

And we do a lot of research; we draw pictures and take the idea out into schools. We pitch to the audience, and we go out and hear what kids have to say and sometimes they say, "I don't like that." That is what they say, literally. Often they will repeat back the story, and a lot of times they will skip over the more educational parts unless you ask them, and then they remember, "Oh yes, we had to find the colors." We are doing all sorts of things with Diego. He is an ecologist, and a paleontologist, and a biologist, and he's eight years old.

Actually, I wasn't sure that I wanted to do this. But then I thought what if you could get kids to aspire to be scientists, because that is a problem that we see. Kids seldom grow up wanting to be a scientist. I started thinking, what we did in *Dora* with Spanish, getting kids across the country speaking a couple words — we wanted to do that with science. Wouldn't it be great if there was a whole generation of kids who said, "I want to work with animals" or "I want to save the planet" or if they are ecologically minded, they are going to see the value of a hybrid car.

Q: *You are giving kids a context for real thinking, which is not usually the case.*

A: That's right. So as a producer, you consider what you really want the show to be about. Sometimes, I just want to show what it's like to be a family living in the 1950s in America, and the family dynamics, *Ozzie and Harriet*. Or something like *Diego*, where there is a real problem with kids liking science. And we also know all the problems we have with the environment, so could we create a character who really tackles this?

Q: *So please talk about how you got to where you are now.*

A: I got out of college, didn't know what I wanted to do. I was a double major in English and in history. And, my Dad was a teacher so I thought, maybe I'll teach. I also loved books, really loved books, so I went into publishing for a while and became a book publicist which, I discovered, I didn't really have any connection with. Then I went back to school and I thought, okay I'll be a teacher, and I got a degree in education. While I was there, I started studying educational technology, either using computers or video.

So, I went back to school, but I knew this time that I would need a job because I couldn't get a third Masters (degree). While I was still in school, I took an internship at Nickelodeon, because I thought, even if I'm not going to be a teacher, I still liked the idea of teaching in some form. The interviewer thought I was insane. They were used to having somebody who is twenty-two, and doesn't mind ordering them lunch. I was working on a thesis film on weekends, and I remember thinking, "this is the most relaxing thing I can do all week is to be your assistant and do all your travel." The people I worked with were both development execs and they oversaw a couple of shows in production. I did that for a year until I started moving up in the ranks and then I was doing development as well.

I actually developed two different projects, one was *Dora the Explorer*, and we piloted them. That got picked up, and at that point I wanted to decide if I was going to stay at the network, which the network wanted me to do. I really felt like I needed to be in the trenches. I think that's something for a lot of people who go the executive route, and stay on the periphery of production. It is a very different sense of accomplishment in what you are doing. I thought, I really want to do this myself, and it's the opportunity of a lifetime. Since I created this thing, *Dora*, it would be easy to hand this off to someone else but then I wouldn't be able to make sure that it was right. So I left with my partner, Chris, and we hired a head writer — that was about five years ago.

From then, I produced that show, a hundred episodes. I probably wrote somewhere between ten and fifteen. I had very different responsibilities from my partner — I don't really do music, and he wanted to work with the composers and the underscorers on the music. I am not an animator myself but I knew what *Dora's* world should look like, especially from a kid's point of view, like what would be fun for a kid, so I oversaw a lot of the designs, the backgrounds, the storyboards. And now on this show, it is much easier to set up the second show, because you've laid the foundation with the first one. More importantly, you've found great people to work with.

You can't do everything yourself, you rely on those other people. You ask yourself, what am I doing? Or is someone going to discover that I'm really flying by the seat of my pants? When I was in grad school, I made a 90-minute feature film for my thesis. It's not watchable, really, but I made it, so it's really more a testament to my producing than to my directing. I remember living through some weekends where everything that could go wrong on a shoot went wrong. And that is something about producing for TV that you have to be able to know: I've never done it before, but I can figure it out, I can handle it. And I think that courage is another one of those defining characteristics of a producer.

Q: *How do you handle being both the producer and the writer?*

A: Just from meeting people in the business who say you've got to write what you want to produce, or at least the first few shows, because otherwise, it will pretty much be taken out of your hands. I didn't want that to happen, so I immediately said "I'm a writer/producer." But, I was always writing. I wrote all through school. Even if you don't have the desire to be a writer, I think you should take writing classes because you should know how a script is put together, even if you are the post-production supervisor. It's a smart thing, to say, "okay, I'm going to write a spec-script for *Will & Grace* just to get through it."

I just interviewed a lot of people to be a writer's assistant, and I was in shock that out of sixteen people, not one had used Final Draft software before. Even if you want to be a director, take a writing class because I do find that people need to think in terms of story. If you're not reading the scripts, you don't know why they made certain choices. If you knew the way the script worked, you would see why we chose to do it that way.

Q: *With* Dora, *each show has such a real story to it.*

A: Dora is our hero. We actually just hired a new head writer for *Diego* and she thought this is so easy because all story is conflict, and the fact that you are an animal rescuer immediately sets the stage for this conflict. But it's true, and I think that people who work in all different aspects of production need to know that. You can buy these great books and teach yourself.

Q: *In what ways do you work with other writers?*

A: For me, it's choice. You've got so many different ideas to chose from, you have to decide which one. There are some times we don't see eye to eye, so we decide by asking the kids what works, the children we tell the stories to. If we think something is too scary for our age group, which is three to five years old, we let the kids tell us. And they do say, "That was too scary" or "I don't like this," or they'll just cover their eyes. In some ways, it is a personal choice for us, and in other ways, we are listening to the most important people — the kids. For me, it's very different because I start working on it, and it's not finished until eighteen months later.

Q: *Can you explain how you produce an animated show?*

A: I am the person in charge of okaying the audio for the show. I'm writing the shows and listening to the actors. Then they start drawing the shows for about six months, then it goes away to Korea to be animated. It comes back and we have color-correction, so it's a long process.

I really have to be in love with each and every show, and I think that's one of the reasons that I've been successful is because that's what I look for. I look for something that I'm going to love and something I'm going to laugh at after eighteen months of the same jokes that I laughed at to begin with. It's a really hard business because you burn out. You're expected to work one day for eight hours and the next day is fourteen, and to keep your energy and enthusiasm up day after day, year after year.

But I don't want it to sound like it is drudgery because I consider myself very lucky being able to do what I love to do. But it really is like a marathon. I think one of a producer's challenges is to keep going and not have your energy wane because if yours does, then there is a trickle down effect. People start coming to meetings later and leaving earlier.

Q: *How do you define a good TV producer?*

A: It might not be flattering. They are able to thrive in situations that have deadlines and other crisis situation. They can walk into chaos and make order out of it, which I think is a really great trait to have. Most of them are really sloppy in their personal lives. Having the ability to wear different hats that they juggle constantly. Within the span of five minutes, I could be answering ten different questions for, say, twenty shows, specific questions having to do with different areas — art, design, writing a song lyric — so the ability to be able to have a good memory and keep track of all that stuff is part of it.

I used to think that being a producer was being the brain because you have to have knowledge of what is going on in all of the other areas. Now, I think it's a lot of different peoples' brains put together. But at times I have thought, "Am I the only one who is responsible for keeping track of this?" because it seemed like everyone was always coming to me. Then I realized that you *do* have to delegate. It will make your life so much easier — find the right people and they can take care of it.

There is no one thing that all producers do. For the most part, they are managing producers, so when my associate producer comes to me with a slew of questions, she knows what needs to be done at what time. She prioritizes what needs to be done with other people's work. It is the step before you do make those decisions. Other associate producers manage down, like dealing with all the production coordinators and PAs, to make sure that someone is available to run all the tapes down to the dub house, or someone else can deal with script distribution. For me, it is important that when somebody who comes to me knows what needs to be done and when, and gets it done.

Q: *How do you develop the premise of a show, like* Diego?

A: First, we make our own standards for the show. We had someone devise our curriculum, a science curriculum. We don't have any kind of PBS-type advisory board because Nickelodeon is not an educational network. Then we go to storybook where we draw pictures from the outline and tell the story in dialogue. We go into preschools and tell the kids the stories in small groups. We always use different kids and different ages, three's and four's and five's. We get their feedback and from there we go back to the script. If we don't get a high level of excitement, we know that there is a problem and it's usually a story problem, because they weren't that excited. Then we do two drafts of the script and a polish, and make any final changes. Only then do we OK it, sign off on it, and it goes off to Korea.

Q: *How does the animation part of production work?*

A: We're an in-house production company at Nick, so we use the in-house animation studio in LA. There are forty or fifty people on staff for our show, and a couple hundred in Korea that work just on this show. This new show is kind of a preschool anime. We have people going to Korea to train the animators; that's why it takes eighteen months. You go over there and it looks like a factory, people working at their desks, very solitary. For me, TV is all about collaboration.

Q: *What are some other traits of a good producer?*

A: A good sense of humor is vital, because sometimes everything is going wrong. You are constantly in a group atmosphere where you need to solve this because nobody goes home until you solve this. Also, being a big picture person and not getting too bogged down in the details. In general, knowing, doing whatever it takes. I feel that women can operate on different levels. There is something about women producers because they don't forget what it was like going up in the ranks, so they are very mindful of other people. I think multitasking is another tricky thing. And, saying "thank you, I know it's annoying but it's your job for now, and you did a good job, and it really helped us."

Q: *Why do you love your job?*

A: I think I love it is because even though I'm not teaching in a classroom, it makes me feel connected to kids, which is my way of teaching. There is a sense of empowering kids that I'm really good at doing and I think they need a lot of positive reinforcement. But there is definitely a good feeling about putting positive role models on TV for kids. For instance, being in a diner in Wisconsin and seeing kids wearing Dora T-shirts was really unbelievable. It was really moving. You can fight things like racism at that young age.

Q: *What do you wish someone had told you about producing when you first began?*

A: Off the top of my head, that there are no wrong answers in producing, only answers that will cost you a lot of money.

Q: *What else is important for a producer to know?*

A: The most important thing to get you through the day, although there are no wrong answers, is that your answer is always the best it can be. I'm on the Web all the time, checking on facts. Something as ridiculous as what size is this animal next to Diego. I use a lot of animal encyclopedias and children's books. In producing there is no bad job, there are jobs you might hate but in the end, each one has taught you something. That's something I like to remind people. You can always quit, but when you do a lot of different jobs, you can always find your niche eventually. The thing I really need is not more money or food, it's five more hours in the day!

Justin Wilkes

Executive producer and producer, including *Jay-Z in Fade to Black*

Q: *How do you define what it is that you do?*

A: I love this question because my mom still asks me this every day: "So you direct the actors?" "No, Mom." "You work the camera?" "No, Mom." "You do the editing?" "No, Mom." There's no simple answer, at least not one that I've ever heard. The best description is (which I can't even take credit for, but since the person who said it is a good friend of mine, I can rip him off): The producer is like the air traffic controller. Your job is to land the plane. Getting into producing is a funny thing and you'll find it's the only profession where you don't really have to do anything to get the title. If you look at a list of every producer on the planet, you'll find that only the smallest percentage of them actually do what I'd consider producing. This is bizarre to me because you can't just wake up one day and say, "I'm a cobbler." First, you have to become an apprentice and work for many years studying the craft. Then finally, after many pairs of shoes, you finally earn the right to call yourself a cobbler. Not so with producing. Anyone can be a producer. You can have money and call yourself a producer. You can have an idea and become a producer. It's truly the easiest title in the world to assume. But I don't suppose you'd be reading this book if the title was all you were interested in. My personal story is that I worked my ass off and did any job I could get my hands on. I got my current job by sitting on the couch in reception until they hired me.

Q: *One premise of this book is that "a producer is a producer is a producer," and that most producing skills can be applied to different areas of television. What's your take on this?*

A: Absolutely. It can even be applied to other mediums. The art of producing is a specific skill set with a different set of tools for each job. Every project is a challenge in its own specific way, but ultimately it's the same. It's like dating.

Q: *Is there a producer's personality?*

A: Incredibly handsome. Deliciously charming.

Q: *What is your day-to-day job description?*

A: As an executive producer in @radical.media's entertainment division, I develop and oversee an assortment of projects ranging from episodic television, one-off's, and feature film projects. It's not as glamorous as it sounds. On any given project, it involves everything from writing, developing, being a liaison to the client/agency/network, scheduling, budgeting, line producing, and overseeing the editorial. Some of @radical.media's recent credits are the feature films, *Jay-Z in Fade to Black, Metallica: Some Kind of Monster,* the Academy Award-winning documentary *Fog of War*, and the Grammy Award-winning *Concert for George.* Our television credits include *The Exonerated* for Court TV; *Nike Battlegrounds: King of the World* for MTV, and *The Life* for ESPN.

Q: *The pitching process is such an integral part of the producer's job. How do you approach writing and presenting a pitch?*

A: I believe there are two main parts to a good pitch. Getting in the door, and then delivering once you get in the door. Both are critical and both require some thought and strategy. Fortunately, we're at the point as a company where we have a reputation for our past work and we've developed relationships with many people at most of the major networks and studios. However, there are still plenty of times where we'll cold-call an assistant to set up a meeting with a development or programming person at a network. Whether there's a relationship or not, it usually takes multiple calls and persistence to actually schedule a meeting (not to mention the constant *rescheduling* that often occurs after an initial time is set).

Now for the pitch itself. We're big fans of not sending our pitch materials ahead of time and instead, showing up with a simple, but well art-directed pitch book that takes the reader through the concept. We'll usually talk through the pitch and refer to the book as we go. Occasionally, we'll use a piece of video or still photos to capture the essence of what we're presenting. The power of a pitch book shouldn't be underestimated. Basically, until your show is produced, the pitch book *is* the show. Everything from the overall look and feel, to the writing, to the design should be reflected in the book. It becomes a great presentational tool and a great way to solidify your own vision of the project.

Q: *What is it about producing that you love?*

A: I love bringing talented people together. There's no greater feeling than standing on a shoot, sitting in an edit session, or watching the final product on TV, knowing that you as the producer pulled together an incredible, hard working group of people to create it.

Q: *What is it about producing that you don't love?*

A: I hate how slow development takes. I hate raising money. I hate people who say they're going to do something and then don't.

Q: *What does the future of television look like from your perspective?*

A: There will be a continual increase in channels and other methods of delivery. You'll receive so much content through your cable, satellite dish, Internet, cell phone, car, washing machine, and toaster that you'll finally turn the damn thing off and read a good book. In the world of advertising, we're seeing a return to one of the earliest forms whereby a brand goes beyond sponsorship of a program and actually owns the content embedded within it.

Q: *The producer's job is a hard and demanding one. How do you keep a balance between your job and your other life?*

A: What's the other life? Have you actually seen it? Oh, please tell me what's it like!

Q: *What would be on your Top Ten list of what a producer should know?*

TOP TEN

Top Ten List of What a Producer Should Know

1. You're always going to come in over budget, so budget accordingly.
2. The network/client will always ask you to make an impossible change at the last minute and you have to make it possible.
3. Put your day-to-day problems into a larger project context when making decisions.
4. Lawyers and agents are not producers. Many would like to be. Many others think they are. But they're not.
5. Your lawyer works for you (not the other way around). Best advice I ever got from another producer.
6. You set the vibe for the entire production. If you yell, others will yell. Lead by example.
7. Great ideas are easy to come by. Actually *making* great ideas is the challenge.
8. Learn every job. A good producer knows how to shoot, edit, gaff, grip, and hold a boom. Not only do people in those positions respect you for knowing something about their craft, but it is invaluable when you're figuring out production logistics and budgeting.
9. Craft Services is the key to success.
10. Don't date the PA. I know you want to. But don't do it.

> To be nobody-but-yourself — in a world which is doing its best, night and day, to make you everybody else — means to fight the hardest battle, which any human being can fight; and never stop fighting.
>
> —e. e. cummings

I. Chapter Review Questions

1. Choose two producers from this chapter and compare and contrast their views on the qualifications and responsibilities of a producer.

2.   Examine the roles and skills sets of various types of producers (i.e., line producer versus supervising producer).

3.   How does a good producer prepare for post-production?

4.   From your perspective, what should a good producer's chief concerns be?

5.   Research the concept of "convergence" and discuss its current and future effects on television.

6.   What genre most interests you? Research two notable producers and their projects in that genre and briefly discuss what made them stand out.

7.   What are five internship opportunities available to you? Get the contact names and addresses for these possibilities.

8.   Who do you know? You may know someone, somewhere, who works in media. If so, arrange for an interview. Ask what his/her responsibilities are now, and the steps taken to get to this position. Write a brief report, or tape a short piece, on this process.

9.   Design a pitch for a project and examine its possible outlets (broadcast network, cable channel, pay-per-view, film festival, direct-to-video release, etc.). Explain how you would tailor your pitch for each outlet.

10.   Research the pilots created for your favorite channel in the last season. Look for patterns between the shows that were picked up for air versus those that were not.

Glossary

24P 24 frames per second, progressive scan.

5.1 audio Refers to the positions in a five-speaker setup, with five speakers placed to the right, center, left, right rear, and left rear of the TV set. This kind of mixing is also called AC3 and Dolby Digital, and is prominent in DVDs, theatrically released films using SDDS and DTS systems, and in some television broadcasts. 5.1 audio requires a specially-equipped television set to hear it at home.

A

Above-the-line People on a project — also called the "creatives" — who are paid a fixed amount, such as producers, writer(s), director(s), primary actors, and legal counsel. Each requires a negotiated fee, including union affiliation, time required, special perks, and more. This cost area also includes acquisitions to script rights.

Account (key budget category) The primary accounts on a budget, including all the departments, all costs above- and below-the-line, and all expenses.

Acoustics The quality of sound and noise found in an enclosed environment used for recording sound during a shoot, such as a soundstage, or a location.

Actual In a budget, the amount actually spent as opposed to estimated.

ADR (automatic dialogue replacement) Also known as looping, actors record, or rerecord their dialogue in the controlled conditions of a recording studio or sound stage. Clean dialogue is recorded to replace lines with noise interference, a bad reading, or a new line not in the original performance. Actors match their performances in the scene by synchronizing to lip movements on a monitor in the studio.

AEA (Actors Equity Association) A union for on-stage actors.

AFTRA (American Federation of Television and Radio Actors) A union that represents actors in television and radio.

Agent (for talent) A talent agent suggests the actors or performers that he or she represents to casting directors, producers, and/or directors. The agent sets up auditions, negotiates contracts, and is responsible for the actor's schedule, make-up and wardrobe calls, call times, etc. The agent is generally franchised by Screen Actors Guild (SAG) and AFTRA, and commonly receives 10% of the actor's earnings.

AGVA (American Guild of Variety Artists) A union that represents performers such as fire jugglers, sword acts, etc.

Ambient sound Background sound or noise natural to the location.

Angle The direction at which a camera or microphone is aimed at the subject that it is recording.

Art director Assists the production designer or, when there is no production designer, serves as the production designer.

Assistant Director (AD) Depending on the project, the AD might hire and be in charge of background extras, as well as direct any action in the background. In a studio shoot, the AD works with the director in the control room and communicates the director's orders to the crew on the studio floor.

Associate Producer (AP) Also called the assistant producer, she or he does specific jobs that the producer assigns such as production schedules, budgets to departments, books talent and/or crew, research, interviews talent, finds locations, supervises union-related functions, etc.

Attached An actor, director, or other talent who has committed to be involved in a project, thus adding extra value to a project's viability.

Audio crew The sound mixer and boom operators on the set/location.

Audio editing Includes editing, positioning, and mixing dialogue, music, sound effects, and other audio components.

Audio log A form kept by the producer and/or post-production supervisor with details pertinent to the audio mix such as the tape number with time codes (in and out point numbers), the scene number, and the take number with a short description of what's been recorded.

Audio mixer (or audio editor) The person responsible for mixing all audio sources such as dialogue, music, and sound effects.

B

B-roll Extra footage that isn't the primary shot, used for montages, background, or cutaways.

Back-end Revenue that comes at the end of the project, such as percentages, royalties or fees for participation.

Background People walking in the background, eating at tables around the actors, or as audience members in a talk show. They lend extra credibility and energy to the project.

Back light One of three main light sources, the back light helps illuminate the background and allows the subject to stand out.

Bars Color bars that are generated by the video camera and help in the edit process.

Below-the-line Costs primarily involved in the production and post-production stages. They are more easily predicted and cover crew and equipment, resources, special effects, editing and audio mixing, and other standard expenses like overhead, insurance, etc.

Bible A standard set of guidelines for a television series or soap opera that include character outlines, plot progressions, and elements that can and can't go into the show.

Bins Digital storage folders in an NLE system in which sequences, clips, and blocks of footage are named and described to make editing easier.

Blocking Comparable to a sequence of steps and actions, like choreography in dance, the director or producer "blocks the scene" before shooting. Blocking examines the positions between actors that the camera is shooting, as well as the movement that takes place, where the camera is going to be, and what is it shooting. The final placement of the actors is often marked with masking tape on the floor as reminders.

Blue screen (or green screen) A screen or background material that is blue (or green) against which the action is shot. These screens can be hundreds of feet long, or can be 8 × 8 feet mobile traveling screens. In editing, the subject is "lifted" off the background and combined with other visual effects. This process is called a chroma-key effect.

Boom A microphone at the end of a long pole that is held over or under the audio source.

Boom operator Responsible for operating the microphone boom that records an actor's dialogue during the filming of a scene. The boom operator follows the action with the microphone as the actors move around the set or location.

Bounce light Indirect light that results from deflected light off special reflectors, white cards, or set pieces.

Branding The specific process of attaching an image, a personal association, and/or a powerful meaning to a product or company. Branding results in higher consumer comfort for buying the product or using the company's services.

Break down At the end of a shoot, the crew disassembles, or breaks down, all the lights, cameras, audio equipment. Whatever else that's not needed for the next shot is packed away. On locations the crew removes tarps, protective coverings, and masking tape; puts items back in their original positions; and thoroughly clears up the location.

Breakdown sheet A form used by the producer, director, and/or key department heads that lists all the elements needed in a scene such as actors, furnishings, props, etc.

Business Physical movements and actions performed by an actor that add to the character's nuance, such as smoking a cigarette in anger.

C

C-stand (century stand) A metal pole with a secure base that is strong enough to hold lighting equipment, sound blankets, and other devices during production.

Call back Second or third audition for an actor for the same part.

Call sheet Daily production schedule that tells each person in the cast and crew what time to arrive on set or location and what scenes are scheduled to be shot.

Camera crew Works under the direction of the director of photography to capture action on film/video of the scene as it will appear on film. The camera operator answers to the DP and may assist him or her in lining up the shot with the director.

Camera operator Camera man or woman who operates the camera. Also called the shooter. Works with the DP or doubles as the DP.

Camera setups Each time the camera and microphone is moved for a new angle.

Casting Finding actors for all the principle roles, as well as supporting actors and extras through the audition process.

Casting director A professional who is familiar with a variety of actors and their performance range. She or he first interests the actor's agent or manager in the role, arranges for auditions, and works with the producer and director in the selection process.

Cathode-ray tube (CRT) An electronic vacuum tube that transmits a focused stream of electrons onto a phosphorous screen, and results in an image on a television set, computer monitor, and other devices.

CCD (charge coupled device) An electronic chip in most video cameras that converts light and images to electrical impulses. For example, a three-chip video camera that has three separate CCDs produces a sharper, higher quality color picture than the standard single-chip cameras with only one CCD.

CG (character generator) Often called chyron, the CG is used to "write" text electronically on the video picture in opening and closing credits, show titles, and in the lower third of the picture to identify a speaker or what's happening on the screen.

CGI (computer generated imagery) Creation and manipulation of images through digital computer technology.

Character actor An actor or performer who specializes in playing secondary roles that are more focused on character than star power.

Choreographer The person responsible for the planning and staging of the dance number(s) for a show.

Chroma A video term relating to true color, with no blacks or grays.

Chroma-key backdrop See *Blue screen*.

Clearance Obtaining legal written permission to use music, a script, footage, or other aspects necessary in a project.

Close-up (CU) A camera frame that shows a close view of a face or an object.

Closing credits Text that details the cast and crew of a program, along with other information.

Coexecutive producer An additional executive producer who may share some of the responsibilities of executive producing, or who may bring funding or other added value to the production.

Color bars The traditional test of a video signal, this series of vertical bars — white, yellow, cyan, green, magenta, red, blue, and black — appears at the beginning of a reel.

Color-correction Changing or correcting the color, hues, or tones of footage by using a color-corrector or time base corrector.

Completion bond A kind of "insurance" that guarantees that the project, usually a film, will be finished on schedule; otherwise the bank and/or investors will get their money back.

Component video A video signal that separates the chrominance (the color) from the luminance (the blacks and whites), resulting in sharper detail and color.

Composer Responsible for the project's musical score. Works closely with the producer and director to find the musical direction of the project and writes music that matches picture, as well as opening and closing themes.

Composite video The luminance and chrominance are combined to form one analog signal.

Compression A digital video storage system that reduces, or compresses, the data in the footage which facilitates storage space.

Conform In the editing process, the editor takes the final cut from the NLE or off-line and matches it with the original, high-resolution footage in an online session.

Conglomerates Large corporations that are involved in and control a variety of media such as television stations, film studios, newspapers, magazines, and more.

Content Another word for a show, program, or project for cable, network, or distribution.

Content provider Media company or independent producer who produces program material, or content, for delivery.

Contingency Back-up funds, usually about 10% of the final budget total, that cover mistakes on the shoot, bad weather days, and other realities in production.

Continuity Seamless movement from one shot or scene to the next that isn't interrupted by mismatched clothing, actions, set pieces, etc. Also see *Script supervisor.*

Cookie (kukaloris) In lighting, a thin panel with cutouts of shapes, either regular or irregular, that permit light to be directed through them, forming patterns on a background.

Coproduction Partnership or joint venture formed for the production of a specific project or projects.

Copyright The exclusive legal right of a writer, author, composer, artist, or publisher to control and dispose of his or her work for a 70-year period.

Courtesy credit Acknowledgment of contributors, investors, or services by listing their names or businesses in the closing credits.

Cover set A fully-dressed interior location that the production can move to in case of sudden problems from an exterior location such as equipment failure or bad weather.

Coverage The variety of angles at which a scene is shot.

Craft services Catered food, snacks, and beverages brought on set or on location; also, the person(s) who is in charge of providing food for the cast and crew.

Crane Similar to a dolly, a crane moves the camera using a balanced arm. Unlike a dolly, a crane has more mobility to rise or descend.

Crawl (also known as **end credits** or **closing credits**) The graphic text information moves vertically or horizontally on the screen.

Creatives Above-the-line personnel such as writers, actors, directors, or other key union members.

Credits Complete list of all the cast and crew who worked on a project, from its beginning to end, and who are given "credit" for their work.

Cross-boarding Shooting scenes consecutively from two or three different episodes that all take place on the same set or location.

Cross-cutting See *Parallel editing.*

Cross fade In an audio mix, one sound is faded out as another sound fades in; similar to a visual dissolve.

Cue sheet A list of any music used on a project that includes the titles of the music selections, the names of the composers and performing rights society affiliation, etc.

Cutaway A shot that is inserted between two other shots. It can prevent a jarring jump cut, enhancing and adding to the edited sequence.

Cyc (cyclorama) A backdrop, like a curtain, that acts as a background for action.

D

Dailies The footage shot by the end of each working day.

DAT (digital audio tape) A high-quality system for recording digital sound with no distortion, used in professional audio recording and for storing computer data.

DAW (digital audio workstation) An electronic system that uses digital audio for mixing sounds, dialogue, music, and effects.

Deal memo An agreement between two parties, usually between the producer and the cast, crew, writer, director, or other people who are part of the production. It defines the time to be worked and the rates to be paid.

Deferment payment When, or if, a project makes money down the line, all who agreed to defer their payments are paid later, often with interest or bonuses on top of their original salary agreement.

Demo reel Similar to a portfolio; a selection of short clips from a producer's projects that gives a potential client examples of the producer's work.

Demographics A precise measurement of a specific population to determine their level of interest, as consumers or viewers.

Deregulation Removing government restrictions on media-related industries.

Detailed budget This budget addresses every aspect of the project's production. Each detail in a project translates into a cost that's part of a key budget account.

DGA (Directors Guild of America) A union representing directors.

Dialogue track An audio track on which an individual actor's dialogue is recorded and stored. There is no other interference of music or sound effect.

Digitize To download footage into data storage.

Directional microphone A microphone that is pointed at a specific actor or source of sound, and picks up only that dialogue or sound.

Director In some television programs (such as dramatic series, sitcoms, movies of the week, etc.), the director is the primary artistic influence, or is more of a technical director who works from a control room.

Director of Photography (DP) Works with the producer and/or director to design the visual images and texture of the footage and shoot the action. The DP may supervise the camera operator(s), or may double as the operator. She or he plans and sets up camera angles and shots, and oversees lighting, etc.

Dissolve The overlap of one shot over another, one fades out and the other fades in.

Distributor A company or individual who owns or licenses the rights to a project for rentals, lease, broadcast, or final sale.

Dolly A small vehicle, like a mobile platform with stabilized wheels, on which a camera is mounted.

Domestic territory Specifically, the United States and Canada, usually referred to as North American territory.

Downconversion The HD footage is converted to an NTSC, or standard definition, tape that can be downloaded into your NLE system.

Download The transfer of digital data into an NLE storage system.

Draft A version, or revision, of a script or program idea.

Dubs Both audio and video are duplicated and copied onto a variety of video formats.

E

E&O Insurance (errors and omissions) An insurance against third-party claims, such as ownership, chain of title, as well as protection from unanticipated problems.

Editor Person responsible for the assembly of the various video, graphic, and audio elements into a cohesive and creative finished piece.

EDL (edit decision list) A sequential list compiled by the editor of all reel numbers, time code locations, music cues, and other data in the final cut.

Effects track A track of audio that is assigned to a specific audio effect, such as chirping crickets or background conversations.

Equalizer An audio device that can increase, decrease, or modulate high, medium, or low frequencies when mixing dialogue, music, ambient sound, etc.

Establishing shot (also called a **master shot**) Usually the opening scene, it sets up the scene and what's happening in it. It's generally a wide shot that establishes the action.

Executive producer The job various considerably from project to project. Often, she or he has the final word on decision making, and maintains overall control over a TV project from acquisition and financing, developing and selling an idea, marketing it, to its final delivery to network. On certain projects, the executive producer is often called the *showrunner*.

Exteriors A location that is outside, rather than inside (interiors).

Extras People who provide a nonspeaking background atmosphere to a production, like passersby in a street scene or as background people in a crowd scene.

Eyeballs An informal term used as measurement for viewers watching a show.

Eye-line The line of attention that begins from an actor's eyes and follows the direction that the actor is looking in.

F

Fade in An image slowly emerges from a black screen.

Fade out An image slowly fades into a black screen.

Fields A video frame is made of two parts, or *fields*.

Fill light Light that is positioned or reflected to fill in shadows on a face or location that are cast by the key light.

Filmlook A special effects design program used in post-production that can treat video footage to give it the grain, texture, and scratches usually associated with film.

Film-to-tape A process of transferring film (super 8, super 16, 16- or 35-mm) to video via a *telecine*, also called a *film chain*.

Final cut The last and final version that reflects all visual and sound edits and creative decision.

First look deal A network or production company that has the right to be the first to option or buy certain rights to the project.

Flag See *Gobo*.

Floor plans An overview of a location, drawn to scale and usually from an overhead perspective, that guides the crew in positioning the cameras, lights, and actors.

Foley Additional sound effects that are performed like footsteps or doors closing.

Foley mixer See *Foley*. Mixes and records the sounds created by the Foley artists.

Format (1) Includes several genres — a quiz show, reality-adventure, talk show — that have specific script formats, sets, musical themes, and lighting, that can be packaged, sold, and adapted by local programmers, usually internationally.

Format (2) The aspect ratio or size of a television screen.

Format (3) An image can be recorded on a video format such as DVPro, BetaSP, DigiBeta, etc.

FPS (frames per second) Speed of camera.

Framing An aspect of composition of an image in the camera's frame. The framing can range from a close-up to an extreme long shot.

Freelancers Independent contractors who are employed on a per-project or an as-needed basis, with no benefits or full-time compensation.

Freeze frame A single frame of video is held, or *frozen*, on the screen.

Fringe benefits The extra costs for union personnel and talent, they include pension and welfare (P&W), health benefits, union payments, etc.

G

Gaffer Often the primary lighting technician who works with electricity. Assists the DP, adjusting the angles and "barn doors" on free-standing and suspended lights.

Gels (gelatins) Durable, translucent material that is available in various colors and hues. Gels are positioned in front of lights to create different colored light.

Genny (generator) A supplemental source of electricity for video equipment, usually used on location.

Genre In television, the format, style, content, and pacing of a show puts it into a category, or genre, such as a sitcom, drama, soap opera, talk show, etc.

Gobo Durable, opaque material that hangs from an adjustable arm on a stand with a firm base, and directs or deflects light to specific areas. Sometimes called a *flag* when it protects the lens from direct light.

Graphic artist Person trained in visual artistic representation through illustration, painting, drawing, font design, photography, and/or printing.

Green light Getting the OK from a client or network to start a project.

Green room An area set aside for actors and talent that is private, comfortable, and quiet.

Greens Plants, real and/or fake, that are used in a scene, from simple houseplants to re-creating a life-size garden.

Greens person Individual responsible for all plants, foliage, and greenery seen on the screen.

Grid In a studio or sound stage, an overhead system of pipes from which hang lights, lighting equipment, and occasionally, microphones.

Grip Works with the camera and camera equipment, and other mechanical aspects of production, like setting up C-stands, maintaining and moving the dolly, and tripods.

H

Handheld camera A camera that is held in the shooter's hand or on the shoulder, rather than on a tripod.

Hard light Lighting that is strong and directed, resulting in sharp-edged, distinct shadows.

HDTV (high-definition television) Video signals with a high resolution (roughly twice the lines of standard TV) and a sharp visual clarity similar to film.

Headshots Professional $8\frac{1}{2} \times 11$ photographs of actors and talent. They are usually close-up vanity shots with a resume of their experiences on the back.

High-key light Lighting produced by the combination of less key light and more fill light, resulting in almost no shadows.

Honey wagon A vehicle with several portable toilets, sinks, and showers for on-location shooting.

Hook An aspect of an idea that is unique enough to grab the reader's attention.

Hyphenate Double tasking, such as a writer-producer, writer-director, etc.

I

Independent production company A small business usually formed by a producer(s) that produces programming for a network, studio, or corporate client, and handles all the administrative and technical requirements needed to satisfy the client.

Indirect costs Additional money that is factored into a production budget that covers areas such as legal fees, accounting services, insurance, and contingency fees.

In-point In the editing process, the starting point of a specific edit.

Insert shot A shot, usually a close-up, that reveals an important detail in a scene.

J

Jib A crane that has an adjustable arm controlling a camera at the end. It can swoop over an audience or into a set or location, and is controlled either manually or by remote.

Jump cut An obvious edit, cutting two very similar images together that share identical angles and framing.

K

Key The head, or most important person, of each department.

Key light The most important light source in the three-point lighting system. Its illumination of a subject is bright and hard, and produces deep shadows.

Kinescope A process developed before the invention of videotape; a 16-mm camera was placed in front of a television screen and filmed television programs that were broadcast live.

L

Lavaliere (lav) An easily concealed small microphone that clips onto clothing; it's generally omnidirectional and picks up dialogue clearly.

Layback In post-production, the process of joining the final completed audio track to the finished picture.

Letterbox format On a television screen, a black strip above and below the picture that frames the image in a film-style aspect ratio.

Lighting board The equipment that controls all the lighting dimmers in a studio or remote location.

Lighting director Person responsible for the design and implementation of the lighting during production.

Line item Each entry in a budget that relates to a specific cost.

Line producer Beginning in preproduction and continuing through completion of principal photography or through the completion of post-production, the line producer is responsible for the day-to-day running of the production.

Linear editing A traditional system of editing video in which shots are edited together in a linear fashion, moving forward.

Lip sync To speak or sing in synchronization with a picture, with the appearance of an exact match.

Load in The transfer or *download*, of footage and audio into a data storage device, such as a nonlinear editing system, to be digitized for editing.

Location scout Person responsible for finding the necessary locations for a project, as well as securing permits, negotiating location agreements and rentals, and obtaining all other permissions required for filming.

Locked When the editing has been finalized, the project is considered "locked."

Locked down camera A camera that is stationary, usually on a tripod or a pedestal, and not handheld.

Log Taking notes of each pertinent shot with its description and time code number.

Log line (also called a **one-liner** or **tag line**) A log line is a concise sentence that cleverly sums up a project's main idea, and is an attention grabber.

Logo A distinctive graphic designed to give a television show a graphic identity.

Long form contract A substantial, detailed agreement that includes all the provisions of the contract.

Long shot (LS) Camera framing that captures an image from a distance, usually from a substantial distance.

Long take A continual, uninterrupted shot, usually lasting at least 20 to 30 seconds or longer.

Low-key lighting A style of lighting produced by the contrast between key light and fill lights, resulting in darker light marked by shadows and occasional high-light.

Lower thirds Electronic text that appears on screen, under a person's face, and spells out his or her name, location, profession, etc.

Luminance In a video image, the measurement of pure white in the picture.

M

M&E (music and special effects) Two important areas of audio components in a mix.

Magic hour Twilight, or dusk, a limited time between sunset and dark when the light has a special luminescent quality to it that's ideal for certain shots.

Make-up artist The person who works closely with the producer and director to design the make-up for the cast, including special effects, aging, wounds, etc.

Making the day Accomplishing what's been planned for each day's shoot.

Manager The manager oversees an actor's career, and may hire an agent, lawyer, accountant, etc. She or he works with the actor on career decisions, such as scripts to review, and advises in a range of professional areas.

Marketing Presenting an idea or product to potential viewers or consumers, using methods that sway or convince the target audience.

Markup fee A percentage added to the overall costs, covering office overhead and personnel.

Master In video, the original footage; also, the completed high-quality first-generation version of a project that is used for dubbing.

Master shot (also called an **establishing shot**) Establishes the scene and the actors' movements and their relationships to each other.

Matching time code The time code on the original footage is exactly the same on the screening cassette. It's visible time code, also called *vizcode* or *VTC*, that's displayed in a small box on the bottom or top of the screen.

Media buy Purchasing airtime (usually in 30- or 60-second blocks) on a network or channel in which to air a commercial.

Medium shot A camera framing in which the person or object is shown almost in its entirety.

Merchandising Adapting the likeness of a popular TV or film character to nonmedia products — T-shirts, hats, pencils — and cashing in on that character's branding.

Mic (mike) A shortened version of microphone.

Mix The combining together of various audio tracks — dialogue, music, effects — and merging them into a single track.

Montage A story-telling device that can compress time or impose a narrative over images, and is built by editing together a series of quick shots to tell the story.

MOS (mit out sound) Shooting video only, with no audio being recorded.

Most favored nation (MFN) A legal agreement in which everyone involved in a project is paid the same amount, or in other ways share in equal parity; no one person has an advantage over another.

Motion control camera (also called **title camera**) A computer-controlled camera designed to pinpoint and shoot small details with zooms, pans, and other camera angles; often used to add dimension and movement to still photos or flat art work.

Music clearance Written legal permission to use preexisting music in a project.

Music director Works with the preexisting music (including popular recordings) to craft together a musical score for a production.

Music supervisor The supervisor of the creation of a musical score using original music and/or existing or prerecorded music. Often responsible for the legal clearances and licensing of any music needed in the project, and compiles the music cue sheet, found in the attached CD.

N

Narration *Voice-over* or narration is provided by an off-camera person who records the script at a recording studio.

Needle drop During audio post-production, various sound effects and music cues from a sound effects or music library might be added and dropped into the mix.

Network A national broadcasting entity made up of many stations in various locations, usually larger cities.

Neutral-density (ND) filters A grayish filtering material often used in shooting video, placed over windows to filter the natural outdoor light that can intrude on a shot.

Niche marketing A television market with precise demographics and specific interests, such as cooking or golf, for which a producer creates programming. Also called *narrowcasting*.

NLE (nonlinear editor) Referring to both the editor and the editing system itself, a digital system that edits footage in a random, nonsequential way similar to film-style editing.

Noise In video, noise on the video signal is created by distortion, and results in the visual effect of "snow" or a hissing sound in the audio.

NTSC (National Television Standards Committee) NTSC is a national standard for American color television, consisting of 525 interlaced scan lines per frame, and runs at 30 fps.

O

Off-line edit Versions of an edited project, cut at a low resolution that require much less storage space and usually conformed in an online session.

Omnidirectional A microphone that can pick up audio from all directions.

Online edit The final cut from the off-line session is brought into an online session during which the original high-resolution footage is assembled. The final audio track along with graphics or other elements are also married to the picture.

On-set dresser Person responsible for furnishing, or dressing, a set with appropriate fittings, furniture, and other objects needed in the scene.

One-off A program that is self-contained, usually one or two hours in length. An example might be a documentary or a news-oriented special.

Opening titles (opening credits) The name of the show and a limited list of the creatives — the producer, writer, director, principal actor(s), etc. — that are seen in text at the beginning of the program.

Option/optioning Obtaining exclusive ownership and/or temporary rights to a script, book, or story for a period of time long enough to develop and hopefully sell as a project. Option payments vary, depending on the situation.

Orphan works Material — footage, photographs, music — whose copyright holders can't be located.

Out of sequence During a shoot, scenes are seldom shot in the sequence in which they appear in the script. Instead, they are shot out of sequence to accommodate schedules and budgets.

P

PA (production assistant) Entry-level position on a project that involves every aspect of work, from running errands to making copies to getting lunch.

PAL (phase alternating line) Video format used in the UK, Australia, China, and parts of Western Europe. This video format is 625 lines and runs at 25 fps.

Pan A camera movement in which the camera moves smoothly, horizontally (from right to left or left to right) or vertically (from top to bottom or bottom to top).

Paper cut or paper edit (editing storyboard) A paper cut is prepared by the producer for the edit session, giving the editor the sequence of shots for the final product. Items on the paper cut include exact in-points of selected shots, their descriptions, time code locations, reel numbers, graphic and audio information, and the duration of each shot.

Parallel editing Two separate yet somehow related events appear to be happening at the same time, shifting back and forth between one scene and another.

Pay-or-play A contractual agreement stating that if the talent or *creative* is not used in a project for whatever reason, she or he will still be paid the agreed-upon fees.

Pay-per-view (PPV) In television, paying a fee for watching a single program or event on a specific PPV channel.

Perma-lancers Permanent freelancers who are employed full-time, though are not paid employee benefits or given any contractual certainty.

Petty cash (PC) Cash kept on hand during a production that pays for expenses such as meals, supplies needed for the crew, props, and other costs that arise.

Pistol grip Special mounting device for a handheld camera.

Pitch Selling an idea for a television show to a network, client, independent producer, or other end user. Also, a written proposal that acts as a selling tool for the idea.

Pixels (picture element) The smallest resolvable rectangular area of an image, made of three close dots of color — red, green, and blue.

Point of view shot (POV shot) A shot that reflects what an actor or character might be seeing; the camera angle is shot from the actor's perspective.

Post-production supervisor In larger or more complex projects, this person is the producer of post-production and is responsible for the coordination of all aspects of post-production.

Presale contracts Selling specific rights of a project, such as international sales or for DVD distribution, in order to interest investors or to obtain a loan.

Prime time In television, the hours in the programming schedule that attract the highest number of viewers, usually 7:30 to 11 p.m.

Principal cast The main actors or central characters in a television show.

Principal photography The actual shooting that begins when everything is ready to start.

Producer Handles the creative and technical logistics, administrative details, and often hires the talent, writers, and director, additional producers, and others. May create or acquire the idea, and obtains funding or sale to a broadcaster, and most or all details, from the beginning to the end of the project. May be a producer who is part of a larger team of producers on complex or long-term projects.

Product placement The use of a specific product (such as a cereal box, a car, sports gear) in a TV show or film in return for a fee.

Production designer Creates the environment for a project and designs the space in which the action takes place. Hires the set builders, scenic artists, set dressers, and prop masters to actualize the design plans, and more.

Prompter Individual who helps actors or talk-show talent when needed by holding up signs, or cue cards, on which their lines are written in large print.

Prop master Designs, buys, or rents each prop needed in a production. Generally, the head of the property department.

Proposal A written prospectus or *pitch* that details the idea of a project, given to a network or potential buyer or investor.

Props An object on a set or on location that is handled by the actor as part of the action, such as a telephone, glasses, or a laptop.

Protection copies Exact copies of original footage or the final master that are backup protections in case of damage or loss in shipping.

Public domain When the copyright has elapsed on specific footage, it has no legal owner and can be used without obtaining legal clearances or paying royalty fees.

R

Rack focus A shot in which the camera changes focus from a person or object in the foreground to the background or vice versa.

Ratings A measurement that determines what programs TV viewers are watching and at what times.

Reaction shot A close-up of an actor's face that registers a reaction to the shot before it or to actions in the story line.

Reality TV A form of television program that is theoretically unscripted, and relies on "real people" in real-life situations.

Recce (recky) A shortened version of "reconnaissance" in the preproduction phase that involves scouting for a location and related location details.

Reel A cassette or tape in video and audio.

Reflected light During a shot, light that is deflected or bounced off objects.

Release A legal agreement that gives a producer the right to use someone's likeness, location, artistic material, or other object in ways that are detailed on the release.

Resolution In video, the level of detail and clarity in an image.

Re-stripe Replacing the original time code on the footage with new time code, making it easier to work with and to log in editing.

RGB (red, green, blue) In video, the primary colors of red, green, and blue.

Room tone Refers to sounds that are a natural part of each and every set or location.

Rotoscope An animation process that involves projecting live action by an actor, frame by frame, onto a software drawing pad.

Rough cut Reflects the overall sequence of shots and audio in editing, with the approximate in- and out-points of the edits and the order in which they'll appear.

Royalty A fee paid to an actor, author, composer, performer, or other artist, for the use of his or her copyrighted material.

S

Safety In video, the inner area of the television screen that will be seen on a broadcast or standard monitor.

SAG (Screen Actors Guild) Union protecting on-camera actors and talent. The SAG contract also protects members of AFTRA and AGVA.

Scale The lowest minimum wage allowed under a union contract.

Scene A segment in a program that happens in one space and period of time, and consists of one or more shots. A scene is also called a *sequence*.

Scenic artist Paints sets, ages walls or floors, creates the look of stone or other materials, and achieves textures or moods on a set.

Scratch track A preliminary track of narration read by the producer or someone else that helps determine final timings and beats in a rough cut. It is later replaced by a professional narration track.

Screen time A period of time in which events are happening on screen. It might be an hour, a day, or a longer time span, depending on the storyline.

Script supervisor Also called the *continuity person*, the script supervisor is on set, observing each shot for details of continuity from one scene to the next, including wardrobe, props, and camera angles, and taking notes on every aspect of the shoot for the director and editor.

SECAM (sequential color with memory) The video standard of 625 lines that runs at 25 fps, used in Russia, Eastern Europe, and France.

Second assistant director (2nd AD) Helps the director and 1st AD, usually prepares the call sheets for the next day's shoot.

Second unit A smaller production team that shoots extra footage, like exteriors, background reactions, etc., that are tied into primary scenes in the editing process.

Set decorator Creates the visual look of the project, including the purchase, rental, and placement of furnishings that add to the set environments.

Set designer Takes the production designer's rough drawings and creates working blueprints and construction drawings that guide the building of the sets.

Set dressing The physical and aesthetic placement of furnishings and props in preparation for rehearsals and the actual shoot.

Set mixer Records the dialogue and any other production sound that is produced on the set as clearly as possible.

Setup All the elements needed for a specific shot, such as the placement of the camera, the lenses and microphones, and the composition of the frame.

Shooter See *Camera operator*.

Shooting out In production, all the shots needed in one location are grouped together and shot before moving on to the next location.

Shooting ratio The amount of footage shot in production compared to the amount of footage used in editing the final piece. Twenty hours of footage for a one-hour documentary has 20:1 ratio, for example.

Shooting schedule A mapped-out plan for the shoot, generally given to all cast and crew for each day's shoot.

Shorts Projects that are under a half-hour in length.

Shot A short, single take that is edited with other shots into a longer sequence or scene.

Showrunner S/he might also be the executive producer of a weekly television show, and is responsible for the creative direction of a series, guiding the writers along with the script, casting the actors, pitching a show idea to a network, etc.

Signatory A person or company that has agreed to comply with the regulations of a union with which they want to work, including those that cover writers, directors, talent, and/or crew members.

Silks Medium to large squares of translucent material that can be strategically hung and positioned to filter the sunlight and maintain lighting consistency.

Single system The audio that is recorded directly onto the videotape.

Slow motion (slo-mo) In video, the speed of a shot is slowed down to create a slower action or other desired effect.

SMPTE (Society of Motion Picture and Television Engineers) The acronym for this organization SMPTE, also represents time code, the standard 8-digits used in video that represents hours, minutes, seconds, and frames per second — 01 02 03 45.

Soft lighting (also called diffuse lighting) The lighting on a subject that avoids extreme bright and dark areas, a gradual transition between highlights and shadows.

Sound blankets Large moving blankets made of a dense absorbent material that can be hung or placed on a set or location to muffle sound.

Sound effects (SFX) This track includes natural sounds from the production such as background ambience, Foley, or audio effects from a sound effects library.

Soundstage A building specially equipped for shooting a production that is generally sound-proof and often furnished with video and audio equipment, lighting grids and equipment, rooms for talent, set construction, and other amenities.

Spec script A script written on speculation. The writer uses it as a sample of his or her work, and does not get paid unless the screenplay is sold.

Special effects make-up Might include artificial wounds or body parts (prosthetics) used to change an actor's appearance.

SPFX (special effects) Effects that are created on the set or location — fog, rain, snow, an open flame — instead of being added in post-production.

Split screen The screen is divided into boxes or parts that are all active at the same time. Each box shows an image that relates to the story line.

Splits During production, the producer might divide the day and night shooting into shifts, or splits, that are then sectioned into a half-day and half-night shift.

Spotting session During the audio post-production phase, the producer or director reviews the project for areas in which to add music, narration, ADR, Foley, and SFX.

Stand-in A person who bears a strong resemblance to an actor stands-in for the actor in technical rehearsals and often in a long shot when the actor isn't available.

Star The lead actor or performer in a production.

Steadicam A counterbalanced rig worn by a camera operator that allows for smoother camera movement — midway between handheld and tripod camera mounts.

Step deal A contract for writers that indicates a series of incremental payments for each version of a script or story.

Still photographer Takes photographs during rehearsals or actual production that may be used for publicity or archiving purposes.

Stills The photographs taken with a still camera that catalog various aspects of the production, like actors in scenes, the director working with the actors and crew, etc.

Stock Unused clean videotape or audio tape on which images or sound is recorded.

Stock footage Preexisting, high-quality footage that is sold by a stock footage company for a negotiated fee and licensing agreement that is dependent on its final use.

Stock music Royalty free prerecorded music that is sold by a stock music company. The fees for its use depend on its final use.

Storyboard Simple, cartoon-like sketches of each scene in a script; also, a paper cut detailing the cuts and their time codes and reel locations for the editor in an edit session.

Storyboard artist Responsible for rendering a sequence of drawings based on a script to aid in planning and coordinating action, drawn by hand or with software.

Striking the set The breaking down of a set, including the removal of furnishings and props after shooting and disassembling the equipment.

Stunt double Substitutes for an actor to perform difficult or dangerous action sequences, and superficially resembles the actor.

Superimpose The layering of one image over another.

Supporting actors Secondary cast members in a production whose characters and roles support those of the primary cast.

Sweetening In audio post-production, the process of mixing the audio tracks of narration, music, and sound effects with the master audio track.

Swish pan (also called a whip pan) A camera movement that pans rapidly from right to left or left to right, and can be an editing or narrative transition from one scene to another.

Sync (synchronization) An exact match of the audio to the image on video.

Synopsis A brief and compelling distillation of a story idea into a short form, usually in one or two paragraphs. It is an essential aspect of the pitching process.

T

Take Each time a specific scene is shot until the producer and/or director is satisfied.

Talent Anyone who appears on camera, such as an actor, performer, host, guests, etc.

Target audience   Specific audience for whom a show is developed or produced.

Technical director   The person, generally in the control room of a studio, who takes in the various camera feeds, graphics, and special video effects, and "edits" them live.

Telecine (also called a film chain)   This device facilitates the transfer of film to videotape. During this process, film images and audio are converted to a format that is used by a broadcast network or for nonlinear editing purposes.

Teleprompter   A small monitor that is mounted directly under the camera lens that displays the performer's lines in a roll-down scroll.

Textless copy   A "clean" copy of the final project with no text or graphics superimposed on it.

Thirteen outline   A comprehensive outline of the first thirteen episodes of a series, written and agreed upon by the producers, prior to start of production.

Three-point lighting   A standard lighting setup that utilizes the three sources of lighting — key light, fill lights, and back lights.

Time code (TC)   A signal "burned on" the videotape that gives every frame a specific number in hours, minutes, seconds, and frames per second.

Time-of-day time code   TC that can be set in the camera itself that records the actual time of day as opposed to an arbitrary time code numbering system.

Top sheet   A quick summary of the budget costs in each department that provides an overview of necessary information at a glance.

Tracking shot   Usually accomplished by mounting the camera on a dolly, crane or a jib. The shot travels forward, backward, or laterally through space to capture movement.

Trades   Entertainment industry publications, such as *Variety* and *The Hollywood Reporter*.

Transition   In editing, the moving of one shot or scene to the next by using a cut, dissolve, wipe, etc.

Treatment   An abbreviated narrative outline of a script, story or idea. Shorter in length than a script.

TRT   The **total running time** of a program or show.

Turnaround   When a studio or network has abandoned a project and removed its support for further development, a producer is free to take it to another studio that can buy it by reimbursing the original studio or network for any incurred costs.

Turnaround time   Actors' unions requirement for a 12-hour break of time between the end of one shooting day and the call time for the next day.

Two-shot   A scene with two people in the frame. Three-shots and four-shots have three and four people in the frame.

U

Underlighting   Placing lights under the people or objects in a scene.

Up-fronts   An annual gathering of the networks and their affiliates during which new shows and pilots are unveiled and previewed.

UPM (unit production manager)   The right hand of the producer(s). Works with administrative below-the-line issues, technical equipment, and the needs of the crew.

V

VCR A machine that can play and/or record on $\frac{1}{2}$-inch VHS tapes.

Video monitor In production, a small video monitor attached by a cable to each camera that shows what the camera sees as it's being shot. Can also provide instant playback of what was just shot.

Visible time code (also called **vizcode** or **VTC**) Time code that matches the original footage and is visible on a screen.

Voice-over (VO) A recorded voice of a "commentator" in a documentary or a "narrator" of a story line.

VTR A **videotape recorder.**

W

Wardrobe designer Does a wardrobe breakdown of all characters and their roles, their time period, the time that wardrobe or costumes are needed, and more.

Wardrobe supervisor Supervises the costume department with the wardrobe designer, keeps track of the budget, maintains the wardrobe, and more.

WGA (Writers Guild of America) Union that represents and protects writers of film, television, and radio projects.

White balance In shooting video, a white card or piece of paper is often held in front of the camera lens to adjust its sensitivity to a light source.

Windscreen An absorbent fuzzy material that can be wrapped around a microphone to deflect or absorb interfering noise from wind or breezes.

Wipe A special effects transition used in video editing that wipes out one scene and brings in another, such as a page turn or one image that drops down over another.

Wireless microphone (also known as a *radio microphone*) A cordless microphone that operates on a battery-powered pack hidden on the person speaking, under clothing.

Wrangler A specially trained person who manages the activities and work of a specific kind of talent, such as a child, an animal, or a stunt person.

Wrap the project Tying up all the loose ends, after completion of the production.

Writer Creates the story, action, and characters for TV narrative programs like sitcoms, drama series, and mini-series. She or he may have created the original material or been brought in to work with an existing script or story outline.

Z

Zoom A movement by the camera lens that either moves quickly into an image (zoom in) or moves quickly away from it (zoom out).

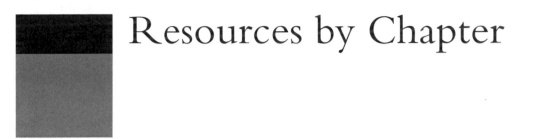

Resources by Chapter

PART ONE

Although the following resources are specific to each chapter, many references can also apply to more than one chapter or area of a producer's responsibilities. The reader is also encouraged to consult the CD for more extensive resources, forms and agreements, books, publications, and Web sites.

CHAPTER 1: What Does a TV Producer *Really* Do?

Cury, Ivan. *Directing & Producing for Television: A Format Approach, 2nd Edition*. Focal Press, 2001.

Gardner, Howard. *Multiple Intelligences for the 21st Century*. Basic Books, 2000.

Goleman, Daniel. *Primal Leadership: Learning to Lead with EQ*. Harvard Business School Press, 2004.

Lee, John J. *The Producer's Business Handbook* (Book & CD-ROM). Focal Press, 2000.

Litwak, Mark. *Dealmaking in the Film and Television Industry From Negotiations Through Final Contracts: 2nd Edition Expanded and Updated*. Silman-James Press, 2002.

Rea, Peter and David K. Irving. *Producing & Directing the Short Film and Video, 2nd Edition*. Focal Press, 2001.

Resnik, Gail and Scott Trost. *All You Need to Know About the Movie and TV Business, 5th Edition*. Fireside, 1996.

Schreibman, Myrl A. *The Indie Producer's Handbook: Creative Producing from A to Z*. Lone Eagle Publishing Company, 2001.

Tompkins, Al. *Aim for the Heart: Write for the Ear, Shoot for the Eye: A Guide for TV Producers and Reporters*. Bonus Books, 2002.

Vachon, Christine. *Shooting to Kill*. Avon Books, 1998.

Wiese, Michael. *Producer to Producer: Insider Tips for Success in Media*. Michael Wiese Productions, 1997.

CHAPTER 2: TV: Past, Present — and Future

Barnouw, Erik. *A History of Broadcasting in the United States*. New York: Oxford University Press, 1968.

Barnouw, Erik. *Tube of Plenty: The Evolution of American Television, 2nd Edition*. Oxford University Press 1990.

Barnouw, Erik. *Conglomerates and the Media*. New Press, 1998.

Bianculli, David. *Teleliteracy*. Ungar Pub Co, 1992.

Boyd, Andrew and Stephen Duncombe."The Manufacture of Dissent: What the Left Can Learn from Las Vegas." *The Journal of Aesthetics and Protest* Vol. 1, #3, 2004.

Fisher, David E. *Tube: The Invention of Television*. Harvest Book, 1997.

Herman, Edward S. and Noam Chomsky. *Manufacturing Consent: The Political Economy of the Mass Media*. Pantheon, 2002.

Lechner, Jack. *Can't Take My Eyes Off of You: 1 Man, 7 Days, 12 Televisions*. Crown, 2000.

MacDonald, J. Fred. *One Nation Under Television*. Pantheon, 1990.

McChesney, Robert W. *Corporate Media and the Threat to Democracy (Open Media Pamphlet Series)*. Seven Stories Press, 1997.

McChesney, Robert W. *The Problem of the Media: U.S. Communication Politics in the Twenty-First Century*. Monthly Review Press (March 1, 2004).

Miller, Mark Crispin. *Boxed in: The Culture of TV*. Northwestern University Press, 1988.

Postman, Neil. *Amusing Ourselves to Death: Public Discourse in the Age of Show Business*. Penguin Books, 1986.

Schwartz, Evan. *The Last Lone Inventor: A Tale of Genius, Deceit, and the Birth of Television*. HarperCollins, 2002.

Stashower, Daniel. *The Boy Genius and the Mogul: The Untold Story of Television*. Broadway, 2002.

Tinker, Grant with Bud Rukeyser. *Tinker in Television: From General Sarnoff to General Electric*. Simon & Schuster, 1994.

Watson, Mary A. *Defining Visions: Television and the American Experience since 1945*. Wadsworth Publishing, 1997.

Weaver, Sylvester L. ("Pat"). *The Best Seat in the House: The Golden Years of Radio and Television*. Knopf, 1994.

CHAPTER 3: Script and Project Development: The Big Idea

Blumenthal, Howard J. and Oliver R. Goodenough. *The Business of Television*. Billboard Books, 1991.

Branston, Gill and Roy Stafford. *The Media Student's Book, 3rd Edition*. Routledge, 2003.

Brody, Larry. *Television Writing from the Inside Out: Your Channel to Success*. Applause Books, 2003.

Jones, Laurie Beth. *The Path: Creating Your Mission Statement for Work and for Life*. Hyperion, 1996.

Longworth, James L. *TV Creators: Conversations with America's Top Producers of Television Drama (The Television Series)*. Syracuse University Press, 2002.

McKee, Robert. *Story*. Regan Books, 1997.

Pepper, Steven. *The Basis of Criticism in the Arts*. Harvard University Press, 1956.

Resnik, Gail and Scott Trost. *All You Need to Know About the Movie and TV Business*. Fireside, 1996.

Seger, Linda. *Making a Good Script Great, 2nd Edition*. Samuel French Trade, 1987.

Straczynski, J. Michael. *The Complete Book of Scriptwriting*. Writer's Digest Books, 1996.

Tierno, Michael. *Aristotle's Poetics for Screenwriters*. Hyperion, 2002.

Trottier, David. *The Screenwriter's Bible*. The Screenwriting Center, 1995.

Vogler, Christopher. *The Writer's Journey: Mythic Structure for Storytellers and Screenwriters*. Michael Wiese Productions, 1992.

Research and Internet Resources

- The ABC/Disney Fellowship (818) 560-6894 http://www.members.tripod.com/disfel

- *Daily Variety* (213) 857-0494 http://www.variety.com

- Hollywood Creative Directory (800) 815-0503

- *Hollywood Reporter* (213) 525-2150 http://www.hollywoodreporter.com

- *New York Screenwriter Monthly* (800) 415-5737

- Nickelodeon Fellowship Program (212) 258-7532

- Script Writer's Network http://www.scriptwritersnetwork.com

- Warner Bros. Writers Workshop (818) 954-7906

- Writer's Guild of America http://www.wga.org

CHAPTER 4: Breakdowns, Budgets, and Finance: Connecting the Dots

Cleve, Bastian. *Film Production Management, 2nd Edition*. Focal Press, 2000.

Honthaner, Eve Light. *The Complete Film Production Handbook, 3rd Edition*. Focal Press, 2001.

Lee, John J. *The Producer's Business Handbook*. Focal Press, 2000.

Moore, Schuyler M. *The Biz, 2nd Edition*. Silman-James Press, 2002.

Newton, Dale and John Gaspard. *Digital Filmmaking 101*. Michael Wiese Productions, 2000.

Schreibman, Myrl. A. *The Indie Producer's Handbook: Creative Producing from A to Z*. Lone Eagle Publishing, 2001.

Simens, Dov S.-S. *From Reel to Deal*. Warner Books, 2003.

Wiese, Michael. *Producer to Producer: Inside Tips for Success in Media*. Michael Wiese Productions, 1997.

CHAPTER 5: Legalities and Rights: Welcome to Reality

Cleve, Bastian. *Film Production Management, 2nd Edition.* Focal Press, 2000.

Donaldson, Michael C. *Clearance and Copyright.* Silman-James Press, 1996.

Erickson, Gunnar, Harris Tulchin, and Mark Halloran. *The Independent Film Producer's Survival Guide: A Business and Legal Sourcebook.* Schirmer Trade Books, 2004.

Honthaner, Eve Light. *The Complete Film Production Handbook, 3rd Edition.* Focal Press, 2001.

Krasilovsky, M. William, Sidney Shemel, and John M. Gross. *This Business of Music: The Definitive Guide to the Music Industry, 9th Edition.* Billboard Books, 2003.

Moore, Schuyler M. *The Biz: The Basic Business, Legal and Financial Aspects of the Film Industry, 2nd Edition.* Silman-James Press, 2002.

Newton, Dale and John Gaspard. *Digital Filmmaking 101: An Essential Guide to Producing Low-Budget Movies.* Michael Wiese Productions, 2001.

Schreibman, Myrl A. *The Indie Producer's Handbook: Creative Producing from A to Z.* IFILM Corporation, 2001.

Research and Internet Resources

- Center for the Study of the Public Domain at Duke University http://www.law.duke.edu/ip
- Copyright Public Information Office (202) 707-3000
- The Copyright Office, Library of Congress (202) 707-9100 http://www.lcweb.loc.gov/copyright
- Creative Commons http://www.creativecommons.org
- The Norman Lear Center at USC http://www.entertainment.usc.edu
- Public Knowledge http://www.publicknowledge.org
- Volunteer Lawyers for the Arts (VLA) (212) 319-ARTS or http://www.vlany.org

Music Clearance Resources

- ASCAP (American Society of Composers and Publishers) (212) 621-6000 http://www.ascap.com
- BMI (Broadcast Music, Inc.) (212) 586-2000 http://www.bmi.com

Video Clearances

- Motion Picture Licensing Corp. (800) 462-8855 http://www.mplc.com

Cartoons Clearances

- Universal Press Syndicate (816) 932-6600 http://www.uexpress.com
- United Media (212) 293-8500 http://www.unitedmedia.com

Print Clearances

- Copyright Clearance Center (978) 750-8400 http://www.copyright.com

- Media Image Resource Alliance (MIRA) (978) 739-9022 http://www.mira.com

Public Domain Clarification

- Copyright Office, Reference and Bibliography Section, LM-451, Copyright Office, Library of Congress, Washington, D.C. 20559.

Fair Use

- Center for Social Media http://www.centerforsocialmedia.org

- Stanford University http://www.fairuse.stanford.edu

Television-Related Unions

- The Screen Actors Guild (SAG) (213) 954-1600 or (212) 944-1030 http://www.sag.com

- The Directors Guild of America (DGA) (800) 421-4173 http://www.dga.org

- The Writers Guild of America (WGA) (212) 767-7800 or (213) 951-4000 http://www.wga.org/www.wgaeast.org

- The National Association of Broadcast Engineer Technicians-Communication Workers of America (NABET-CWA) (800) 882-9174 http://www.nabet-cwa.org

- The American Federation of Television and Radio Artists (AFTRA) (212) 532-0800 or (213) 634-8100 http://www.aftra.org

- The American Federation of Musicians (AFM) (212) 869-1330 http://www.afm.org

- The Producers Guild of America (PGA) (310) 358-9020 http://www.producersguild.org

CHAPTER 6: Pitching and Selling the Project

Brody, Larry. *Television Writing from the Inside Out: Your Channel to Success.* Applause Books, 2003.

Eastman, Susan Tyler and Douglas A. Ferguson. *Broadcast/Cable/Web Programming: Strategies and Practices.* Wadsworth, 2002.

Litwak, Mark. *Dealmaking in the Film and Television Industry: From Negotiations to Final Contracts.* Silman-James Press, 1994.

Resnik, Gail and Scott Trost. *All You Need to Know About the Movie and TV Business.* Fireside/Simon & Schuster, 1996.

Yoneda, Kathie Fong. *The Script-Selling Game: A Hollywood Insider's Look at Getting Your Script Sold and Produced.* Michael Wiese Productions, 2002.

CHAPTER 7: Preproduction: The Plan

Branston, Gill and Roy Stafford. *The Media Student's Book, 3rd Edition*. Routledge, 2003.

Campbell, Drew. *Technical Film and TV for Nontechnical People*. Allworth Press, 2002.

Cury, Ivan. *Directing & Producing for Television: A Format Approach, 2nd Edition*. Focal Press, 2001.

Newton, Dale and John Gaspard. *Digital Filmmaking 101: An Essential Guide to Producing Low-Budget Movies*. Michael Wiese Productions, 2001.

Rea, Peter and David K. Irving. *Producing and Directing the Short Film and Video, 2nd Edition*: Focal Press, 2001.

Young, Jeff. *The Master Director Discusses His Films (interviews with Elia Kazan)*. Newmarket Press, 1999.

Additional Resources

* *StoryBoard Artist* and *StoryBoard Quick* — PowerProduction Software http://www.powerproduction.com

Cast and Talent

* Academy Players Directory http://www.playersdirectory.com
* The Screen Actors Guild (SAG) (213) 954-1600 or (212) 944-1030 http://www.sag.com
* The American Federation of Television and Radio Artists (AFTRA) (212) 532-0800 or (213) 634-8100 http://www.aftra.org

Booking Crews

* Crew Connection (303) 526-4900 http://www.crewconnection.com
* Crews Control (800) 545-CREW http://www.crews-control.com
* Crew Star, Inc. (508) 481-2212 http://www.crewstar.com

CHAPTER 8: Production: The Shoot

Branston, Gill and Roy Stafford. *The Media Student's Book, 3rd Edition*. Routledge, 2003.

Campbell, Drew. *Technical Film and TV for Nontechnical People*. Allworth Press, 2002.

Cury, Ivan. *Directing & Producing for Television: A Format Approach, 2nd Edition*. Focal Press, 2001.

Newton, Dale and John Gaspard. *Digital Filmmaking 101: An Essential Guide to Producing Low-Budget Movies*. Michael Wiese Productions, 2001.

Rea, Peter and David K. Irving. *Producing and Directing the Short Film and Video, 2nd Edition*: Focal Press, 2001.

Schreibman, Myrl. A. *The Indie Producer's Handbook: Creative Producing from A to Z*. Lone Eagle Publishing, 2001.

Information Resources

- http://www.sony.com

- http://www.panasonic.com

- http://www.videouniversity.com

Digital Video Professionals Association

- http://www.dvpa.com

- HD Expo http://www.hdexpo.net

Production Software Programs

- Jungle Software (818) 508-7090 http://www.junglesoftware.com

CHAPTER 9: Post-Production: The Final Product

Berger, John. *Ways of Seeing*. Penguin Books, 1995.

Button, Bryce. *Nonlinear Editing: Storytelling, Aesthetics, & Craft*. CMP Books, 2002.

Campbell, Drew. *Technical Film and TV for Nontechnical People*. Allworth Press, 2002.

Giannetti, Louis D. *Understanding Movies, 10th Edition*. Prentice Hall, 2004.

Murch, Walter. *In the Blink of an Eye, Revised 2nd Edition*. Silman-James, 2001.

Rea, Peter and David K. Irving. *Producing and Directing the Short Film and Video, 2nd Edition*. Focal Press, 2001.

Schreibman, Myrl. A. *The Indie Producer's Handbook: Creative Producing from A to Z*. Lone Eagle Publishing, 2001.

Additional Resources

Stock Footage and Archival Footage

- Video University (845) 355-1400 http://www.videouniversity.com

- Royalty-free stock footage http://www.footagesources.com

- Getty Images http://www.gettyimages.com (wide variety)

- Corbis Motion Brands http://www.corbismotion.com

- Image Bank http://creative.gettyimages.com (high-quality commercial footage)

- Archive Films by Getty Images http//creative.gettyimages.com (historical footage, images)

- Artbeats Digital Film Library http://www.artbeats.com (graphics and backgrounds, faces, aerials, scenic, lifestyles)

- DVArchive.com (diverse collection of royalty-free downloadable DV footage)
- Historic Films http://www.historicfilms.com (historical footage from around the globe, 1930s–80s)
- IMAX http://www.imax.com
- The National Archives http://arcweb.archives.gov/arc/baxic_search.jsp (government footage and collections)
- Focal International http://www.focalint.org/ (trade association representing over 120 libraries in 20 countries)
- Footage.net
- Footage.info
- Prelinger Archives
- Second Line Search
- Sony Pictures http://www.SonyPicturesStockfootage.com
- ABCNews VideoSource http://www.abcnewsvsource.com (their news material libraries date back to 1898)
- *National Geographic* http://www.ngtlibrary.com (over 25,000 hours of *National Geographic* film that dates back to the mid-1960s)
- Discovery Communications http://www.discovery.com
- Independent Television News or ITN http://www.itnarchive.com (300,000 hours of news material)
- UCLA Film and Television Archive (323) 466-8559 http://www.itnarchive.com
- WPA Film Library (800) 777-2223 http://www.wpafilmlibrary.com
- *FilmLook* http://www.filmlook.com

Stock Music and Original Music Composers

- SandBlast Productions http://www.sandblastproductions.com
- David Schwartz Music http://www.davidschwartzmusic.com

CHAPTER 10: It's a Wrap! Then, Next Steps

Branston, Gill and Roy Stafford. *The Media Student's Book, 3rd Edition*. Routledge, 2003.

Fitzsimmons, April. *Breaking and Entering: Land Your First Job in Film Production*. Lone Eagle Publishing Co., 1997.

Landau, Camille and Tiare White. *What They Don't Teach You at Film School*. Hyperion, 2000.

Rea, Peter and David K. Irving. *Producing and Directing the Short Film and Video, 2nd Edition*. Focal Press, 2001.

Rowlands, Avril. *The Television PA's Handbook*. Focal Press, 1987.

Organizations — Networking, Information, Seminars

• Association of Independent Video and Filmmakers (AIVF) http://aivf.org

• Independent Film Project (IFP) http://www.ifp.org

• International Documentary Association (IDA) http://www.ida.org

Festivals — Web Sites, Publications, and Organizations

• Festivals for television http://www.televisionfestivals.com

• *Film Festival Today* http://www.filmfestivaltoday.com (quarterly publication and online resource for festivals and grant information)

• Film Festivals.com http://www.filmfestivals.com

• FilmBuzz http://www.filmbuzz.com

• *Filmmaker Magazine* http://www.filmmakermagazine.com

• International Documentary Association (IDA) http://www.ida.org

• Without A Box http://www.withoutabox.com ·

Grants

• http://www.filmfestivaltoday.com/grants.asp

Starting Your Own Business

• Internal Revenue Service (IRS) (800 829-3676) Forms and publications such as *Your Business Tax Kit,* can be accessed at http://www.irs.gov.

Index

LIMITED WARRANTY AND DISCLAIMER OF LIABILITY

ELSEVIER, INC. AND ANYONE ELSE WHO HAS BEEN INVOLVED IN THE
CREATION OR PRODUCTION OF THE ACCOMPANYING CODE ("THE
PRODUCT") CANNOT AND DO NOT WARRANT THE PERFORMANCE OR
RESULTS THAT MAY BE OBTAINED BY USING THE PRODUCT. THE PRODUCT
IS SOLD "AS IS" WITHOUT WARRANTY OF MERCHANTABILITY OR FITNESS
FOR ANY PARTICULAR PURPOSE. ELSEVIER WARRANTS ONLY THAT THE
MAGNETIC DISC(S) ON WHICH THE CODE IS RECORDED IS FREE FROM DEFECTS
IN MATERIAL AND FAULTY WORKMANSHIP UNDER THE NORMAL USE AND
SERVICE FOR A PERIOD OF NINETY (90) DAYS FROM THE DATE THE PRODUCT
IS DELIVERED. THE PURCHASER'S SOLE AND EXCLUSIVE REMEDY IN THE VENT
OF A DEFECT IS EXPRESSLY LIMITED TO EITHER REPLACEMENT OF THE DISC(S)
OR REFUND OF THE PURCHASE PRICE, AT ELSEVIER'S SOLE DISCRETION.

IN NO EVENT, WHETHER AS A RESULT OF BREACH OF CONTRACT,
WARRANTY, OR TORT (INCLUDING NEGLIGENCE), WILL ELSEVIER OR ANYONE
WHO HAS BEEN INVOLVED IN THE CREATION OR PRODUCTION OF THE
PRODUCT BE LIABLE TO PURCHASER FOR ANY DAMAGES, INCLUDING ANY
LOST PROFITS, LOST SAVINGS OR OTHER INCIDENTAL OR CONSEQUENTIAL
DAMAGES ARISING OUT OF THE USE OR INABILITY TO USE THE PRODUCT OR
ANY MODIFICATIONS THEREOF, OR DUE TO THE CONTENTS OF THE CODE,
EVEN IF ELSEVIER HAS BEEN ADVISED ON THE POSSIBILITY OF SUCH DAMAGES,
OR FOR ANY CLAIM BY ANY OTHER PARTY.

ANY REQUEST FOR REPLACEMENT OF A DEFECTIVE DISC MUST BE POSTAGE
PREPAID AND MUST BE ACCOMPANIED BY THE ORIGINAL DEFECTIVE DISC,
YOUR MAILING ADDRESS AND TELEPHONE NUMBER, AND PROOF OF DATE
OF PURCHASE AND PURCHASE PRICE. SEND SUCH REQUESTS, STATING THE
NATURE OF THE PROBLEM, TO ELSEVIER CUSTOMER SERVICE, 6277 SEA
HARBOR DRIVE, ORLANDO, FL 32887, 1-800-321-5068. ELSEVIER SHALL HAVE NO
OBLIGATION TO REFUND THE PURCHASE PRICE OR TO REPLACE A DISC BASED
ON CLAIMS OF DEFECTS IN THE NATURE OR OPERATION OF THE PRODUCT.

SOME STATES DO NOT ALLOW LIMITATION ON HOW LONG AN IMPLIED
WARRANTY LASTS, NOR EXCLUSIONS OR LIMITATIONS OF INCIDENTAL OR
CONSEQUENTIAL DAMAGE, SO THE ABOVE LIMITATIONS AND EXCLUSIONS
MAY NOT APPLY TO YOU. THIS WARRANTY GIVES YOU SPECIFIC LEGAL
RIGHTS, AND YOU MAY ALSO HAVE OTHER RIGHTS WHICH VARY FROM
JURISDICTION TO JURISDICTION.

THE RE-EXPORT OF UNITED STATES ORIGINAL SOFTWARE IS SUBJECT TO THE
UNITED STATES LAWS UNDER THE EXPORT ADMINISTRATION ACT OF 1969 AS
AMENDED. ANY FURTHER SALE OF THE PRODUCT SHALL BE IN COMPLIANCE
WITH THE UNITED STATES DEPARTMENT OF COMMERCE ADMINISTRATION
REGULATIONS. COMPLIANCE WITH SUCH REGULATIONS IS YOUR
RESPONSIBILITY AND NOT THE RESPONSIBILITY OF ELSEVIER.